Athens
&
Jerusalem

Athens

&

Jerusalem

LEV SHESTOV

Translated, with an introduction, by Bernard Martin

SECOND EDITION

Edited, with a new introduction and annotations, by Ramona Fotiade

OHIO UNIVERSITY PRESS · ATHENS

Ohio University Press, Athens, Ohio 45701
ohioswallow.com
First edition © 1966 by Ohio University Press
Second edition © 2016 by Ohio University Press
New introduction © 2016 by Ramona Fotiade
All rights reserved

To obtain permission to quote, reprint, or otherwise reproduce or distribute material from
Ohio University Press publications, please contact our rights and permissions department at
(740) 593-1154 or (740) 593-4536 (fax).

Printed in the United States of America
Ohio University Press books are printed on acid-free paper ⊗ ™

26 25 24 23 22 21 20 19 18 17 16   5 4 3 2 1

Library of Congress Cataloging-in-Publication Data
Names: Shestov, Lev, 1866–1938, author. | Martin, Bernard, 1928– translator,
  writer of introduction. | Fotiade, Ramona, editor, writer of introduction.
Title: Athens and Jerusalem / Lev Shestov ; translated, with an introduction,
  by Bernard Martin.
Other titles: Afiny i Ierusalim. English
Description: Second edition / edited, with a new introduction and
  annotations, by Ramona Fotiade. | Athens, Ohio : Ohio University Press,
  2016. | Includes bibliographical references and index.
Identifiers: LCCN 2016040552| ISBN 9780821422199 (hardback) | ISBN
  9780821422205 (pb) | ISBN 9780821445617 (pdf)
Subjects: LCSH: Religion—Philosophy. | Philosophy and religion. | BISAC:
  PHILOSOPHY / General. | PHILOSOPHY / Movements / Phenomenology. |
  PHILOSOPHY / Movements / General.
Classification: LCC BL51 .S52273 2016 | DDC 210—dc23
LC record available at https://lccn.loc.gov/2016040552

To Nancy, Rachel, and Joseph Martin

Quid ergo Athenis et Hierosolymis?

—Tertullian

Contents

Lev Shestov—The Thought from Outside

Ramona Fotiade

An influential forerunner of French Existentialism, best known for his unique blend of Russian religious philosophy and Nietzschean aphoristic thought, Lev Shestov (1866–1938) elaborated a radical critique of rational knowledge from the point of view of individual existence. His view of philosophy as "the most worthy" (τὸ τιμιώτατον) was inspired by Plotinus's flight "beyond reason and knowledge" in order to grasp the meaning of life, free from the constraints of logical and ethical thinking, which pose death as the ultimate limit of temporal existence.

One of the precursors of the generation of Absurdist playwrights and essayists (most notably acknowledged in the works of Camus and Ionesco), Shestov fought against the disparagement of real, individual beings and personal experience in a world rendered absurd by the drive toward absolute knowledge and scientific objectivity. He saw the effects of the dehumanizing search for mathematical certainty in the gradual confinement of philosophical investigation to abstract, logical matters, which culminated in Husserl's phenomenology. "Philosophy as rigorous science" (defined along the principles of Kant's *Critique of Pure Reason*) not only confirmed the nonexistence of real, temporal entities, from the point of view of scientific thought, but also restated the equivalence between thought and true being, on the one hand, and true being and meaning, on the other. Within this framework, the search for truth becomes a search for meaning (achieved through intentional constitution), and whatever cannot be "constituted" in the same manner as mathematical objects (e.g., the rule of "2 x 2 = 4"), or concepts (such as the idea of "table" in general), falls outside the category of true being and has no intelligible meaning and no place in philosophical discourse. Shestov sought to restore the rights of the living individual against the rise of the scientific mentality that discarded insoluble metaphysical questions and viewed life in a necessary relationship to death and destruction.

If he frequently recalled Plato's definition of philosophy as "practice for death" and meditation on dying, Shestov did so in order to remind readers and contemporary philosophers that reflection on ultimate realities is not a disinterested pursuit of knowledge but a constant struggle against the logical certainty of one's fleeting passage through time and eventual annihilation. Philosophy, in Shestov's view, is more akin to a combat strategy, a "fight against self-evidence" (which echoes the revolt of Dostoevsky's underground man against the rule of "2 x 2 = 4" as a principle of death), and leads to spiritual awakening. The notion of "awakening," which Shestov takes up from Plotinus, corresponds to the "second sight" that man acquires when "the corporeal eyes begin to lose their sharpness" (according to Plato's *Symposium* 219A). This metaphorical description of a shift in one's thinking points to the fact that the soul lies sleeping in the body, and that it takes a considerable effort to change the way one normally sees the world, a process which Shestov compares with the experience of a dreamer struggling to awaken from a nightmare. Two contradictory, yet equally convincing, perceptions of reality are confronted in the dreamer's consciousness: one places the subject in an impersonal environment, which is indifferent to human suffering and desires, and within which events pursue their course in an implacable manner; the other opens up the possibility of freeing oneself from logical principles and awakening to a reality in which the cries of Job and of the Psalmist are heard and answered. However curious this may seem, as Shestov remarks, the impression of internal consistency and necessity accompanies not only the dreamer's absurd experience of the world (as he imagines, for instance, that "he is the Emperor of China and that . . . he is engraving monograms on the surface of a sphere with one dimension only") but also the perception of the world of the man who "is only guided by reason" in the waking state and who cannot conceive the existence of a reality unfettered by the laws of causality, temporal irreversibility, and death.

We are like sleepwalkers in a world whose logic and a priori principles seem unsurpassable and prevent us from seeing the incongruities and arbitrary connections which make up the fabric of our daily lives. It takes an extraordinary effort of the will to break the spell of self-evident truths and awaken from the nightmare of one's powerless submission to misfortune, injustice, suffering, and death. Being able to reject Spinoza's Stoical injunction "do not laugh, do not curse or mourn, but understand" amounts to a radical choice: a choice confronting every individual who has become aware of the unbearable nature of the human condition. One can either try to come to terms with the "logical necessity" of death or refuse to accept the a priori law of temporal existence and adopt instead the contradictory belief that man is destined for a "higher lot," and that he can overcome death. This opposition between two modes of thinking and two philosophical traditions is perfectly captured by Tertullian's famous dictum ("What has Athens to do with Jerusalem?"), which serves as a springboard for Shestov's argument in his final and most compelling "essay of religious philosophy."

Written over a period of twelve years and published shortly before the author's death in 1938, Shestov's philosophical testament, *Athens and Jerusalem*, sets up a gripping confrontation between the two symbolic poles of ancient wisdom: "Athens" (i.e., Greek thought as source of Western European philosophy) and "Jerusalem" (i.e., the Judeo-Christian tradition based on Biblical revelation). Before Shestov made it his favorite theme of reflection, the tension between rational analysis and faith had been a subject of theological debate and literary writing from the early Fathers of the Church to the founder of modern existential philosophy, Søren Kierkegaard. Shestov's project of a study devoted to the philosophy of religion and inspired by Tertullian's remark dates back to 1909–10, when Shestov was writing his article on Tolstoy (entitled "Destroyer and Builder of Worlds") and working on a book on Luther, *Sola Fide,* which he never finished (due to the outbreak of World War I), but whose arguments and themes were later incorporated into *Potestas Clavium* (1923), a critique of the Catholic doctrine of salvation through works in opposition to the doctrine of salvation through "faith alone." The circumstances in which Shestov first discovered Tertullian's antirationalist statement of belief ("I believe because it is absurd") are also indicative of the evolution of his thought prior to his encounter with Husserl's phenomenology and his polemic against the rising scientific strand in philosophical enquiry.

According to the recollection of his friend and disciple Benjamin Fondane, Shestov came across the famous passage from the treatise on the incarnation (*De Carne Christi*) in his youth, most probably in the 1900s, given that the earliest mention of Tertullian crops up in Shestov's controversial volume of aphorisms, *The Apotheosis of Groundlessness* (1905), subtitled "Essay in Adogmatic Thinking," which was published in English translation as *All Things Are Possible* (1920):

> I was young, I was searching, I lacked daring. And then I found that text by Tertullian (*Et mortuus est Dei filius: non pudet quia pudendum est. Et sepultus resurrexit: certum est quia impossibile*—"and the son of God died: we are not ashamed, because it is shameful; he was buried and rose again: I believe it because it is absurd.") You know where I found it? In a big book by Harnack, in the footnote, at the bottom of the page. Harnack cites it as some sort of oddity—good enough for the basement, not good enough to insert in the main text.[1]

In his preface to *All Things Are Possible,* D. H. Lawrence highlighted the gaping rift between Russian "rootless" vitalism and European culture that Shestov's free-spirited critique of Western idealism brought into view. The less conspicuous opposition between Greek rationalism and Biblical revelation, which subtended the ideological and stylistic dismantling of the Western metaphysical discourse in Shestov's collection of aphorisms, came across indirectly in Lawrence's recurrent reference to the radical alterity of Russian religious thought: "[Russia's] genuine Christianity, Byzantine and Asiatic, is incomprehensible to us. So with her true philosophy." If "Russia will certainly inherit the future," in Lawrence's view, it is because the paradoxical message Russia brings comes from outside the tradition of Western speculative thought and testifies to the existence of an alternative tradition, a "rootless" and "nomad" undercurrent of philosophical reflection, which includes not only Tertullian but also Dostoevsky, Tolstoy, and Nietzsche. More recently, Gilles Deleuze and Félix Guattari also remarked on the figure of the "nomad" (in "Treatise on Nomadology"[2]) and on the striking discontinuity that Shestov's Russian brand of paradoxical thinking introduces in the European tradition of rationalist discourse. Within the lineage of "private thinkers" (alongside Nietzsche and Kierkegaard), Shestov's use of aphoristic style corresponds to the subversive strategy of a "thought from the outside" (as first Foucault and then Deleuze have termed the attempts at overcoming the Western metaphysical discourse and setting "the interiority of our philosophical reflection and the positivity of our knowledge"[3] in relation to an irreducible exteriority). Some of Shestov's assertions in *All Things Are Possible* (*The Apotheosis of Groundlessness*) fully justify D. H. Lawrence's odd contention that Russia has been "infected" with the virus of European culture and has struggled to assimilate and overcome it before articulating its distinctive, if dissonant, message:

> Scratch a Russian and you will find a Tartar. Culture is an age-long development, and sudden grafting of it upon a race rarely succeeds. To us in Russia, civilization came suddenly, whilst we were still savages. At once she took upon herself the responsibilities of a tamer of wild animals, first working with decoys and baits, and later, when she felt her power, with threats. We quickly submitted. In a short time we were swallowing in enormous doses those poisons which Europe had been gradually accustoming herself to, gradually assimilating through centuries.[4]

Subsequently, Shestov has often used the metaphor of the "savage," ignorant dissenter, epitomized by Dostoevsky's "underground man," to designate the resistance to European civilization and its tradition of Greek speculative thought. From this perspective, Tertullian, the North African Christian apologist, belongs to the "savage" camp, along with maverick European personalities such as Luther, Kierkegaard, and Nietzsche, given that the tension between Athens and Jerusalem relates to an all-pervasive inner antinomy of speculative philosophy when confronted with biblical revelation. The process that led to the gradual suppression of the biblical strand of reflection in European culture is described by Shestov with reference to the "Hellenization of Christianity" started by Philo of Alexandria (25 BCE–50CE), a Jewish thinker and educator who strove to reconcile Greek philosophy and biblical exegesis in an attempt at emancipating the Jewish population and protecting their civil rights. As the apex of Jewish-Hellenic synchretism, Philo is diametrically opposed to Tertullian, whose view of the conflicting aims of the Greek and Jewish traditions focused on the Old Testament source of biblical revelation. The importance that Shestov attached, for instance, to the story of the Maccabees, the leaders of the successful Jewish revolt against the Hellenization of Judea,[5] bears out well his defiant philosophical disengagement with Greek wisdom.

In *Athens and Jerusalem,* Tertullian's contradictory statement "I believe because it is absurd" is referred back to its biblical source, and in particular to St Paul's Epistle to the Romans (14:23), which Shestov quotes in the foreword to bring out the opposition between Greek wisdom, according to which virtue is the "highest good," and revelation, which condemns the speculative substitution of the living God with the moral idol, as well as any notion of salvation in the absence of faith:

> The fundamental opposition of biblical philosophy to speculative philosophy shows itself in particularly striking fashion when we set Socrates' words, "The greatest good of man is to discourse daily about virtue" (or Spinoza's *gaudere vera contemplatione*—"to rejoice in true contemplation") opposite St Paul's words, "Whatsoever is not of faith is sin."[6]

In citing Kierkegaard's interpretation of the Pauline conception of faith in the second part of *Athens and Jerusalem* ("the opposite of sin is not virtue but faith" and "the opposite of freedom is guilt"[7]), Shestov sets into question the speculative interpretation of the Fall of Man from the point of view of Hegel's philosophy. Given the absence of a genuine "critique of pure reason" within the history of modern thought, Shestov's position consists in tracing back the fundamental link between knowledge and death to its origin in the story of Genesis (2:17):

The words that God addressed to Adam, "As for the tree of knowledge of good and evil, you shall not eat of it, for on the day that you eat thereof you shall surely die," are in complete disagreement with our conception of knowledge as well as our conception of good and evil. But their meaning is perfectly clear and admits of no tortured interpretation. I repeat once more: they constitute the only true critique of pure reason that has ever been formulated here on earth. God clearly said to man that he must not put his trust in the fruits of the tree of knowledge, for they carry with them the most terrible dangers.[8]

The opposition between faith and knowledge does not refer in this case to the distinction between the virtue of obedience and the transgression that led to the fall, but signals the chasm that separates the freedom beyond good and evil before the fall and the condition of the man subjected to the laws of reason and ethics. In Shestov's view, man traded his status as being created in God's image, sharing in God's creative power and divine free will, for the status of a slave to necessity:

> The serpent said to the first man: "You shall be like God, knowing good and evil." But God does not know good and evil. God does not *know* anything, God *creates* everything. And Adam, before his fall, participated in the divine omnipotence. It was only after the fall that he fell under the power of knowledge and at the same moment lost the most precious of God's gifts—freedom. For freedom does not consist in the possibility of choosing between good and evil, as we today are condemned to think. Freedom consists in the force and power not to admit evil into the world.[9]

Similarly, in quoting a passage on the transient nature of knowledge from 1 Corinthians 13 in the preface to *Potestas Clavium,* Shestov traces back the tension between Athens and Jerusalem not to the polemics between Greek philosophers and Christian theologians (which marked the evolution of Western metaphysics throughout the early Middle Ages and beyond) but to its biblical sources:

> If I speak the tongues of men or of angels, but do not have love, I am only a resounding gong or a clanging cymbal. If I have the gift of prophecy and can fathom all mysteries and all knowledge and if I have a faith that can move mountains, but do not have love, I am nothing. . . . Love never fails. But where there are prophecies, they will cease;

where there are tongues, they will be stilled; where there is knowledge, it will pass away.[10]

The announced disappearance of knowledge, which will give way to *agàpe* (brotherly love or charity), the most important of the three Christian virtues (faith, hope, and charity), heralds the victory of Jerusalem over the wisdom of Athens. However, within the realm of temporal existence, the only vision that fallen man can have of transcendent reality is reminiscent of the shadows cast on the wall of the cave in Plato's *Republic,* and Shestov aptly comments in the first part of *Athens and Jerusalem* that "Plato would hardly need to change a single word to his myth of the cave. . . . The world would remain for him, 'in the light' of our 'positive' sciences, what it was—a dark and sorrowful subterranean region—and we would seem to him like chained prisoners."[11] In St Paul's words, the distance that separates man from the sources of truth after the fall alters the image of reality in the manner of an obscure reflection glimpsed in a mirror: "For now we see only a reflection as in a mirror [*per speculum in enigmate*— through a glass darkly]; then we shall see face to face. Now I know in part; then I shall know fully, even as I am fully known" [1 Corinthians 13:12].

The meaning of the apostle's analogy implies a complete reversal of our conception of knowledge and of our hierarchy of values, which is similar to Nietzsche's "transvaluation of all values" and which occurs, according to Shestov, only at a time of great spiritual upheaval or in a limiting situation when all our certainties and hopes begin to crumble. The encounter with death, as well as any catastrophic event that undermines the foundation of our speculative reasoning, plays the role of a catalyst and an eye-opener. Shestov often makes reference to Tolstoy's *Master and Man* and *The Death of Ivan Ilitch* as an example of the radical transformation of convictions that the author himself had gone through. He talks about this process in his book *The Good in the Teaching of Tolstoy and Nietzsche* (1900) but also in his article published on the great novelist's eightieth birthday and entitled "Destroyer and Builder of Worlds."[12] Published the year before Shestov's visit to Iasnaia Poliana, in 1910, this article analyzes the effects of the tragic experience that Tolstoy went through and of his two encounters with death, which led him to believe that "it suffices to know that God exist in order to live; and it suffices to forget him, no longer to believe in him, in order to die," or in other terms, that "faith is an intelligence of the meaning of life which prompts man not to destroy himself, but to live. Faith is the source of life."[13]

Shestov then cites a passage from Luther's *Commentary on Paul's Epistle to the Galatians* that he later mentions several times in *Potestas Clavium* and *Athens and Jerusalem,* concerning man's presumptuous belief in his self-justification, or in other words, in his reason as a means of salvation, which God must break with a hammer. The *malleus Dei*, which falls on the foundation of autonomous ethics, on the principles of sufficient reason, as *bellua qua non occisa homo non potest vivere* (this beast without whose killing man cannot live),[14] acts as a liberating force. As long as man remains a prisoner of appearances and places his trust in his ability to reach truth and find salvation "through reason alone," divine grace intervenes in a paradoxically violent manner to smash and annihilate "the stubborn and impenitent beast," whose archetype is none other than the serpent of the Bible, and the desire engendered by the fruits of the tree of knowledge. The meaning of the crisis and the transformation of convictions that Tolstoy, as well as Dostoevsky and Chekhov, have gone through at some point in their lives is thus related to the violent irruption of a transcendent force in personal existence. The sudden collapse of rational certainties is accompanied by a complete reversal of values resulting from the trangression of the limit posed to human temporal reflection. The article marking Tolstoy's eightieth anniversary is preceded by a motto that takes on an immense significance in Shestov's critique of scientific knowledge over the years and in his polemic with Husserl: "The time is out of joint"[15] becomes the epitome of the sudden inner transformation that man experiences in contact with the radical alterity of God or in a limiting situation (extreme suffering, madness, death).

The idea of the liberating potential of near-death experiences runs through Shestov's entire work from his article on Tolstoy to his first writings in exile, and in particular his landmark work on Tolstoy and Dostoevsky entitled "The Revelations of Death,"[16] whose foreword alludes to the famous passage from Plato's *Phaedo* (64A), to which Shestov returns in the first part of *Athens and Jerusalem*:[17] "those who pursue philosophy study nothing but dying and being dead," and whose motto is a quotation from Euripides: "Who knows if life is not death and death life?" According to Gorky's recollection, it was with reference to Shestov's book on the idea of the good that Tolstoy made his well-known remark about the source of genuine philosophical reflection (which resonates with Plato's *meletê thanatou*—"practice for death"): "If only a man has learnt to think, whatever the object of his thoughts may be, he always thinks of his own death. It has been like this for all philosophers. And what truth can there be if there is death?"[18] In *Athens and Jerusalem*, Shestov takes up the Platonic definition of philosophy as "practice for death" and makes it the focus of the preface and of the first part of his book, "Parmenides in Chains," which deals with the absence of freedom within the realm of our rational experience of reality, and the possibility of "awakening" or acquiring a "second sight" through philosophical reflection, following a tragic descent into the depths of human despair:

But the philosopher who has arrived at the boundaries of life and passed through the school of death, the philosopher for whom *apothnêskein* (dying) has become the present reality and *tethnanai* (death) the reality of the future, has no fear of threats. He has accepted death and become intimate with it, for dying and death, by weakening the corporeal eye, undermine the very foundation of the power of Necessity, which hears nothing, as well as of the evident truths which depend on this Necessity. The soul begins to feel that it is given to it not to submit and obey but "to lead and govern." [*Phaedo*, 80A] In fighting for this right it does not fear to pass beyond the fateful limit where what is clear and distinct ends and the Eternal Mystery begins. Its *sapientia* (wisdom) is no longer a *meditatio vitae* (meditation on life) but a *meditatio mortis* (meditation on death).[19]

Death, which forces man to abandon the well-trodden path of rational analysis and wander off into the underground or the desert, acts in the same violent and paradoxical manner as the *malleus Dei*: it both destroys man's self-righteousness and restores his freedom. As in the legend of the Angel of Death, which Shestov mentions in the first part of his book on Dostoevsky and Tolstoy,[20] man is endowed with a second pair of eyes following the limiting experience of a near-death experience. The courage or the paradoxical weakness needed to accept the destruction of one's old world and the birth of a new vision of reality (a process that Tolstoy captures in his description of Brekhunov's death in *Master and Man*) is in fact the source of a transformation that closely resembles the terrifying, yet marvellous, metamorphosis of a caterpillar into a butterfly:

> But in Tolstoy, just as in Plato and Plotinus, the thought of death is accompanied by a particular sentiment, by a kind of consciousness that, even while horror rose before them, wings were growing in their backs. Probably something similar happens with the chrysalis when it begins to gnaw at its cocoon. It gnaws because it is growing wings.[21]

If, as Shestov remarked, "the entire history of philosophy, and philosophy itself, should be and often has been simply a 'wandering through human souls,'"[22] death is not a value in itself, and the author of "The Revelations of Death" opposed the philosophies of finitude, which define being in relation to its temporal limitation and, consequently, freedom as *Freiheit zum Tode* (freedom toward death).

In attempting to reverse the rational judgment of living beings as inessential and linked to inevitable destruction, Shestov traces Tertullian's remarks on the death and resurrection of Jesus Christ back to their biblical source, and to the prophet Isaiah and Saint Paul's refusal to reconcile Greek wisdom (Athens) and revelation (Jerusalem).[23] The Christian allegory of the chrysalis that depicts the paradoxical destruction leading to the liberation of the soul after death takes on the meaning of a profound transformation of beliefs (similar to Nietzsche's "transvaluation of all values"), whereby an individual reverses his judgement of Greek wisdom as "the highest good" and discovers the self-affirming power of "madness" and biblical revelation as source of truth. In discussing Nietzsche's attacks on classical metaphysics and epistemology, Shestov does not hesitate to relate Luther's interpretation of *malleus Dei* to the notion of "philosophizing with a hammer," and goes as far as to say, "Does not then Nietzsche's *Will to Power* express under another form Luther's *sola fide?*"[24] For it is the human will that has been paralyzed by the drive toward knowledge, and it is the will that needs to be freed by the destructive-creative intervention of an alternative type of thinking—the "philosophy of tragedy" (in Shestov's terms) or "philosophy with a hammer" (according to Nietzsche). "A great struggle awaits us," Nietzsche wrote with reference to the Eternal Return. "For it is required a new weapon, the hammer, to bring on a terrible decision" (*The Will to Power* §1054).[25] Breaking the causal connection between events and overcoming temporal irreversibility is the actual aim of the thought of Eternal Return, and not the endless mechanical repetition of the same, as Shestov pointed out in comparing Nietzsche's and Luther's revolt against the idolatry of reason and autonomous ethics:

> Behind Nietzsche's Eternal Return is hidden, it seems, a force of infinite power that is also prepared to crush the horrible monster who rules over human life and over all being: Luther's *Creator omnipotens ex nihilo faciens omnia*. The omnipotent creator is not only beyond good and evil but also beyond truth and falsehood. Before his face (*facie in faciem*), both evil and falsehood cease to exist and are changed into nothingness, not only in the present but also in the past. They no longer are and never have been, despite all the testimonies of the human memory.[26]

Philosophy, as "the second dimension of thought" according to Shestov, is not the disinterested contemplation of the impersonal laws that dictate the conditions of being, but an actual fight against the "supernatural enchantment and slumber" (as Pascal qualified it) that has taken over the human mind after the fall:

Religious philosophy is not the search for the eternal structure and order of immutable being; it is not reflection (*Besinung*); it is not an understanding of the difference between good and evil. . . . Religious philosophy is the final supreme struggle to recover original freedom and the divine *valde bonum* (very good) which is hidden in that freedom and which, after the fall, was split into our powerless good and our destructive evil.[27]

From the point of view of the existential critique of the ethical foundation of speculative thought, Lev Shestov's final work can be ultimately understood as an essay devoted to the question of freedom. In terms of its elaboration and structure, *Athens and Jerusalem* is an argumentative and stylistic *tour de force* that effortlessly combines more discursive, historical forms of exegesis and shorter, aphoristic fragments, strongly reminiscent of Nietzsche. The preface, as often is the case, was written last, in April 1937. As Shestov himself explained: "A foreword is basically always a post-word. This book, developed and written over a long period of time, is at last finished. The foreword now seeks to formulate as briefly as possible what has given direction to the author's thought over the course of several years."[28] The short introductory essay, entitled "Wisdom and Revelation," is indeed a synthesis of the arguments in Shestov's major preceding works of the exile period (namely, *Potestas Clavium, In Job's Balances,* and *Kierkegaard and Existential Philosophy*). The epigraph to the foreword, composed of two citations from Plato (*Apology,* 38A) and Saint Paul (Romans, 14:23), encapsulates the opposition between Greek wisdom and biblical revelation that provides the guiding thread for the ensuing "essay in religious philosophy." In refusing to reduce the essential interrogation over the meaning of life to a question of moral justification, Shestov chooses to oppose faith and knowledge, while recalling the distance that has always separated "the God of Abraham, of Isaac and of Jacob" from the "God of philosophers." The power to suspend the reign of immutable ethical principles and to transcend temporal irreversibility belongs to the Creator alone and remains inaccessible to the idol with which human morality and reason have replaced the Living God. Shestov thus refers the notion of "created truth" to Peter Damian's conception that "God could bring it about that that which had been had not been." And from this point of view, not only the fall of man but the entire

history of humanity—or, more precisely, all the horrors of the history of humanity—is, by one word of the Almighty, "annulled"; it ceases to exist . . . : Peter did not deny; David cut off Goliath's head but was not an adulterer; the robber did not kill; Adam did not taste the forbidden fruit.[29]

In his preliminary study of Tertullian's work, Shestov drew attention to the significance of the rift between knowledge and life which was clearly brought to light by the first pages of Genesis: "'Quid ergo Athenis et Hierosolymis?'—Tertullian exclaimed—and, of course, he was right: the truth of Athens has not been reconciled and cannot be reconciled with the truth of Jerusalem, in the same way in which the fruits of the tree of knowledge of good and evil could only block man's access to the tree of life."[30]

In the first part of the volume, "Parmenides in Chains (On the Sources of Metaphysical Truths)," Shestov focused precisely on the link between knowledge and man's loss of freedom. The elaboration of this long section of the book starts in 1926, when Shestov was writing *In Job's Balances*. The essay on Pamenides initially was intended for a series of conferences at the University of Frankfurt and at the Kant-Gesellschaft in Halle in 1930. It was first published in French in the *Revue philosophique de la France et de l'étranger* (July–August 1930, no. 7/8), then in Russian, as a brochure, with YMCA-Press, in 1931.

The first chapter of "Parmenides in Chains" deals with the same topic as the last two aphorisms in *Athens and Jerusalem* ("Looking Backwards" and "Commentary on That Which Precedes"), which in turn correspond to the philosophical debate between Shestov and Husserl. If, from Shestov's point of view, "philosophy is a struggle, the ultimate struggle" for recovering the freedom before the fall and the sources of life opposed to the knowledge of good and evil, according to Husserl "philosophy is reflection" on the foundation of scientific truth. In June 1930 Shestov gave a paper on this topic to the Nietzsche-Gesellschaft, which was published, alongside fourteen aphorisms from *Athens and Jerusalem,* under the title "Kampf und Besinnung" [Fight and reflection] in the magazine *Neue Rundschau* in October 1930.

Shestov and Husserl met for the first time at a conference in Amsterdam, in 1928, and then at regular intervals over the following decade. In the obituary[31] that Shestov completed in 1938, only a couple of months before he himself died, the author of *Athens and Jerusalem* remembers that, despite their radically opposed views on the sources of truth and the aims of philosophy, Husserl recommended "Parmenides in Chains" for publication in the prestigious German periodical *Logos.*[32] Echoes of their initial debate and of their ensuing discussion during Husserl's visit to the Sorbonne in 1929 (which Shestov helped organize) resonate through the inaugural lecture that Heidegger gave the same year at the University of Freiburg, entitled "Was ist Metaphysik?" [What is metaphysics?]. The meetings and correspondence between Shestov, Husserl, and Heidegger at this time are particularly important for the elaboration of Shestov's book on Kierkegaard and existential philosophy (first published in 1936), whose problematics is equally evoked in the second part of *Athens and Jerusalem*. According to Shestov's recollection of his first meeting with Heidegger in Freiburg, in 1928, their discussion turned around aspects of the existential critique of speculative thought, which the author of *Being and Time* had borrowed from Kierkegaard (something which Shestov ignored as he had not yet read the Danish philosopher):

> When I met Heidegger at Husserl's, I quoted a few of his texts which, as I thought, ought to have shattered his system. I was absolutely certain. I had no idea then that these texts reflected Kierkegaard's influence and that Heidegger's input consisted in his determination to fit these ideas into the Husserlian framework. After Heidegger left, Husserl approached me and *made me promise* that I would read Kierkegaard. I couldn't understand *why* he was so adamant about it—Kierkegaard's thought has nothing to do with Husserl's, and I don't think Husserl even liked him. Today I think that he probably wanted me to read Kierkegaard so I may *better understand* Heidegger.[33]

In the first part of *Athens and Jerusalem,* Shestov brings out the contrast between two conceptions of truth, with reference to their positioning in relation to the famous equivalence which Parmenides first established between being and thought (ε ἶ ναι—einai and νοε ἶ ν—noein):

> Philosophy has always meant and wished to mean reflection, *Besinung,* looking backward. Now it is necessary to add that "looking backward," by its very nature, excludes the possibility and even the thought of struggle. "Looking backward" paralyzes man. He who turns around, who looks backward, must see what already exists, that is to say, the head of the Medusa; and he who sees Medusa's head is inevitably petrified, as the ancients already knew. And his thought, a petrified thought, will naturally correspond to his petrified being.[34]

Contrary to Hegel's conception, which draws on the equivalence between being and thought established by Parmenides, religious philosophy starts from the premise that being is not "situated entirely and without residue on the level of resasonable thought,"[35] and that the fight against self-evidences aims to retrieve the "irrational residue of being"[36] that the entire history of speculative thought has sought to obliterate—that is, the living individual as well as the living God.

The title of the second part of *Athens and Jerusalem*, "In the Bull of Phalaris," refers to the story of Phalaris (570–540BCE), the tyrant of Agrigento (in Sicily), whose reputation of extreme cruelty was derived from the punishment he devised for his victims, who were roasted alive by being shut in a brazen bull, beneath which a fire was kindled. In Shestov's philosophical argument, the criticism of the Stoical attitude, which advises the calm contemplation of all misfortunes and suffering, often points to the remarks on self-restraint and endurance in Aristotle's *Nicomachean Ethics*, Book 7. Stoicism is contrasted with Job's revolt, and his decision to confront God while refusing to accept the unjust suffering he is condemned to endure. "The second part, the most difficult, as Shestov remarks in the Foreword, reveals the indestructible bond between knowledge, as philosophy understands it, and the horrors of human existence."[37]

Written in 1931, the essay on knowledge and freedom, "In the Bull of Phalaris," bears out Shestov's decisive encounter with Kierkegaard's work. The last three chapters in the second part of *Athens and Jerusalem* correspond to Shestov's first article on the Danish philosopher, which was also included in a slightly modified version in the central section of *Kierkegaard and the Existential Philosophy*, where Shestov writes:

> Kierkegaard asked that men imitate Christ in their own lives, and seek from life, not joy, but sorrow. The Greek *katharsis* could be summed up, without exaggeration, as an imitation of Socrates, and the Greeks taught of the wise man's bliss in the bull of Phalaris.[38]

The meditation on necessity and freedom in *Athens and Jerusalem* leads to a surprising parallel interpretation of Nietzsche's and Kierkegaard's conceptions in light of Luther's critique of dogmatic theology. If Nietzsche's notions of the Eternal Return and "the will to power" seem to abolish necessity and recover the free will of the *Creator omnipotens*, in agreement with Luther's own view of salvation, it is nevertheless apparent that any attempt at providing a speculative foundation to such unsystematic, subversive reflections on time and self-awareness prompts a return to ethical reasoning, and to "amor fati":

> And Nietzsche could not escape the fate of all; the idea of Necessity succeeded in seducing him also. He bowed his own head, and called all men to prostrate themselves, before the altar or throne of the "monster without whose killing man cannot live."[39]

Kierkegaard's similar evolution, from his initial faith in the Absurd (which he took up from Tertullian), to his later submission to Socratic ethical principles, brings out the fallen man's inability to save himself as he "puts all his trust in knowledge, while it is precisely knowledge that paralyzes his will and leads him inexorably to his downfall."[40] The existential philosoper, according to Shestov, should aspire to think in the categories in which he lives, rather than constantly strive to do the opposite. Autonomous ethics renders the idea of God in man's image, that is to say within the bounds of bare reason. From Luther's point of view, *de servo arbitrio* [the bondage of the will] concerned only man, whereas "for Kierkegaard, as for Socrates and Spinoza, *de servo arbitrio* extends likewise to God."[41] The second part of *Athens and Jerusalem* was initially published in several isues of the *Revue philosophique de la France et de l'étranger*, from January to April 1933.

The elaboration of the third part of *Athens and Jerusalem*, concerning the philosophy of the Middle Ages, dates back to 1934 and reflects Shestov's interest in the work of Etienne Gilson, following from the analysis he devoted to dogmatic theology and to its relationship to speculative philosophy in *Potestas Clavium*. In the Foreword, Shestov summarizes the intent of this section: "In the third part, [subtitled] 'Concupiscentia Invincibilis' [Invincible desire], the fruitless efforts of the Middle Ages to reconcile the revealed truth of the Bible with the Hellenistic truth are dealt with."[42] The presence of a number of arguments that featured in Shestov's unfinished book on Plotinus, which he started writing in 1923 and partially published in the magazine *Versti* [Miles] in Paris, as well as in the Russian and German editions of his book *In Job's Balances*, printed in 1929, indicates the slow elaboration of a critique of the Greek heritage of medieval philosophy that gained momentum during the polemic with Jean Hering on the incompatibility between revelation and Husserl's phenomenological method. The possibility of a religious philosophy that breaks with the tradition of scholastic thought and decides to oppose Athens and Jerusalem consists in the decision to replace self-evident, immutable truth with the notion of "created truth," as Shestov argued:

> Only such a philosophy can call itself Judaeo-Christian, a philosophy which proposes not to accept but to overcome the self-evidences and which introduces into our thought a new dimension—faith. . . . This is why the Judaeo-Christian philosophy can accept neither the fundamental problems nor the principles nor the technique of thought of rational philosophy.[43]

Just as the difference between Descartes and Damian consisted in the former's dismay at offending reason (even when he admitted the possibility that God could have created man so that his limited understanding cannot allow for the existence of a mountain without a valley), Duns Scotus's and William of Occam's attacks against the edifice of Greek wisdom aimed to restore God's omnipotence without fear of the "wicked and lawless arbitrariness" of the rationally unkownable Creator. However, it was not until the Reformation that the extent to which Greek thought had taken over the medieval conception of faith and salvation fully came to light:

> And yet Luther is strictly connected to the medieval philosophy,
> in the sense that the very possibility of his appearance presupposes
> the existence of a Judaeo-Christian philosophy which, setting as its
> task to proclaim the idea—hitherto unknown—of a created truth,
> continued to cultivate the fundamental principles and technique of
> the ancient thought.[44]

The fourth and final part of *Athens and Jerusalem,* composed of sixty-six aphorisms in the German and French first editions of 1938, though including two more short texts in the posthumous Russian edition (YMCA-Press, 1951), was the first one to be elaborated, starting with 1925, as indicated by the date inscribed on the manuscript notebooks kept in the Shestov Archives at the Sorbonne. All the aphorisms in "The Second Dimension of Thought" were published in various magazines: in Russian in *Chisla* [Numbers], no. 1, 1930, and *Sovremennye zapiski* [Contemporary papers], no. 43, 1930; in French and English in *Forum philosophicum* (no. 1, 1930), which mainly gathered the aphorisms related to Shestov's polemic with Husserl. One of the two aphorisms which were not included in the French, English, and German editions of *Athens and Jerusalem,* entitled "The Choice," was also published in the same issue of *Forum philosophicum.* This is aphorism LXIV in the Russian edition, whose first few lines recall the opposition between the two originary myths of mankind, one which conceives individual life as illegitimate daring leading to inevitable destruction, the other which sets particular being under the protection of divine creation: "The appearance of man on earth is an impious audacity. God created man in His own image and likeness and, having created him, blessed him."[45] In fact the same text features twice, in slightly modified versions and with two different titles (LXIV "The Choice" and XXVIII "On the Sources of 'Conceptions of the World'"), in the Russian edition, whereas the English and the French editions include only the final version, which is also the most elaborate.[46]

In contrasting the Greek myth of the origin of mankind (as illustrated by Anaximader's conception) and the biblical story of Genesis, Shestov highlights the opposition between Athens and Jerusalem or, more specifically, between the rational explanation of life and its source in God's creation. The same topic had been dealt with in the third part of *In Job's Balances,* which provides a critique of the Greek conception of the origin of evil as "audacious" and unforgivable birth of particular beings doomed to disappear in order to expiate their sin.[47] The biblical account of man's creation in God's image, of the advent of the God-Man, of his death and resurrection, proposes an alternative, soteriological view of individual existence after the fall, which is also present in Dostoevsky's often misunderstood writings:

> Everyone is convinced, in fact, that Dostoevsky wrote only
> the several dozen pages devoted to starets Zosima, to Alyosha
> Karamazov, etc. and the articles in the *Journal of a Writer* where
> he explains the theories of the Slavophiles. As for *Notes from the
> Underground,* as for *The Idiot,* as for *The Dream of a Ridiculous Man,*
> as for the nine-tenths of all that constitutes the complete works
> of Dostoevsky—all that was not written by him but by a certain
> "personage with a regressive physiognomy"[48] and only in order to
> permit Dostoevsky to cover him with shame.[49]

The only aphorism that was not reproduced in the English, French, or German editions of *Athens and Jerusalem* is entitled "The Fourth Gospel" and deals with the Hellenization of Christianism starting from the doctrine of the Logos, which finds its source in 1 John 1: "In the beginning was the Word, and the Word was with God, and the Word was God." In *Potestas Clavium* Shestov had already exposed the speculative argument that led to the identification of God as Logos to reason and Greek wisdom, in line with the conception of Philo, the Hellenized Jew.[50] It is also noteworthy that this question played a significant part in Shestov's polemic with Jean Hering concerning the sources of truth and the object of philosophical enquiry. When the Protestant theologian quotes the "words of the Logos-Messiah" in order to underpin his defense of Husserlian phenomenology, Shestov replies:

> It is true that God is called *logos* in the Gospel, but can the *logos* of the
> Gospel be equated with that of the philosophers? [. . .] Husserl's ar-
> gument is based on self-evident truths; has it then a right to enlist the
> support of the Gospel commandments? Dostoevsky was able to take

the passage in Saint John (12:24) as motto for his *Brothers Karamazov;* but Dostoevsky is hardly a fitting mate for Husserl.[51]

The famous line in the Fourth Gospel about "the kernel of wheat that falls to the ground and dies," which has a special place in Shestov's work, crops up in a philosophical argument seemingly dominated by the rational, speculative grounding of faith. The conclusion of the aphorism devoted to the Gospel of John in the Russian edition of *Athens and Jerusalem* emphasizes the link between the conceptual approach to religion and the doctrine of the Logos:

> And we must not forget that theologians draw mainly on the Fourth Gospel. Theology is a science of faith. But a science must prove its statements and, therefore, cannot do without rational arguments, or in other words, it reduces "revelation" to rational arguments: theology does not need God, but *verbum Dei* and *Deus dixit* [God's word and God said].[52]

It is also interesting to note Shestov's significant and deliberate misquotation of a phrase he often liked to mention to Fondane as his "literary will." In the preliminary drafts of the aphorism on the Fourth Gospel, Verlaine's well-known "prends l'éloquence et tords-lui le cou" [take eloquence and break its neck] becomes "prends la raison et tords-lui son cou" [take reason and break its neck],[53] which aptly renders the equivalence between the "logos" and speculative discourse, or "eloquence" and "reason," according to Shestov.

Athens and Jerusalem, Shestov's posthumously published work, written during the last years of his life (and in the runup to World War II), enables the reader to appreciate the lasting impact his work had on the evolution of Continental philosophy and European literature in the twentieth century, given his interaction with major European writers (e.g., André Gide, Albert Camus, D. H. Lawrence, David Gascoyne, Thomas Mann) and his legacy on the postwar literary diaspora (Czeslaw Milosz and Joseph Brodsky).

In the anglophone world, Shestov became known even before he was forced into exile by the Bolshevik revolution in 1921, thanks to several translations published in London, Dublin, and Boston, which were prefaced by high-profile personalities of the time such as D. H. Lawrence and John Middleton Murry (a close friend of D. H. Lawrence and Katherine Mansfield's husband). Three collections of articles came out in quick succession: *Anton Tchekhov and Other Essays* (published by Mansel & Co., in 1916), *Penultimate Words and Other Essays* (published by W. Luce, also in 1916), and *All Things Are Possible* (the first translation of the volume originally entitled *The Apotheosis of Groundlessness,* published by Martin Secker in 1920, with an introduction by D. H. Lawrence). Shestov's work had a powerful influence on the British poet David Gascoyne, who was briefly associated with the Surrealist movement in Paris in the 1930s before becoming Fondane's close friend and disciple. Gascoyne later published a long essay on Shestov (in the magazine *Horizon* in 1946) and an account of his encounter with Fondane (and, indirectly, with Shestov's philosophy), which first came out in French in 1987, and was then collected in a volume of *Existential Writings* (published by Amate Press, Oxford, in 2001). Nevertheless, half a century passed between the first English translations of Shestov's essays in 1916 and the more recent editions of his works starting with *Chekhov and Other Essays* prefaced by Sidney Monas in 1966 (for the University of Michigan Press), and *Athens and Jerusalem,* which Bernard Martin edited and published with Ohio University Press the same year. From that moment on the list of available titles by Shestov from Ohio University Press grew steadily, reaching a peak in the late 1960s and mid-1970s, but suddenly coming to a halt in 1982—the year that *Speculation and Revelation* was published. Four decades after the last publication of a book by Shestov in English translation, most of his major works (such as *Dostoevsky, Tolstoy and Nietzsche, In Job's Balances, Potestas Clavium*) have long been out of print.

The new edition makes once again available Shestov's masterpiece of religious existential philosophy, which is frequently referenced in Continental philosophy, religion, and interfaith studies. The recent renewal of interest in his work has been sparked by comparative studies in phenomenology, existentialism, and the philosophy of religion that have brought out Shestov's influence on the evolution of twentieth-century luminaries such as Albert Camus, Vladimir Jankélévitch, Emile Cioran, Leszek Kolakowski, Michel Henry, and Gilles Deleuze. Deleuze and Guattari brought to light Shestov's preeminent role in the postmodern attempt at breaking with the tradition of speculative thought and overcoming the limits of the scientific account of being, in order to establish a new type of thinking, most aptly defined as "the thought from the outside" or the "nomad thought":

> Noology, which is distinct from ideology, is precisely the study of images of thought, and their historicity. . . . But noology is confronted by counterthoughts, which are violent in their acts and discontinuous in their appearance, and whose existence is mobile in history. These are the acts of a "private thinker," as opposed to the public professor: Kierkegaard, Nietzsche, or even Shestov. Wherever they dwell, it is the

steppe or the desert. . . . "Private thinker," however, is not a satisfactory expression, because it exaggerates interiority, when it is a question of outside thought. . . . There is another reason why "private thinker" is not a good expression. Although it is true that this counterthought attests to an absolute solitude, it is an extremely populous solitude, like the desert itself, a solitude already intertwined with a people to come, one that invokes and awaits that people, existing only through it, though it is not yet here.[54]

Shestov's solitary journey far from the beaten tracks of speculative discourse, across the wastelands of reason, presents the reader not so much with the riddle of a voice crying out in the desert, but with the call addressed to nomad thinkers and explorers who have, at different times, and in discontinuous yet persistent manner, set out in search of the impossible figure of an "eternal return" without repetition, outside of time.

Prefatory Note

Bernard Martin

The present translation includes the entire text of *Athens and Jerusalem* except for some of Shestov's quotations in the original languages from Greek, Latin, French and German authors. All of these quotations have here been rendered into English. In some cases, where this was deemed necessary for a full appreciation both of Shestov's substance and style, the original languages have also been retained.

I am grateful to Shestov's daughters, Madame Tatiana Rageot and Madame Natalie Baranov of Paris, who supplied me with much valuable biographical information about their father and read large parts of my translation. The translation was read in its entirety by Professor Stanley Green of Ohio University and in part by Professor George Kline of Bryn Mawr College, to both of whom I would express my appreciation. Responsibility for any errors in the translation is entirely my own. I am grateful, also, to Professor Paul R. Murphy of Ohio University for transliterating a large number of Greek quotations in the text, to Miss Jane Ann Caldwell for preparing the index and to Mr. Mark McCloskey and the late Mr. Cecil Hemley of the Ohio University Press for their unfailing kindness and courtesy.

The Life and Thought of Lev Shestov

Bernard Martin

I

Lev Shestov (1866–1938) belongs to the small company of truly great religious philosophers of our time and his work deserves the closest attention of all who are seriously concerned with the problems of religious thought.

Unfortunately, Shestov's stature has not hitherto been generally recognized nor has his work been widely studied. Even in Europe—where his genius was acknowledged by such figures as Nikolai Berdyaev and Sergei Bulgakov in Russia, Jules de Gaultier, Lucien Lévy-Bruhl and Albert Camus in France, and D. H. Lawrence and John Middleton Murry in England—he did not enjoy any great popularity in his lifetime and now, a quarter of a century after his death, his writings are little read. In America his name is practically unknown to the general public, and even many professional philosophers and theologians are unacquainted with his work.

It is regrettable that this is so, and yet the fact itself is hardly surprising. Shestov established no school and had no real disciples[1] to carry on his work. He did not believe that he had created any clearly defined, positive body of philosophic or religious thought that could simply be handed on to students, to be expounded and taught. Whatever insights or wisdom his own life-long spiritual striving had brought him could not be transmitted by intellectual processes to others; their appropriation of his existentially acquired "truths" could come about only through the same kind of intensive personal struggle and search on their part. But perhaps an even more important reason for the relative obscurity into which Shestov has fallen is the fact that he is stubbornly and unrelentingly anti-modern. The gods of Nineteenth and Twentieth Century man—science, technology, the idea of inevitable historical progress, autonomous ethics and, most of all, rationalist systems of philosophy—were for him idols, devoid of ultimate meaning but terrible in their potentiality for destruction.

It is Shestov's revolt against scientism and philosophic rationalism, a revolt carried on with immense polemical passion and extraordinary dialectical skill, that has drawn attention to his work but at the same time repelled most readers. Some, to be sure, have found that what Shestov has to say is extremely important and worth listening to. His diatribes against the untested assumptions of rationalist metaphysics and positivist science, as well as his superb and penetrating analyses of the singular, the inexplicable and the extraordinary in the human psyche, made a profound impression on at least a few of the important figures of the French Existentialist movement who were developing their philosophical outlook just at the time when his works were appearing in France. Albert Camus, for example, has noted the intensity and concentrated power of his work in this connection.

> Shestov . . . throughout a wonderfully monotonous work, constantly straining toward the same truths, tirelessly demonstrates that the tightest system, the most universal rationalism always stumbles eventually on the irrational of human thought. None of the ironic facts or ridiculous contradictions that depreciate reason escapes him. One thing only interests him, and that is the exception, whether in the domain of the heart or of the mind. Through the Dostoevskian experiences of the condemned man, the exacerbated adventures of the Nietzschean mind, Hamlet's imprecations, or the bitter aristocracy of an Ibsen, he tracks down, illuminates, and magnifies the human revolt against the irremediable. He refuses reason its reasons and begins to advance with some decision only in the middle of that colorless desert where all certainties have become stones.[2]

For Shestov, however, his rebellion against rationalism and scientism was only, as Camus recognized,[3] a preliminary step. It was a clearing of the way for his bold and fervent affirmation, in the mature and final phase of his life, of the truth of the biblical message. Only a reappropriation of the faith of Scripture— which proclaims that man and the universe are the creation of an omnipotent, personal God and that this God made man in His own image, endowing him with freedom and creative power—could, Shestov came to believe, liberate contemporary humanity from the horrors of existence. But such faith, in the face of the mechanist and rationalist assumptions underlying modern scientific and philosophical thought and now entirely dominating the mentality of Western man, is attainable only through agonized personal struggle against what has come to be regarded as "self-evident" truth. Shestov undertook to show the way by his own battle against the self-evident. With a mastery not only of the entire Western philosophic tradition but also of modern European literature, he used his vast erudition, as well as the ardent passion of his entire being and his extraordinary literary talents (D. S. Mirsky says of Shestov's writing that "it is the tidiest, the most elegant, the most concentrated—in short, the most classical prose—in the whole of modern Russian literature")[4] to forge a blazing indictment of rationalist and scientist metaphysics in order to regain for man what he considered the most precious of human gifts: the right to God and to the primordial freedom which God has given man.

American and British readers, to whom the life and work of this great Russian Jewish thinker are now virtually unknown,[5] can profit from becoming acquainted with him. For, as William Barrett has said of Shestov's work, it "can show us what the mind of western Europe, the heir of classicism and rationalism, looks like to an outsider—particularly to a Russian outsider who will be satisfied with no philosophic answers that fall short of the total and passionate feelings of his own humanity."[6]

II

Shestov was born Lev Isaakovich Schwarzmann on January 31, 1866 (February 13, according to the old Russian calendar) in Kiev, where his father, Isaak Moisseevich Schwarzmann, a wealthy merchant and manufacturer, had established a large textile business known throughout southwest Russia. In his youth, spent with two younger brothers and four sisters in a large house in the Podol quarter of Kiev, Lev Isaakovich received instruction in Hebrew and Jewish literature from a tutor engaged by his father. The father himself, while generally regarded as something of a free thinker by the more orthodox Jews of Kiev, was a lover of Hebrew literature and had a strong loyalty to Judaism and Jewish tradition. At one time there was talk of expelling him from the Kiev synagogue for his alleged blasphemies and for his irrepressible tendency to joke about the narrowmindedness of his fellow Jews, but Isaak Moisseevich is reported to have said, "At the time of the high holidays, when they carry the scrolls of the Torah into the synagogue, I always kiss them." The young Lev Isaakovich—his brother-in-law, Herman Lowtzky, tells us[7]—delighted in hearing his father repeat stories and legends from ancient Jewish literature.

In order to obtain for their son the privileges accorded educated Jews by the Tzarist government, his parents enrolled Lev Isaakovich in the Gymnasium of Kiev but, after becoming involved in a political affair, he had to leave. He finished his Gymnasium studies in Moscow, whereupon he entered the university there, studying first under the Faculty of Mathematics and later under the Faculty of Law. After a run-in with the notorious Inspector of Students, Bryzgalov, Shestov was obliged to return to Kiev, where he finished his studies in 1889 with the title of Candidate of Laws. In his university days he was primarily interested in economic and social questions and, while studying in Moscow, wrote a lengthy paper on the problems of the Russian worker with the subtitle "Factory Legislation in Russia." His doctoral dissertation at Kiev was concerned with the condition of the Russian working class. Though accepted by the University of Kiev, the dissertation was suppressed by the Committee of Censors in Moscow as revolutionary. Hence Shestov could not become a doctor of law. He was inscribed on the official list of advocates at St. Petersburg but never practiced the legal profession and later lost most of his interest in the law.

To the Schwarzmann home in Kiev in the early 1890s, attracted by the young Shestov's brilliance, came many of the leading intellectual figures of the city. As his lifelong friend Bulgakov wrote:

> In the hospitable Schwarzmann home at Kiev one could meet many of the representatives of the local intelligentsia, as well as writers and artists from the capital passing through Kiev. People gathered there to exchange ideas and to listen to music. Life at that time (I am speaking of the 1890s) still flowed equably and calmly, but only up to 1905, when, after the revolution, there broke out in Kiev one of the first pogroms, which we felt in all of its tragedy. In those years I had, along with Berdyaev, to struggle with the local representatives of positivism and atheism in defense of a religious outlook. Shestov was in sympathy with us, though he did not himself participate in the discussions. From Kiev our group moved north, and our ties with Shestov were continued and consolidated in Moscow. In the midst of new literary, philosophic and religious movements, Shestov remained his old self, with the same paradoxical philosophy, and invariably loved by all . . . [8]

After finishing his studies at the university, Shestov entered his father's textile firm. Though bored by business affairs, he managed to acquire enough skill in merchandising and accounting to stave off the bankruptcy then threatened by his father's overextension of the firm's credit. At the same time he maintained his literary interests and began to write for the avant-garde press of Kiev. He published several articles, including an essay on the work of Soloviev and one entitled "Georg Brandes and Hamlet,"[9] which was to serve as the basis for his first book.

Having put the family business on a firm footing, Shestov turned its management over to his brothers-in-law and younger brothers, and in 1895 went to Rome. There in 1896 he married a young medical student, Anna Eleazarovna Berezovsky. Two daughters were born of the marriage, Tatiana in 1897 and Natalie in 1900. In 1898 Shestov and his wife moved to Switzerland where Anna finished her studies under the Faculty of Medicine at the University of Berne. At this time Shestov considered pursuing a career as a singer but, according to his brother-in-law, Lowtzky, a pupil of Rimsky-Korsakov and Gabriel Fauré who became an eminent musicologist, Shestov's teacher ruined his splendid singing voice. This did not, however, destroy his interest in music. Music and poetry (though he was not satisfied with his own attempts at writing verse) continued to be his major interests. The French poets—Musset, Baudelaire and

Verlaine—were great favorites of Shestov's at this period, but he soon abandoned poetry and music for what Plato called "the highest music"—philosophy.

In 1898 Shestov returned to Russia for a brief stay in St. Petersburg. Here he became part of a circle of talented young writers and artists, including Dmitri Merezhkovsky, Vasily Rozanov, Nikolai Berdyaev, David Levin and Sergei Diaghilev, the great creator of the modern Russian ballet. Diaghilev welcomed Shestov as a contributor to the noted journal *Mir Iskusstva* (*The World of Art*) which he was then editing.

Shestov had brought back with him two completed book manuscripts. The first, *Shakespeare and His Critic Brandes,* was published in 1898. In it he attacked the positivism and skeptical rationalism of the famous Danish critic and essayist in the name of a vague moral idealism. The second, *Good in the Teaching of Tolstoy and Nietzsche: Philosophy and Preaching*, which appeared in 1900, was characterized by a very different outlook. Shestov's first reading of Nietzsche had been a shattering intellectual and emotional experience. He was greatly moved by the paradoxical ideas of the solitary German thinker and prophet. In his volume comparing him with the Russian writer, Shestov contrasted Nietzsche's supposedly cruel, unpitying and amoral philosophy with the pretentious moralistic preaching of Tolstoy. The book's closing lines express the central idea that came to dominate all of Shestov's later thought and writing: "Good—we now know it from the experience of Nietzsche—is not God. 'Woe to those who live and know no love better than pity.' Nietzsche has shown us the way. We must seek that which is *above* pity, *above* Good. We must seek God."

Shestov's profound interest in Nietzsche inspired a third book comparing the German philosopher with Dostoevsky. This volume, entitled *Dostoevsky and Nietzsche: The Philosophy of Tragedy*, was published in St. Petersburg in 1903 and enhanced the author's growing reputation as a creative and original thinker. The systematic presentation of ideas, however, was growing burdensome to Shestov. In his next volume, *The Apotheosis of Groundlessness,* published in St. Petersburg in 1905, he turned to the aphoristic style which remained one of his favorite literary forms throughout the remainder of his life. This was a book containing over 160 brief essays, some no more than a paragraph in length, dealing with philosophy, science and literature. Shestov here revealed himself as a keen satirist and polemicist, a master of the ironic style and of the indirect mode of discourse that characterizes much of Kierkegaard's writing. Though at this time Shestov had not even heard of Kierkegaard or of what a few years later came to be called *Existenz-philosophie*, it is interesting to note that *The Apotheosis of Groundlessness* already adumbrates a number of the chief characteristics of existentialist thought. It contains not only a vigorous attack on the speculative metaphysics of the neo-Kantian and Hegelian idealist variety that dominated European academic philosophy at the time but also a radical challenge to the pretensions of scientific positivism and its basic assumptions, namely, the principle of unalterable regularity in the sequence of natural phenomena and the idea of causal necessity that is supposed to govern them. Shestov further denied the value of autonomous ethics and passionately insisted on the need for subjectivity and inwardness in the search for truth. In this book he also displayed a profound appreciation of those unique insights in the work of Tolstoy, Dostoevsky, Chekhov and Ibsen which later critics were to regard as distinctively "existential."

The Apotheosis of Groundlessness was not warmly received either by the general public or by the author's friends in the literary circles of St. Petersburg and Moscow. Though the classic simplicity of Shestov's language and his stylistic brilliance evoked widespread admiration, the Russian public by and large saw in the book mere libertinism and sarcasm. Even the critics emphasized its apparently nihilistic message and strongly decried its anti-rationalism; only a very few—among them Shestov's friend, Berdyaev understood the significance of what he was saying and recognized the promise implicit in the book. However, in all fairness it must be admitted that *The Apotheosis of Groundlessness* is largely a negative work. Shestov was merely beginning his struggle against the ideas dominating European thought which he felt had to be overcome in order to provide room for what was later to be the chief burden of his positive message—the reality of the living God of the Bible and the possibility of the restoration of human freedom through religious faith.

The Apotheosis of Groundlessness was translated into English by S. S. Koteliansky and published in London and New York in 1920 under the title *All Things Are Possible.* In his foreword to this edition, D. H. Lawrence said of Shestov:

> "Everything is possible"—this is his really central cry. It is not nihilism. It is only a shaking free of the human psyche from old bonds. The positive central idea is that the human psyche, or soul, really believes in itself, and in nothing else.
>
> Dress this up in a little comely language, and we have a real new ideal that will last us for a new, long epoch. The human soul itself is the source and well-head of creative activity . . . No ideal on earth is anything more than an obstruction, in the end, to the creative issue of the spontaneous soul. Away with all ideals. Let each individual act spontaneously from the forever-incalculable prompting of the creative well-head within him. There is no universal law. Each being is, at his purest, a law unto himself, single, unique, a Godhead, a fountain from the unknown.

This is the ideal which Shestov refuses positively to state, because he is afraid it may prove in the end a trap to catch his own free spirit. So it may. But it is none the less a real, living ideal for the moment, the very salvation. When it becomes ancient, and like the old lion who lay in his cave and whined, devours all its servants, then it can be dispatched. Meanwhile it is a really liberating word.[10]

Lawrence declared that what Shestov had rendered explicit in *The Apotheosis of Groundlessness* was just what had been implied in the work of the great Russian novelists, namely, a rejection of and rebellion against "the virus of European culture and ethic" that had worked in the Russian soul "like a disease." Shestov, he suggested, in "tweaking the nose of European idealism," was expressing the last prenatal struggle of the real Russia about to be born and presently engaged in "kicking away from the old womb of Europe."[11]

In the years preceding the First World War Shestov made his home alternately in Russia and in Switzerland or Germany. From 1908 to 1909 he and his family lived in the German university town of Freiburg and from 1910 to 1914 in the Swiss town of Coppet on Lake Geneva. These were for Shestov years of continued literary and philosophical study and writing. In 1908 his book, *Beginnings and Endings*, containing two perceptive essays on Chekhov and Dostoevsky as well as a number of striking aphorisms, was published in St. Petersburg. Three years later, in 1911, another book, *Great Vigils*, appeared.

Beginnings and Endings was translated into English and published in 1916 in London under the title *Anton Chekhov and Other Essays* and in Boston under the title *Penultimate Words*. In his introduction to the English version John Middleton Murry, writing under the deeply felt impact of the war in which Europe was then embroiled, insisted on the need for men to "learn honesty again: not the laborious and meagre honesty of those who weigh advantage in the ledger of their minds, but the honesty that cries aloud in instant and passionate anger against the lie and the half-truth, and by an instinct knows the authentic thrill of contact with the living human soul."[12] Murry suggested that the work of Shestov could well teach such honesty. He noted the deep passion, the courage, the authenticity, the rebellion against tyranny and dogmatism and the refusal to be deceived that motivated both Shestov's personal reflections and his criticism of other men's ideas. Shestov, he declared,

is aware of himself as a soul seeking an answer to its own question; and he is aware of other souls on the same quest. As in his own case he knows that he has in him something truer than names and divisions and authorities, which will live in spite of them, so towards others he remembers that all that they wrote or thought or said is precious and permanent in so far as it is the manifestation of the undivided soul seeking an answer to its question.[13]

In 1914 Shestov felt the need to return to his homeland and again immerse himself in the life of the Russian people. He went with his wife and children to Moscow, where they lived through the stormy years of the war. Anna Eleazarovna, who had passed her state medical examinations in Moscow in 1905, worked in a hospital and their daughters attended secondary school. The war brought him one great personal sorrow when, in 1915, his handsome and gifted illegitimate son, Sergei Listopadov, was killed in action. Shestov traveled to the front to trace him but his mission was unsuccessful.

During the war years Shestov remained largely indifferent to political controversies. He continued his writing, working on a book which was to be called *Potestas Clavium* and which was dominated by the religious interest in the direction of which his thought had been increasingly turning. He also maintained contact with a group of philosophers and writers including Chelpanov, Gershenson, Bulgakov, Lurie, Berdyaev and Ivanov.

The democratic revolution of February 1917 left Shestov unaffected, but when the Bolsheviks seized power in October, life in Moscow became precarious. Shestov and his family fled to Kiev, which was not yet under Communist rule and there, in January 1919, he finished *Potestas Clavium*. By this time Kiev, too, had acceded to the Soviets, and the authorities refused permission to publish the book unless the author added an introduction—be it only half a page—defending Marxist doctrine. Shestov stubbornly refused and the volume never appeared in Russia. Despite the disfavor in which he stood with the authorities, Shestov was permitted to teach and in the winter of 1918–19 gave a course of lectures on Greek philosophy at the People's University of Kiev. During this period he also received an honorary doctorate from the University of Simferopol. A growing discontent with the Bolshevik regime, however, finally led him to the decision to leave Russia. In the fall of 1919 he and his family began a long and difficult overland journey with stops at Rostov, Yalta and Sevastopol, where they boarded a French steamer with visas obtained by an older sister who lived in Paris. After visiting the home of the Lowtzkys in Geneva, they arrived in Paris in 1920, where a large colony of Russian *émigrés* had settled and where the Shestovs were to live for the next ten years. During this period Shestov resumed his quarrelsome but enduring friendship with Berdyaev, who was later to call him "one of the most remarkable and one of the best men it was my fortune to meet in my whole life."[14]

When Shestov first came to Paris he was virtually unknown in French literary and philosophical circles. But in 1921 he wrote a brilliant article commemorating the one hundredth anniversary of Dostoevsky's birth. When it appeared in *La nouvelle revue française,* a number of distinguished French philosophers and men of letters became aware of Shestov's existence and recognized the originality and profundity of his thought. This article, *"La lutte contre les évidences,"* was combined in 1923 with one on the late work of Tolstoy called *"Le jugement dernier"* under the title *"Les révélations de la mort"* and published in book form in Paris early that year. A few months later a remarkable essay commemorating the three hundredth anniversary of Pascal's birth appeared in Paris as a small book entitled *"La nuit de Gethsémani."*[15] On the strength of these essays Shestov was invited to contribute to the *Revue philosophique* by its well-known editor, Lucien Lévy-Bruhl, who for many years published his articles and papers.

The middle 1920's brought Shestov increasing fame not only in France but throughout Europe. In addition to continuing his research and writing, which had for some years now been concentrated on the Bible and on an intensive study (he called it a "pilgrimage through souls") of the work of such great religious thinkers as Plotinus, St. Augustine, Spinoza, Luther and Pascal, Shestov taught at the Institut des Etudes Slaves and served as a lecturer in the extension division of the Sorbonne. He also joined the Academy of Religious Philosophy which had been founded by Berdyaev in Berlin in 1922 with the help of the American YMCA and transferred to Paris in 1925. The YMCA Press, of which Berdyaev was the director, published several of his books, and a number of his essays appeared in the Russian-language periodical *Put,* also sponsored by the YMCA. With the financial support of his friend, Max Eitingon, Shestov undertook in 1926 the preparation of a complete edition of his works in French. Though sales were small, his works were thereby made available to interested readers everywhere on the Continent. The German Nietzsche-Gesellschaft, recognizing his stature, elected him its honorary president, along with Thomas Mann, Heinrich Hilferding, Heinrich Wolfshagen and Hugo von Hofmannsthal, and in 1926 published a splendid German translation of his *Potestas Clavium.* Under the auspices of the Nietzsche-Gesellschaft Shestov was also invited to lecture in Berlin, Halle, and Freiburg. Invitations from other countries as well came to him, and he addressed philosophical meetings in Prague, Cracow, and Amsterdam. In Amsterdam Shestov met Edmund Husserl, with whom he maintained a close friendship for some years. Though they differed radically in their philosophical orientation and sharply attacked each other's point of view, they had a profound respect for each other. It was at Husserl's home in Freiburg that Shestov, when he came to the German university town to lecture in 1929, met Martin Heidegger. When

Heidegger left the house after a long philosophical discussion, Husserl urged Shestov to acquaint himself with the work of Kierkegaard, hitherto entirely unknown to him, and indicated that some of Heidegger's fundamental ideas had been inspired by the Nineteenth-Century Danish thinker.

Shestov plunged into a study of Kierkegaard and immediately recognized that he had found a deeply kindred spirit. His own thought, influenced by his reading of Dostoevsky, Nietzsche, Pascal, Luther and, above all, the Bible, had for a long time been moving in the very directions in which, as he now discovered, Kierkegaard had preceded him. The rejection of Hegelian idealism as mere word-play of no ultimate significance to the living individual; the insistence that man's salvation lies in subjective, rationally ungrounded faith rather than in objective, verifiable knowledge; the awareness that the root of sin is in man's obsession with acquiring knowledge through the exercise of reason and through empirical procedures; the conviction that science and speculative philosophy have not, despite their inordinate pretensions, liberated man but served rather to destroy the freedom with which God had originally endowed him; the unshakable belief that for God—the God of the Bible, not of the philosophers—"all things are possible" and that indeed it is just this boundless possibility that constitutes the operational meaning of the reality of the living God of Scripture—all this that Shestov found in his reading of Kierkegaard had already been for some time his own passionately held convictions. To be sure, there was much here that did not please him— Kierkegaard, he felt, did not go far enough and at crucial moments had "lost his nerve"—but, on the whole, he found him deeply congenial.

The fruit of Shestov's study of the founder of modern religious existentialism was one of his finest works, *Kierkegaard and Existential Philosophy: Vox Clamantis in Deserto,* published in France in 1936 by a committee of eminent French and Russian *émigré* men of letters organized to honor the author on the occasion of his seventieth birthday.

That year also saw the fulfillment of one of Shestov's long-cherished dreams. At the invitation of the Cultural Department of the Histadrut, he traveled to Palestine, where his grandfather lay buried on the Mount of Olives, to deliver a series of lectures. His appearances in Jerusalem, Tel Aviv and Haifa evoked an enthusiastic response from audiences who recognized the aged Shestov as one of the great Jewish philosophers of the century.

Shestov's home in Boulogne-sur-Seine, where he moved in 1930, was the meeting place of a considerable number of distinguished representatives of the French as well as the Russian émigré literary and philosophical worlds, but he had few intimate friends or genuine disciples with the exception of Benjamin

Fondane, a talented young Rumanian Jewish poet and essayist with whom he became acquainted a few years after settling in Paris. Fondane was to be Shestov's most appreciative pupil and closest confidant during the last years of his life. The notes he kept of his meetings with the philosopher and his correspondence with him provide valuable insights into Shestov's intellectual interests and motivations. They were found among Fondane's papers after his death at the hands of the Nazis in the gas chambers of Birkenau in 1944.[16]

Shestov's last years were shadowed by the approach of war, but he continued his work until the very end. He had finished the manuscript of his major work, *Athens and Jerusalem,* in the spring of 1937 at Boulogne-sur-Seine and had personally supervised the preparation of French and German translations of the Russian text. The German language edition was barely published in Graz and distributed to libraries throughout Europe before Hitler annexed Austria.

The summer of 1938 was spent in Châtel-Guyon which had been Shestov's much loved vacation home for a number of years, but he went there a tired and sick man and returned to Paris in the fall already mortally ill. Despite his illness and fatigue, however, Shestov persisted in the last weeks of his life in working on an article on Husserl who had just died and, when he was too tired to write, whiled away the hours by reading Indian philosophy. On November 14 he was taken to the Boileau Clinic in Paris and there, six days later, died peacefully. At his bedside was an open Bible and the Deussen translation of the Vedas open at the chapter *"Brahma als Freude"* where he had underlined the following passage: *Nicht trübe Askese kennzeichnet den Brahmanwisser, sondern das freudig hoffnungsvolle Bewusstsein der Einheit mit Gott* [It is not somber asceticism that marks a sage but a confident and joyous awareness of unity with God]. He was buried in the mausoleum of the new cemetery at Boulogne-Billancourt, where his mother and brother lay, on November 22, 1938.

III

In his last years Shestov brooded incessantly over what he called, in a letter to Bulgakov, "the nightmare of godlessness and unbelief which has taken hold of humanity." He was convinced that only through "the utmost spiritual effort," as he termed it, could men free themselves from this nightmare. His own life was concentrated on a passionate struggle against the "self-evident" truths of speculative philosophy and positivistic science which had come to dominate the mind of European man and made him oblivious to the rationally ungrounded but redeeming truths proclaimed in the Bible. This struggle is most fully reflected in his last and greatest book, the monumental *Athens and Jerusalem,* on which he worked for many years and completed just a year before his death.

Athens and Jerusalem is the culmination of Shestov's entire lifetime of intellectual inquiry and spiritual striving. It brings together all the diverse strands that had appeared in his earlier writings. His largely negative work of thirty years before, such as *The Apotheosis of Groundlessness,* may be regarded in retrospect as prolegomena and preparation for the positive message of the great work on which Shestov's permanent fame as a religious thinker will undoubtedly rest. In it he set himself the task of critically examining the pretension of human reason to possession of the capacity for attaining ultimate truth—a pretension first put forth by the founders of Western philosophy in Athens two and a half millennia ago, maintained ever since by most of the great metaphysicians of Europe, and still defended by many philosophers today. This pretension, he concluded, must be firmly rejected. Reason and its by-product, scientific method, have their proper use and their rightful place in obtaining knowledge concerning empirical phenomena, but they cannot and must not be allowed to determine the directions of man's metaphysical quest or to decide on the ultimate issues— issues such as the reality of God, human freedom and immortality.

The scientists and most of the philosophers, Shestov repeatedly insists in *Athens and Jerusalem* as well as in some of his earlier works,[17] have been concerned with discovering self-evident, logically consistent, or empirically verifiable propositions which they take to be eternal and universal truths. For them, man is merely another link in the endless chain of phenomena and lives in a universe totally governed by the iron laws of causal necessity. They assume, whether they say so explicitly or not, that human liberty is largely an illusion, that man's freedom to act and his capacity for self-determination are sharply limited by the network of unchangeable and necessary causal relationships into which he has been cast and which exercise an insuperable power over him. Consequently, the path of both virtue and wisdom for man, they believe, lies not in useless rebellion against necessity but in submissive obedience and resignation.

European man, according to Shestov,[18] has languished for centuries in a hypnotic sleep induced by the conviction that the entire universe is ruled by eternal, self-evident truths (such as the principles of identity and non-contradiction) discoverable by reason, and by an everlastingly unalterable and indifferent power which determines all events and facts. This power is commonly known as "necessity." God Himself, for a thinker like Spinoza, has no power to transcend the necessary structures that express His being. And Spinoza is only the culmination of the mechanistic philosophy that has dominated European metaphysics since Aristotle. To be sure, there have been solitary figures here and there, Shestov points out,[19] who have protested against the pretensions of reason and its self-evident truths and have stubbornly refused to accept the dictates of the natural sciences concerning what is possible and what is impossible, but theirs were voices crying in the wilderness." Tertullian's was such a voice, and so also was St. Peter Damian's. In modern times, Shestov declares,[20] it is Dostoevsky who, in his passionate *Notes from the Underground,* has presented the strongest and most effective "critique of reason." The world as logic and science conceive it, governed by universal and immutable laws and constrained by the iron hand of necessity, is for Dostoevsky a humanly uninhabitable world. It must be resisted to the utmost, even if the struggle seems a senseless beating of the head against a stone wall. Shestov finds an immense nobility and heroism in the cry of Dostoevsky's protagonist in his *Notes from the Underground:*

> But, good Lord, what do I care about the laws of nature and arithmetic if I have my reasons for disliking them, including the one about two and two making four! Of course, I won't be able to breach this wall with my head if I'm not strong enough. But I don't have to accept a stone wall just because it's there and I don't have the strength to breach it.
>
> As if such a wall could really leave me resigned and bring me peace of mind because it's the same as twice two makes four! How stupid can one get? Isn't it much better to recognize the stone walls and the impossibilities for what they are and refuse to accept them if surrendering makes one too sick?[21]

To resist the self-evident truths of science and philosophy, to stop glorifying and worshipping them, however, is not necessarily an exercise in futility. If man will attend to the ancient message of the Bible, Shestov maintains, he will find there a conception of God, of the universe and of himself that not only lends meaning to such resistance but also makes of it the first and most essential step in becoming reconciled with God and regaining his freedom. For the Bible, in opposition to Western science and philosophy, proclaims that God is the omnipotent One for whom literally nothing is impossible and whose power is absolutely without limits, and that He stands not only at the center but at the beginning and end of all things. God, according to the Bible, created man as well as a universe in which there is no defect, a universe which—indeed—He saw to be "very good." Having created man, God blessed him, gave him dominion over all the universe and bestowed upon him the essentially divine and most precious of all gifts, freedom. Man is not, unless he renounces his primordial freedom (as all men, in fact, tend to do in their obsession with obtaining rational explanation and scientific knowledge) under the power of universal and necessary causal laws or unalterable empirical facts. Unlike both traditional philosophy and science, which have sought to transform even single, non-recurring facts or events into eternal and unchangeable truths, the Bible refuses to regard any fact as ultimate or eternally subsistent but sees it rather as under the power of God who, in answer to man's cry, can suppress it or make it not to be. For biblical faith, knowledge—whether it is concerned with what have been called "truths of reason" or "truths of fact"—is not, as it is for traditional philosophy and science, the supreme goal of human life. Against their assumption that knowledge justifies human existence, the existential philosophy which takes its rise from the Bible will insist that it is from man's living existence and experience that knowledge must obtain whatever justification it may have.[22]

There can be no reconciliation, Shestov contends,[23] between science and that philosophy which aspires to be scientific, on the one side, and biblical religion, on the other. Tertullian was right in proclaiming that Athens can never agree with Jerusalem—even though for two thousand years the foremost thinkers of the Western world have firmly believed that a reconciliation is possible and have bent their strongest and most determined efforts toward effecting it. The biblical revelation not only cannot be harmonized with rationalist or would-be "scientific" metaphysics but is itself altogether devoid of support either from logical argument or scientific knowledge. For biblical man based his life totally and unreservedly on faith, which is not, as has often been suggested, a weaker form of knowledge (knowledge, so to speak, "on credit," for which proofs, though presently unavailable, are anticipated at some future time), but rather a completely different dimension of thought. The substance of this faith, emphatically denied both by science and philosophy, is the daring and unsupported but paradoxically true conviction that all things are possible. Shestov was haunted for years by the biblical legend of the fall. As he interpreted it, when Adam ate the fruit of the tree of knowledge, faith was displaced by reason and scientific knowledge. The sin of Adam has been repeated by his descendants, whose relentless pursuit of knowledge has led not to ultimate truth but to the choking of the springs of life and the destruction of man's primordial freedom.

According to Shestov, speculative philosophy beginning in wonder or intellectual curiosity and seeking to "understand" the phenomena of the universe, leads man to a dead end where he loses both personal freedom and all possibility of envisioning ultimate truth. It is, in a sense, the Original Lie which has come into the world as a consequence of man's disobedience of God's command to refrain from eating of the tree of knowledge. Its narrowness, its lack of imagination, its preoccupation with "objectivity" and its wish to extrude from thought all human emotion, its conviction that there is nothing in the world that is essentially and forever mysterious and rationally inexplicable, its refusal even to entertain the possibility of a universe in which the rules of traditional logic (such as the principles of non-contradiction and identity) do not hold sway—all this condemns it to sterility. If philosophy is to serve the human spirit rather than destroy it, it must—Shestov maintains[24]—abandon the method of detached speculation and disinterested reflection (what Husserl called *Besinnung*); it must become truly "existential" in the sense of issuing out of man's sense of helplessness and despair in the face of the stone walls of natural necessity. When philosophy becomes, as it must, a passionate and agonized struggle against the self-evident, necessary truths that constrain and crush the spirit, when it refuses, for instance, to refrain from drawing any distinction between the propositions, "the Athenians have poisoned Socrates" and "a mad dog has been poisoned" and to regard both with the same "philosophic" indifference— then it may make man receptive to the supernatural revelation of Scripture and to the possibility of redemption that is to be found there. "Out of the depths I cried unto Thee, O Lord" and "My God, my God, why hast Thou forsaken me?"—the experience reflected in these agonized cries of the Psalmist, Shestov maintains, must be *the starting point of true philosophy.*

When his philosophy has taught man to reject all *veritates aeternae* as illusions, to confront unflinchingly the horrors of his historical existence, to experience his despair authentically and without evasion, to realize his mortality and his insignificance in a universe that seems bent on his destruction, then it may perhaps succeed in preparing him for that act of spiritual daring which is faith and which can bring him to the God who will restore to him not only a center of meaning for his life but also his primordial freedom. As Shestov states it in *Athens and Jerusalem*:

> . . . to find God one must tear oneself away from the seductions of reason, with all its physical and moral constraints, and go to another source of truth. In Scripture this source bears the enigmatic name "faith," which is that dimension of thought where truth abandons itself fearlessly and joyously to the entire disposition of the Creator: "Thy will be done!" The will of Him who fearlessly and with sovereign power returns to the believer, in turn, his lost power: ". . . what things so ever you desire . . . you shall have them." (Mark 11:24)[25]

Faith, for Shestov, is *audacity,* the daring refusal to accept necessary laws, to regard anything as impossible. It is the demand for the absolute, original freedom which man is supposed to have had before the fall, when he still found the distinction between truth and falsehood, as well as between good and evil, unnecessary and irrelevant. Through faith, Shestov seems to suggest, man may become, in a sense, like God himself for whom neither intellectual nor moral grounds and reasons have any reality. "Groundlessness," he writes,

> is the basic, most enviable, and to us most incomprehensible
> privilege of the Divine. Consequently, our whole moral struggle,
> even as our rational inquiry—if we once admit that God is the last
> end of our endeavors—will bring us sooner or later (rather later,
> much later, than sooner) to emancipation not only from moral
> evaluations but also from reason's eternal truths. Truth and the
> Good are fruits of the forbidden tree; for limited creatures, for
> outcasts from paradise. I know that this ideal of freedom in relation
> to truth and the good cannot be realized on earth—in all probability
> does not need to be realized. But it is granted to man to have
> prescience of ultimate freedom.
>
> Before the face of eternal God, all our foundations break together,
> and all ground crumbles under us, even as objects—this we know—
> lose their weight in endless space, and—this we shall probably learn
> one day—will lose their impermeability in endless time.[26]

But Shestov's God—the God of whom the Bible speaks and before whom all human foundations crack and crumble—is not the God of Spinoza or of Kant or of Hegel. Against all metaphysical and rationalist theologies, Shestov declares, "We would speak, as did Pascal, of the God of Abraham, the God of Isaac, the God of Jacob, and not of the God of the philosophers. The God of the philosophers, whether He be conceived as a material or ideal principle, carries with Him the triumph of constraint, of brutal force."[27] The God of the Bible is not to be found as the conclusion of a syllogism. His existence cannot be proved by rational argument or inferred from historical evidence. "One cannot demonstrate God. One cannot seek Him in history. God is 'caprice' incarnate, who rejects all guarantees. He is outside history, like all that people hold to be *to timôtaton*."[28] How shall one arrive at this *Deus absconditus*, this hidden God? "The chief thing," says Shestov, "is to think that, even if all men without exception were convinced that God does not exist, this would not mean anything, and that if one could prove as clearly as two times two makes four that God does not exist, this also would not mean anything."[29] To the complaint that it is not possible to ask men to take a position which negates a universal conviction of the race and flies in the face of logic, Shestov replies, "Obviously! But God always demands of us the impossible . . . It is only when man wishes the impossible that he remembers God. To obtain that which is possible he turns to those like himself."[30]

Shestov suggests, as we have already indicated, that modern man can perhaps reach the God of the Bible only by first passing through the experience of his own nothingness and by coming to feel, as did Nietzsche and others, that God is not. This feeling is a profoundly ambiguous one, capable of leading men in diametrically opposite directions.

> Sometimes this is a sign of the end and of death. Sometimes of the beginning and of life. As soon as man feels that God is not, he suddenly comprehends the frightful horror and the wild folly of human temporal existence, and when he has comprehended this he awakens, perhaps not to the ultimate knowledge, but to the penultimate. Was it not so with Nietzsche, Spinoza, Pascal, Luther, Augustine, even with St. Paul?[31]

Our task, if we would enter upon the road which leads to true reality and ultimately to the God revealed in Scripture, consists "in the Psalmist's image, in shattering the skeleton which lends substance to our old ego, melting the 'heart in our bowels.'"[32] Experiencing the abyss that opens before him when all his laws, his "eternal truths" and his self-evident certainties are taken away, the desperate soul feels that "God is not, man must himself become God, create all things out of nothing; all things; matter together with forms, and even the eternal laws."[33] When he has experienced this complete abandonment to himself and to boundless despair, then a man—as such irreconcilable enemies as St. Ignatius Loyola, the founder of the Jesuits, and Luther, the renegade monk, both have testified—may, through faith, direct his eyes toward ultimate reality and see the true God who will restore to him the limitless freedom with which he was created and again make all things possible for him.

Man, Shestov concludes, must choose: Athens *or* Jerusalem. He cannot have both. Athens—with its constraining principles, its eternal truths, its logic and science—may bring man earthly comfort and ease but it also stupefies, if it does not kill, the human spirit. Jerusalem—with its message of God and man for both of whom nothing is impossible, with its proclamation that creativity and freedom are the essential prerogatives of both the divine and human—terrifies man, but it also has the power of liberating him and ultimately transforming the horrors of existence into the joys of that paradisiacal state which God originally intended for His creatures.

Shestov has been dismissed by some critics as a wild irrationalist, a willful protagonist of the absurd, who wished to abandon reason entirely in order to make
room for a trans-rational revelation. But the case is hardly so simple as this. His
polemics against scientific knowledge and reason, as even the most superficial
reading of his work reveals, are themselves peculiarly lucid and rational. They
are also based on a masterful knowledge of the entire Western philosophical
tradition. Shestov, as *Athens and Jerusalem* and his other books powerfully attest, was completely at home in the thought of all the great European philosophers from Heraclitus to Husserl. Furthermore, given his predilection for irony
and overstatement and his proclaimed intent forcibly to awaken his readers,
to drive them through shock out of comfortable ruts into new and unfamiliar
paths, it may be doubted that he meant categorically to reject objective knowledge, i.e., logic and science, as such. His real concern seems to have been rather
to emphasize that these are hardly the unmixed blessing they have commonly
been taken to be and that they assuredly do not exhaust the possible approaches
to truth. What they tend, rather, to do is to lead those who concentrate on them
away from the ultimate reality given in revelation.

In addition to the partial and preliminary truths of science and logic, Shestov wished to make it clear, there are infinitely more significant "personal" and
"subjective" truths which can neither be objectively demonstrated nor empirically verified, and among these are the biblical affirmations concerning God
and human freedom. If the latter are declared absurd before the bar of reason
and experience, then the truths approved by these judges are themselves foolishness before God.

What Shestov was fundamentally concerned with doing throughout his
lifetime was to criticize the timidity and lack of imagination of traditional philosophy, with its view that metaphysical truth flows solely from obedience and
passive submission to the structures of being given in experience, and to insist
instead that ultimate reality transcends the categories of rationalist metaphysics
and scientific method and that the truth about it is to be discovered through
the untrammeled soaring of the spirit and through daring flights of the imagination. It may be said that so to insist is to abandon philosophy for poetry and
art, but Shestov himself always maintained that philosophy is indeed, or rather
should be, more art than science.

Shestov criticized science because it subordinates man to impersonal necessity. But it is fairly clear that he did not mean to question the preliminary
value and significance of scientific knowledge in everyday life. What he insisted, rather, was that the limits of science must be clearly understood and

that the scientists and the would-be scientific philosophers must not pretend that their essentially "soulless and indifferent truths"[34] alone will satisfy the ultimate needs of the human spirit. More than anything else Shestov was troubled by the tendency of the scientists and the rationalist philosophers to bless and glorify their "constraining truths." Granted that there is a great deal of physical constraint in the world, why must man worship and adore it? Why should he not rather fiercely resent and ceaselessly challenge its authority? To sing praises not only to that measure of necessity and constraint that obviously exists but to go further and maintain that everything in the universe is necessarily and eternally as it is—this tendency of rationalist thought, he contended, does the greatest violence to the spirit. Furthermore the belief, inculcated by scientism and rationalism, in an eternally necessary and unchangeable order of things is, in a sense, a "self-fulfilling" conviction. Men who accept it will do nothing to affirm even that degree of creative freedom which they have within the limits of natural necessity, much less expand it; and their freedom, as well as their capacity for attaining that realm of authentic being which—Shestov believed—lies forever beyond "reasonable explanation," will consequently atrophy and disappear. That true, existential philosophy must be a continuous and agonizing struggle against constraint, against the immoderate pretensions of the logically self-evident, against the deliverances of common consciousness, is one of the dominant as well as one of the most valuable motifs in Shestov's thought.

Shestov also performed a useful service in forcibly and repeatedly drawing our attention to the fact that not all questions are of the same kind.[35] A physical question such as "What is the speed of sound?" differs essentially and in kind from a metaphysical question such as "Does God exist?" Against the positivists he maintained that questions such as the latter are genuine and, indeed, of ultimate importance, but that their significance lies precisely in the fact that they do not admit of ordinary answers, that such answers kill them.

In the specifically religious thought of his mature and final period, Shestov seems to have been motivated basically by an unremitting awareness of what Mircea Eliade has appropriately called "the terror of history." He was obsessed by the fact that Socrates, the best and wisest of men, was poisoned by the Athenians and that, in the understanding of historicist and rationalist philosophies, this fact is on the same level as the poisoning of a mad dog. The despair which an awareness of the terror of history entails can be overcome, he concluded, only through faith. In this he was in complete agreement with Eliade who has written:

> Since the "invention" of faith, in the Judeo-Christian sense of the
> word (for God all is possible), the man who has left the horizon of

archetypes and repetition can no longer defend himself against that terror except through the idea of God. In fact, it is only by presupposing the existence of God that he conquers, on the one hand, freedom (which grants him autonomy in a universe governed by laws or, in other words, the "inauguration" of a mode of being that is new and unique in the universe) and, on the other hand, the certainty that historical tragedies have a trans-historical meaning, even if that meaning is not always visible for humanity in its present condition. Any other situation of modern man leads, in the end, to despair.[36]

Faith in God was, for Shestov, the ultimate source of man's deliverance from despair and the guarantee of his own freedom in a universe all of whose energies seem bent on denying it. Such faith, he held, as we have seen, lies beyond proofs and is in no way affected by logical argument.[37] In this he was surely right. Like Kierkegaard, he recognized that faith can no more be destroyed by logical impossibility than it can be created by logical possibility. If faith is not pre-existent, if it does not precede all of a man's reasoning and argumentation, then these will never lead him to God. Scripture itself, he pointed out, does not demand faith; it presupposes it.[38]

But the question may be raised—How is faith obtained? By man's own wishing and striving for it? Though Shestov's definition of faith as "audacity" seems to suggest that it is produced by an affirmation of human will, he plainly denied that man can by himself obtain faith.[39] Faith is a gift of God, a manifestation of His grace. Echoing the Calvinistic doctrine of predestination and applying it to faith, Shestov seems to have believed that it is mysteriously given to some and denied to others by God. Even one to whom it is given may, of course, reject it, but none by his own unaided endeavor can obtain it. Must it be sought in order to be found? Yes, according to Shestov. The first movement of faith, he wrote, involves "a spiritual exertion"[40] on the part of man and, as we have already heard him say, "to find God one must *tear oneself* away from the seductions of reason."[41] Man must begin by questioning all laws, by refusing to regard them as necessary and eternal. But whether Shestov believed that even this can be done without the grace of God is something that is not altogether clear.

For modern man—Shestov, as we have seen,[42] suggested—God may perhaps be reached only by first passing through the experience of despair, through a sense of utter abandonment. But if one feels that "God is not, man must himself become God, create all things out of nothing; all things; matter together with forms, and even the eternal laws"—what guarantee is there that this will not end in pagan titanism? Is there any assurance that man will not arrogantly put himself in the place of God, or that he will go beyond self-exaltation and recognize God as his own and the universe's Lord and Creator? Indeed, Shestov himself seems at times to blur any ultimate distinction between God and the individual who is in the condition of faith. Through faith, he appears to have believed, man becomes—in an important sense—like God. For the man of faith, too, "all things are possible," and this, according to him,[43] is the operational definition of God.

Has this notion of radical, unlimited freedom, this conception that *all* things may become possible for man, any validity or significance? We may agree with Shestov that science and rationalist philosophy have, indeed, often exceeded their proper bounds and manifested an unjustified tendency to pronounce arbitrary judgment over what is possible and what is impossible. We may agree also that science has deliberately overlooked "miracles" and willfully ignored much that is fortuitous, extraordinary, and incapable of being assimilated into its accepted categories of explanation. But does this entitle us to go to the opposite extreme and deny, as Shestov at times appears to do, that there are any norms, principles or laws governing the phenomena of the universe? Shestov may also be right in holding that scientific knowledge has often tended to enslave man or at least diminish his freedom to act, and we may concur in his suggestion that, by transcending science and returning to the biblical outlook, man may find the scope of his liberty greatly enlarged and discover that many things he formerly believed impossible are quite possible. But does his freedom thereby become, as Shestov seems to believe, absolute and unlimited? Faith, he claims, gives man absolute freedom. But how? By what means does faith produce this astounding result? And can Shestov, or anyone else who accepts the literal truth of the promise proclaimed in Mark 11:23–24, point to anyone either in the past or present in whom this promise has been fully actualized? And furthermore, should he not in all fairness have conceded that while science (or rather, an excessive worship of science) may have at times enslaved man, it has also given him a greater measure of power over nature and thereby broadened the range of his freedom?

Faith, Shestov maintained, results in the liberation of man not only from all physical compulsion but also from all moral constraint. In faith man, to employ the terminology of Nietzsche, moves "beyond good and evil." He is freed from subjection to all ethical principles and moral valuations, and returns to the paradisiacal state in which the distinction between good and evil and between right and wrong is non-existent. But, granted that man's awareness of moral distinctions imposes heavy burdens upon him and restricts his freedom, is a return to the condition of Adam before the fall possible? And granted also that the God of the Bible is degraded and, indeed, denied if He is reduced to the position of guarantor of bourgeois morality, with the selfishness and cruelty that it has often served to cloak, can it be denied that the biblical God is in fact represented as a Lawgiver who has a moral will for man and that man's freedom in the Bible is understood as his capacity to respond affirmatively or negatively to God's call? Aside from the question whether he has, in his concept of "moral freedom," fairly portrayed the character of the God of Abraham, Isaac and Jacob of whom he purported to speak, it may be asked of Shestov whether it makes any sense to assert that man can live entirely without ethical norms or principles. Or was it, perhaps, his belief that a life "beyond good and evil" cannot be lived in man's present existence but only in some transcendent realm? On this he is not clear. In any case, the tendency to formless anarchism that is to be discerned in his friend Berdyaev and that seems to have been part of the mental furniture of a good many other Russian thinkers and writers of his time did not leave him untouched.

For all its ambiguities, exaggerations and inconsistencies, Shestov's work remains of vital contemporary significance. Here was a thinker thoroughly schooled in the Western philosophical tradition who rejected that tradition with passionate intensity when he discovered the deadly threats to the human spirit implicit in it and who, in the style of the prophet, not the theologian or religious apologist, summoned men to turn away from Athens and seek their salvation in Jerusalem.

Not only to the irreligious and non-religious man of the Twentieth Century, but also to him who claims to live by the faith of the Bible yet whose understanding of that faith has inevitably been encumbered and distorted by centuries of rationalist philosophical and theological commentary, Shestov offers a fresh appreciation of the terror and promise of the biblical message. In his own lifetime his was "a voice crying in the wilderness," but it is time that this voice be heard again.

Bernard Martin
Western Reserve University
January, 1966

Athens
&
Jerusalem

Wisdom and Revelation

"The greatest good of man is to
discourse daily about virtue."

—Plato, *Apology,* 38A

"Whatsoever is not of faith is sin."

—St. Paul, Romans 14:23

I

A foreword is basically always a post-word. This book, developed and written over a long period of time, is at last finished. The foreword now seeks only to formulate as briefly as possible what has given direction to the author's thought over the course of several years.

"Athens and Jerusalem," "religious philosophy"—these expressions are practically identical; they have almost the same meaning. One is as mysterious as the other, and they irritate modern thought to the same degree by the inner contradiction they contain. Would it not be more proper to pose the dilemma as: Athens *or* Jerusalem, religion *or* philosophy? Were we to appeal to the judgment of history, the answer would be clear. History would tell us that the greatest representatives of the human spirit have, for almost two thousand years, rejected all the attempts which have been made to oppose Athens to Jerusalem, that they have always passionately maintained the conjunction "and" between Athens and Jerusalem and stubbornly refused "or" Jerusalem and Athens, religion and rational philosophy, have ever lived peacefully side by side. And this peace was, for men, the guarantee of their dearest longings, whether realized or unrealized.

But can one rely on the judgment of history? Is not history the "wicked judge" of popular Russian legend, to whom the contending parties in pagan countries found themselves obliged to turn? By what does history guide itself in its judgments? The historians would like to believe that they do not judge at all, that they are content simply to relate "what happened," that they draw from the past and set before us certain "facts" that have been forgotten or lost in the past. It is not the historians who pronounce "judgment"; this rises of itself or is already included in the facts. In this respect the historians do not at all distinguish themselves, and do not wish to be distinguished, from the representatives of the other positive sciences: the fact is, for them, the final and supreme court of judgment; it is impossible to appeal from it to anyone or anything else.

Many philosophers, especially among the moderns, are hypnotized by facts quite as much as are the scientists. To listen to them, one would think that the fact by itself already constitutes truth. But what is a fact? How is a fact to be distinguished from a fiction or a product of the imagination? The philosophers, it is true, admit the possibility of hallucinations, mirages, dreams, etc.; and yet it is rarely recognized that, if we are obliged to disengage the facts from the mass of direct or indirect deliverances of the consciousness, this means that the fact by itself does not constitute the final court of judgment. It means that we place ourselves before every fact with certain ready-made norms, with a certain "theory" that is the precondition of the possibility of seeking and finding truth. What are those norms? What is this theory? Whence do they come to us, and why do we blithely accord them such confidence? Or perhaps other questions should be put: Do we really seek facts? Is it facts that we really need? Are not facts simply a pretext, a screen even, behind which quite other demands of the spirit are concealed?

I have said above that the majority of philosophers bow down before the fact, before "experience." Certain among the philosophers, however—and not the least of them—have seen clearly that the facts are at best only raw material which by itself furnishes neither knowledge nor truth and which it is necessary to mould and even to transform. Plato distinguished "opinion" (*doxa*) from "knowledge" (*epistêmê*). For Aristotle knowledge was knowledge of the universal. Descartes proceeded from *veritates aeternae* (eternal truths). Spinoza valued only his *tertium genus cognitionis*[1] (third kind of knowledge). Leibniz distinguished *vérités de fait* from *vérités de raison*[2] and was not even afraid to declare openly that the eternal truths had entered into the mind of God without asking His permission. In Kant we read this confession, stated with extraordinary frankness: "Experience, which is content to tell us about what it is that it is but does not tell us that what is is necessarily, does not give us knowledge; not only does it not satisfy but rather it irritates our reason, which avidly aspires to universal and necessary judgments." It is hard to exaggerate the importance of such a confession, coming especially from the author of *The Critique of Pure Reason*. Experience and fact irritate us because they do not give us knowledge. It is not knowledge that fact or experience brings us. Knowledge is something quite different from experience or from fact, and only the knowledge which we never succeed in finding either in the facts or in experience is that which reason, *pars melior nostra* (our better part), seeks with all its powers.

There arises here a series of questions, each more troubling than the other. First of all, if it is really so, wherein is the critical philosophy distinguished from the dogmatic? After Kant's confession, are not Spinoza's *tertium genus cognitionis* and Leibniz's *vérités de raison* (those truths which entered into the mind of God without His permission) confirmed in their hallowed rights by a centuries-old tradition? Did the critical philosophy overcome that which was the content, the soul even, of the pre-critical philosophy? Did it not assimilate itself to it, having concealed this from us?

I would recall in this connection the very significant conflict, and one which the historians of philosophy for some unknown reason neglect, between Leibniz and the already deceased Descartes. In his letters Descartes several times expresses his conviction that the eternal truths do not exist from all eternity and by their own will, as their eternity would require, but that they were created by God in the same way as He created all that possesses any real or ideal being. "If I affirm," writes Descartes, "that there cannot be a mountain without a valley, this is not because it is really impossible that it should be otherwise, but simply because God has given me a reason which cannot do other than assume the existence of a valley wherever there is a mountain." Citing these words of Descartes, Bayle agrees that the thought which they express is remarkable, but that he, Bayle, is incapable of assimilating it; however, he does not give up the hope of someday succeeding in this. Now Leibniz, who was always so calm and balanced and who ordinarily paid such sympathetic attention to the opinions of others, was quite beside himself every time he recalled this judgment of Descartes. Descartes, who permitted himself to defend such absurdities, even though it was only in his private correspondence, aroused his indignation, as did also Bayle whom these absurdities had seduced.

Indeed, if Descartes "is right," if the eternal truths are not autonomous but depend on the will, or, more precisely, the pleasure of the Creator, how would philosophy or what we call philosophy be possible? How would truth in general be possible? When Leibniz set out on the search for truth, he always armed himself with the principle of contradiction and the principle of sufficient reason, just as, in his own words, a captain of a ship arms himself on setting out to sea with a compass and maps. These two principles Leibniz called his invincible soldiers. But if one or the other of these principles is shaken, how is truth to be sought? There is something here about which one feels troubled and even frightened. Aristotle would certainly have declared on the matter of the Cartesian mountain without a valley that such things may be said but cannot be thought. Leibniz could have appealed to Aristotle, but this seemed to him insufficient. He needed proofs but, since after the fall of the principles of contradiction and of sufficient reason the very notion of proof or demonstrability is no longer anything but a mirage or phantom, there remained only one thing for him to do—to be indignant. Indignation, to be sure, is an *argumentum ad hominem* [an argument directed at the man]; it ought then to have no place in philosophy. But when it is a question of supreme goods, man is not too choosy in the matter of proof, provided only that he succeeds somehow or other in protecting himself . . .

Leibniz's indignation, however, is not at bottom distinguished from the Kantian formulas—"reason aspires avidly," "reason is irritated," etc. Every time reason greatly desires something, is someone bound immediately to furnish whatever it demands? Are we really obliged to flatter all of reason's desires and forbidden to irritate it? Should not reason, on the contrary, be forced to satisfy us and to avoid in any way arousing our irritation?

Kant could not resolve to "criticize" reason in this way and the Kantian critique of reason does not ask such questions, just as the pre-critical philosophy never asked them. Plato and Aristotle, bewitched by Socrates, and, after them, modern philosophy—Descartes, Spinoza, Leibniz, as well as Kant—seek, with all the passion of which men are capable, universal and necessary truths—the only thing, according to them, which is worthy of being called "knowledge." In short, it would hardly be extravagant to say that the problem of knowledge, or more exactly, knowledge as a problem, not only has never drawn the attention of the most notable representatives of philosophical thought but has repelled them. Everyone has been convinced that man needs knowledge more than anything else in the world, that knowledge is the only source of truth, and especially—I emphasize this particularly and insist upon it—that knowledge furnishes us with universal and necessary truths which embrace all being, truths from which man cannot escape and from which there is consequently no need to escape. Leibniz said that the "eternal truths" are not content to constrain but do something still more important: they "persuade." And it is not, of course, only Leibniz personally whom they persuade but all men; Leibniz would not have ascribed any value to truths capable of persuading him but incapable of persuading others or even of constraining them.

In this respect there is hardly any difference between Leibniz and Kant. The latter has told us that reason avidly aspires to necessary and universal judgments. It is true that, in the case of Kant, the element of constraint seems to play a decisive and definitive role: even if there should be men whom the truths do not persuade, whom they irritate as experience irritates Kant, this would be no great misfortune; the truths would nevertheless constrain them and thus fully succeed in justifying themselves. And, in the last analysis, does not constraint persuade? In other words, truth is truth so long as it has demonstrative proofs at its disposal. As for indemonstrable truths, no one has any need of them and they appear to be incapable of persuading even a Leibniz.

It is this that determines Kant's attitude towards metaphysics. It is known that according to Kant, who speaks of this more than once in his *Critique of Reason*, metaphysics has as its object three problems—God, the immortality of the soul, and freedom. But suddenly it appears that the final result of the Kantian critique is that none of these three metaphysical truths is demonstrable and that there can be no scientific metaphysics. One would have thought that such a discovery would have shaken Kant's soul to its deepest foundations. But it did nothing of the sort. In his Preface to the Second Edition of *The Critique of Pure Reason*, Kant declares calmly, almost solemnly: "I had to renounce knowledge (*Wissen*) in order to make room for faith (*Glauben*)." So Kant speaks in this same Preface, where we read the following lines: "It will always be a scandal for philosophy and human reason in general that we must accept the existence of things outside ourselves merely *on faith*[3] and that, if someone should take it into his head to doubt it, we would be incapable of setting before him any sufficient proof." It is impossible to prove the existence of God, the immortality of the soul, or free will, but there is nothing offensive or disturbing in this either for philosophy or for human reason; all these will get along without proof and will content themselves with faith, with what Kant and everyone call faith. But when it is a question of the existence of objects outside ourselves, then faith does not suffice, then it is absolutely necessary to have proof. And yet, if one admits Kant's point of departure, the existence of objects outside ourselves is hardly in a more enviable situation, as far as proof is concerned, than God, the immortality of the soul, or free will. At best, the existence of objects outside ourselves can be postulated or be an object of faith. But it is this that Kant cannot endure, just as Leibniz could not endure Descartes' mountain without a valley. And Kant, not having at his disposal any convincing demonstration, just like Leibniz, did not recoil before the use of an *argumentum ad hominem,* before indignation: if we do not succeed in knowing that things exist outside ourselves, then philosophy and reason are forever covered with shame; it is a "scandal! . . . "

Why did Leibniz so passionately defend his eternal truths, and why was be so horrified at the idea of subordinating them to the Creator? Why did Kant take to heart the fate of objects outside ourselves, while the fate of God, of the soul and of freedom left him untouched? Is it not just the opposite which should have happened? The "scandal" of philosophy, one would think, consists in the impossibility of proving the existence of God. One would also think that the dependence of God on the truths would poison man's mind and fill it with horror. So one would think; but in reality it was the contrary of this that occurred. Reason, which aspires eagerly to necessity and universality, has obtained all that it wished and the greatest representatives of modern philosophy have expelled everything which could irritate reason to the region of the "supra-sensible" from which no echo comes to us and where being is confounded with non-being in a dull and dreary indifference.

Even before *The Critique of Pure Reason* Kant wrote to Marcus Herz that "in the determination of the origin and validity of our knowledge the *deus ex machina* is the greatest absurdity that one could choose." Then, as if he were translating Leibniz's objections to Descartes: "To say that a supreme being has wisely introduced into us such ideas and principles (i.e., the eternal truths) is completely to destroy all philosophy." It is on this that all of the critical philosophy, just like the pre-critical philosophy, is built. Reason does not tolerate the idea of what

Kant calls a *deus ex machina*[4] or "a supreme being"; this idea marks the end of all philosophy for reason. Kant could not forgive Leibniz for his modest "pre-established harmony" because it conceals a *deus ex machina*. For once one accepts the existence of a *deus ex machina*—this is to say, a God who, even though from afar and only from time to time, intervenes in the affairs of the world—reason would be obliged to renounce forever the idea that what is is necessarily just as it is, or, to use Spinoza's language, that "things could not have been produced by God in any other way or order than that in which they were produced."

Kant (in this, also, agreeing with Leibniz) was very unhappy when he was compared with Spinoza. He, like Leibniz, wanted people to consider him (and they did indeed consider him) a Christian philosopher. But for all his piety, he could not accept the idea that God can and must be placed above the truths, that God can be sought and found in our world. Why was this idea unacceptable to him? And why, when he spoke of the "dogmatic slumber" from which his "critiques" had permitted him to escape, did it not occur to him to ask whether the certitude with which he affirmed the autonomy of the truth, as well as his hatred for "experience," did not flow from the "dogma" of the sovereignty of reason, a dogma devoid of all foundation and one which is an indication not of slumber but of profound sleep, or even—perhaps—the death of the human spirit? It is a terrible thing to fall into the hands of the living God. But to submit to impersonal Necessity which (no one knows how) has been introduced into being—this is not at all terrible, this calms and even rejoices! But then, why did Kant need to distinguish himself from Leibniz, and why did both Kant and Leibniz need to distinguish themselves from Spinoza? And why, I ask once more, do the historians of philosophy—one might almost say, does the history of philosophy—continue up to our own day to guard so carefully that boundary which Kant drew between himself and his immediate predecessors, between his philosophy, on the one hand, and the medieval and ancient philosophy, on the other hand? His "critiques," in fact, have not at all shaken the foundations on which the investigative thought of European man has rested. After Kant, as before Kant, the eternal truths continue to shine above our heads like fixed stars; and it is through these that weak mortals, thrown into the infinity of time and space, always orient themselves. Their immutability confers upon them the power of constraint, and also—if Leibniz is to be believed—the power of persuading, of seducing, of attracting us to themselves, no matter what they bring us or what they demand of us, while the truths of experience, whatever they may bring, always irritate us, just as does the "supreme being" (that is to say, *deus ex machina*) even when he wisely introduces into us eternal truths concerning what exists and what does not exist.

II

The critical philosophy did not overthrow the fundamental ideas of Spinoza; on the contrary, it accepted and assimilated them. The *Ethics* and the *Tractatus Theologico-Politicus* remain alive, though implicitly, in the thought of German idealism quite as much as in the thought of Leibniz: the Necessity which determines the structure and order of being, the *ordo et connexio rerum,* does not constrain us but persuades us, draws us along, seduces us, rejoices us, and bestows upon us that final contentment and that peace of soul which at all times have been considered in philosophy as the supreme good. "Contentment with one's self can spring from reason, and that contentment which springs from reason is the highest possible."[5] Men have imagined, it is true—and certain philosophers have even supported them in this—that man constitutes in nature a kind of state within a state. "After men have persuaded themselves that everything that happens happens for their sakes, they must consider as most important in everything that which is for them most useful, and they must value most that by which they would be best affected." Consequently, *flent, ridunt, contemnunt vel quod plerumque fit, detestantur*[6] (they weep, laugh, scorn or—what happens most of the time—curse). It is in this, according to Spinoza, that there lies the fundamental error of man—one could almost say man's original sin, if Spinoza himself had not so carefully avoided all that could recall the Bible even if only externally.

The first great law of thought which abolishes the biblical interdiction against the fruits of the tree of knowledge is *non ridere, non lugere, neque detestari, sed intelligere*[7] (not to laugh, not to lament, not to curse, but to understand). Everything is then transformed before our eyes. In contemplating life "in the perspective of eternity or necessity," we accept whatever we encounter on our road with the same tranquility and the same feeling of good will. "Even if these things are inconvenient, they are nevertheless necessary and have determinate causes through which we seek to understand their nature, and the mind rejoices just as much over their true contemplation as over the knowledge of those things that are pleasing to the senses."

In contemplating the necessity of everything that happens in the universe, our mind experiences the highest joy. How does this differ from the statement of Kant, who says that our reason aspires eagerly to universal and necessary judgments? Or from Leibniz's affirmation that the truths not only constrain but persuade? Or even from the famous Hegelian formula, "All that is real is rational?" And is it not evident that for Leibniz, Kant and Hegel— quite as much as for Spinoza—the pretensions that man makes of occupying a special, privileged place in nature are ungrounded and absolutely unjustified, unless recourse is had to a "supreme being" who does not exist and has never existed? It is only when we forget all "supreme beings" and repress, or rather tear out of our soul, all the *ridere, lugere, et detestari* [laughing, lamenting, and cursing], as well as the absurd *flere* [crying] which flows from them and which comes to the ears of no one—it is only when we recognize that our destiny and the very meaning of our existence consist in the pure *intelligere*, that the true philosophy will be born.

Neither in Leibniz nor in Kant do we find, to be sure, the equivalent of the *Tractatus Theologico-Politicus* which established what is now called "biblical criticism," but this does not mean that they had taken any less care than Spinoza to protect themselves from the biblical contamination. If everything that Kant said about *Schwarmerei* and *Aberglauben* (fanaticism and superstition) or that Leibniz wrote on the same subject were brought together, one would completely recover the *Tractatus Theologico-Politicus*. And conversely, all the effort of the *Tractatus* is bent to ridding our spiritual treasury of the ideas which Scripture had introduced there and which nothing justifies.

The *non ridere, non lugere, neque detestari, sed intelligere* [not to laugh, not to lament, not to curse, but to understand] of Spinoza, who abrogated the ban placed by the Bible on the fruit of the tree of knowledge, constitutes at the same time a reasonable reply to the *De profundis ad te, Domine, clamavi* (out of the depths I cried unto Thee, O God) of the Psalmist. The Psalmist could cry to God, but the man *qui sola ratione ducitur*[8] (who is led by reason alone) knows well that it is absolutely useless to cry to God from the depths. If you have fallen into an abyss, try to get out of it as best you can, but forget what the Bible has told us throughout the centuries—that there is somewhere, "in heaven," a supreme and omnipotent being who is interested in your fate, who can help you, and who is ready to do so. Your fate depends entirely on the conditions in which chance has placed you. It is possible, in some measure, to adapt yourself to these conditions. You may, for example, prolong your earthly existence by working to earn your bread or by taking it away from others. But it is a question only of prolongation, for it is not given anyone to escape death. An ineluctable eternal truth says: "Everything that has a beginning has also an end." The man of the Bible was unwilling to accept this truth; it did not succeed in "persuading" him. But this shows only that he did not allow himself to be led "by reason alone," that he was deeply bogged down in *Schwarmerei* and *Aberglauben* [fanaticism and superstition]. The man who has been enlightened—a Spinoza, a Leibniz, a Kant—thinks quite otherwise. The eternal truths do not simply constrain him; they persuade him, they inspire him, they give him wings. *Sub*

specie aeternitatis vel necessitates[9] [in the perspective of eternity or necessity]—
how solemnly these words resound in Spinoza's mouth! And his *amor erga rem
aeternam* (love of what is eternal)—does not one feel ready to sacrifice for this
the entire universe, created (if one may believe the doubtful, or rather, quite
frankly, false teachings of this same Bible) by God for man? And then there is
Spinoza's "we feel and experience that we are eternal,"[10] and the statement which
crowns his *Ethics*: "Happiness is not the reward of virtue but virtue itself."[11]
Are these words not worth our abandoning all the passing and changing goods
which life promises us?

We touch here precisely upon that which deeply distinguishes the biblical
philosophy, the biblical thought—or, better, the mode of biblical thought—
from the speculative thought that the vast majority of the great philosophers
of historic humanity represent and express. The *ridere, lugere, and detestari*,
along with the accompanying *flere* that are rejected by Spinoza, the most audacious and sincere of these philosophers, *constitute that dimension of thought*
which no longer exists, or more accurately, which has been completely atro-
phied in the man "who is led by reason alone." One could express this still
more strongly: the prerequisite of rational thought consists in our willingness
to reject all the possibilities that are bound up with *ridere, lugere, et detestari*
and especially with *flere*. The biblical words "And God saw that it was very
good" [*valde bonum*] seem to us the product of a fantastic imagination, as does
the God who reveals Himself to the prophet on Mount Sinai. We, enlightened
men, put all our trust in autonomous ethics; its praises are our salvation, its re-
proofs our eternal damnation. "Beyond" the truths which constrain, "beyond"
good and evil, all interests of the mind come, in our opinion, to an end. In the
world ruled by "Necessity" the fate of man and the only goal of every reasonable
being consist in the performance of duty: autonomous ethics crowns the autonomous laws of being.

The fundamental opposition of biblical philosophy to speculative philosophy
shows itself in particularly striking fashion when we set Socrates' words, "The
greatest good of man is to discourse daily about virtue" (or Spinoza's *gaudere
vera contemplatione*—"to rejoice in true contemplation") opposite St. Paul's
words, "Whatsoever is not of faith is sin." The precondition of Socrates' "greatest good," or of Spinoza's "true contemplation," is the willingness of the man
"who knows" to renounce God's "blessing" by virtue of which the world and
everything that is in the world were destined for man's use. The ancients already
had seen the "eternal truth" that man is only one of the links of the chain, without beginning or end, of phenomena; and this eternal truth—constraining, of
course, and coming from the outside—in antiquity already had at its disposal

the power of constraining the philosophical intelligence and also of seducing it, or, as Leibniz puts it, persuading it. And it is here that there arises the essential philosophical question, which unfortunately did not attract the attention of philosophers—neither of Leibniz nor of all those who, before or after him, considered implicite or explicite that the eternal truths not only constrain but also persuade. It is the question of knowing what is essential in our relationship to the truths: is it the fact that they constrain or the fact that they persuade? To put the matter in another way: *if the truth which constrains does not succeed in persuading us, does it thereby lose its status as truth?* Is it not enough for the truth to have the power of constraining? As Aristotle says of Parmenides and the other great philosophers of antiquity, they are "constrained by the truth itself." (*hyp' autes aletheas anankazomenoi*). It is true that he adds, with a sigh, *tên anankên ametapeiston ti einai*, "Necessity does not allow itself to be persuaded," as if he were replying in advance to Leibniz, who said that the truth does more than constrain, that it persuades. But Aristotle ended by repressing his involuntary sigh and began to glorify the constraining truth, as if it were not content to constrain but also persuaded.

In modern philosophy, such expressions as Leibniz's "persuasion" or Spinoza's *vera contemplatione gaudere* constitute, in a way, a substitute for the flere and for the biblical "God blessed," a substitute smuggled into the domain of objective thought which seemed to have been so carefully and once for all cleansed of all the *Schwarmerei* and *Aberglauben* to be found in the neighborhood of Scripture and its revelations.

But this was not enough for philosophy, or, more precisely, for the philosophers; they wished, and still wish, to think, and they try by all means to suggest to others, to make them think, that their truths possess the gift of persuading all men without exception and not only themselves who have uttered them. Reason recognizes as true only these truths. They are the truths that it seeks. It is these alone that it calls "knowledge." If someone had proposed to Spinoza, Leibniz or Kant that they limit their pretensions, in the sense of recognizing that the truths are true only for those whom they persuade and cease to be truths for those whom they do not succeed in persuading, would the truths of Leibniz, Spinoza and Kant have retained their earlier charm in the eyes of these philosophers? Would they have continued to call them truths?

Here is a concrete example (the fundamental opposition between Hellenistic and biblical thought bursts forth fully only in concrete examples): The Psalmist cries to the Lord out of the depths of his human nothingness, and all his thought is oriented—just as the truths that he obtains are determined—not by what is "given," by what "is," by what one can "see" be it even by means of the eyes of the mind (*oculi mentis*), but by something quite different—something to which what is given, what is, remains, despite its self-evidence, subordinate. Thus, the immediate deliverances of consciousness do not circumscribe the goal of the Psalmist's searchings; the facts, the given, experience—these do not constitute for him the final criterion which serves to distinguish truth from falsehood. A fact is for him something which rose one day, which had a beginning, and consequently may, if not must, have an end. We know from history that almost twenty-five hundred years ago Socrates was poisoned in Athens. "The man who is led by reason alone" must bow down before this "fact," which not only constrains but also persuades him; he will feel calm only when reason will have guaranteed that no force in the world could destroy this fact, i.e., when he will have perceived in it the element of eternity or necessity. It seems to him that by succeeding in transforming even that which happened only once into an eternal truth, he acquires knowledge, the true knowledge which concerns not what begins and ends, what changes and passes, but what is forever immutable. Thus he elevates himself to the understanding of the universe sub specie aeternitatis vel necessitatis. He attains, with a flap of his wings, the regions where truth lives. And what this truth brings with it is then altogether indifferent to him, whether it be the poisoning of the wisest of men or the destruction of a mad dog. The important thing is that he obtain the possibility of contemplating eternal, immutable, unshakable truth. The mind rejoices over the eternity of truth; as for its content, to this it remains quite indifferent. *Amor erga rem aeternam* fills the human soul with happiness, and the contemplation of the eternity and necessity of everything that happens is the greatest good to which man can aspire.

If someone had taken it into his head to tell Spinoza, Leibniz, or Kant that the truth "Socrates was poisoned" exists only for a definite term and that sooner or later we shall obtain the right to say that no one ever poisoned Socrates, that this truth, like all truths, is in the power of a supreme being who, in answer to our cries, can annul it—Spinoza, Leibniz and Kant would have considered these words a sacrilegious attack on the sacred rights of reason, and they would have been indignant, just as Leibniz was when he recalled Descartes' mountain without a valley. The fact that on earth righteous men are poisoned like mad dogs does not at all trouble the philosophers, for they believe it in no way threatens philosophy. But to admit that a "supreme being" can rid us of the nightmare of the eternal truth "Socrates was poisoned"—this would appear to them not only absurd but revolting. This would not satisfy or persuade them but, on the contrary, irritate them to the last degree. Of course, they would have preferred that Socrates had not been poisoned but, since he was poisoned, it is necessary to submit and to be content with thinking up some theodicy; this, even if it does not make us completely forget the horrors which fill human existence, will perhaps succeed in somewhat weakening their impression. To be sure a theodicy—Leibniz's or anyone else's—must rely on some eternal truth which, in the final analysis, reduces itself to Spinoza's sub specie aeternitatis vel necessitatis. It will be said that everything that is created cannot be perfect by reason of the very fact that it was created and that, consequently, the world that was created can only be the "best of all possible worlds"; we must then expect to find in it many bad things, even very bad things.

Why should creation not be perfect? Who suggested this idea to Leibniz, who imposed it on him? To this question we will not find any answer in Leibniz, just as we will not find in any philosopher an answer to the question how a truth of fact is transformed into an eternal truth. In this respect, the enlightened philosophy of modern times is hardly to be distinguished from the philosophy of the "benighted" Middle Ages. The eternal truths constrain and persuade all thinking beings equally. When in the Middle Ages the voice of Peter Damian rang out, proclaiming that God could bring it about that that which had been had not been, it seemed like the voice of one crying in the wilderness. No one, neither of our time nor even of the Middle Ages, dared to admit that the biblical "very good" corresponded to reality, that the world created by God had no defect. Even more: it may be said that medieval philosophy, and even the philosophy of the Church Fathers, was the philosophy of people who, having assimilated Greek culture, thought and wished to think *sub specie aeternitatis vel necessitatis*. When Spinoza says, in ecstasy, "the love for the eternal and infinite feeds the mind with joy alone, and this itself is free from every sorrow, which is greatly to be wished and striven after with every power," he is only summing up the teaching of the philosophers of the Middle Ages who had passed through the severe school of the great Greek thinkers. The only difference is that Spinoza, in order to trace the way which would lead him to *res aeterna et infinita*, believed that it was his duty as a thinker to sharply separate himself from Scripture, while the scholastics made superhuman efforts to save for the Bible the authority which belonged to it as a divinely inspired book.

But the more men occupied themselves with the authority of the Bible, the less they took account of the content of the sacred book; for, indeed, authority demands finally nothing but respect and veneration. Medieval philosophy never stopped repeating that philosophy is only the handmaid of theology and always referred to biblical texts in its reasonings. And yet as competent a historian as Gilson is obliged to recognize that the medieval philosopher, when he read Scripture, could not fail to recall Aristotle's words about Homer, "The poets lie a great deal." Gilson also cites the words of Duns Scotus: "I believe, Lord, what your great prophet has said, but if it be possible, make me understand it." So the *doctor subtilis*, one of the greatest thinkers of the Middle Ages, speaks. When he hears the words, "Rise, take up your bed and go," he replies, "Give me my crutches that I may have something upon which to lean." And yet Duns Scotus surely knew the words of the Apostle, "Whatsoever is not of faith is sin," as well as the biblical account of the fall of the first man, who renounced faith in order to attain knowledge. But, just as later on in the case of Kant, there never occurred to him the thought of seeking in the biblical legend the "critique of reason," the critique of the knowledge which pure reason brings to man. Is it possible that knowledge leads to the biblical "you shall die" while faith leads to the tree of life? Who will dare admit such a "critique?"[12] The truth that knowledge is above faith, or that faith is only an imperfect kind of knowledge—is not this an "eternal truth," a truth to which Leibniz's words, "it not only constrains but also persuades," could be applied *par excellence*! This truth had already seduced the first man, and ever since, as Hegel very rightly says, the fruits of the tree of knowledge have become the source of philosophy for all time. The constraining truths of knowledge subdue and persuade men, while the free truth of revelation, which has not and does not seek any "sufficient reason," irritates men, just as experience irritates them. The faith which, according to Scripture, leads us to salvation and delivers us from sin introduces us, in our view, into the domain of the purely arbitrary, where human thought no longer has any possibility of orienting itself and where it cannot lean upon anything.

And even if the biblical "critique" of reason is right, even if knowledge, by introducing itself into being, leads inevitably to all the horrors of existence and to death—even then, the man who has once tasted the forbidden fruits will never consent to forget them and will not even have the power to do so. Such is the origin of Spinoza's rule: *non ridere, non lugere, neque detestari, sed intelligere*. To "understand" we must turn away from all the things to which our joys, our sadnesses, our hopes, our anxieties, and so on are bound. We must renounce the world and that which is in the world. "Constrained by the truth itself," Spinoza, following the example of antiquity and of the Middle Ages, turns away from the world created by God; everything that exists in the world is reduced for him to "wealth, honors and sensuality." Everything that exists in the world passes away, is condemned to disappear. Is it worth the trouble to hold on to such a world? Were not the ancient and medieval philosophers, who preferred the ideal world created by human reason to the world created by God and who saw in the former the "greatest good" of man, right? *Amor erga rem aeternam* is the only thing that can be called "very good," that is, capable of justifying being in the eyes of man.

There is then, on the one side, Socrates with his "knowledge" who has withdrawn into his ideal world and, on the other side, the biblical legend of the fall of the first man and the Apostle who interprets this legend by declaring that "whatsoever is not of faith is sin." The task which I have set for myself in this book, *Athens and Jerusalem*, consists in putting to proof the pretensions to the possession of truth which human reason or speculative philosophy make. Knowledge is not here recognized as the supreme goal of man. Knowledge does not justify being; on the contrary, it is from being that it must obtain its justification. Man wishes to think in the categories in which he lives, and not to live in the categories in which he has become accustomed to think: the tree of knowledge no longer chokes the tree of life.

In the first part, "Parmenides in Chains" (*Parmenidês desmôtês*), I try to show that, in pursuing knowledge, the great philosophers lost the most precious of the Creator's gifts—freedom; Parmenides was not a free man but one enchained. The second part, the most difficult, "In the Bull of Phalaris," reveals the indestructible bond between knowledge, as philosophy understands it, and the horrors of human existence. The immoralist Nietzsche glorifies unpitying cruelty and swears eternal fidelity to fate with all its ineluctabilities; and he rejoices and prides himself on the bargain of his submission to fate, forgetting his "beyond good and evil," his "will to power," and all that he had said about the fall of Socrates: the praises and threats of morality have seduced him also. In Kierkegaard mild Christianity loses its mildness and is impregnated with a ferocity which transforms it by ancient destiny—away from the moment where the "fact" has obtained the sovereign right of determining both the will of man and of the Creator. In the third part, "Concupiscentia Invincibilis," the fruitless efforts of the Middle Ages to reconcile the revealed truth of the Bible with the Hellenistic truth are dealt with. The fourth part, "On the Second Dimension of Thought," begins by assuming that the truths of reason perhaps constrain us but are far from always persuading us and that, consequently, the ridere, lugere, et detestari and the flere which flows from them not only do not find their solution in the intelligere but, when they attain a certain tension, enter into a struggle against the intelligere—a terrible, desperate struggle—and sometimes overthrow and destroy it. Philosophy is not a curious looking around, not *Besinnung*, but a great struggle.

A similar purpose underlies all four parts of the book: to throw off the power of the soulless and entirely indifferent truths into which the fruits of the tree of knowledge have been transformed. The "universality and necessity" to which the philosophers have always aspired so eagerly and with which they have always been so delighted awaken in us the greatest suspicion; in them the threatening "you will die" of the biblical critique of reason is transparent. The fear of the fantastic no longer holds us in its power. And the "supreme being," transformed by speculation into a *deus ex machina,* no longer signifies for us the end of philosophy but rather that which alone can give meaning and content to human existence and consequently lead to the *true philosophy.* To speak as did Pascal: the God of Abraham, the God of Isaac, the God of Jacob, and not the God of the philosophers. The God of the philosophers, whether he be a material or ideal principle, carries with him the triumph of constraint, of brutal force. That is why speculation has always so obstinately defended the universality and necessity of its truths. The truth spares no one, no one can escape it; it is this, this alone, that has enticed the philosophers. Leibniz's "persuasion" was only a hypocritical mask behind which the longed-for "constraint" hid itself. It is said in Scripture, "You shall receive according to your faith." Would Leibniz or any other philosopher have ever had the audacity to say, "You shall receive according to your truth"? Athens could not bear such a truth. It does not constrain, it does not constrain at all; it will never obtain ethical approval. How could human reason be enticed by it?

But Jerusalem holds only to this truth. The constraining truths, and even the truths which seek the approbation and fear the reprobation of autonomous ethics—those eternal truths which, according to Leibniz, were introduced into the mind of God without asking His permission—not only do not persuade Jerusalem but are, on the contrary, the abomination of desolation. Within the "limits of reason" one can create a science, a sublime ethic, and even a religion; but to find God one must tear oneself away from the seductions of reason with all its physical and moral constraints, and go to another source of truth. In Scripture this source bears the enigmatic name "faith," which is that dimension of thought where truth abandons itself fearlessly and joyously to the entire disposition of the Creator: "Thy will be done!" The will of Him who, on his side, fearlessly and with sovereign power returns to the believer his lost power: . . . "what things soever ye desire . . . ye shall have them."[13]

It is here that there begins for fallen man the region, forever condemned by reason, of the miraculous and of the fantastic. And, indeed, are not the prophecy of the 53rd chapter of Isaiah, "the Lord hath laid upon him the iniquity of us all," and what the New Testament tells of the fulfilment of this prophecy, fantastic? With a sublime daring and unheard power Luther says of this in his *Commentary on the Epistle to the Galatians:* "All the prophets saw this in the spirit: that Christ would be the greatest robber, thief, defiler of the Temple, murderer, adulterer, etc.—such that no greater will ever be in the world." The same thought was expressed by Luther in a still plainer, more naked, and truly biblical fashion in another passage of the same commentary: "God sent his only begotten son into the world and laid upon him all the sins of all men, saying: 'Be thou Peter, that denier; Paul, that persecutor, blasphemer and doer of violence; David, that adulterer; that sinner who ate the apple in paradise; that thief on the cross—in sum, be thou the person who committed the sins of all men.'"

Can we "understand," can we grasp, what the prophets and the apostles announce in Scripture? Will Athens ever consent to allow such "truths" to come into the world? The history of humanity—or, more precisely, all the horrors of the history of humanity—is, by one word of the Almighty, "annulled"; it ceases to exist, and becomes transformed into phantoms or mirages: Peter did not deny; David cut off Goliath's head but was not an adulterer; the robber did not kill; Adam did not taste the forbidden fruit; Socrates was never poisoned by anyone. The "fact," the "given," the "real," do not dominate us; they do not determine our fate, either in the present, in the future or in the past. What has been becomes what has not been; man returns to the state of innocence and finds that divine freedom, that freedom for good, in contrast with which the freedom that we have to choose between good and evil is extinguished and disappears, or more exactly, in contrast with which our freedom reveals itself to be a pitiful and shameful enslavement. The original sin—that is to say, the knowledge that what is is necessarily—is radically uprooted and torn out of existence. Faith, only the faith that looks to the Creator and that He inspires, radiates from itself the supreme and decisive truths condemning what is and what is not. Reality is transfigured. The heavens glorify the Lord. The prophets and apostles cry in ecstasy, "O death, where is thy sting? Hell, where is thy victory?" And all announce: "Eye hath not seen, non ear heard, neither have entered into the heart of man, the things which God hath prepared for them that love Him."[14]

The power of the biblical revelation—what there is in it of the incomparably miraculous and, at the same time, of the absurdly paradoxical, or, to put it better, its monstrous absurdity—carries us beyond the limits of all human comprehension and of the possibilities which that comprehension admits. For God, however, the impossible does not exist. God—to speak the language of Kierkegaard, which is that of the Bible—God: this means that there is nothing that is impossible. And despite the Spinozist interdictions, fallen man aspires, in the final analysis, only to the promised "nothing will be impossible for you"; only for this does he implore the Creator.

It is here that religious philosophy takes its rise. Religious philosophy is not a search for the eternal structure and order of immutable being; it is not reflection (*Besinnung*); it is not an understanding of the difference between good and evil, an understanding that falsely promises peace to exhausted humanity.

Religious philosophy is a turning away from knowledge and a surmounting by faith, in a boundless tension of all its forces, of the false fear of the unlimited will of the Creator, that fear which the tempter suggested to Adam and which he has transmitted to all of us. To put it another way, religious philosophy is the final, supreme struggle to recover original freedom and the divine *valde bonum* [very good] which is hidden in that freedom and which, after the fall, was split into our powerless good and our destructive evil. Reason, I repeat, has ruined faith in our eyes; it has "revealed" in it man's illegitimate pretension to subordinate the truth to his desires, and it has taken away from us the most precious of heaven's gifts—the sovereign right to participate in the divine "let there be"—by flattening out our thought and reducing it to the plane of the petrified "it is."

This is why the "greatest good" of Socrates—engendered by the knowledge that what is is necessarily—no longer tempts or seduces us. It shows itself to be the fruit of the tree of knowledge or, to use the language of Luther, *bellua qua non occisa homo non potest vivere* (the monster without whose killing man cannot live). The old "ontic" critique of reason is re-established: *homo non potest vivere*, which is nothing but the "you will die" of the Bible, unmasks the eternal truths that have entered into the consciousness of the Creator, or rather of the creation, without asking leave. Human wisdom is foolishness before God, and the wisest of men, as Kierkegaard and Nietzsche, however unlike each other, both perceived, is the greatest of sinners. Whatsoever is not of faith is sin. As for the philosophy that does not dare to rise above autonomous knowledge and autonomous ethics, the philosophy that bows down will-lessly and helplessly before the material and ideal "data" discovered by reason and that permits them to pillage and plunder the "one thing necessary"—this philosophy does not lead man towards truth but forever turns him away from it.

Lev Shestov
Boulogne s. Seine
April, 1937

I

Parmenides in Chains

[On the Sources of the Metaphysical Truths]

"Necessity does not allow
itself to be persuaded."

—Aristotle, *Met.,* 1015A, 32

"The beginning of philosophy is the
recognition of its own powerlessness and
of the impossibility of fighting against Necessity."

—Epictetus, *Dissert.,* II, 11

I

We live surrounded by an endless multitude of mysteries. But no matter how enigmatic may be the mysteries which surround being, what is most enigmatic and disturbing is that mystery in general exists and that we are somehow definitely and forever cut off from the sources and beginnings of life. Of all the things that we here on earth are the witnesses, this is obviously the most absurd and meaningless, the most terrible, almost unnatural, thing—which forces us irresistibly to conclude either that there is something that is not right in the universe, or that the way in which we seek the truth and the demands that we place upon it are vitiated in their very roots.

Whatever our definition of truth may be, we can never renounce Descartes' *clare et distincte* (clarity and distinctness). Now, reality here shows us only an eternal, impenetrable mystery—as if, even before the creation of the world, someone had once and for all forbidden man to attain that which is most necessary and most important to him. What we call the truth, what we obtain through thought, is found to be, in a certain sense, incommensurable not only with the external world into which we have been plunged since our birth but also with our own inner experience. We have sciences and even, if you please, Science, which grows and develops before our very eyes. We know many things and our knowledge is a "clear and distinct" knowledge. Science contemplates with legitimate pride its immense victories and has every right to expect that nothing will be able to stop its triumphant march. No one doubts, and no one can doubt, the enormous importance of the sciences. If Aristotle and his pupil Alexander the Great were brought back to life today, they would believe themselves in the country of the gods and not of men. Ten lives would not suffice Aristotle to assimilate all the knowledge that has been accumulated on earth since his death, and Alexander would perhaps be able to realize his dream and conquer the world. The *clare et distincte* has justified all the hopes which were founded upon it.

But the haze of the primordial mystery has not been dissipated. It has rather grown denser. Plato would hardly need to change a single word of his myth of the cave. Our knowledge would not be able to furnish an answer to his anxiety, his disquietude, his "premonitions." The world would remain for him, "in the light" of our "positive" sciences, what it was—a dark and sorrowful subterranean region—and we would seem to him like chained prisoners. Life would again have to make superhuman efforts, "as in a battle," to break open for himself a path through the truths created by the sciences which "dream of being but cannot see it in waking reality."[1] In brief, Aristotle would bless our knowledge while Plato would curse it. And, conversely, our era would receive Aristotle with open arms but resolutely turn away from Plato.

But it will be asked: What is the force and power of the blessings and curses of men, even if these men be such giants as Plato and Aristotle? Does truth become more true because Aristotle blesses it, or does it become error because Plato curses it? Is it given men to judge the truths, to decide the fate of the truths? On the contrary, it is the truths which judge men and decide their fate and not men who rule over the truths. Men, the great as well as the small, are born and die, appear and disappear—but the truth remains. When no one had as yet begun to "think" or to "search," the truths which later revealed themselves to men already existed. And when men will have finally disappeared from the face of the earth, or will have lost the faculty of thinking, the truths will not suffer therefrom. It is from this that Aristotle set out in his philosophical researches. He declared that Parmenides was "constrained to follow the phenomena." In another place,[2] speaking of the same Parmenides and of other great Greek philosophers, he wrote, they were "constrained by the truth itself." This Aristotle knew definitely: the truth has the power to force or constrain men, all men alike, whether it be the great Parmenides and the great Alexander or Parmenides' unknown slave and the least of Alexander's stable-men.

Why does the truth have this power over Parmenides and Alexander, and not Parmenides and Alexander who have power over the truth? This is a question that Aristotle does not ask. If someone had asked it of him, he would not have understood it and would have explained that the question is meaningless and obviously absurd, that one can say such things but one cannot think them. And this is not because he was an insensible being who was indifferent to all and to whom everything was the same, or that he would have been able to say of himself, like Hamlet, "I am pigeon-livered and lack gall to make oppression bitter." For Aristotle oppression is bitter. In another passage of the same *Metaphysics* he says that it is hard to bow down before Necessity: "everything which constrains is called necessary and that is why the necessary is bitter, as Evenus says: 'every necessary thing is always painful and bitter.' And constraint is a form of necessity—as Sophocles also says: 'But an invincible force necessitates me to act thus.'"[3] Aristotle, we see, feels pain and bitterness at ineluctable Necessity, but, as he himself adds immediately, he distinctly knows that "Necessity does not allow itself to be persuaded." And since it does not listen to persuasion and is not to be overcome, one must submit to it—be this bitter or not, painful or not—submit and henceforth renounce useless struggle: *anankê stênai*, "cry halt before Necessity."

ATHENS AND JERUSALEM

Whence comes this "cry halt before Necessity"? Here is a question of capital importance which contains, if you wish, the *alpha* and *omega* of philosophy. Necessity does not allow itself to be persuaded, it does not even listen. The injustice cries to heaven, if there is no longer anyone here to whom one can cry. It is true that in certain cases and even very often, almost always, the injustice will cry and protest only to end up by becoming silent; men forget both their sorrows and their cruel losses. But there are injustices that one cannot forget. "If I forget thee, O Jerusalem . . . let my tongue cleave to the roof of my mouth."[4] For two thousand years we have all repeated the Psalmist's oath. But did the Psalmist not "know" that Necessity does not allow itself to be persuaded, that it does not listen to oaths or prayers, that it hears nothing and fears nothing? Did he not know that his voice was and could be only the voice of one crying in the wilderness? Of course he knew it, he knew it quite as well as Aristotle. But, doubtless he had something more than this knowledge. Doubtless when a man feels the injustice as deeply as did the Psalmist, his thought undergoes, in a way that is completely unexpected, incomprehensible and mysterious transformations in its very essence. He cannot forget Jerusalem, but he forgets the power of Necessity, the omnipotence of this enemy so terribly armed—one does not know by whom or when or why; and, without thinking of the future, he begins a terrible and final, battle against this enemy. This is surely the meaning of Plotinus' words: "A great and final battle awaits human souls." And these words of Plato have the same meaning: "If it is necessary to dare everything, should we not dare to defy all shame?"[5] Man decides to take up the struggle against all-powerful Necessity only when there awakens in him the readiness to dare everything, to stop before nothing. Nothing can justify this boundless audacity; it is the extreme expression of shamelessness. One has only to look at Aristotle's *Ethics* to be convinced of this. All the virtues are placed by him in the middle zone of being, and everything which passes beyond the limits of "the mean" is an indication of depravity and vice. "Cry halt before Necessity" rules his *Ethics* as well as his *Metaphysics*. His final word is the blessing of Necessity and the glorification of the spirit which has submitted to Necessity.

Not only the good but the truth as well wishes man to bow down before it. All who have read the famous Twelfth Book, especially the last chapter, of the *Metaphysics* and the Ninth and Tenth Books of the *Ethics* know with what fervor Aristotle supplicated Necessity which does not allow itself to be persuaded and which he had not the power to overcome. What irritated him or, perhaps, disturbed him most in Plato was the latter's courage or rather, to use his own expressions, Plato's audacity and shamelessness, which suggested to him that those who adore Necessity only dream of reality but are powerless to see it in the waking state. Plato's words seemed to Aristotle unnatural, fantastic, deliberately provoking. But how to silence Plato, how to constrain him not only to submit to Necessity in the visible and empirical world but also to render to it in thought the honors to which, Aristotle was convinced, it is entitled? Necessity is Necessity, not for those who sleep but for those who are awake. And the waking who see Necessity see real being, while Plato, with his audacity and shamelessness, turns us away from real being and leads us into the domain of the fantastic, the unreal, the illusory, and—by that very fact—the false. One must stop at nothing in order finally to extinguish in man that thirst for freedom which found expression in Plato's work. "Necessity" is invincible. The truth is, in its essence and by its very nature, a truth that constrains; and it is in submission to the constraining truth that the source of all human virtues lies. "Constrained by the truth itself," Parmenides, Heraclitus and Anaxagoras accomplished their work. It has always been so, it will always be so, it must be so. It is not the great Parmenides who rules over the truth but the truth that is the master of Parmenides. And to refuse obedience to the truth that constrains is impossible. Still more: to do other than bless it, whatever be the thing to which it constrains, is impossible. Herein lies the supreme wisdom, human and divine; and the task of philosophy consists in teaching men to submit joyously to Necessity which hears nothing and is indifferent to all.

II

Let us stop and ask ourselves: why does the truth that constrains need men's blessing? Why does Aristotle put himself to so much trouble to obtain for his Necessity men's blessing? Can it not get along without this blessing? If Necessity does not listen to reason, is it more receptive to praises? There is no doubt that constraining Necessity listens no more to praises than to prayers or curses. The stones of the desert have never replied "Amen" to the inspired sermons of the saints. But this is not necessary. What is necessary is that to the silence of the stones—is not Necessity, like the stones, indifferent to everything?—the saints should sing hosannas.

I would recall in this connection the chapters already mentioned of the *Metaphysics* and *Ethics* of Aristotle, the high priest of the visible and the invisible church of "thinking" men. We are asked not only to submit to Necessity but to adore it: such always has been, and such is still, the fundamental task of philosophy. It is not enough that philosophy should recognize the force and power, in fact, of such or such an order of things. It knows and it fears (the beginning of all knowledge is fear) that empirical force, that is, the force that manifests itself in constraining man only once, may be replaced by another force that will act in a different way. Even the scientist, who refuses to philosophize, has, finally, no need of facts; the facts by themselves give us nothing and tell us nothing. There has never been a genuine empiricism among men of science, as there has never been a genuine materialism. What scientist would study facts merely for the sake of facts? Who would wish to observe this drop of water suspended from a telegraphic wire, or this other drop that glides over the window-pane after a rain? There are millions of such drops and these, in and of themselves, have never concerned the scientists and could not concern them. The scientist wishes to know what a water-drop in general is or what water in general is. If, in his laboratory, he decomposes into its constituent elements some water drawn from a brook, it is not in order to study and know what he has at this moment in his hands and under his eyes but in order to acquire the right to make judgments about all the water that he will ever have occasion to see or never will see, about that which no one has ever seen and no one ever will see, about even that which existed when there was not a single conscious being or even any living being on earth. The man of science, whether he knows it or not (most often, obviously, he does know it), whether he wishes it or not (ordinarily he does not wish it), cannot help but be a realist in the medieval sense of the term. He is distinguished from the philosopher only by the fact that the philosopher must, in addition, explain and justify the realism practiced by science. In a general way, since empiricism is only an unsuccessful attempt at philosophical justification of the scientific, i.e., realistic, methods of seeking the truth, its work has, in fact, always led to the destruction of the principles on which it was based. It is necessary to choose: if you wish to be an empiricist, you must abandon the hope of founding scientific knowledge on a solid and certain basis; if you wish to have a solidly established science, you must place it under the protection of the idea of Necessity and, in addition, recognize this idea as primordial, original, having no beginning and consequently no end—that is to say, you must endow it with the superiorities and qualities that men generally accord to the Supreme Being. As we have seen, that is what was done by Aristotle, who thus deserves to be the consecrated pope or high priest of all men who think scientifically.

Doubtless Kant did not exaggerate Hume's merits when he wrote in his *Prolegomena* that since the beginning of philosophy no one had ever discovered a truth equal in importance to that which Hume discovered. As if scales had suddenly dropped from his eyes, Hume saw that the "necessary" bonds established by men between phenomena are only relationships of fact, that there is no "necessity" in the world, and that those who speak of necessity only "dream of being" but cannot see it in waking reality. Hume was too balanced a man—and one, moreover, who valued his equilibrium more than anything else in the world—to be able to appreciate and utilize the great discovery that he had made. One may, if one wishes, say as much of all those men whose eyes have been opened and who have been permitted to see extraordinary things; the sun of truth blinds the inhabitants of the kingdom of darkness with its brilliance. Hume ended up by restoring to Necessity almost all its sovereign rights; but Kant, not being able to bear the "almost" that no one had noticed, accomplished his Copernican task and directed our thought anew into that "sure and royal way" which mathematics had followed for centuries.

Hume's sudden discovery had awakened Kant from his dogmatic slumber. But is it given to men to be awake on earth? And is "nature that does not sleep,"[6] to use Plotinus' term, man's natural state? On the other hand, does not "to dream in sleep or while awake mean to take that which resembles (reality) not for something that resembles (reality) but for the reality that it resembles?"[7] Necessity resembles what really exists like two drops of water resemble each other, but it is not what really exists; it only seems really to exist for him who dreams. Hume's barely perceptible "almost" would have been able to render immense services to thinking and searching humanity if it had been preserved under the form in which it first appeared to the Scottish philosopher. But Hume himself was afraid of what he had seen and hastened to throw away everything that had fallen to his hand so as to have it no longer under his eyes. As for Kant, he found that this was still not enough and he transferred Hume's "almost" outside the limits of synthetic judgments *a priori* into the transcendental and noumenal—i.e., completely inaccessible, without relationship to us and without usefulness for us—world of things in themselves (*Ding an sich*). The shock that he had received from Hume awakened the great philosopher of Königsberg from his sleep. But Kant understood his mission and destiny to mean that he must at all costs defend himself and others against the eventuality of sudden and brutal shocks that interrupt the peace of our somnolent waking, and he proceeded to create his "critical philosophy." At the same time as Hume's "almost," all metaphysics was transferred outside the limits of synthetic judgments *a priori* which, since Kant, have inherited all the rights of the old Necessity and have, for a century and a half, guaranteed to European humanity undisturbed sleep and faith in itself.

It is obvious that for Aristotle the most intolerable and distressing of thoughts was that our earthly life is not the last, definitive, truly real life and that an awakening, be it only in a certain measure, is possible—an awakening similar to that which we know in coming out of sleep. When he attacked Plato's "ideas" he was trying above all to rid himself of this eventuality which was, to him, worse than a nightmare. And his distress was, in a certain sense, completely justified, as was Kant's distress when Hume, with his "almost," so brutally awakened him from his dogmatic slumber. Plato's "they dream," quite like Hume's denial of any necessary bonds between phenomena, undermines the very foundations of human thought. Nothing is impossible. Anything that one wishes can flow from anything that one wishes and the principle of contradiction, which Aristotle wished to consider as "the most unshakable of principles," begins to totter, discovering to the frightened human mind the kingdom of the absolutely arbitrary which threatens to destroy the world and the thought which seeks to know the world; *einai kai noein* (being and thought) become phantoms. How could Plato have permitted himself to speak of his cave? How could he have imagined it? How could Hume have dared to deny the rights of Necessity? And does not humanity owe an eternal debt of gratitude to Aristotle and to Kant, to the first for having put an end, by his severe criticism and indignant cries, to the fantastic tendencies of his teacher, and to the second for having led our thought back into its natural groove by his doctrine of synthetic judgments *a priori?*

There cannot be two answers to these questions. Aristotle is the founder not only of the positive sciences but also of the positive philosophy. It is not for nothing that the Middle Ages saw in him the only guide through the labyrinth of life and did not dare to open the books, written without him (and perhaps also not for him), of the Old and New Testaments. The new philosophy has always followed, and still continues to follow, the paths that he marked out. One can say the same thing of Kant: he subdued the disquieting spirit of doubt and "forced it to bow its rebellious head before the angelic visage of the universal and the necessary.

Necessity has obtained its justification—a justification of which it had no need at all. The celebrities of science, like all the ordinary scientists, glorify Necessity, even though it be as indifferent to blame as to praise. Only the wicked or the foolish can doubt its sovereign rights. But has this human defense rendered it stronger and more vigorous? Or should we not, perhaps, put the question differently: does not its force come from the fact that men have taken it under their protection and have surrounded it with an insurmountable wall made of formulas of incantation forged through the centuries?

III

Although Seneca may not have been an original philosopher, he succeeded quite well at times, as is known, in expressing the thought of others. Everything discussed in our preceding chapters was formulated by him in a few words that have become famous: *Ipse omnium conditor et rector . . . semper paret, semel jussit* (The founder and guide of all things . . . always obeys, but has commanded only once). So thought Seneca, so thought the ancients, so all of us think. God commanded only once and, thereafter, He and all men after Him no longer command but obey. He commanded a long time ago, an infinitely long time ago, so that He Himself has forgotten when and under what circumstances there occurred this absurd, unique of its kind, and consequently unnatural, event. Perhaps, having taken on this habit of passive and submissive existence, God has even forgotten how to command; perhaps, like us ordinary mortals, He can only obey. In other words, the will to act that He once manifested forever exhausted His creative energy, and now He is condemned, like the world that He created, to fulfill His own prescriptions, prescriptions that He Himself can no longer violate. To put it still differently, the Creator of the world has Himself become subordinate to Necessity which He created and which, without at all seeking or desiring it, has become the sovereign of the universe.

I repeat: Seneca's formula belongs unquestionably to him, but the thought that he expresses is not his own. So thought and so continue to think all the learned men of all countries. Why do they think so? Were they witnesses of the world's creation, or did the Creator reveal his secret to any of them? No one was present at the creation of the world, no one can any longer boast of any special intimacy with the Creator. The thought expressed by Seneca allured men because the mysterious and inconceivable moment of command (*jubere*) as pushed back into the eternity of the past and declared unique (*semel jussit*), while for ordinary usage men chose obedience, the *parere*, which seems to be the comprehensible, natural, and normal fate not only of the creature but also of the Creator Himself. And, indeed, Seneca was right: in the parere everything is comprehensible, clear to all, and—consequently—natural, while in the *jubere* everything is mysterious, arbitrary and—consequently—fantastic, eternally inconceivable and puzzling.

Had it been possible, Seneca and those from whom Seneca learned to "think" would have preferred not to remember the mysterious *jubere* at all. No one has ever commanded anything, all have always done nothing but obey; for there has never been anything supernatural or mysterious, either in the remotest times or in our own day. Everything has always been dear and natural. And the task of philosophy is then to strengthen and sustain Necessity by all the means at its disposal. But what are these means? It is not given mortals to change anything whatsoever of the nature of Necessity, to enhance or strengthen it in its own being. There remains, then, only one thing to do: to convince men by reasoning or by incantations that, on the one hand, Necessity is omnipotent and to fight it serves no purpose; on the other hand, that Necessity is of divine origin (that is why the *semel jussit* is preserved) and that it is impious and immoral to refuse it obedience. This same Seneca is inexhaustible in his praise of God who has forgotten how to command and of men who manifest a boundless submission. "I do not obey God, I agree with Him; I follow Him with all my soul, but not because it is necessary." Or again, in the famous translation of the words of the Stoic Cleanthes which Cicero so admired: "the fates lead the willing, but the unwilling they drag." One could cite hundreds of pages from Seneca or Cicero filled with reflections of this kind.

It will be said that Seneca, as well as Cleanthes on whom Seneca relied, expresses the ideas of the Stoic school, and that we have no right, in speaking of Aristotle, to refer to the Stoics whose narrowness of mind was already well known to the ancients. But I believe that Dilthey was right when he frankly admitted that the modern age received the philosophy of antiquity through Cicero and Seneca, and that it is with their eyes that we see the ancients. It is even more exact to say that the narrow philosophy of the Stoics and the overly simple logic of the Cynics at times reveal to us the essence of ancient thought (and of our own) better than the works of Plato and Aristotle. The Stoics are regarded with scornful condescension, but it cannot even be imagined what would have become of European thought if the ideas sown in the world by the Stoics had not produced so abundant a harvest. The Stoics at times were only too frank. Now, many ideas are admitted only if they agree not to show their true face and, when necessary, to deny it. Ham, who turned around to look at his father's nakedness, has been nailed to the pillory by history. But how many have turned around without anyone thinking of blaming them? To turn around, to reflect, *besinnen*, is considered one of the most honorable of things; Hegel's entire philosophy reduces itself finally to a looking around. It will be said that the "nakedness of the father" did not interest Hegel. I would answer that he looked at nakednesses that are even more criminal to contemplate than one's father's. But Hegel knew what one can say and what must be passed over in silence. This knowledge was foreign to the Stoics, and even more so to the Cynics. The Cynics' whole error derives from the fact that they had an absolute confidence in reflective human reason. Other men, almost all, especially the philosophers, have committed the same mistake. Who does not trust reason? But others knew how to keep to themselves the greatest part of what they had received in payment for their absolute confidence in reason, and they are praised as sages while the Cynics are called "dogs." Noah's third son, the Cynics and, to some extent, the Stoics are not reproached for turning around and looking at the completely "naked" truth; this is permitted and even encouraged. What is not forgiven them is only their calling things by their right names, their saying that they are looking around when they are looking around and that nakedness is nakedness.

Blessed are those who look around and are silent, blessed are those who see but hide what they see. Why is this so? No one can answer. It seems that every man, like Socrates, has at his side a demon who, in decisive moments, demands of him judgments and acts whose meaning remains incomprehensible to him and forever hidden. But if such a demon exists in nature and if even the most courageous of men dare not disobey him, how can one not ask whence, from what worlds, this mysterious being has come to us? But no one greatly desires to ask this. People know that there is someone (or perhaps even something: it is not known in advance how the demon should be spoken of, whether as a thing or as a being) that has received or has arrogated the right to present to men completely unmotivated demands, and they are satisfied with that. The demon prescribes, men obey. And all are happy that a power should finally be found which binds and decides, which delivers us from freedom of the will, and that one can, one should, one must stop—"cry halt before Necessity."

Again it will be said that I have exceeded the limits, that I began by speaking in the name of "all" and ended with the words of a famous philosopher. For the phrase, "cry halt before Necessity," that I have just quoted belongs to Aristotle. But the average person is not so far removed from the philosopher. Somewhere, at the beginning or at the end, in the depths or at the surface, the average man and the philosopher meet. Seneca, who proclaimed his *paret semper, jussit semel* as the last word of the philosophers' wisdom, was only paraphrasing Aristotle. Quite like the average man, Aristotle wishes to know nothing of commanding (*jubere*); he needs only to obey (*parere*) in order to accomplish, in obeying, what he believes, what all men believe, to be the destiny of man. It does not matter to him at all whence the commandment comes—all the more so since, as Seneca has frankly admitted to us, the sources of *jubere* are now forever dried up. No one in the world will ever again command, all will forever obey—the great and the small, the righteous and the sinners, men and gods. "Truth" does not make any distinctions; it constrains all alike, the great Parmenides as well as the humblest day laborer.

"Parmenides is constrained" and the day laborer is constrained. The gods themselves are in the power of Necessity: "Not even the gods fight against Necessity."[8] It is impossible to investigate whence Necessity derives this power of constraining all living beings. One cannot even ask what the nature of this Necessity is and why it must constrain living beings. Not only will it not reply, but it will not even hear the questions that are addressed to it. And still less is it capable of allowing itself to be persuaded or convinced. Aristotle himself, like no one else, knew how to look around and investigate what was before him and behind him; he tells us that "Necessity does not allow itself to be persuaded."

Whatever field of philosophical thought we approach, we always run up against this blind, deaf and dumb Necessity. And we are convinced that philosophy begins only where the kingdom of strict Necessity discloses itself. Our thought, in the final analysis, is only the search for this strict Necessity. And still more, it is not for nothing that Parmenides affirmed "being and thought are one and the same." To think is necessarily to take cognizance of the necessity of everything that forms the content of being. Whence comes Necessity? Does it come from being and end in thought? Or does it come from thought and end in being? We do not know. We do not even raise this question, knowing—doubtless instinctively—that such questions not only would not reconcile the theory of Knowledge which is concerned with "thought" (*noein*) with the ontology which is concerned with "being" (*einai*) but would forever separate them and set them at enmity with each other. No one wishes to take upon himself the responsibility for the results to which so ancient and universally recognized an idea as that of Necessity may lead. Thought would have preferred to consider Necessity a creation of being, that being, which by its very nature is more turbulent, might easily repudiate Necessity and declare it to be the child of pure thought. Being, despite what Parmenides says, is not the same as thought. But, on the other hand, being, at least within the bounds of philosophical systems, has not been able to find any adequate expression outside of thought. Even though it is not always submissive to Necessity, its attempts at struggle do not reach the domain of philosophy. We have said that philosophy has always meant and wished to mean reflection, *Besinnung*, looking backward. Now it is necessary to add that "looking backward," by its very nature, excludes the possibility and even the thought of struggle. "Looking backward" paralyses man. He who turns around, who looks backward, must see what already exists, that is to say, the head of Medusa; and he who sees Medusa's head is inevitably petrified, as the ancients already knew. And his thought, a petrified thought, will naturally correspond to his petrified being. Spinoza was in error when he said that if the stone were endowed with consciousness it would imagine that it falls to the ground freely. If someone had endowed the stone with consciousness, at the same time preserving for it its nature as a stone (this is obviously possible—the authority of the sober-headed Spinoza is sufficient guarantee for it), it would not for a single moment have doubted that Necessity is the primordial principle upon which all being in its totality—not only the real, but also the possible—is based. Is not the idea of Necessity the most adequate expression of petrification? And would not the thought and being of a stone endowed with consciousness be completely exhausted by the content that we find in the idea of Necessity?

But let us go further. Philosophy—we have seen—was, is, and wishes to be, a looking backward. To look backward does not at all mean, and we know this well, merely to turn the head. When Noah's third son turned around he drew upon himself universal scorn. When the Cynics turned around they became dogs. But even worse things happen: one who turns around sees the head of Medusa and is changed into a stone. I know that the philosophers do not believe much in the possibility of such miraculous transformations and do not like to have them spoken of. But this is why I have reminded myself of Socrates' demon. If Socrates had prejudices, if Socrates was superstitious, if Socrates sought protection against the light of his reason in the fantastic, if Socrates fled the clear and distinct world of ideas that he had himself created in order to take refuge with his demon—have we not the right, are we not obliged, even if it be only once in our life and only for a moment, to doubt, not our existence (there is no need for us to doubt this, any more than there was for Descartes), but that our thought, which we have become accustomed to consider as the only possible thought, leads us precisely to the sources of the final truths? Should we not tell ourselves that to think means not to look backward, as we habitually believe, but to look forward? And that we may even not look at all but proceed venturously forward with eyes closed, without foreseeing anything, without asking anything, without being disturbed by anything, without being concerned with adapting ourselves to the laws, great and small, the observance of which has always appeared to men as the condition of the possibility of seeing truths and the realities which these truths uncover? In general, must we forget fear, apprehension, anxiety?

It will be said that this is not given to man. But, then, let us recall once more the divine Plato, the great pupil of a great teacher, and his lesson: "everything must be dared." We must try to stand up against Necessity itself, try to free the living and feeling Parmenides from dead and altogether indifferent power. To Necessity all things are indifferent, but to Parmenides all things are not indifferent. On the contrary, it is infinitely important to him that certain things should be and that certain other things should not be—for example, that the hemlock should be dependent on Socrates and not Socrates on the hemlock. Or rather, to make the matter still clearer, let us say this: in the year 399 B.C. the aged Socrates, condemned to death by his fellow citizens, took from the jailer's hands the cup of hemlock and in that very moment, by Socrates' will, the hemlock became a healthful drink. And this is not imagination or fantasy but reality, that which actually was. Imagination and fantasy, rather, are all that is related of Socrates' death in the history manuals. And similarly, what Aristotle teaches us, "Necessity does not allow itself to be persuaded," is also only an invention. Necessity

ATHENS AND JERUSALEM

does listen and does allow itself to be persuaded, and it cannot oppose itself to Socrates; it cannot in general oppose itself to any man who has discovered the secret of its power and has enough audacity to command it without turning backward, to speak to it as "one who has power."

Aristotle would certainly have paid no attention to thoughts of this kind. And Seneca and Cleanthes would have completely ignored them as being of no concern to themselves. But Epictetus, perhaps because he was more sensitive or perhaps because he was less well-bred, would have been enraged by them. Is this not an attempt to escape the principle of contradiction? In his eyes, as in Aristotle's, this was clearly a mortal sin, and he considered that he had the right in this instance to give free reign to his anger. "I should have wished," he said, "to be the slave of a man who does not admit the principle of contradiction. He would have told me to serve him wine; I would have given him vinegar or something still worse. He would have become angry and complained that I did not give him what he asked. But I would have answered, 'You do not recognize the principle of contradiction; hence, wine, vinegar or any loathsome thing are all the same. And you do not recognize Necessity; therefore, no one has the power to compel you to regard the vinegar as something bad and the wine as something good. Drink the vinegar as if it were wine and be content!' Or again, the master orders me to shave him, and I cut off his nose or his ear with the razor. He would again cry out, but I would repeat to him my argument. And I would do everything in the same way until I forced my master to recognize the truth that Necessity is invincible and the principle of contradiction omnipotent."

We see that Epictetus repeats what Aristotle said or, more precisely, gives a commentary of Aristotle's words. And, as almost always happens with the Stoics, Epictetus, in commenting, discovers what in Aristotle had been intentionally left in the dark, and so betrays the secret of the philosophical foundation of the Aristotelian truths. The principle of contradiction, as well as Necessity and the truth itself, with a capital letter or a small letter, are supported only by threats: one cuts off your ears or your nose, one pierces your eyes, etc. . . . Before such constraint all living beings—men and devils and angels, and even the gods—find themselves equal. Epictetus speaks of an imaginary master, but he would say the same thing of Heraclitus, of Parmenides, of Socrates and of God Himself.

IV

"Parmenides constrained, Socrates constrained": it seems to Aristotle—no, it does not seem to him, it is obvious to him (and he is convinced that the whole world considers it obvious along with him)—that the truth has the power to constrain the great Parmenides, the great Socrates, anyone whomsoever. And (this is the most important thing) it is also obvious to him that it is completely absurd to ask who endowed the truth with this extraordinary power, and still more absurd to fight against this power. Whence came this conviction to him? From experience? But experience—Aristotle knew from Plato—is never the source of eternal truths. Experiential truths are just as limited and contingent as experience itself. "Necessity does not allow itself to be persuaded"—the source of this truth is not experience but something else.

Even the most ordinary experiential truth, even what is called the establishment of a fact, does not wish to be a relative and limited truth; the truths of fact claim, and indeed successfully, the title and dignity of eternal truths. I have given examples of this. In the year 399 B.C. Socrates was poisoned at Athens. This is a truth of experience, the establishment of a fact. But it does not wish to remain in this state. "That Socrates drank a cup of poison is, it is true, something that in reality happened once; but the historical truth that this was so will remain for all time, independently of the fact whether it is forgotten or not"—this is what we read in a book by a very prominent modern philosopher. No one will ever again have the right to say, "No, it was not so. It did not happen. Socrates was not poisoned." Whether it be a question of the poisoning of Socrates or the poisoning of a mad dog is of no importance. The eternal truth, just like the necessity of which it was born, does not listen and does not allow itself to be persuaded. And, just as it does not hear or listen to anything, it does not make any distinctions: that Socrates should have been poisoned or that a mad dog should have been poisoned is absolutely indifferent to it. It automatically affixes the seal of eternity on both events and thus forever paralyses the seeker's will. Once Necessity has intervened, man no longer dares to doubt, to be indignant, to contradict, to struggle and say, for example, "Yet it is not a dog but Socrates, the best and the wisest of men, a saint, who has been poisoned!"

Even if one agrees to recognize the proposition "a dog has been poisoned" as a truth which, though it establishes something that happened only once, is nevertheless an eternal truth, one cannot willingly resolve to fix the seal of eternity on the proposition "Socrates has been poisoned." It is already quite enough that this truth should have subsisted for a long period of history. It has lived in the world all too long—almost twenty-five hundred years. But to promise it immortality, an existence outside of time that no forgetfulness will ever be able to destroy—who has taken upon himself the right to give such promises? And why does philosophy, which knows that everything that has a beginning must also have an end, forget this "eternal truth" and grant everlasting existence to a truth which did not exist before the year 399 B.C., which was born in 399 B.C.? Aristotle did not ask himself such questions. For him the truth was more precious than Plato, more precious than Socrates, more precious than everything in the world. Plato and Socrates, having had a beginning, must therefore have an end, while the truth which had a beginning, quite like the truth which had no beginning, will never have an end. And, if you should try to argue with Aristotle or to persuade him, it would be in vain; he would not hear, as Necessity does not hear. Even Aristotle is *ti* "something" (not *tis,* "someone," but *ti,* "something") that "does not hear"; he can but will not, or perhaps he cannot and will not, listen to any argument. He has lived so long in the company of "the truths" that he has assimilated their nature; he has himself become like a truth and sees the essence of his being, of all being, in "constraining and being constrained." And if anyone should refuse obedience to him he would—as the honest Epictetus has told us—cut off his ears or his nose. He would force him to drink vinegar, and if all this were not enough, he would present him the cup of hemlock which, as we know, finally and once and for all (an eternal truth!) finished Socrates himself. Whatever one might say to him, Aristotle would not renounce his statement, "Necessity does not allow itself to be persuaded." And he does not rely, I repeat once more, on experience; experience does not give us eternal truths, it gives us only empirical, provisional, temporary truths. The source of his truths is something quite other.

In 399 B.C. the Athenians poisoned Socrates, and Plato his disciple, "constrained by the truth itself," could not do other than think that Socrates had been poisoned. He speaks of Socrates' death in the *Crito,* in the *Phaedo* and in his other dialogues. But in everything that he writes, there is always apparent this question: is there really in the world a power to which it is given to constrain us finally and forever to admit that Socrates was poisoned in 399? For Aristotle such a question, which in his eyes was obviously absurd, did not exist. He was convinced that the truth "Socrates was poisoned," quite like the truth "a dog was poisoned," is beyond all divine or human objections. *The hemlock makes no distinction between Socrates and a dog.* And we, "constrained to follow the phenomena, constrained by the truth itself," are obliged in our judgments, whether mediate or immediate, to make no distinction between Socrates and a dog, even between Socrates and a mad dog.

Plato knew this no less than Aristotle. He also, let us recall, wrote: "Not even the gods fight against Necessity." Nevertheless he himself did struggle against Necessity all his life. From this derives the dualism for which he has always been reproached; from this come his contradictions and paradoxes which so infuriated Aristotle. Plato was not content with the sources of truth that satisfied the curiosity of his great pupil. He knew that it is difficult to find "the Father and Creator of all the universe" and that "if one finds Him, one cannot show Him to everyone." Nevertheless, he strained all his powers in an attempt to overcome these difficulties as well as this impossibility.

It seems at times that it is only difficulties that attract Plato, that his philosophical genius deploys its full activity only before the impossible. "It is necessary to dare everything," and it is all the more necessary to dare when there are fewer chances, in the eyes of the average man, of obtaining anything. There is no hope of wresting Socrates from the power of the eternal truth, which is as indifferent to Socrates as to a mad dog and which has swallowed him up forever. Therefore, philosophy and the philosophers must think of nothing other than to deliver Socrates. If one cannot do this otherwise, he must go down to the netherworld, as Orpheus did. He must implore the gods, as Pygmalion once did, whom the inert Necessity which directs the natural course of things would not hear. Pygmalion's desire to animate the statue that he had made—was this not and is it not still, for logical thought, the height of madness and immorality? But before the tribunal of the gods, who, unlike Necessity, know how and are willing to allow themselves to be persuaded, the impossible and the senseless become possible and sensible. God thinks and speaks quite otherwise than Necessity. "Everything that is bound," says God in the works of Plato, "may be dissolved; but only the wicked can wish to dissolve that which is well bound and holds together as it should. This is why, in general, you who were created are not protected against dissolution and are not immortal; but you will not be dissolved and you will not experience the fate of mortality because, by my will, you will receive a more lasting strength than that which you had at your birth."[9]

Not only Aristotle but no one, not even the most ardent admirers of the Platonic truth, can read these words without irritation or resentment. What is this "my will" which arrogates to itself the right and power to change the natural course of things? We "understand" Necessity, and we "understand" also that "Necessity does not allow itself to be persuaded" (why we understand it and who the "we" are who understand—these questions we do not even wish to raise). But when "by my will" intervenes, the whole spiritual nature of thinking man, his soul (in general the soul does not exist, but for this occasion it will be rehabilitated), is indignant at the daring and impudence of these pretensions. "By my will" is nothing else than the *deus ex machina*; but we think, with Kant (can we think otherwise?), that "in the determination of the origin and validity of our knowledge, the *deus ex machina* is the greatest absurdity that one could choose." Or as the same Kant says elsewhere with still greater force, "to say that a supreme being has wisely introduced into us such ideas and principles *a priori* is completely to destroy all philosophy."

Why does Necessity which does not listen and does not allow itself to be persuaded seem to us a reasonable supposition, while the *deus ex machina* seems to us to open the way to, and protect, all kinds of caprices (*jeder Grille . . . Vorschub gibt*) and appears to us so absurd? The *deus ex machina* threatens to destroy the very possibility of knowledge. But Kant's task was not to defend and glorify knowledge at all costs. He had undertaken the "critique" of pure reason. He should therefore have put, before everything else, this question: are our knowledge and that which people ordinarily call philosophy so precious that we must take up their defense at the cost of any sacrifice, no matter how great? On the contrary, perhaps, since knowledge is so intimately bound to Necessity that it becomes impossible when one admits the *deus ex machina* (*höheres Wesen*), would it not be better to renounce knowledge and seek the protection of the "caprice" that so frightened Kant? To show oneself ready to renounce knowledge—is this not the only means (or at least the first step) to free oneself from that so greatly detested Necessity (which as we know, sometimes made Aristotle himself groan), from that Necessity which is not even afraid to offend the gods?

What Kant and all of us after Kant judge to be the most absurd of suppositions allows us to entertain the possibility of freeing mortals and immortals from that implacable power which, by some unknown miracle, has conquered the world and subjugated all living beings. Can it be that the *deus ex machina* might put an end to the hateful *parere* (obedience) and return to men the creative *jubere* (commanding) which the gods themselves had to renounce at some mysterious and terrible moment of the distant past? Can it be that the fall of Necessity would bring about the fall of the other usurpers to whom we feeble slaves, accustomed to the *parere*, have handed over our destiny? The principle of contradiction and the principle of identity have also been introduced into the world without authorization to act as masters therein. When we affirm that sound is heavy, these principles intervene and immediately oppose their veto: "we do not permit this, therefore it is not so." But when it is said "Socrates has been poisoned," these two principles remain passive and even give their blessing to this judgment and confer upon it, as we recall, eternity. But does there not exist somewhere in the depths of being a "reality" wherein the nature of the principles of contradiction and identity undergoes a radical transformation, wherein it is not they but man who commands, wherein they obey man's commandments, i.e., wherein they do not intervene when sounds become heavy but protest when righteous men are put to death? Then the proposition "sound is heavy" would not seem absurd, while the proposition "Socrates has been poisoned" would become contradictory and, by that very fact, non-existent.

If such things be possible, if it be possible that Necessity which does not allow itself to be persuaded bows down before the caprice (*Grille*) of man, if the principles of contradiction and identity cease to be principles and become merely executive instruments, if the impossible becomes possible—what is then the value of the "eternal truths" accumulated by thinking humanity? It will be asked: how is one to know if such a reality is possible? That is just it: how is one to know? Once we begin to ask, we shall be told, as we have already been told, that such a reality is impossible; that Necessity, the principle of identity, the principle of contradiction and the other principles have ruled, do rule and will forever rule in our world as well as in all the worlds which have existed and will ever exist; that there never have been and never will be heavy sounds; that people have put to death and will continue to put to death wise men; and that the power of the gods themselves has limits that cannot be transcended.

But what if we do not ask anything of anyone? Are we capable of such daring and of so realizing the free will with which the philosophers entice us? Or better still, do we desire such freedom—a freedom such that the principles of contradiction and of identity and Necessity itself should be under our command? It seems that we have no great desire for it and that we should be afraid to grant such freedom to God Himself.

V

Aristotle and Epictetus submitted to Necessity and reconciled themselves to it. Plato did not reconcile himself to Necessity, even though he understood, quite as well as Aristotle and Epictetus, what dangers threaten the man who refuses to submit to this power. Plato saw quite well, just as all of us see, that in the year 399 Socrates was poisoned. And nevertheless, or rather precisely because he had seen it, because he had been "constrained" to see it with his own eyes, he suddenly had for the first time that deep, indestructible suspicion which is so incomprehensible to men: are our own eyes, then, really the source of the final metaphysical truths? In the *Symposium* he writes: "The spiritual eye becomes keen when the corporeal eyes begin to lose their sharpness" (219A).

It may be assumed that when this idea came to his mind for the first time Plato himself was frightened by it and, before deciding to express it aloud, had more than once to give himself courage by remembering "it is necessary to dare everything." And indeed, if there are two kinds of eyes, who will say with which eyes we see truth and with which error? With all the good will in the world we should never be able to answer this question. Is it the corporeal eye that discovers the truth or is it the spiritual eye? The one supposition is as admissible as the other. The physical eyes can distinguish truth from error. Epictetus could force a man to distinguish vinegar from wine, shaving from cutting, etc., but Epictetus, quite like Aristotle, had no power over the spiritual eyes. For both of them relied on Necessity, both of them were "constrained by the truth itself," and they wished and were able also "to constrain" others. But this was possible only so long as those to whom they addressed themselves were beings equipped with corporeal eyes. These one can constrain by threats. Necessity has power over them. But he who has lost his corporeal eyes, who, instead of corporeal vision, possesses "spiritual vision"—does Necessity have any power over him? Is it not in this that that miracle of transfiguration which was mentioned above consists? Parmenides is no longer constrained but rather constrains; the principle of contradiction does not command but obeys; the vinegar becomes wine, the razor does not cut, etc. And the whole arsenal of Aristotle's and Epictetus' threats loses, like salt which ceases to be salty, all sense and meaning.

I think that there cannot be two opinions on this matter: Plato's "spiritual vision" is nothing other than a desperate attempt to tear himself away from the power of Necessity which has been throughout all time the foundation of human thought. The best commentary on the passage of the *Symposium* that we have quoted is found in the words of Plotinus: "Thought was granted to the divine, but not to the best beings, as an eye intended to correct their natural blindness. But what would it serve for the eye to see what is, if it were itself the light? And so if someone has need of eyes, it is that, being himself blind, he seeks the light."[10] "Spiritual vision" is no longer vision in the proper sense; that is, the passive consideration and acceptance of truth prepared in advance, imposed by an external constraint—as truth, according to Aristotle or Epictetus, is imposed. *What appears to the latter as the essential moment of truth, the power of constraining all men, is found to be a mere accident.* Circumstances change and this constraint becomes at first useless, inconvenient, intolerable, then finally *a distortion of the very nature of truth*—at least of the metaphysical truth concerning which we are here speaking. The truth of the corporeal eye maintains itself by force, by threats. Sometimes it also employs allurements. It forces the disobedient to drink vinegar; it cuts off their noses, their ears, etc. . . . It does not know any other means of bringing it about that men should agree to recognize it. If you deprive such a truth of the means of coercion that it has at its disposal, who would then be willing to follow it? Who would recognize of his own free will that Socrates has been poisoned? Who would delight in seeing the phenomena lead the great Parmenides, as if he were not Parmenides but a horse or a mule? All that is human in the living being imperiously demands that no one should be permitted to touch Socrates, and that the phenomena should not lead the great Parmenides as they wish but rather docilely and trustingly follow Parmenides.

Spinoza's stone endowed with consciousness would have approved, one may believe, the order of existing things or, rather, the *ordo et connexio rerum* visible to the corporeal eye. But the living person will never accept this order. And if, nevertheless, many have sincerely sought to secure such a state of affairs *in saecula saeculorum,* it is not at all necessary to deduce therefrom what people ordinarily deduce: namely, that one can see the final truths with the corporeal eye and that Necessity has at its disposal a miraculous power, a supernatural force, to transform the temporal into the eternal. It is necessary to draw therefrom a conclusion which will perhaps seem at first sight paradoxical and consequently completely inadmissible for our *ignava ratio* (lazy reason) but which, it is to be believed, is the only truth: "Not all are created under the same conditions but to some eternal life is preordained, to others eternal damnation." Or, if you do not care for theology and Calvin, the same thought may be formulated using Spinoza's words: most men only resemble men, in reality they are not men but stones endowed with consciousness. And what we customarily call "the laws of thought" are only the laws of the thought of stones endowed with consciousness. Or again: it seems that, in the course of man's brief existence, each of us often has occasion to see himself transformed into a stone endowed with consciousness—and this precisely when he turns backward, inquires, and begins to reflect. Plato sadly felt this and sought with all the powers of his soul to escape the petrification that threatened him. For Aristotle, on the other hand, to try to fight what he considered the natural order of things and, consequently, the final and definitive reality, was the height of folly.

Can it be hoped that the enfeebled physical eye may be replaced by a spiritual eye that will permit us to see another world and no longer that which we have always seen and shall always and everywhere see? It is here that there begins, for Aristotle, the domain of the fantastic, against which he defends himself and others by means of his logic as well as his metaphysics and his ethics, by his categorical statement "Cry halt before Necessity." Plato, on the contrary, drew his inspiration from the fantastic. For Plato, the corporeal vision was so intimately bound to the idea of "constraining and being constrained," to the idea that the death of Socrates is an eternal truth in the world where it is the corporeal eyes that discover the truth, that it did not seem to him sufficient to weaken our physical vision and our physical being in general. As long as we exist physically we are under the domination of Necessity. One can put us to the torture and force us to recognize anything whatever.

I shall recall again—for one repeats these things in vain, people always forget them—how the noble Epictetus treated all those who were unwilling to follow him, how he pierced their eyes and cut off their noses and ears, and how

Aristotle forced the great Parmenides to accept his truths. Can one live in a world where the truth—i.e., that which, according to us, is the most powerful, the best, and the most desirable thing on earth—tortures men and transforms them into stones endowed with consciousness? We must flee this world, flee it as quickly as possible, flee it without turning backward, without asking where we are going and without considering what the future will bring us. We must burn, tear out, and destroy in ourselves everything that stupefies, petrifies, crushes, and draws us towards the visible world, if we wish to save ourselves from the terrible danger (*damnatio aeterna*) that lies in wait for us. Not only the corporeal eye but all of the "corporeality" through which we arrive at the constraining truths must be torn out of man, so that the vinegar may become wine and that a new eye may arise in place of the pierced eye. But how can we do this? Who can do it? Plato replies: this is the task of philosophy, of a philosophy that is no longer science and no longer even knowledge but, as he says in the *Phaedo, meletê thanatou,* "the practice of death"—of a philosophy capable of replacing the natural eye of man by a supernatural eye, i.e., *an eye which sees not what is but thanks to which what one sees "by one's will" becomes what is.*

Aristotle does not understand Plato's "practice of death," even though this "thought," if one may call it a thought, is developed in the *Phaedo* and emphasized with all the force of which Plato was capable. Plato says that all those who sincerely devoted themselves to philosophy were doing nothing but preparing themselves by degrees for death and to die. It is true that he adds immediately afterwards that the philosophers generally hide this from the whole world. But there was no need even, it seems, to hide it. Plato did not hide it: he proclaimed his "practice of death" aloud and yet no one understood it. Before as after Plato, the whole world is convinced that truths and revelations are not to be sought in death but that death is rather the end of revelations and truths.

People do not argue with Plato or contradict him, but almost no one speaks of the "practice of death." The only exception is Spinoza, who, like Plato, was not afraid "to dare everything" or to approach the limits of being. As if in answer to Plato, he declares: "a free man thinks of death least of all things, and his wisdom is a meditation not of death but of life."[11] This is basically what Aristotle would already have had to say. Here is the only way of freeing oneself from Plato with his spiritual eye and his "preparation for death." There are no eyes other than the corporeal eyes, and even Spinoza's *oculi mentis* (eyes of the mind) are in a certain sense only the corporeal eyes arrived at a higher degree of evolution or, if you wish, the corporeal eyes par excellence. The *oculi mentis* bring us to the *tertium genus cognitionis* (third kind of knowledge), to *cognitio intuitiva* (intuitive knowledge), that is, precisely to the kind of knowledge where Necessity shows itself to us in all its omnipotence and terrible magnificence. *Sub specie necessitatis* is transformed, through Spinoza's will, into *sub specie aeternitatis,* that is, Necessity becomes an ideal at the same time that it is a reality. It comes from reason, which Spinoza, forgetting his promise to speak of everything as the mathematicians speak of lines and surfaces, calls "the greatest gift and the divine light," and to which he erects an altar as the only god worthy of veneration: "what altar will he build for himself who insults reason's majesty?" Reason alone can give us that "one thing necessary" which, as all the wise men have taught, makes man, whom we see and who exists, and the gods, whom no one has ever seen either with corporeal eyes or with spiritual eyes, to live. "Contentment with one's self can spring from reason, and that contentment which springs from reason is the highest possible."[12]

Spinoza did not like Aristotle, perhaps because he did not know him well enough but more perhaps because even in Aristotle he discovered too obvious traces of that "mythological" thought of which he wished to believe himself completely freed. Spinoza endeavored to create not the "best philosophy" but the "true philosophy." He assured everyone else as well as himself that man has no need of the "best," that it is enough for him to have the "true." But Spinoza was doubly wrong. Aristotle, as we have seen, believed in the sovereign rights of truth and never attempted in his philosophical and scientific researches to protest against the subordinate and dependent situation to which the very conditions of our existence condemn us. He spoke, it is true, of the purposes of creation, he said that nature does nothing in vain, etc. But this was only a methodological procedure, a procedure for seeking truth, just as his *primum movens immobile* (first unmoved mover) was no longer a living god inhabiting Olympus or any other place in the real universe, however distant from us, but only an active force determining the formation and succession of all the observable phenomena of the external world. For him, the *summum bonum* (highest good) of men is limited by the possible, and the possible is determined by reason.

And if Aristotle found this *summum bonum* in our world, Spinoza in this respect is hardly far from Aristotle. His "contentment with oneself which springs from reason" is not essentially distinguishable from the Aristotelian ideal of wisdom, from his *noêsis noêseôs* (thinking of thought). So that it is rather Spinoza (did he not affirm that his task was the search for the "true philosophy" and that he was not concerned with the needs and aspirations of men, for men are to him only perpendiculars or triangles and do not deserve to be considered in any way other than perpendiculars or triangles?) whom one could accuse of being untrue to his principles by erecting an altar to reason, by glorifying ratio as the "greatest gift and the divine light," by singing the praises of "contentment with oneself," etc. But it is precisely because Spinoza, quite like Aristotle, permitted himself this inconsequence, whether unconsciously or deliberately, that he succeeded in reaching the goal that he had set himself: to convince men that the ideal of human existence is the stone endowed with consciousness. Why? Even if it is correct that the stone endowed with consciousness is best fitted to perceive the truths, why address oneself to living men and demand of them that they accomplish such a transformation of themselves? And why did neither Aristotle nor Spinoza attempt (what at first appears easier), by means of their incantations and their sorceries, to endow with consciousness the inanimate objects which have not and cannot have any motive for opposing such attempts? But no one has ever attempted anything of the kind. No one is interested in seeing that the stones are transformed into thinking beings, but many are interested in seeing that living men are transformed into stones. Why? What is finally in question here?

VI

Here I have only touched lightly on the philosophy of Spinoza; elsewhere I speak of it in greater detail. I wished only to emphasize the basic opposition between the tasks Plato and Spinoza set for themselves. The one sees in philosophy the "practice of death" and declares that the true philosophers have always done nothing other than *apothnêskein kai tethnanai* (prepare themselves for death and to die). For Plato, philosophy is not knowledge or science—one cannot call the "practice of death" a science—but something of a completely different order. He wishes to render the human vision not more penetrating but, on the contrary, less so—that vision to which, according to general opinion, it is given to discover the ways that lead to the sources of all truths. "Have you not noticed," he writes, "in observing those of whom it is said that they are wicked but intelligent men the keen vision that a soul such as theirs has, how well it sees what it looks at, and how the capacity for sight that it possesses is considerable; but it is obliged to serve the evil, and the keener its vision the more evil it does."[13]

The faculty of seeing (*Einsicht, intuitio*), even if it be very great, does not bring man to the truth; on the contrary, it leads him away from it. *Cognitio intuitiva,* bestowed by reason and bringing us "contentment with oneself which is the highest possible"—Plato knew quite well that here was the supreme wisdom for men, but he also felt in the depths of his being that under this "contentment with oneself" was hidden the most terrible thing that there is in life. He tells us that Socrates, his teacher, said of himself that he was a gadfly and considered that his task was not to calm men but ceaselessly to irritate them and bring into their souls an intolerable restlessness. Spinoza's *ratio* brings men "contentment with oneself" and a peace "which is the highest possible." This means that *ratio* threatens us with the greatest of dangers, that we must fight against it night and day without shrinking before any difficulties or sacrifices. Plato, the father of dialectic, possessed a remarkable vision. But the sources of philosophical knowledge were not, for him, either in dialectic or in the faculty of discerning what others do not discern. Vision and dialectic can be in the service of the "evil," and then of what use are they? The better we see, the more deeply do we sink into evil. Perfect vision would thus end in the definitive triumph of evil in the world.

It is of this, and of this alone, that Plato's myth of the cave speaks to us. The inhabitants of the cave see clearly and distinctly everything that takes place before them, but the more firmly and solidly they believe in what they see, the more desperate does their situation become. They should seek neither what is clear and distinct nor what is fixed and lasting. On the contrary, they should experience the greatest suspicions, the deepest unrest. It is necessary that their spiritual tension reach the ultimate limits so that they can break the chains which bind them to their prison. The clarity and distinctness which seduce all minds and not only Descartes' (Descartes merely formulated what led men astray long before him) and which, in the eyes of all, are a guarantee of the truth, seem to Plato forever to hide the truth from us. The clear and distinct draw us not toward the real but toward the illusory, not toward what exists but toward the shadow of what exists.

If you ask where Plato learned this and how he, being himself an inhabitant of the cave wherein all of us live, could divine that what he saw was not reality but only the shadow of reality and that real life begins elsewhere, beyond the limits of the cave—you will not get any answer. Plato has no proofs for this and yet, it must be recognized, he exhausts himself in searching for proofs. It was for this purpose that he invented his dialectic; and in his dialogues he tried by all dialectical means to obtain from his imaginary interlocutors that they recognize the truth of his revelations. But it is precisely because and inasmuch as Plato wished to make his revelation a truth that constrains, a truth obligatory for all, that he laid himself open to Aristotle's criticisms.

As long as it was a question of the *anankazein kai anankazesthai* (to constrain and be constrained), it seemed that Aristotle, and not only Aristotle but Epictetus as well, were invincible. We have no means of constraining a man to recognize that his reality is not real. On the contrary, as we recall, all the means of constraint are on the side of those who see in reality the final and only possible reality. This reality is sufficiently protected against the attempts that might be made to disqualify it not only by the threats of Epictetus but also by the all-powerful principle of contradiction. He who doubts reality also doubts his doubt, for the doubter, together with all his doubts, belongs to this reality. Plato well knew this irrefutable argument, which later tempted two men as dissimilar as Saint Augustine and Descartes. Plato himself used it more than once to refute the Sophists, and he realized very well that his myth of the cave, as well as his theory of ideas, were shot through and through with contradictions. He understood this and yet he did not renounce his ideas and sought all his life to escape from the cave. What does this mean? Is it that "the practice of death" bestows upon man the mysterious gift of no longer fearing the principle of contradiction? Does he learn, in general, to fear nothing and "to dare everything"? Dialectic was not at all necessary for Plato and his revelations, and he used them not so much because his revelations could not do without them but because the men before whom he set forth his truths could not do without them. Men are accustomed to think that, by the very nature of things, where there is no force there is no truth; that force, whenever it wishes (by its own caprice), authorizes or does not authorize the truth to "be," but that it itself exists without asking authorization of anything whatsoever (and especially of truth). In Spinoza's terminology: it is necessary to seek the "true philosophy" and not the "best philosophy."

This problem runs through all of Plato's work, but nowhere is it posed with as much clearness and sharpness as in the *Phaedo*, where Plato tells us that philosophy is "the practice of death." And this is not merely an accident. In the presence of Socrates, who awaits death, one cannot speak of anything else. If philosophy is really "the practice of death," then a man who awaits death can still meditate and philosophize. But if the truth is with Spinoza and if "a free man thinks of death least of all things," then the sentence of the judges forever closed Socrates' mouth, even before he had drunk the hemlock. The human thought which wishes and is able to look death in the face has other dimensions than the thought of those who turn away from death and forget death. To put it in another way: the truths that Plato sought have no place on the plane of reason. They presuppose another dimension, a dimension which is generally not taken into consideration.

When Plato found himself before the dilemma, the "true philosophy" or the "best philosophy," he did not hesitate: he has no need of the "true philosophy." Thus, he seeks and finds the "best philosophy." If he had been asked who gave him the right to choose, if there had been demanded of him what the lawyers call *Justus titulis* and which the philosophers also ordinarily desire to obtain, he certainly would not have known how and perhaps would not even have wished to answer this question. Or else he would have answered this question by another question: *Does anyone have the right to grant what the lawyers* (i.e., men who by their vocation and their mentality are called to defend the pseudo-reality they have discovered in the cave) *call "Justus titulis"?* And, indeed, who or what determines the fate of men? As long as we obtain no answer to this question, all our truths will have only a conditional significance. We say "who" or "what." This means that the *justi tituli* are at the disposal perhaps of a living being who feels and chooses or, perhaps, of something that is interested in nothing and in no one. This something that is without will and indifferent to everything automatically pronounces—without hearing anything, without taking account of anything—judgments that are definitive and without appeal. And if this indifferent and inanimate "something" is the source of life and of truth, then what meaning, what importance, can human choice have? In that case, choice is only a delusion, an auto-suggestion, a shameless insolence that will inevitably be uncovered and severely punished at the first conflict of man with reality.

We could lengthen the list of these questions, but it is obvious that *on the plane where they were born and developed we shall obtain no answer.* Or worse still: *on this plane all these questions are decided in advance.* There is no "who" at the sources of being; therefore there is no "who" at the sources of truth. And even if there once was a "who," long ago, in time immemorial, he renounced both himself and his sovereign rights by handing over their eternal use to the inanimate "what" from whose stony hand the power cannot be wrested, no matter how great our efforts and our daring may be. This is the meaning of the *semper paret, semel jussit* (He always obeys but has commanded only once), this is the meaning of all the "constraining and being constrained" which were discussed above. Reasoning and dialectic, quite like prayers and persuasion, can do nothing here. If true reality is found on the two-dimensional plane of the "what" and if the thought expressive of this reality knows only two dimensions [*einai* (being) = *noein* (thought)], then there is no escape: we must give up free choice, submit to Necessity, and no longer receive any truths without its consent and authorization. Necessity does not authorize choice. If you wish to acquire the right and freedom to choose, you must abandon the plane where Necessity realizes its power, without allowing yourself to be stopped by any impossibilities and, above all, despising all the *justi tituli* which fetter not only our thought but also our being. Without asking anything of anyone, on our own initiative, we must oppose to the Necessity which does not allow itself to be persuaded the authority of the "by my will." So that the "Parmenides constrained" of Aristotle becomes the Parmenides who speaks "as one who has power." For it is written: the kingdom of God is conquered only by violence.

It will be said that this amounts to fighting the self-evident. But Plato, all his life, did nothing but fight the self-evident. To subdue it he went to the most distant boundaries of being, where no one ventures, where—according to general opinion—life even no longer is or can be, where death, which puts an end to everything, reigns. To be sure, this is great daring, the greatest of daring, the final impudence of which man is capable. But what other means is there of obtaining the "by my will"? That "Necessity does not allow itself to be persuaded" was, I repeat once more, quite as incontestable for Plato as for Aristotle. But what death is, no one knows. It is true that it is uncanny to behold. But "the beautiful is difficult." Spinoza himself did not deny this: "all sublime things are as difficult as they are rare." That is how he concluded his *Ethics*. It may be that, behind the difficulties and the horrors of death, there is hidden something that we need much more than the facilities and pleasantries of daily life. We have nothing more to lose. We have appealed to Necessity, questioned it and begged it; it has not budged and will not budge. As long as it preserves its power, the judgment "Socrates has been poisoned" will remain an eternal truth, quite like the judgment "a mad dog has been poisoned." But if one becomes intimate with death, if one passes through the needle's eye of final and terrible solitude, of forsakenness and despair, then one may perhaps succeed in recovering the sacred "by my will," the primordial and powerful *jubere* that we have exchanged for the weak, automatic and soothing *parere*. We must overcome fear, summon up all our courage, go toward death and try our luck with her. Ordinary thought, the thought of the man who obeys and recoils before threats, gives us nothing.

The first step is to accustom oneself to take no account of "sufficient reason." If Epictetus or anyone else threatens to cut off our ears, pierce our eyes, make us drink vinegar or hemlock, we will not listen to his threats—just as Necessity does not listen to our supplications. "The human soul," says Plato, "when it feels pleasure or pain in connection with something is constrained to consider this thing as the most evident and the most true, even though it is not really so . . . Each pleasure and pain is like a nail and rivets the soul to the body, fixes it to the body and makes it similar to the body, so that it begins to consider as true what the body considers as true."[14] As if he were defending himself in advance against Aristotle and Epictetus, for whom the *anankazein* (constraint) and the endless *lupethênai* (eyes pierced, ears cut off, vinegar, hemlock, etc.) were the final court of appeal in the conflict between truth and error, Plato tries not to refute them but rather to flee from the places where arguments of this kind have, and can have, any force. The body and all that is related to the body is subordinated to Necessity and fears its threats. As long as man is afraid, he can be terrorized; and once he is terrorized, he can be constrained to obedience. But the philosopher who has arrived at the boundaries of life and passed through the school of death, the philosopher for whom *apothnêskein* (dying) has become the present reality and *tethnanai* (death) the reality of the future, has no fear of threats. He has accepted death and become intimate with it, for dying and death, by weakening the corporeal eye, undermine the very foundation of the power of Necessity, which hears nothing, as well as of all the evident truths which depend on this Necessity. The soul begins to feel that it is given to it not to submit and obey but "to lead and govern."[15] In fighting for this right it does not fear to pass beyond the fateful limit where what is clear and distinct ends and the Eternal Mystery begins. Its *sapientia* (wisdom) is no longer a *meditatio vitae* (meditation on life) but a *meditatio mortis* (meditation on death).

VII

Such was the way that Plato followed. In the *Phaedo* Socrates relates that when he was a young man he was present at a reading of fragments of the work of Anaxagoras. Having heard that reason was the orderer and cause of all, he felt a tremendous joy and told himself that here was precisely what he needed and that he would not be willing to exchange this doctrine for all the treasures of the world. To ascribe such a power to reason meant, according to him, that it is given to reason to find for everyone what best agrees with him. Consequently man has the right to expect that there will come to him nothing but happiness and good. But how disillusioned Socrates was when, having probed Anaxagoras' words to the depths, he saw that Anaxagoras' reason seeks and discovers in the world only the natural relationships of things! Socrates found this deeply offensive and, turning away from Anaxagoras, began to seek at his own risk and peril the principles and sources of all that exists.

By what right did Socrates so decide? Was reason obliged to furnish Socrates an explanation of the universe in which "the best" would also be the strongest? Does reason possess the faculty of discovering everywhere only the "good" and not what is—the evil as well as the good? We have no right, i.e., we have no ground, to be certain that reason will find in the world more good than evil. It may be that it finds more good, or it may be that it finds more, even enormously more, evil. Aristotle also knew Anaxagoras, but Anaxagoras was quite agreeable to him; he considered him "a sober man among the drunken." Are the notion of reason and the notion of "the best" juxtaposable? Should it not be admitted, on the contrary, that the notion of "the best" must be deduced from the notion of reason? The best may not be reasonable, and the reasonable may exclude the best. It is completely reasonable, not to take any other example, that the judgment "Socrates was poisoned" should be an eternal truth, quite like the judgment "a mad dog was poisoned." It is similarly reasonable that the stone endowed with consciousness and the divine Plato, who would have given everything in the world to wrest his master from the clutches of this eternal truth, should be equally constrained to recognize the reality of this judgment. One could cite an endless number of examples of this kind. Did not Plato and Socrates know this quite as well as we? Had they so wished, they would have been able to say, as people now say: "The inferior categories of being are the strongest, the superior the weakest." And even if there were only a little good here, even if there were no good at all, this would have been completely reasonable. It would have been well if the superior categories were the strongest. But to demand of reason that it recognize that the superior categories *are* the strongest, would this not be to "constrain" reason? And does reason submit to force, wherever it may come from? People can say to us, as they have said to us, "Parmenides constrained" or even "God constrained." But to say "reason constrained," even if it be by the good itself—no matter how highly one glorifies the good and even if one affirms, following Plato, "the good is not essence but that which is beyond essence and surpasses essence both in value and in power"[16]— who would dare say such a thing? Who would have the courage to declare that the truth "Socrates was poisoned" will cease to exist in some near or distant future and that (this is what is now most important for us) reason itself will have to recognize this, and not on its own initiative but "constrained" by something stronger than itself? Is there a power capable of ruling over the truths?

There cannot be two opinions on this matter: there is no such power. And yet Plato sought this power and followed it even into death where, according to the general opinion, one cannot find anything. But it must be recognized: *Plato did not find what he was seeking.* Or, to be more exact: *Plato did not succeed in bringing back to men what he had found beyond the limits of all possible knowledge.* When he tried to show men what he had seen, the thing changed itself mysteriously under his eyes into its contrary. It is true that this "contrary" beguiles and charms us through the reflection of the ineffable, which awakens in mortals the remembrance of the primordial, infinite and supernatural fullness and beauty of being. But the ineffable remains ineffable. "To see the Creator of the world is difficult, to show Him—impossible." The ineffable is ineffable because and inasmuch as it is opposed by its very nature not to realization in general, as people are inclined to believe, but to definitive and final realization. It does realize itself but it cannot and does not wish to be transformed into knowledge. For knowledge is constraint, and constraint is submission, loss, and privation, which finally hides in its depths the terrible threat of "contentment with oneself." Man ceases to be man and becomes a stone endowed with consciousness. The Parmenides "who is constrained by the truth itself," the Parmenides who turns around to look at the truth, is no longer the Parmenides who, as Plato later did, dares to penetrate into the land which is known by no one but only promised to men, to seek there the golden fleece or some other treasure that in no way resembles those that men know. He is no longer the living, restless, insubmissive, tortured and—by that very fact—great Parmenides. The Medusa's head, which he saw in turning backward, brought him a deep and final repose.

Plato himself writes: "But the pleasure which is to be found in the knowledge of true being is known only to the philosopher."[17] But he has explained to us what pleasure is: pleasure is the nail by means of which man is riveted to his illusory, shadow-like, and mortal being. Now if contemplation brings pleasure, whatever the contemplation may be, we shall not escape the fateful payment. And Plato, as if he were doing it purposely, as if he wished to emphasize that it is not given to man to go beyond "pleasure" and that pleasure is the recompense and goal of all our efforts, repeats again on the following page: "All pleasure, except that which a reasonable man feels, is impure and shadow-like." And later he expatiates with still more warmth on the pleasure which this same contemplation brings to us.[18] Everything that Aristotle later said with so much eloquence about "contemplation being what is most pleasant and best"[19] is taken from Plato. And in Plotinus also we find not a few eloquent pages of the same kind. By means of pleasure man is effectively nailed, as with enormous nails, to that place of being where he was obliged by chance to begin his existence. And accordingly, fear, armed with threats of every kind, does not permit him to tear himself away, be it only in imagination, from the earth and to rise above the plane which our thought has become accustomed to consider as containing everything real and everything possible.

We have preserved this mysterious thought of Heraclitus: "For God everything is good and just, while men consider certain things just and certain other things unjust." This thought is also found in Plotinus. He repeats it in the last, chronologically, of his *Enneads* (I, VII, 3): "for the gods there is only good, there is no evil." And again (I, VIII, end): "there, there is no evil," as if he were echoing to us the no less mysterious "it was very good" of the Bible. But this "absurd" thought, whose very absurdity makes it so seductive, does not find any root in the world where pleasures and pains have power over us, where pleasures and pains are a "sufficient reason" for the acts and thoughts of man, where it is they that determine what is significant and important for us. For it is also a "fundamental law" that pleasures and pains here on earth come not when and for as long as a man calls them but when they themselves wish. Then they make themselves masters of a man's soul and, as Plato taught us, nail him to the subterranean place which was prepared for him in advance, by suggesting to him the invincible conviction that this was and always will be so, that even among the gods everything happens as it does on earth, that pleasures and pains govern and command while no one governs or commands them. In Spinoza's terminology: good and ill fortune is distributed indifferently among the just and the wicked. Socrates' statement that no good can come to the wicked and no evil to the good is only an "empty babbling," a "poetic image" that he picked up on the street or some place still worse (Socrates went everywhere and disdained no one); it was certainly not drawn from the sources whence the eternal truths flow for man.

It is not difficult to guess where Socrates found his pseudotruth and to what source he went to seek it. It obviously flows from the "by my will," from the primordial *jubere,* which men and gods have forgotten and of which they do not dare to remind themselves. Socrates' conviction was born of his desire, but what good can there be in an idea derived from such low parentage? Socrates turned away from Anaxagoras because the latter glorified the reason (*nous*) which does not take any account of human desires and is indifferent to "the best." The universe is maintained only by obedience: "Law is the king of all, of mortals and immortals."[20] There is no way of escape from this. Wherever one looks there are laws, demands, commandments that rest on the "sufficient reasons" of which we have heard so much said by Aristotle and Epictetus. Plato and Socrates dared to defy the laws and Necessity, and opposed to them "by my will." But—and here is the most terrible and mysterious of all the "buts" that have ever limited man—they were not able to renounce pleasure, not even the pleasure that forms the essence and content of "contentment with oneself." How could it be otherwise? If "by my will" remains itself, for as long as it remains itself, one cannot show it, as one cannot show men the Demiurge who is the source of all "by my will." No eye, either corporeal or spiritual, can see either the Demiurge or the commandments that emanate from him. Here vision ends, here begins the mysterious region of the no less mysterious *participation.* Here constraint ends, for the commandments of the Demiurge, contrary to the commandments of Necessity which is indifferent to all, do not constrain anyone. They call to life, make gifts, enrich suddenly.

The more the Demiurge commands, the less it is necessary to obey. The Demiurge calls the man enchained by Necessity to ultimate freedom. He is not even afraid, no matter how strange this may appear to the human thought based upon fear—but the Demiurge fears nothing—to give all his endless power and all his creative forces which are also endless to another being whom he has created in his image. "For God everything is very good." For men it is otherwise; for them the "very good" is the greatest of absurdities. "Daily experience" teaches us that it is necessary to be afraid, that everything surrounding us hides endless dangers in itself. And to avoid these dangers we take refuge behind the ramparts, created by ourselves, of "eternal, self-evident truths." Plato himself, despite his desperate struggle against Necessity maintained in the depths of his soul the clear and irreducible conviction that "Necessity does not allow itself to be persuaded," that one may at times outwit its vigilance and trap it but that it is finally given no one to escape its power. Without pleasures one cannot live; but pleasures come and go, not when we desire but when they themselves please. And if one wishes to enjoy them, he must go and seek them at all-powerful Necessity; he must reluctantly renounce the sovereign *jubere* (command) and return to the *parere* (obedience) that has been admitted throughout all time.

As soon as Plato turned away from the Demiurge—even if it were only to show him to others, to show him to all—the "by my will" grew dim and became a shadow, a phantom. But when Plato, in communing with him, discovered the Demiurge, he lost the possibility and faculty of giving men truths "capable of being proved." Communion presupposes "the flight of the one to the One," as Plotinus was later to say. It begins with the "true awakening" and carries man "beyond reason and knowledge," beyond the limits of the world "given" once for all that is "the condition of the possibility" of knowledge and where the conditions of the possibility of knowledge were created by Necessity which does not allow itself to be persuaded and which exists especially for this. And indeed, if Necessity were not deaf and blind, the idea of knowledge would lose all meaning. Truth could not be in the *adaequatio rei et intellectus* (agreement between thing and intellect), for how could one take as the standard a thing that is not at the disposal of deaf and, by that very fact, unchangeable Necessity but depends on the will of a relenting, susceptible to persuasion and, consequently, "capricious" being (Kant's *deus ex machina* or *höheres Wesen*)?

If one drove Necessity from the world, knowledge would become a dream as unrealizable as it is useless. At present, as we recall, even empirical, *a posteriori* judgments have obtained the exalted rank of eternal truths; but if Necessity disappeared, *a priori* judgments themselves would return to the subaltern state of perishable beings. The very gods would no longer be omniscient. Can one accept such a state of things? "Contemplation is what is most pleasant and best," we have heard Aristotle say above. And Plato spoke the same way. In return, however, we should once again possess the "by my will," the primordial freedom. And *to ariston* (the best), as well as *to hêdiston* (the most pleasant) would come not when they wish but when we called them! And pleasures would no longer enchain us but rather follow us into that world where laws do not rule over mortals and immortals but where the immortals and the mortals whom they have created would, by their divine will, themselves make and unmake laws, where the proposition "a mad dog has been poisoned" would really be an eternal truth while the proposition "Socrates has been poisoned" would be a temporary and provisional truth, where for men also "everything is very good."

I repeat once more: Plato sought only this—to flee from the cave where the shadows pretend to reality and where one cannot look at the illusory reality because it petrifies. Indeed, *it is necessary that our corporeal eyes forget how to see when it is given us to penetrate into the region where the gods live with their tes ernês boulêseôs (limitless freedom) and without our knowledge, without even the perfect knowledge that we call omniscience.* Plato, I say, sought only this. But Necessity does not merely refuse to let itself be persuaded. In the course of its millennial relationships with the men over whom it had power it acquired consciousness from them. If many men are changed into stones endowed with consciousness, Necessity—although preserving its stony and altogether indifferent nature—also finds itself provided with consciousness. And it succeeded in deceiving Plato himself, in persuading him that in the "other" world also only he who is on good terms with Necessity can exist, that the gods do not fight against Necessity, that the world was born of the union between reason and Necessity.

It is true that, according to Plato, reason convinced Necessity of many things and seems to have succeeded even in gaining ascendancy over Necessity; but this domination was illusory and conditioned by the tacit recognition of the primordial rights, and even the birthright, of Necessity. Still more: in order to "achieve dominion" over Necessity, reason had to give way on the most important and most essential point; it had to agree that all conflicts between truths should be resolved by "force" (*bia*) and to admit that truth is truth only when and for as long as it is given to it to constrain men. Through their corporeal eyes men are bound to their prison; "the spiritual vision" must then also bind, "constrain."

The disciples of Socrates gathered around their condemned master to receive from his mouth not simply the truth but the truth that constrains—not through the corporeal eyes, it is true, but through the spiritual eyes. Its power of constraint, however, is not weakened thereby but further augmented. In the presence of death and preparing to die, Socrates gives proofs, proofs, and again proofs. He cannot do otherwise: "unbelief is proper to the masses." If one does not furnish them with proofs, the masses will not believe. But who are *hoi polloi*, "the masses"? The disciples of Socrates are not *hoi polloi*; they are the elect. But the elect are no exception; they do not wish, and are not able, to "believe." *Hoi polloi*—these are "all of us," not only the mob but also the disciples of Socrates, not only the disciples of Socrates but Socrates himself. Socrates also wishes first to see, be it only by "the spiritual vision" or by the "eyes of the mind," and only thereafter to accept and believe. This is why he listens so attentively to the objections of his interlocutors. This is why the divine Plato, who took over his intellectual heritage, could not, to the very end of his days, renounce dialectic. Dialectic is as much a "force" as physical force; it is a death-dealing weapon, like the sword or the arrow. It is a question only of knowing how to use it, and the whole world will be at our feet. "The whole world" means all men. All men will be obliged to repeat what you proclaim as the truth.

I insist upon this: in the presence of "all," Socrates and Plato did not dare to go back to the sources of their truths. In the presence of "all," they also became like everyone else, like *hoi polloi,* of whom it is said that unbelief is proper to them, who accept only the proven truth which constrains—the apparent, visible, evident truth. Beyond the limit of what is visible either to the spiritual or the physical eye, there is no longer anything to seek, there is no longer anything to expect. Under the pressure of Necessity, Socrates had to give way on this point. He offered his disciples "the vision of what is" and "the pleasure" that depends on the vision of what is. He offered these to his disciples in place of the various pleasures which are bound, for the inhabitants of the cave, to the perception of that subterranean reality where Plato suddenly felt the presence of corrupting, destructive elements (*damnatio aeterna*). And he regarded this "vision" as "a great gift to men of the gods, who will not give them and have never given them any greater."[21]

The "masses" have obtained what they desired. They desired to receive their reward immediately, even before Socrates had closed his eyes, and they did receive it. "Philosophy" makes this categorical declaration to us in the *Phaedo*: "to believe no one except oneself." But he who believes only in himself, only in his own eyes, even if they be the spiritual eyes, will inevitably become the vassal of Necessity and be condemned to content himself with the leavings that it hands over to mortals and immortals. Without realizing it Plato let himself slide (or was carried away) from the heights that he had attained when—"the one before the One"—he forgot, thanks to the practice of and meditation on death, all fear and all the threats that close for men the gateway to the final truth, and fell back again to the place where the great Parmenides himself, "constrained to follow the phenomena," does not dare to seek anything other than the pleasure obtained by the contemplation of that which is, of that which was created and formed without him and before him. And not only Parmenides but the gods themselves, "constrained by the truth," have refused to create or to change anything whatever in the universe. Plato did not succeed in "persuading" Necessity; Necessity outwitted Plato. For the "pleasure" of being with all and of thinking like all, he had to surrender everything to it. Necessity remained the sovereign of the world; the whole world belongs to it while the "by my will" became transformed into a shadow. And at the same time the cave, as well as everything that happens in the cave, became again the kingdom of the sole and final reality, outside of which there is neither being nor thought.

VIII

Aristotle won a complete victory over Plato, and what he established and constructed has remained standing to our day. Nicholas of Cusa wrote: "The difference between the divine mind and our own is similar to that between making and seeing. The divine mind creates through thinking, our own imitates through thinking or through intellectual vision. The divine mind is creative power, our own is imitative power."

It seems that there is repeated here that thought of Philo's which was based on the Bible: "For God creates in speaking, His word being already an act." But we know that Philo, in his desire to reconcile Holy Scripture with Greek wisdom, had already weakened the meaning and scope of the biblical "and God spoke." With Nicholas of Cusa, who appears at the threshold of modern history, the relationship between creation and thought is completely broken. He already thinks like a Greek, and if one separated the quotation that we have just cited from its superficial stratum of Christian theology, that is to say, from that which derives from the Bible, one could easily find there the *semper paret, semel jussit* that we know so well. Nicholas of Cusa felt that God is far away, so far away that it is better not to try to reach Him but rather to accept, once for all, our mortal destiny not to create (*facere*) but only to see (*videre*) and to imitate through thought (*concipiendo assimilare*). And he believed that for man the principle of agreement between thing and intellect (*adaequatio rei et intellectus*) is the universal principle for seeking truth, whether it be a question of ordinary positive truths or the final problems of metaphysics. And if Nicholas of Cusa—who still held close to the Biblical conceptions of the Middle Ages, though he is justly considered the forerunner of the new philosophy—thought thus, what shall we say of modern times and how they have come to limit the rights and possibilities of human thought?

It is true, and this is something that must never be forgotten, that the fear of freedom is undoubtedly the basic characteristic of our perhaps distorted but nonetheless real human nature. At the depths of our souls we aspire to limit

God Himself, to curtail His creative activity, His right to the *jubere,* to the "by my will." It seems to us that even for God it would be better not to command but to obey, that the will of God—if it be not subordinated to some "eternal" principle—will fall into arbitrariness and caprice. I am not yet speaking of St. Thomas Aquinas, who could not and would not consider the Scriptures otherwise than in the framework of Aristotelian philosophy and who taught the generations that followed to value this framework as much as what it contained. But a thinker as thoroughly free and Christian as Duns Scotus felt at peace only when he succeeded in convincing himself that above God there exists something which binds Him, that for God Himself the impossible exists: *lapidem non potest (Deus) beatificare nee potentia absoluta nee ordinata* (He—God—cannot make a stone blessed either through absolute or through ordered power). Why did he need to say this? He could, had he wished, easily have recalled what is related in Genesis: God created man out of the dust and He blessed man whom He created out of the dust. Whether He did it *potentia ordinata* or *potentia absoluta* matters little; whatever Duns Scotus says, He did it. But Duns Scotus is afraid to grant God a limitless sovereignty; he imagines perhaps that God Himself is afraid of such sovereignty. I think that if we would question Duns Scotus we would discover that God not only cannot *beatificare lapidem* (make a stone blessed) but that He is incapable of doing many other things besides. Duns Scotus would certainly have repeated after St. Augustine: "God's justification can be without your will, but it cannot be in you against your will. . . . He, therefore, Who created you without yourself does not justify you without yourself. So He creates you without your knowing it and justifies you with your will." And, after Aristotle, he would have repeated Agathon's words:

> For one thing only is impossible to God: to make undone that which has been done.[22]

One could discover many other things that are "impossible" to God, and the philosophy which takes for its point of departure the principle that the knowledge of the possible precedes the knowledge of the real at last obtains what it needs when it comes up against obstacles that are as insurmountable for God as they are for men. These are what we call *vérités de raison* [truths of reason] or *veritates aeternae:* for what is insurmountable for God is so definitively and forever. And, most important, not only is it given to man to know that there are insurmountable obstacles before which God Himself must bow, but it is also given to man to discern (obviously by means of his spiritual eyes) these insurmountable things in being and in reality. We have heard that God cannot *beatificare lapidem,* that He cannot save man against his will, and that He cannot make what has been not to have been. There are many such "impossibles" which stand over God as well as over men: *ex nihilo nihil fit* (nothing comes from nothing), the principle of contradiction, etc. . . . The totality of these "impossibles" and of the "possibles" that correspond to them forms a whole science. This science, which precedes every other knowledge, which precedes reality itself, is the basic philosophical science. And both men and gods must again learn it from the very Necessity which itself learns nothing, knows nothing, and wishes to know nothing, which is not concerned with any thing or any person and which despite this—without wishing or seeking it—has been reared so high above everything existing that gods and men all become equal before it, equal in rights or, more correctly, equal in the lack of all rights.

This is what Hegel has admirably expressed in his Logic with the prudent and clever courage that characterizes him: "Consequently one must regard logic as the system of pure reason, the kingdom of pure thought. This kingdom is the truth without veils, as it is in itself and for itself. Therefore one can say that its content is the image of God, such as it is in its eternal essence before the creation of the world and of a finite spirit." Some dozen pages further, Hegel, as if he had forgotten that he wrote God with a capital letter, tells us: "The system of logic is the kingdom of shadows, the world of simple essences, free of all concrete and sensible being." Obviously Hegel could have himself brought together the two passages that we have just cited, instead of separating them by a dozen pages. Then the reader would have more clearly understood what the unveiled truth is and what kind of God He is who existed before the creation of the world and of the concrete spirit. But Hegel, the most daring of philosophical smugglers, was the child of his time and knew how, when necessary, to pass over certain things in silence, as he also knew how to avoid useless bringings together. Logic is "the image of God such as He was before the creation of the world"; "logic is the kingdom of shadows" (of shadows and not of spirits, it is expressly said). Then God, such as He is, is the kingdom of shadows? Not at all, many admirers of Hegel will tell you: Hegel was a believer, a convinced Christian. He adored God in spirit and in truth, as Holy Scripture demands.

This is undeniable: in no other philosopher does one so frequently encounter the words "spirit" and "truth." And besides, Hegel called Christianity the absolute religion, declared that the Word had become flesh, recognized the Trinity and the sacraments and "almost" everything that Christianity teaches, and sought to give it a philosophical foundation. This is all correct. And it is still more correct that Hegelian Christianity, like the entire Hegelian philosophy that is based upon Aristotle, corresponds, in a way that cannot be improved upon, to the disposition of the modern mind. It is possible, it is even very probable, that if Hegel had been a Catholic, he would have been recognized as a *doctor ecclesiae* and would have replaced St. Thomas Aquinas, who, in large measure, is dated and needs to be corrected or, as is said in order to avoid conflicts, "interpreted." But read a page of Hegel's *Philosophy of Religion* and you will know what the essence of this Christianity is, or, more precisely, how Christianity must "transform" itself in order to satisfy at the same time "the reason and conscience" of European man educated by the Aristotelian Necessity; or, still more precisely, how the Christianity which has fallen under the power of Necessity has been transformed. "It is possible that in a religion faith should begin with miracles, but Christ himself spoke against miracles. He denounced the Jews who demanded miracles of him and said to his disciples, "The spirit will lead you to all truth." The faith that is based on things so external is only a formal faith, and it must give place to the true faith. If this is not so, then *it would be necessary to demand of men that they believe things which, after having attained a certain degree of education, they can no longer believe . . .*[23] Such a faith is a faith that has for its content the finite and the contingent; it is not, therefore, the true faith, for the content of the true faith is not contingent . . . That the guests at the marriage at Cana drank more or less wine is, for example, of no importance. The healing of a paralyzed hand is also only a pure accident; millions of men have paralyzed and crippled limbs and no one heals them. Again, it is said in the Old Testament that at the time of the Exodus the Jews marked their houses with bloody signs in order that the angel of the Lord should be able to recognize them, as if without these signs the angel would not have been able to distinguish the Jewish houses. Such a faith has no interest for the spirit. It is against this faith that the bitterest sarcasms of Voltaire are directed. He says, among other things, that God would have done better to teach the Jews the immortality of the soul than to instruct them how *aller à la selle* [go to the toilet] (Deut. 23:13–15). The places for relieving oneself thus become the content of faith."

Hegel rarely speaks in so free a way. He was undoubtedly at the end of his patience and laid bare almost everything that he had accumulated in his soul in the course of his long apostolate. How can one ask of educated men that they seriously believe in the story of the marriage at Cana, in the healing of paralytics, in the resurrection of the dead, or that they consider as God Him in whose name verses 13 to 15 of the twenty-third chapter of Deuteronomy were written? And Hegel is right: one cannot ask such things, and this not only of cultivated people but also of simple men. But do the Holy Scriptures demand faith? By himself man can no more obtain faith than he could obtain his own being. It is this that Hegel does not even suspect. Such an idea does not enter into the thought of a learned man. Hegel writes: "Knowledge or faith, for faith is only a particular form of knowledge." This is what all of us think. And, indeed, if faith is only knowledge, then the stories of the marriage at Cana or of the resurrection of Lazarus are only absurd inventions against which it is necessary to protect learned as well as unlearned people. And then the Scriptures, the Old as well as the New Testament, are only Inventions and lies; for these books do not demand but presuppose faith in what is incompatible, completely incompatible, with knowledge. Hegel obviously did not go to this length and express his thought completely. But it is not difficult to say it for him, and it is necessary to say it. It is not a question restricted only to Hegel, but refers to all of us, to the thought that is common to all of us. Hegel's argument is not even original; it is not for nothing that he refers to Voltaire. He could have referred to Celsus who, fifteen hundred years before Voltaire, had said everything that can be said against the Holy Scriptures and who, as Was proper for a cultivated man (fifteen hundred years ago there Were already men as cultivated as Hegel and as all of us who have been to Hegel's school), became enraged at the thought that there are men for whom and a Bible in which faith is not identified with, but opposed to, knowledge.

We read in the Bible: "If ye have faith as a grain of a mustard seed, ye shall say to this mountain 'Remove hence to yonder place' and it shall remove, and nothing shall be impossible unto you."[24] Hegel does not mention these words. He feels that they are more difficult to handle than the story of the marriage at Cana and the resurrection of Lazarus, that it is more difficult to rid oneself of them. I say this is wrong: the one thing is as easy or difficult as the other. That the mountain should or should not remove itself at the command of man— this is in the domain of the finite and contingent and consequently is of no great interest to us. And then Hegel nowhere says but surely thinks: mountains are removed precisely by those who lack the faith of which Scripture speaks. This is the secret meaning of his words: "A miracle is nothing but a violation of natural relationships and, by the same token, nothing but a violation of the spirit." Hegel expected nothing from faith: he placed all his hopes on science and knowledge. And if "the spirit" is the incarnation of science and knowledge, then one must agree with Hegel that a miracle is a violation of the spirit.

But we have seen something else. We have seen that science and knowledge were born of Necessity, that the birth of knowledge was a violation of man. Of this Hegel does not speak. He is a daring and truly ingenious smuggler, and he knows how to pass forbidden wares under the eyes of the most vigilant guards. The Evangelist's miracles are a violation of the spirit while the killing of Socrates was perpetrated with the consent and approval of the spirit, because the miracles violate the natural relationships of things while the killing of Socrates does not. One would have thought that it is just the other way around: that it is the natural relationships of things that constitute the greatest violation of the spirit. Here, however, Hegel is powerless. But he does not dare admit his weakness and hides it under the solemn word "freedom."[25] Hegel's mortal enemy, Schelling, thought as did Hegel himself on this matter. And this is quite in the nature of things; he who has turned around to look backwards sees Necessity, and he who sees Necessity is changed into a stone—a stone endowed with consciousness. For such a person the marriage at Cana, the resurrection of Lazarus, the poisoning of Socrates and the poisoning of a dog all become contingent and finite; for such a person the only source of truth is reason, and the only goal is the "contentment with oneself" of which it is said that "it springs from reason and is the highest possible."

IX

Kant is considered the destroyer of metaphysics, while Hegel is regarded as the philosopher who gave back to metaphysics the rights that Kant had torn away from it. In reality Hegel only completed Kant's work.[26] The conviction that faith is knowledge, the hostility to Holy Scripture carefully hidden under the appearance of respect, the denial of the very possibility of any other participation in truth than that which science offers—all these sufficiently testify to the goal that Hegel had set for himself. For him there is only one source of truth; he is "convinced" that all those who wished to find the truth have always and everywhere gone to the sources from which his own philosophy sprang. In his *Logic* he writes: "The quality of the concept consists in negating itself, in holding itself back and making itself passive in regard to what is, in order that the latter be not determined by the subject but be able to show itself as it is in itself." And in the *Philosophy of Religion* he declares: "In faithful prayer the individual forgets himself and becomes filled with his object."

If this is so, it is obvious that "in philosophy religion receives its justification from the thinking consciousness. . . . Thought is the absolute ruler before which the content must prove itself true." And of the very Christianity that he calls the absolute religion, he says in a tone that brooks no contradiction, "the true content of Christian faith is to be justified through philosophy." This means: being is situated entirely and without residue on the level of reasonable thought and everything that suggests—no matter how remotely—the possibility of another dimension must be energetically repressed as fantastic and non-existent. "Just as man must learn to recognize the sensible on the basis that it is there and that it is, just as man must accept the sun because it is there, so man must accept science, man must accept truth."

Whatever Hegel may do, whatever his efforts to convince himself and others that freedom is for him more precious than anything else in the world may be, finally he comes back to the old way, recognized by and comprehensible (that is to say, reasonable) to all: to constraint. In the metaphysical realm where philosophy dwells, as in the empirical realm where the positive sciences live, that Necessity of which Aristotle and Epictetus have told us so much alone rules and governs. Whether one wishes it or not, one must recognize what is given by the senses, just as one cannot escape from the "truths" of the religion that Hegel calls Christianity. Yet Hegel himself has no need of Christianity because the science of logic grasps, without the help of Christianity, the unveiled truth as it is in itself and for itself as well as God's eternal essence before the creation of the world.

I do not know if Hegel inadvertently betrayed himself by uniting in such a tangible way the "truth" of concrete, sensible reality with the religious truths in the general notion of constraining truth, or if he deliberately emphasized the indestructible bonds that exist between metaphysical and positive knowledge. I am inclined to believe that he did it deliberately just as, in speaking of the marriage at Cana and of the healing of the paralytics, he deliberately concluded with the Voltairean *aller à la selle*. But whether it was deliberate or not, it is clear in any case that for him neither metaphysics nor religion can draw their truths from sources other than those which teach us, using the formula of Spinoza, that the sum of the angles of a triangle is equal to two right angles—and this even though already in the *Phenomenology of the Spirit* he speaks with extreme arrogance and scorn of the methods of mathematics. This is why I have said that Hegel only completed Kant's work. It is known that for Kant metaphysics reduced itself to three fundamental problems—God, the immortality of the soul, and free will. When he posed the question "Is metaphysics possible?" he set out from the assumption that metaphysics is possible only if the answer to these three problems will be furnished us by the same authority that enlightens us when we ask if one can inscribe a rhombus in a circumference or if one can make what has been not to have been. Now, according to Kant, to the questions "Can one inscribe a rhombus in a circumference or make what has been not to have been?" we obtain answers that are completely precise and obligatory for all or, as he puts it, universal and necessary: one cannot inscribe a rhombus in a circumference or make what has been not to have been. But to the three metaphysical problems such answers cannot be obtained: it may be that God exists, as it may be that God does not exist; it may be that the soul is immortal, as it may be that it is mortal; it may be that free will exists, or it may be that it does not exist. All the "critique of pure reason" comes down basically to this.

Indeed, if Kant had fully expressed his thought or, rather, if he had formulated his conclusions less cautiously, he would have said: God does not exist, the soul (which also does not exist) is mortal, free will is a myth.

But, beside the theoretical reason, Kant also assumes a practical reason. And when we address the same questions to the practical reason the situation immediately changes: God exists, the soul is immortal, the will is free. Why and how Kant transferred to the practical reason the powers that he had so pitilessly wrested from the theoretical reason is unnecessary to recount; everyone knows it. What is important is that Hegel's metaphysics is basically not at all distinguished from Kant's practical reason. To put it differently, Kant's practical reason already contained, under an incompletely developed form, all of Hegel's metaphysics. This seems almost paradoxical, but it is so and it could not be otherwise, because both of them set out from the traditional conviction that there is only one source of truth and that the truth is that to which every man can be led by constraint.

Almost every page of Hegel's writings reveals to us that his metaphysics was born of Kant's practical reason. Such is the meaning of his ontological proof of the existence of God: with Hegel as with Kant, it is not the theoretical but the practical reason which here "proves." Even more clearly does this come out from the following thought of Hegel: "When a man does evil, this evil is at the same time given as something which in itself is nothing, as something over which the spirit has power, so that the spirit can bring it about that the evil should not have occurred. The meaning of repentance and atonement consists in that the crime, by the fact that its perpetrator has been raised to the truth, is apprehended as something which in itself and for itself has been overcome, which of itself has no power. That what happened should so be made not to have happened cannot come about in a sensible way but rather in a spiritual way, inwardly."

Hegel's entire metaphysics is thus constructed: where the theoretical reason stops, feeling its impotence and incapacity to do anything whatsoever, the practical reason comes to its aid and declares that it has a remedy for everything. Only the terms differ: instead of "practical reason" Hegel says "*Geist*." Obviously no force in the world can bring it about that what has once been should not have been, and the crimes that have been committed—even the most terrible, Cain's fratricide and Judas' betrayal—will remain committed for all eternity. They belong to the domain of pure theoretical reason, and by that very fact are subordinated to the power of the implacable Necessity which does not allow itself to be persuaded. But it is not at all necessary that what has once been should not have been in the sensible and finite world, just as there is no need for the marriage at Cana or the resurrection of Lazarus. All this breaks the natural relationships and is consequently a "violation of the spirit." The practical reason has found something much better: "inwardly," "spiritually," through repentance, it will make what has been not to have been.

Here, as frequently happens in reading Hegel's works, one asks himself if it is really he who is saying what he thinks, or if it is the Necessity that is speaking through its intermediary, after having hypnotized him and changed him into a stone endowed with consciousness. It may even be assumed that Cain and Judas, if they had not known repentance, would have forgotten what they had done and their crimes would have been drowned in Lethe. But repentance is repentance precisely because it cannot come to terms with what has happened. This is the origin of the legend of the Wandering Jew. And if you do not like legends, I recall to you the testimony of Pushkin:

> The long scroll of my memories unrolls before me;
> And in reading my life with disgust,
> I tremble and curse.
> I moan bitterly and bitterly weep,
> But I cannot blot out these overwhelming lines.

Pushkin did not kill a brother or betray a divine master, but he knows that no practical reason, no truth—not even that which, according to Hegel, existed before the creation of the world—can give him that for which his soul longs. It is to be assumed that Pushkin judged otherwise than did Hegel of the marriage at Cana and of the resurrection of Lazarus; it did not seem to him that the stories of Holy Scripture must be submitted to the verification of "our thought, which is the sole judge" and that the breaking of the natural relationships between phenomena was a violation of the spirit.

For Hegel as for Kant, faith, or what he calls "faith," is under the eternal tutelage of reason. "Faith, however, rests upon the testimony of the spirit—not upon miracles but upon the absolute truth, upon the eternal idea, and thus upon a true content. And from this point of view miracles present only a paltry interest." I think it is again necessary to correct the last words of the sentence quoted and to say not that "miracles present only a paltry interest" but that "miracles present no interest at all," as the Stoics said: all that is not in our power is "indifferent." Or again—and here Hegel's true "interest" or, rather, the basic postulate of his thought would appear—it is necessary to say that all miracles, those of which the Bible testifies and those that are recounted in *the Thousand and One Nights,* are only worthless trash, rejected by the theoretical reason and completely unacceptable to the practical reason. Or, as Kant said: the *deus ex machina* is the most absurd of all suppositions, the idea of a supreme being involved in the affairs of men means the end of all philosophy. Kant's thought as well as Hegel's rests entirely on this principle. Even Leibniz's innocent "pre-established harmony" was for them an object of horror and disgust, as idols were for the biblical prophets. The "pre-established harmony" is again nothing but the deus ex machina whose acceptance must sooner or later make man leave the rut of normal thought. Kant and Hegel, to be sure, were unfair to Leibniz. Leibniz never tried to make anyone come out of the norm or the rut. If he admitted a pre-established harmony, it was only for a single time, as did Seneca, for example, with his *semper paret, semel jussit* (He always obeys but has commanded only once). For Leibniz also, the thought based on the *jubere* seemed monstrous and barbarous. *Consensu sapientium* [by the agreement of the wise] the *deus ex machina* and the supreme being have always been driven by the philosophers outside the limits of real being into the region of the eternally fantastic.

But we would ask once again: by what right is the deus ex machina considered an absurd supposition and the supreme being declared the enemy of philosophical researches? When the chemist, the physicist or the geologist turn away from the *deus ex machina* or from the supreme being, they have their reasons for this. But a philosopher, and especially a philosopher who has undertaken the critique of pure reason—why does he not see that the *deus ex machina* has quite as much right to existence as any synthetic judgment whatsoever? And that in any case one cannot *a priori* qualify him as an absurd supposition? And yet, it is enough to grant him certain rights, be they even the most minimal, for the entire "critique" to fall to pieces. Then it would appear that the point on which stands or falls the philosophy of Kant and of all those who followed him depended on a shadow, on an idea having no relationship with reality. Or to put it better: the idea that the *deus ex machina* (*höheres Wesen*) is the most absurd of all possible suppositions was suggested to Kant and to those who followed him by that very Necessity which does not allow itself to be persuaded and has the capacity to change into stones all those who look at it. And its power of suggestion was such that Kant could never—either in reality or in dream, either alone or in the presence of others—tear himself away from the power of this idea. All reality found itself passed somehow into a flattening mill and forcibly introduced into that two-dimensional thought, which in fact does not "admit" (that is to say, refuses to give any place to) either the *deus ex machina* or the *höheres Wesen* and therefore considers as an absurdity everything that bears the stamp of the unforeseen, of freedom, of originality, everything that seeks and desires not passive being but the creative action that is not bound or determined by anything.

It was on this level, too, that there was installed Hegel's "spirit" which, not-withstanding its overly celebrated freedom, was also—probably even before the creation of the world—condemned to turn in the circle "wherein the first is also the last and the last also the first." For Hegel, as for Kant and for Fichte and Schelling (especially the Schelling of the first period), the idea of knowledge and the idea of truth were indissolubly bound to the idea of mechanism. In Fichte and Schelling we even find such expressions as "the mechanism of the human spirit." In The *Critique of Judgment* Kant insists on the proposition that it is absolutely impossible to prove that organisms could not be produced by purely mechanical and natural means. And in *The Critique of Pure Reason* we read: "If we could explore to the bottom all the phenomena of human choice, there would not be any human action that we could not certainly predict and know as necessary from its anterior conditions."

I ask again (and one cannot stop asking this question, even though its con-stant repetition will irritate and fatigue both the author and his readers): Whence did the great German philosophers derive this attachment to "mechanism," as if they had already in infancy taken a Hannibal-like vow not to stop before over-throwing the detestable *deus ex machina?* Whence, more generally, springs the conviction in all the philosophy of all the centuries that it is in mechanism, in *Selbstbewegung* [self-generated movement], in movement in a circle, that we must seek the final mystery of creation? The German idealists always loved to speak of freedom and endlessly glorified freedom. But what freedom can there be where everything is "natural," where mechanism rules? And was not Plato when he spoke to us of his prisoners in the cave, or Luther with his *de servo arbitrio* [bondage of the will], or Spinoza who openly admitted that everything that he wrote was written not because he freely wished it but under the influence of an external constraint, closer to the truth? Such disclosures (as well as the terror that flows from them—"the fear of God"), are signs of at least the presen-timent of awakening and deliverance (here on earth men probably do not know Plotinus' "true awakening") or of a longing for freedom, and show us that we are dealing not with stones endowed with consciousness but with living men.

X

Hegel's metaphysics and Kant's practical reason are nourished from the same source and lie on the same plane. The modern attempts to overcome Kant's for-malism and to construct a material ethic were condemned in advance to failure. To remove formalism from ethics is to destroy ethics. Formalism is the soul of ethics, just as "theory" is the soul of "knowledge." It is formalism alone that makes possible what is called autonomous ethics, the only kind that deserves the name of ethics. Obviously, "law is the king of all, of mortals and immortals": this we have already heard from Plato. But there is something else that is no less essential: ethics has its own laws that are not the same as those which govern the other realms of being. It is this that we must never forget; otherwise, the constructions of Kant and Hegel lose their meaning and their importance. Already in *The Critique of Pure Reason* the role of ethics in Kant's conception of the world is fixed in a precise enough way, just as in Hegel's *Phenomenology of the Spirit* one can easily discern the contours of his philosophy of history and of his philosophy of religion. But it is only in *The Critique of Practical Reason* that the idea of autonomous ethics appears openly under its true aspect. There is room to believe that Hegel, who criticized Kant's ethics so self-assuredly and so pitilessly, owed much to it. It permitted him to keep the precepts of Spinoza that he could never renounce (*sub specie aeternitatis seu necessitates*—in the perspective of eternity or necessity—which Hegel translated as "adoration in spirit and in truth") and to preserve at the same time the attitude, the solemn tone, which the elevation of his thought justifies and which, in the eyes of people in a hurry, brings contemplative philosophy, the vassal of Necessity, close to religion.

Surely if any ethics can pretend to the title "elevated," it is Kant's ethics, based on the idea of pure duty. People often quote the famous phrase of *The Critique of Practical Reason*: "The starry sky above me and the moral law within me." But in my judgment the lyrical digression of the third chapter of the first part of the same *Critique* is still more important: "Duty! Thou sublime and mighty name that dost embrace nothing charming or insinuating but requirest submission and yet seekest not to move the will by threatening aught that would arouse natural aversion or terror, but only holdest forth a law which of itself finds entrance into the mind and yet gains reluctant reverence (though not always obedience)—a law before which all inclinations are dumb even though they secretly work against it: what origin is there worthy of thee, and where is to be found the root of thy noble descent which proudly rejects all kinship with the inclinations and from which to be descended is the indispensable condition of the only worth which men can give themselves?"

This attempt (rather gauche from a literary point of view) to compose a prayer out of the notions derived from "pure reason," does not leave any doubt about what Kant really meant by "ethical formalism." Formalism in Kant is the "adoration in spirit and in truth" of which Hegel, as well as the modern philosophers who go back to Hegel, speak so much. Kant knew quite as well as do our contemporaries how to develop the idea of personality, which was, for him, the condition and foundation of an autonomous morality. In the same chapter, "On the Motives of the Pure Practical Reason," we read: "The idea of personality which awakens respect, which places the sublimity of our nature (according to its definition) before our eyes . . . is natural and easily perceptible even to the most ordinary human reason . . . It is the effect of a respect for something which is completely other than life, in comparison and in opposition to which life with all its charms has no value. He lives, henceforth, only out of duty, not because he finds the least pleasure in living." I do not really know wherein the "duty" before which Kant prostrates himself is distinguished from Hegel's "spirit" and why modern philosophical criticism holds Kant's doctrine of personality to be inadequate. The idea of duty, the idea of the sanctity of the moral law, as well as the idea of the autonomy of the reasonable being, and all the sublimity and solemnity that these ideas bring to man—all these are guaranteed by the *Critique of Practical Reason* no less than universal and necessary judgments are guaranteed to science by the *Critique of Pure Reason.*

Hegel could "think his system to the end" only by introducing into the domain of theoretical reason, with everyone's knowledge and with his customary boldness (Hegel could permit himself all kinds of boldness with impunity, and even an eye as vigilant as that of Schelling who closely surveyed the "dialectic" of his enemy perceived nothing), the lofty ideas procured by Kant's practical reason. "Man," he says in his *Logic*, "must raise himself to the abstract generality in which it is really indifferent to him whether he does or does not exist, that is, whether he does or does not exist in finite life (for it is a question here of a state, a determinate existence, etc.)—so that *si fractus illabatur orbis, impavidum ferient ruinae,* 'if the heavens should crack over him, the ruins would strike him unafraid,' as a Roman said; and the Christian must feel himself still more in this state of indifference." Everyone knows these words of Hegel; he did not hide them, they are placed clearly in evidence. But Hegel's self-assurance is such that it occurs to no one that Hegel's "spirit" is nothing other than Kant's "duty" of which we have just spoken. All are convinced that Hegel overcame Kant's formalism and do not notice that his ontological proof of the existence of God (from which we have extracted the sentence quoted above) is distinguished in absolutely no way from Kant's "postulate of God," just as the Hegelian "spirit" is not at all distinguished from the Kantian "duty."

Kant and Hegel went to seek the final truth in one and the same place. They made great efforts to raise themselves ("*erheben*" [sublime], "*Erhabenheit*" [sublimity] are favorite terms of both Kant and Hegel) to the regions from which the sources of being and of life flow. But they were convinced beforehand that man cannot take a step without turning backward and without looking forward—in short, without assuring himself first that the way which he wishes to follow is open. The *Critique of Pure Reason* was par excellence a looking backward. Kant asked (of whom?): is metaphysics possible? And the response naturally was: No, it is not possible. But, I repeat, *Whom did he ask? Upon whom did he confer the right to decide what is possible and what is impossible?* Experience as the source of metaphysical knowledge had been rejected by Kant. Already at the beginning of the introduction to the *Critique of Pure Reason* (First Edition), Kant definitely says of experience: "It tells us indeed what is but it does not tell us that it must necessarily be so and not otherwise. Therefore it does not give us any true universality, and reason which aspires so avidly to this kind of knowledge is more irritated than satisfied by it." Remarkable words! Kant, as we see, immediately addressed his questions to reason and was sincerely convinced that he was writing a *Critique of Pure Reason.* He did not even ask himself: why must we endeavor to satisfy reason? Reason avidly seeks the universal and the necessary; we must be prepared for everything, prepared to sacrifice everything, in order that it may obtain the necessity which is so dear to its heart, in order that it be not irritated. The question arose before Kant: Is metaphysics possible and from what source can suffering humanity draw the elixir of life (do not forget that, according to Kant, metaphysics deals with God, the immortality of the soul and free will)? But Kant thinks only of pleasing reason, to which God, the soul and free will matter little—provided only that one does not offend Necessity! The positive sciences have justified themselves in the eyes of Necessity; if metaphysics wishes to have the right to exist, it must also assure itself of the goodwill of Necessity. "Necessity and strict universality are sure signs of *a priori* knowledge," which is the only knowledge that man can trust. This is for Kant an evident truth, as it is evident that the *deus ex machina* is the most absurd of suppositions and that if *ein höheres Wesen* (a supreme being) intervenes in human affairs philosophy has nothing more to do in the world.

Who suggested to Kant that he should believe in these "truths?" How are such suggestions possible? You will not find answers to these questions in Kant's "Critiques." Neither will you find them in the philosophical systems which have continued Kant's work. For to whom is one to address these questions? And is it possible to resist Necessity, to persuade it? "Necessity does not allow itself to be persuaded." But in return it has the power, which is quite superfluous to it, of bewitching and conquering men. We have just heard the prayer that Kant addresses to duty: the practical reason only repeats docilely what it has learned from the theoretical reason. For the theoretical reason the source of truth is Necessity; for the practical reason virtue consists in obedience. The supremacy of the practical reason presents no danger. It will not be indignant, it will not betray, and its "commandments" will not at all threaten the order that has been established in the universe without it and in no way for it. It is impossible, for example, to admit the idea of purpose (finality) in nature: such autonomy would recall the *deus ex machina* or the supreme being and would be an incursion into the domain reserved for all eternity to Necessity. But the practical reason is modest and undemanding; it will never make any attempts against the sovereign rights of Necessity and mechanism.

If one at times observes in "experience" phenomena—organisms, for example—that lead men to believe that someone (who is not as indifferent to everything as Necessity) has borne a certain concern for the arrangement of the world, practical reason immediately arises and tells us that it is necessary to mistrust this supposition and that it would be better to admit that things happen in the world as if (*als ob*) someone occupied himself with the destiny of the world. Such an "as if" does not offend the majesty of Necessity and does not make any attempts on its sovereignty. In return, it is permitted to men to speak as much as they wish "of the wise adaptation of man's cognitive faculties to his practical vocation" (such is the title of one of the chapters of the *Critique of Practical Reason*). It will be said: if one speaks of "wise adaptation," is there not then purpose or finality? Will not the *deus ex machina* then reappear despite all interdictions? Not in the least; Kant knows what he is doing. This is not the miracle of Cana and it is not the resurrection of Lazarus. It is only one of those natural "miracles" that Necessity light-heartedly puts at the disposal of the philosophers. Such miracles will not bring you into the metaphysical realm. On the contrary, the more miracles of this kind in the world, the better will men be protected against metaphysics. This is why, as I have just said, the theoretical reason has so readily granted to the practical reason "primacy" and even the uncontrolled right to dispose of "metaphysical consolations." For the role of metaphysical consolations is precisely to permit man to do without metaphysics, that is to say, to obtain without God, without the immortality of the soul, and without free will, the "contentment with oneself that reason produces."

In Hegel the practical reason does not live in the neighborhood of the theoretical reason; it is found at the very heart of the latter. "Man must raise himself to abstract generality": in Hegel this "categorical imperative" flows from "logic." It is necessary to recognize this: Hegel thought Kant through to the end. He knows as well as Kant that metaphysics is impossible—the metaphysics that seeks God, the immortality of the soul and free will. But it is impossible not because reason is limited and because the categories of our thought are applicable only to what is given by the senses. The very act of raising the question of the limits of human reason irritated Hegel, and he apparently had sufficient grounds to believe that for Kant himself such was no longer the task of the "critique of reason." A metaphysics which wishes to discover God, the immortality of the soul and free will is impossible *because as God, the immortality of the soul and free will do not exist;* all these are only bad dreams that are seen by men who do not know how to rise above the particular and the contingent and who refuse to adore in spirit and in truth. It is necessary at all costs to deliver humanity from these dreams and from the "unhappy consciousness" which created them. They are only representations (*Vorstellungen*). As long as man will not tear himself away from them and will not penetrate into the realm of pure concepts (*Begriffe*) given by reason, the truth will remain hidden from him. *Super hanc petram* (on this rock) Hegel's entire philosophy is founded.

XI

So Hegel taught, but he had found all this in Kant. When Kant summoned metaphysics before the tribunal of reason he knew that it would be condemned. And when, later, Fichte, the young Schelling and Hegel wished to obtain from the same tribunal a revision of the case, they also knew that the cause of metaphysics was forever lost and hopeless. Kant strained all the tremendous powers of his dialectic in order to rid the human soul of the strange elements that he called "sensuousness." But dialectic did not suffice. All that is customarily called "proof" loses, beyond a certain limit, the power of constraining and subduing. One can easily "prove" that the sum of the angles of a triangle is equal to two right angles, but how is one to "prove" to a man that if the very sky falls in upon his head he must remain calm under the ruins, for what happened had to happen? To prove such a thing is impossible. *One can only suggest it to himself and to others, as one can only suggest to himself and to others but not prove that the deus ex machina is the most absurd of suppositions and that Necessity has received the sovereign right of driving the great Parmenides on.*

Submitting to his destiny or, to use Hegel's terms, to the spirit of the time, Kant did not disdain suggestion as a means of searching for the truth. The principal thing is to obtain "universality and necessity," the rest is secondary. Suggestion obtains universality and necessity quite as well as do proofs. One would think that there would be no place for prayer where it is a question of the critique of the pure theoretical reason or the critique of the pure practical reason. But Kant asked permission of no one and addressed prayers to duty, and this passes for "proof." One would think that the ancient "anathema" had already long since been banished from the domain of philosophical thought, but when it is a question of ridding the human soul of all that is "pathological" (for Kant the term "pathological" does not mean diseased or abnormal; he uses it as a synonym for "sensuous"), Kant does not disdain anathema and even anathema passes for proof. "Suppose," he writes, "that someone says his lust is irresistible when the desired object and opportunity are present. Ask him whether he would not control his passion if, in front of the house where he has this opportunity, a gallows were erected on which he would be hanged immediately after gratifying his lust. We do not have to guess very long what his answer would be. But ask him whether he thinks it would be possible for him to overcome his love of life, however great it may be, if his sovereign threatened him with the same sudden death unless he made a false deposition against an honorable man whom the ruler wished to destroy under a plausible pretext. Whether he would or not he perhaps will not venture to say; but that it would be possible for him he would certainly admit without hesitation. He judges, therefore, that he can do something because he knows that he ought, and he recognizes that he is free—a fact which, without the moral law, would have remained unknown to him."

What is the meaning of this "argumentation?" And does there not remain here only a shadow of that freedom of which Kant speaks with such eloquence here and elsewhere in his works and which the best representatives of philosophy in their time have proclaimed? To justify his categorical imperatives Kant found no means other than suggestion and incantation. He prayed long and ardently before the altar of duty and when he felt in himself the necessary power—or rather, when he felt that *he had no more power, that he himself no longer existed,* that another power was working through him (when "he raised himself to abstract generality," to speak as Hegel did), and when he became the blind and will-less instrument of this power—then he wrote the *Critique of Practical Reason.*

The theoretical reason cannot be satisfied as long as it has not convinced everyone, as long as it has not dictated its laws to nature. The practical reason leaves nature in peace, but its "will to power" demands that men should submit to it. The fate of men, then, is always the *parere* (obedience) while the *jubere* (commanding) remains at the disposal of the "idea," the "principle." The goal of philosophy thus comes down to this: to suggest to men, in one way or another, the conviction that the living being must not command but obey and that the refusal to obey is a mortal sin punished by eternal damnation. And this is what is called freedom! Man is free to choose the *jubere* instead of the *parere,* but he cannot bring it about that he who has chosen the *parere* should be damned. Here freedom ends, here everything is pre-determined. "Even the author and founder of the universe" cannot change anything of this. His freedom also has been reduced to obedience. Kant goes even further than Seneca: he will not admit that God commanded even once. No one has ever commanded; all have always obeyed. Every command is a *deus ex machina* which signifies the end of philosophy. This he knows *a priori.* But he also proves *a posteriori,* as we have just seen, that the moral law is realized—otherwise, it is true, that the commandments of the theoretical reason, but nevertheless realized: the "voluptuary" will be afraid of the gallows, while the man who obeys the moral law will feel no fear even in the face of the gallows. Why did Kant need to concern himself with such a "realization"? Why threaten the voluptuary with the gallows? Why not give him the "freedom" to follow his inclinations, since freedom is recognized as man's fundamental prerogative? But such freedom is for the philosopher even more hateful than the *deus ex machina* and, in order to kill it, Kant did not disdain even the empirical gallows which, it seems, do not hesitate to become involved in the affairs of pure a priori judgments. But there is a limit to philosophical patience. The noble Epictetus cut off the noses and ears of his intellectual opponents; Kant is prepared to hang them. And they are obviously right; they have no other means at their disposal. Without the help of empirical constraint (Aristotle's *bia*) the "pure" ideas would never obtain the victory and the triumph that they so highly esteem.

And yet Kant "made the reckoning without the innkeeper." The gallows will not help him or, in any case, will not always help him. He speaks of a "voluptuary," that is to say, he clothes the man with his shroud even before his fate is decided. It is permissible to cut off the voluptuary's nose and ears, it is permissible to hang him, but one may not under any circumstances grant him freedom. But try for a moment to come down from the "heights" of pure reason and ask yourself who is this voluptuary whom Kant so implacably executes. Kant will not answer; he prefers to remain in the domain of general concepts. But it is not for nothing that people have always sought to make general concepts pure and transparent. The concept of the voluptuary is the Pushkin who wrote *The Egyptian Nights;* it is the Don Juan of Spanish legend; it is the Orpheus and Pygmalion of ancient mythology; it is also the immortal author of *The Song of Songs.*

If Kant had thought about it—or rather if, before playing the role of hypnotist, he had not himself been hypnotized by omnipotent Necessity—he would have felt that the thing was not so simple and self-evident and that neither his shroud nor his gallows pre-judge or decide anything here. Orpheus was not afraid to go down to Hades to seek out Eurydice; Pygmalion demanded of the gods a miracle; Don Juan pressed the hand of the statue that had come alive; in Pushkin a timid young man gives his life for a night with Cleopatra. And in The Song of Songs we read that love is strong as death. What remains of Kant's suggestions? And what eternal truths can his practical reason, and the moral law that this reason contains, furnish? And is it not clear that true freedom is found infinitely far from the regions that the practical reason has chosen and where it resides? Is it not clear that where the law exists, where the *parere* exists, there is not and cannot be any freedom, that freedom is inextricably bound to that *jubere* which we have become accustomed to consider as the source of all errors, all absurdities, and all that is forbidden? Pygmalion did not ask anyone if he could demand a miracle for himself. Orpheus broke the eternal law and went down to Hades, though he should not and could not have gone there, though no mortal had ever gone down there before him. And the gods approved their daring, and even we others, we cultivated men, when we hear the story of their deeds, sometimes forget all that we have been taught and also rejoice with the gods.

Pygmalion wished the impossible, and because he wished it the impossible became possible, the statue became a living woman. If our "thought" incorporated in itself the ardent passion of Pygmalion, thus acquiring a new dimension, many things considered "impossible" would become possible and what seems false would become true. Then such impossible things would happen as that Kant would cease to characterize Pygmalion as a voluptuary and that Hegel would recognize that a miracle is not a violation of the spirit but, on the contrary, the impossibility of miracles is the Worst violation of the spirit. Or am I deceived and would they continue to repeat what they have always said? Would they continue to suggest to us that the passions and the desires (*Neigungen*) must bow down before duty and that the true life is the life of the man who knows how to rise above the "contingent" and the "temporary?" Was Calvin right: "Not all are created under the same condition, but to some eternal life is preordained, to others eternal damnation"? Who will answer this question?

XII

In one way or another we now understand why Hegel was so afraid to break the "natural relationships of things" and why Kant, without any preliminary "critique," that is to say, not only without discussing the question but without even indicating the possibility of any questions or doubts whatsoever in this matter, submitted metaphysics to the judgment of the positive sciences that had justified themselves and to the synthetic *a priori* judgments on which these are based.

"All the interest of my reason (the speculative as well as the practical) is combined in the following three questions: What can (*kann*) I know? What must (*soll*) I do? What may (*darf*) I hope?," writes Kant in one of the last chapters of his *Critique of Pure Reason*. To whom are these questions addressed? With this Kant is as little concerned as is Hegel. It seems absurd, no doubt, for him to admit that the very readiness to raise these questions binds men in advance and forever. When he studied the positive sciences he asked: What are the highest mountains on earth? What are the dimensions of the sun's diameter? What is the speed of sound or of light? etc. And he became accustomed to think that it is always proper to question, that someone exists who can be questioned, and that it is to him that he must put all questions—him whom he asked concerning the mountains, the sun, the light and the sound—for at his disposal are all the *kann, soll* and *darf*. If metaphysics does not go to seek answers at the same place and does not receive them from the same hands that up till now have distributed all the *kann, soll* and *darf*, it will never obtain truth. The old, pre-critical metaphysics went to seek its truths where it ought not to have gone, and its truths were not truths but *Hirngespinst* (whim) and *Grille* (caprice). But when, after the *Critique*, it went where Kant directed it, it returned with empty hands; all the *kann, soll* and *darf* had already been distributed and there was nothing left for it. Since before the *Critique* metaphysics supplied certain things and since after the *Critique* it no longer supplies anything, it would seem natural to ask if it is not the *Critique* itself which has dried up the metaphysical sources. To put it differently, is it perhaps not metaphysics that is impossible, as Kant concluded, but the *critical* metaphysics, the metaphysics that turns around backwards and looks to the future, that is afraid of everything and asks everyone, that dares nothing (metaphysics as science, in Kant's terminology) that is impossible?

Who suggested to us that metaphysics wishes to be or must be a science? How did it happen that, in asking whether there is a God, whether the soul is immortal, whether free will exists, we declare ourselves prepared in advance to accept the answer that will be given us without even inquiring concerning the nature and essence of that which supplies us with the answer? We are told that God exists, therefore He exists; we are told that God does not exist, therefore He does not exist; and it remains for us only to submit. Metaphysics must be a *parere* (obedience), just like the positive sciences. Parmenides, Plato, Spinoza, Kant, Hegel, "constrained by the truth itself," do not choose and do not decide. Someone has chosen, someone has decided, someone has commanded, without them. And this is what is called the truth. People then consider, as Cleanthes and Seneca taught, that here it is necessary not only to obey but to accept with veneration and joy or, as Kant and Hegel taught, that it is necessary to prostrate oneself and pray and to call others to prayer. All the "reasons"—theoretical and practical, human and superhuman—have always told us, each in particular and all in general, the same thing throughout the millennial development of philosophical thought: one must obey, one must submit.

The metaphysics which goes back to the source, covered by the sand of centuries, from which flows the *jubere* (commanding) terrifies and repels everyone. God Himself, let us recall, dared only once to manifest His arbitrary will; doubtless He could not do otherwise, as the atoms of Epicurus could not turn aside but once from their natural orbit. But since then both God and the atoms humbly obey. For our thought the *jubere*, the "by my will," is completely unbearable.

Kant was horrified by the mere idea of *deus ex machina* or an *höheres* Wesen interfering in human affairs. In Hegel's God, such as He was before the creation of the world, in Spinoza's *causa sui* [one's own cause] there is no trace of the free *jubere*. The *jubere* seems to us to be the arbitrary, the fantastic; what can be more horrible and more repugnant than this? Better Necessity that does not allow itself to be persuaded, that is concerned with nothing, that makes no distinction between Socrates and a mad dog. And if the theoretical reason cannot, when it is a question of metaphysical queries, guarantee for us the inviolability of Necessity—that is to say, give us universal, necessary, obligatory and constraining truths—we shall not, for all that, follow metaphysics to the sources from which the *jubere* flows. We wish at all costs to obey and we shall create for ourselves, in the image of the theoretical reason, the practical reason, which will watch to see that the fire is never extinguished on the altar of the eternal *parere*.

This is the meaning of the philosophical tasks that our "thought" has set for itself from antiquity to Kant and our own contemporaries. The sight of a man who is ready and capable of directing his own destiny at his own risk and peril and following his own will poisons the existence of our reason. God Himself seems to us a monster if He refuses to obey. Philosophy can accomplish its work only if all will forever forget the *jubere*, the "by my will," and erect altars to the *parere*. An Alexander the Great or a Pygmalion could overthrow all the constructions of Aristotle or Kant if they were not constrained to abdicate their will. And the miracle of the marriage at Cana is more dangerous still. Even if one succeeded in establishing historically that Jesus really transformed the water into wine, it would be necessary at all cost to find a way of suppressing this historical fact. Obviously one cannot charge the theoretical reason with such a task. It would never be willing to admit that what has been has not been. But we have the practical reason (Aristotle already knew it long before Kant) which realizes "in the spirit" what the theoretical reason does not dare to accomplish. The marriage of Cana would have been, as Hegel explains to us, a "violation of the spirit," of the spirit of men who—not "freely," even though they think so, but constrained by Necessity—have deified the *parere*. Hence one can and must overcome the miracle of Cana by the spirit. Everything "miraculous" must at all costs be driven out of life, just as the men who seek to save themselves from Necessity by breaking the natural relationships of things must be driven out of it. "Parmenides enchained and constrained," Parmenides transformed by Necessity into a stone endowed with consciousness: this is the ideal of the man who philosophizes as our "thought" represents him.

But it is not given the petrified Parmenides to help man escape from the limited world. And the thought which turns backward will not lead us to the sources of being. Aristotle turned back-ward, Kant turned backward, all those who followed Kant and Aristotle turned backward, and they became eternal prisoners of Necessity. To tear oneself away from its power, it is necessary "to dare everything," to accept the great and final struggle, to go forward without asking and without foreseeing what awaits us. And only the readiness, born out of supreme anguish, to bind oneself in friendship with death (*meletê thanatou*) can fortify man in his mad and unequal struggle against Necessity. In the presence of death human "proofs," human self-evidences, melt away, vanish, and are transformed into illusions and phantoms. Epictetus with his threats, Aristotle with his truths that constrain, Kant and Hegel with their imperatives and their hypnotizing practical reason, are terrible only to those who cling desperately to pleasure, even if it be the pleasure that "contemplation" gives and that bears the noble name "contentment with oneself." The sting of death spares nothing; one must master it in order to direct it against Necessity itself. And when Necessity will be felled, the truths that rested on it and served it will also collapse. Beyond reason and knowledge, where constraint ends, the enchained Parmenides, having participated in the mystery of the being who is eternal and who always commands (*tês emês boulêseôs*), will regain his primordial freedom and speak not as a man "constrained by the truth" but as one "possessed of power." And this primordial *tês emês boulêseôs* (boundless free will), which no "knowledge" can contain, is the only source of metaphysical truth. Let the promise be realized: "Nothing will be impossible for you!"

II

In the Bull of Phalaris

[Knowledge and Freedom]

"Happiness is not the reward
of virtue but virtue itself."

—Spinoza, *Ethics,* V, 42

"Ye shall be as God,
knowing good and evil."

—Genesis 3:5

I

In his preface to his *Phenomenology of the Spirit,* Hegel writes: "Philosophy, however, must beware of wishing to be edifying." As is generally the case with him, he is here only repeating what Spinoza had said when he considered his philosophy not the best but the only true philosophy. It seems at first glance that this declaration came, so to speak, from the depths of the heart. But Hegel, who repeated Spinoza, was no more veridical than the latter. Before as after Socrates, all the great philosophers have always sought to preach to, and edify, their listeners and readers. And it was precisely those among them who preached and edified with the most insistence who proclaimed that their purpose consisted in discovering the truth, and nothing but the truth. I do not think that Socrates himself was an exception in this respect, although he did not, as is known, in any way hide the fact that he wished to better his fellow-men. But he succeeded in so closely fusing knowledge and edification that when he was preaching he appeared only to be seeking the truth, while when he was seeking the truth he was in reality preaching.

To Socrates belongs the merit of having created what was later called "autonomous ethics." But it was also Socrates who laid the foundations of scientific knowledge. He was the first to distinguish the "morally good" from the "pleasant," the "morally evil" from the "bad." At the same time he taught that virtue is knowledge, that the man who knows cannot but be virtuous. But since Socrates there was introduced into philosophy the enigmatic "passing over into another realm" that the opposition of "good" and "evil" (in the moral sense) to "pleasant" and "bad" makes possible. When one begins to speak of the bad, one generally glides—without effort, without wishing it, without even realizing it—into the morally evil, just as one airily substitutes, as if the thing happened of itself, the morally good for the pleasant or *vice versa* . . .

Hegel's words that I have just quoted, as well as Spinoza's declaration, contain a problem that is worth studying closely. Whatever philosophic question is presented to us, we discover in it obvious traces of the confusion that Socrates openly admitted when one identifies knowledge with virtue; and even those philosophers who in no way shared the fundamental postulate of Socratic thought could not, or perhaps did not wish to, avoid this identification. It might be said that this confusion constitutes the "point on which philosophy stands or falls," that philosophy would lose its *raison d'être* if it renounced this mistaken substitution or (what is perhaps still more terrible) if it admitted that it lives only thanks to this substitution. Yet no one today would identify knowledge with virtue. The most limited mind realizes that one can know and at the same time be full of vice just as one can be ignorant and at the same time a saint. How is it, then, that Socrates did not see what common sense today clearly perceives? No one dreams of raising this question. Still less does one dream of asking himself: can philosophy exist if common sense is right, if the wisest among men was grossly deceived when he proclaimed that virtue and knowledge are one and the same thing?

It is generally assumed that German idealism—in the person of Kant and of his successors, Fichte, Schelling and Hegel—finally and definitively overcame Spinozism. This judgment of history is correct only in the sense that toward the end of their careers the German idealists, those even who like Fichte and Schelling could call Spinoza their first philosophic love, tried by every means to draw a sharp line of demarcation between themselves and Spinoza. People esteemed Spinoza but they feared him and moved far away from him. Leibniz argued with Locke in a respectful and friendly tone, while in his polemic against Spinoza an icy hostility breaks through: he did not wish to be confused with the author of the *Ethics*. This hostility is also to be discerned in Kant when he speaks of Spinoza. As for Fichte, Schelling and Hegel, one might believe from their attitude toward Spinoza that they had left him far behind and had completely rid themselves of him. But the development of German philosophy testifies to the contrary. Kant was indeed further removed from Spinoza than his successors. What separated Kant from Spinoza was submitted in the post-Kantian philosophy to the sharpest criticism.

As German idealism developed it drew ever nearer to Spinozism, and we are justified in considering Hegel's "Philosophy of the Spirit," in its content if not in its form, as the *restitutio in integrum* of Spinozism. Hegel affirmed that philosophy must not be edifying. Spinoza said that he was seeking not the best but the true philosophy. As for Socrates, he identified virtue with knowledge, or to use his formula: nothing bad can happen to a virtuous man, nothing good can happen to a wicked man. It seems then that Spinoza and Hegel took their departure from a principle sharply opposed to that of Socrates. Spinoza wrote in the Ethics that daily experience shows us that successes (good) and failures (bad) are distributed equally among the just and the impious. Hegel, of course, was completely in accord with Spinoza in this matter. In his *Philosophy of Religion* he affirms that a miracle, as a breaking of the natural relationships of things, would be violence against the spirit. Hegel shows himself in this case even more Spinozist than Spinoza himself. Spinoza appeals to daily experience which convinces him that successes and failures are distributed indifferently among the good and the wicked. This knowledge, like all empirical knowledge, is still not the highest, true knowledge (the *tertium genus cognitionis, cognitio intuitiva*) that philosophy seeks. Hegel does not in any way appeal to experience; what he knows, he knows before all experiences. He does not need "experience." He, like Spinoza, needs *tertium genus cognitionis,* and he is not content with the simple fact but finds for it a foundation in the very structure of being. If misfortune struck only the impious and if the just alone knew success, this would be a miracle; but a miracle is violence against the spirit. Consequently, since the spirit does not tolerate violence, virtue—to employ the language of Socrates—is one thing and knowledge is another.

This is the meaning of Spinoza's words, this is also the meaning of Hegel's words. And yet, Spinoza and Hegel followed the way opened up by Socrates: throughout their work they never ceased to develop the idea that virtue and knowledge are one and the same thing, that nothing bad can happen to a just man and nothing good to a wicked man. Not only could not and would not their philosophy renounce edification, but it was precisely in edification that it saw its principal, one could even say its unique, task. Spinoza concluded on an inspired note the reflections on God and the soul that he set forth in the first two parts of the *Ethics:* "How useful the knowledge of this doctrine is for the conduct of life. . . . First, inasmuch as it teaches us to act solely according to the decree of God, and to be participants in the divine nature, and so much the more, as we perform more perfect actions and more and more understand God. . . . This doctrine then . . . teaches us wherein our highest happiness or beatitude consists, namely, solely in the knowledge of God. . . . Secondly, inasmuch as it teaches us how we ought to conduct ourselves with regard to the gifts of fortune or things that are not in our power . . . namely, to await and endure both faces of fortune with equanimity."[1]

Hegel is, in this respect, in no way outdone by Spinoza. Having taken up, against Kant, the defense of the ontological argument, he says in his *Logic:* "Man must, through thought, raise himself to a generality in which it is really indifferent to him . . . whether he does or does not exist, that is, whether he does or does not exist in finite life, etc., so that *si fractus illabatur orbis, impavidum ferient ruinae*[2]—as a Roman said, and the Christian must feel himself still more in this state of indifference." Try to remove from Spinoza his *docet* (it teaches) and his *quomodo nos gerere debeamus* (how we ought to conduct ourselves)—what will remain of his philosophy? And what will remain of the ontological argument if man does not consent "to raise himself to a generality in which it is really indifferent to him whether he does or does not exist"—as Hegel translated into his own language Spinoza's suggestion that "we ought to await and endure both faces of fortune with equanimity"?

II

Kant's *Critique of Practical Reason* especially irritated Hegel and his disciples, and precisely because they found in it, carried to the maximum, that edification of what we have spoken above. It is well-known that the *Critique of Practical Reason* is entirely based on the idea of pure duty: what Kant calls the categorical imperative. For Hegel the "critique of reason" (theoretical as well as practical) was generally intolerable. To criticize reason was, in his eyes, a mortal sin against philosophy. He mocked Kant's "critiques" in every way and compared the philosopher of Konigsberg to the scholastic who, before going into the water, wanted to know how to swim.

Jesting remarks often pass for arguments, and Hegel's irony produced a certain effect, even though his comparison was completely false. Did Kant begin by asking himself how he should philosophize, and did he attack philosophic problems only after having obtained an answer to this first question? Kant finished his *Critique of Pure Reason* at the age of fifty-seven; he had already been occupied with philosophy for many years without asking himself whether the methods of searching for truth that he, like everyone else, used in the realm of the exact sciences could be applied to the solution of metaphysical problems. It was only in the sixth decade of his life—whether under the influence of Hume's "skepticism" or struck by the antinomies that he had encountered at the limits of thought—that Kant, as he himself relates, awoke from his dogmatic slumber; it was then that there arose in him the doubt that was to lead him to the "critique" of reason: are the methods of searching for truth that have been elaborated by the exact sciences, and that give such excellent results, inapplicable to metaphysical problems?

It is hardly to be admitted that Hegel himself did not understand how little Kant resembled the ridiculous scholastic. Apparently he simply was not able to answer Kant, and he realized at the same time that, were the "critique" of reason carried through, the very foundations of human thought would be ruined. That this disturbing thought was not entirely strange to Hegel is to be divined from certain reflections in his *Phenomenology of the Spirit:* "Meanwhile, if the fear of making a mistake sets up a distrust of knowledge which, without any such scruples, goes about its work and really knows, it is not to be conceived why, conversely, a distrust of this distrust should not be set up, so that this fear of making a mistake is already itself a mistake."

Distrust and distrust of the distrust! Is there any place in philosophy for such a struggle between distrusts? Kant knew before Hegel—and he spoke of it sufficiently in his book—that the exact sciences have no need of the critique of reason, and they can calmly accomplish their task without at all concerning themselves with the doubts and anxieties of the philosophers; nothing is more foreign to them than distrust of their work. But this is not the meaning of Hegel's remark. The important thing is that there came to Hegel's mind the thought that one could trust knowledge, but one could likewise distrust it. He immediately brushes aside this thought, it is true, by saying "what is called fear of error is rather to be recognized as fear of truth." But it is hardly probable that this consideration can make the reader forget that Hegel himself felt at times uneasily that one could trust knowledge but that one could also refuse to trust it, and to the distrust of knowledge there was nothing else to oppose than distrust of the distrust. For those who make scientific knowledge the ideal of philosophy, "the distrust of distrust" is a truly shattering thought. It turns out, then, that in the last resort knowledge is based on the trust that we accord to it and that it is up to man to decide, to choose freely, whether knowledge deserves his trust or not.

What is to be done with this freedom? And even if it should appear that fear of error in this case is fear of knowledge, this would in no way simplify the situation: if knowledge inspires fear, it is perhaps because it really hides in itself something terrible against which man must guard himself. The fear of knowledge poses a problem as difficult as that which underlies the distrust of knowledge. And, of course, the philosopher must, before everything else, in some way overcome his distrust and his fears. As long as he sought truth naively without suspecting that there could be in his methods of search a defect which prevents man from recognizing truth even when he encounters it on his way, as long as he was also naively convinced that knowledge must be beneficial for man, the philosopher could calmly give himself over to his task. It seemed to him that trust is founded only on knowledge and that knowledge alone is capable of driving away all terrors. But suddenly it turns out that knowledge cannot found itself on itself, that it demands that trust be placed in it, and that not only does it not drive away terrors but on the contrary provokes them.

If Hegel had decided to plumb this thought to its depths, perhaps he would have seen that Kant's sin was not in having criticized reason but in never having been able to decide to fulfill the promise he had made of giving us a critique of reason. Spinoza said: "What altar will he who insults the majesty of reason build for himself?" Kant could have taken this phrase as the motto of his "critique." And, indeed, to criticize reason—is this not to commit an offence against its sovereign rights and to render oneself guilty of *laesio majestatis?* Who has the right to criticize reason? What is the power that will dare put reason in its place and deprive it of its scepter? Kant, it is true, affirmed that he had limited the rights of reason in order to open the way to faith. But Kant's faith is a faith within the limits of reason; it is reason itself but under another name. Hegel, who spoke of "distrust of distrust," was—if you please—more radical, more daring than Kant; but, of course, in words only. In fact Hegel had neither the audacity nor the desire to stop for a moment and ask himself why he had such trust in reason and knowledge and whence this trust came to him. More than once he brushed up against this question but always passed it by.

A strange thing! Hegel hardly appreciated the Bible; he did not like the New Testament, and as for the Old, he despised it. And yet, when there arose before him the fundamental philosophic problem, forgetting all that he said about Scripture, he sought support in the biblical account of original sin. Hegel writes: "This is found in another form in the old story of the fall of man—the serpent did not, according to it, deceive the man; for God says, 'See, Adam is become as one of us, to know good and evil.'" Again in his meditations on the fate of Socrates (in the same *Lectures on the History of Philosophy*), we read: "The fruit of the tree of the knowledge of good and evil—of the knowledge that is of reason out of itself—[is] the universal principle of philosophy for all later times."

It is not only Hegel who thinks thus. All of us are persuaded that the serpent who enticed our primal forefathers to taste of the fruits of the tree of the knowledge of good and evil did not deceive them, that the deceiver was God who had forbidden Adam to eat of these fruits in the fear that the man would become like God. Whether it was proper for Hegel to appeal to Scripture is another question. Hegel could permit himself everything and his disciples, whom the atheism (or pantheism) of Spinoza angered, listened piously to Hegel's discourses and almost considered his philosophy the only possible apology for Christianity. Yet here again, Hegel was only repeating Spinoza's thought, with the difference that Spinoza declared openly and forthrightly that there is no truth in the Bible and that the sole source of truth is reason, whereas Hegel spoke of revelation at the very moment when in the "dispute" between God and the serpent he took the side of the latter. There is no doubt that if the problem of truth had been posed in this form to Spinoza, he would have given his full approval to Hegel. If it is necessary to choose between God who warns us against the fruits of the tree of the knowledge of good and evil and the serpent who extols these fruits to us, the educated European cannot hesitate; he will follow the serpent. Daily experience convinces us that learned people enjoy great advantages over the ignorant. Consequently, he who seeks to discredit knowledge in our eyes lies, while the truth speaks through the mouth of him who glorifies knowledge. To be sure, as I have already said, according to Spinoza and to Hegel who followed him in everything, experience does not give us perfect knowledge (*tertium genus cognitionis*). Thus, when it is a question of choosing between the serpent and God, we are in the same situation as when we must choose between distrust of knowledge and distrust of distrust. In difficult moments reason refuses to guide us, and then we are obliged to decide at our own risk and peril without any guarantee that our decision will be justified by its results.

III

I know, certainly, that not only Spinoza and Hegel but even Kant would never have admitted that reason could refuse to guide man. "Reason avidly seeks universal and necessary judgments," says Kant at the beginning of his *Critique of Pure Reason* (First Edition). And not once in the course of his work does he ask himself: Why must we exert ourselves to furnish reason what it so avidly seeks? And who or what is this reason that possesses so great a power over man? Moreover, the fact that reason is possessed by a passion like every limited being should already suffice to put us on the alert and render reason and the universal and necessary judgments to which it aspires suspect in our eyes. But, I repeat, reason remains above all suspicion, even for the author of the *Critique of Pure Reason.*

Such has always been the tradition of human thought: distrust of reason has always been considered a crime oflaesio majestatis. Plato said that the greatest misfortune that could come to a man was to become a "hater of reason." For Aristotle, knowledge is universal and necessary knowledge (*katholou gar hai epistêmai panton, ex anankês ara estin to epistêton*). From Socrates on, we have once and for all renounced what constitutes the essential problem of knowledge and, at the same time, the metaphysical problem. The aim of the Socratic thought was precisely to protect knowledge from every attempt at criticism, as appears in that statement which at first glance appears precisely the condition and the beginning of all criticism—"I know that I know nothing" (a statement which, according to Socrates' own testimony, made the oracle declare him the wisest of all men)—but which actually kills in the germ the very possibility of all criticism. Indeed only he who is convinced that knowledge is the sole source of truth will say he knows that he knows nothing. Not for nothing did Hegel, in connection with Socrates' fate, recall the tree of knowledge and the words of the tempting serpent, "You shall be like God." Only he who has tasted the fruits of the tree of the knowledge of good and of evil is capable of handing himself over so unreservedly to the enchantments of knowledge. For Socrates, to despise knowledge was a mortal sin. He reproached the poets, mocking them for seeking to attain truth by ways other than those of knowledge. And he could not find words harsh enough for those who, knowing nothing, believed that they did know something. Whence comes this unshakable assurance that knowledge alone brings man the truth? And what does this assurance that we have all inherited from Socrates mean? Did the oracle seduce Socrates as the biblical serpent had once seduced Adam? Or did the seduction lie elsewhere, and did Pythia, like Eve, only offer Socrates the fruit that she had herself tasted at the suggestion of a power that escapes our sharpest notice?

However this may be, after Socrates the most noted representatives of human thought could not do other than identify truth with the fruits of the tree of knowledge. This is the meaning of Plato's warning against the "hater of reason." This is the meaning of Aristotle's "in general" (*katholou*) and "of necessity" (*exanankês*), of Descartes' "everything is to be doubted" and "I think, therefore I am," of Spinoza's "the true is the index of itself and of the false." This is why Kant declares at the beginning of his "critique" that reason avidly seeks universal and necessary judgments.

All this constitutes the heritage of Socrates. Since Socrates the truth, for men, has been confounded with universal and necessary judgments. Everyone is convinced that thought has the right to stop only when it has come up against Necessity, which puts an end to all searchings and all curiosity. And at the same time no one doubts that thought, in penetrating to the necessary relationships of things, accomplishes the supreme task of philosophy. So that Hegel, in short, saw quite rightly when he sought to demonstrate that there are not "philosophies" but "philosophy," that all the philosophers have always understood in the same way the mission that fate had imposed upon them. All of them sought to discover the rigorous and unchangeable order of being, for all of them—even those who, like Socrates, knew that they knew nothing—were completely hypnotized by the idea that this order which depends on no one must exist, that it is impossible that it should not exist, just as there must exist a science which reveals this order to man.

Socrates said, it is true, that perfect knowledge belongs only to the gods and that the knowledge of man is incomplete. But in saying this he exalted knowledge still higher, for his words meant, in short, that the freedom of the gods was no longer absolute: knowledge sets limits to them by fixing the bounds not only of the possible and the impossible but even of the permitted and the forbidden. In the *Euthyphro*, written by Plato while his master was still alive, Socrates demonstrates that it is not given even to the gods to choose: they are not free not to love the just, as mortals are not free not to love it. Mortals and immortals are equally subject to duty and to Necessity. This is why the task of philosophy consists of revealing the necessary relationships of things, that is to say, in obtaining knowledge, in order to convince men that one cannot argue with Necessity, that one must obey it. Of course, the exact sciences also establish the necessary relationships of things and teach men obedience, but philosophy is not content with this. It is not enough for philosophy that men accept Necessity and accommodate themselves to it; philosophy wishes to bring it about that men should love and venerate Necessity, as they once loved and venerated the gods.

It may be that the essential difference between Socrates and the Sophists, a difference which history has carefully hidden from us, consists precisely in the fact that, when the Greeks of the second half of the Fifth Century discovered that the Olympian gods were the work of the imagination and that "constraints" of every kind came not from living beings who took the fate of men to heart but from Necessity which is indifferent to everything, the Sophists (as St. Paul was later to do) reacted violently: if constraints come not from the gods but from Necessity, then nothing is true, everything is permitted. Protagoras' "man is the measure of all things" has the same meaning, it seems, as St. Paul's phrase, "if the dead rise not, let us eat and drink"[3]; in short, let us do whatever occurs to us, let us live just as we wish. No more than the Sophists did Socrates admit the existence of the gods. And this is quite understandable: he who is afraid of becoming a "hater of reason," who sees in knowledge the sole source of truth, cannot agree to recognize the gods. With a naivete perhaps very alluring but hardly appropriate to a philosopher who wished to prove everything and to question everything, Socrates turned away disdainfully from the poets and the artists only because, even if they happen at times to discover high truths, they do not obtain these from knowledge but from some other source and are incapable of explaining how they have found them. Socrates had no confidence in men "inspired by the gods": how can one place confidence in them when it is known that the gods do not exist? Or—if Hegel's later commentary is admitted—when one knows that God deceived man, as He Himself admitted when the serpent, having penetrated His secret intentions, revealed them to our primal forefathers? In any case, if one wishes to be prudent, it is better to hold on to Protagoras: "As for the gods, I do not know whether they exist or whether they do not exist."

Before his judges, who had to pronounce judgment concerning the accusation of atheism brought against him by Anytus and Meletus, Socrates said in short the same thing as did Protagoras; but, since he spoke of the immortality of the soul and not of the existence of the gods, many people even today believe that Socrates thought otherwise than Protagoras. In reality, both of them set out from the same idea but reacted differently to it, though with the same passion. Protagoras said: if the gods do not exist, if the soul is not immortal, if human life is no more than this brief terrestrial existence which begins with birth and ends with death, if we are not bound by invisible threads to superior beings—in short, if everything that begins in the world also ends there—then what is it that can bind man's caprice and in the name of what shall man renounce his caprice? Why, in this case, should not man give free rein to his desires and passions? He is at times obliged to submit to force, insofar as he cannot conquer or escape it by any ruse. But to submit to it still does not mean to recognize its supreme and final rights. Let us—to speak as did St. Paul—eat, drink and rejoice.

Socrates' attitude in regard to the truth that he had discovered is completely different. Like Protagoras, he does not doubt for a moment that it is for reason to decide the question of the gods' existence; and, with the intellectual honesty that characterized him and in which he saw (and we also after him) the highest virtue of the philosopher, he had to recognize that in the sight of reason one could as well admit the existence of the gods and the immortality of the soul as deny them. Furthermore—Socrates did not say this but it may be believed that he thought it—since science is incapable of providing a positive answer to these questions, since a scrupulous examination leads him as well as Protagoras (so different from him in all respects) to the same conclusion—it may be that the gods exist or it may be that they do not exist—then the cause of the gods is in a bad way: there is every reason to believe that they were invented by men. Yet, the solution proposed by Protagoras was unacceptable to Socrates, just as he would have indignantly rejected the words of St. Paul if he had been able to know them. Anything was better in Socrates' eyes than Protagoras' *homo-mensura* or the apostle's "let us eat and drink." What remains to be measured by man if everything that is measurable is transitory and subject to change? And how can one think of rejoicing when he knows that his days are numbered and that no one is certain of tomorrow?

Long before Socrates the great philosophers and poets of Greece considered with terror the agonizing uncertainty of our transient and sorrowful existence. Heraclitus taught that everything passes, that nothing remains. With a power that has never been surpassed the tragedians portrayed the horror of human life. And yet, as if across the centuries he were echoing the prophet Isaiah and St. Paul who repeated Isaiah, Heraclitus could still say that what the gods have prepared for us surpasses all the dreams and hopes of men. But it was no longer given to Socrates to speak thus. We do not know what awaits us after death: is it not then shameful to speak of what one does not know? Heraclitus, Isaiah and St. Paul were as unacceptable to Socrates, enthralled by knowledge, as was Protagoras who glorified the arbitrary. It is obvious that the men of the Bible and the philosophers of Heraclitus' type drew their wisdom from sources extremely doubtful; they were like the poets who, in a burst of unjustified enthusiasm, proclaimed things that they themselves did not understand. Without knowledge there can be neither truth nor goodness. Consequently, knowledge is the only source of everything that is important to man; it gives man, and cannot do otherwise, the "one thing necessary." To be sure, if knowledge revealed to us the gods and the immortality of the soul, this would not be at all bad; but since it is otherwise, we shall have to get along without these. So it was that Socrates understood the task that devolved on him. He saw quite as well as Aristotle that a man of knowledge could be wicked. But he had discovered that our existence ends in death. Since this is so, the biblical serpent and Pythia were right: virtue resides only in knowledge. In the eyes of all, publicly, Socrates had to repeat the act which, according to the ancient myth that no one can attest, Adam had committed.

IV

The serpent did not deceive man. The fruit of the tree of the knowledge of good and evil (i.e., as Hegel has explained to us, reason, which draws everything from itself) has become the principle of philosophy for all time. The "critique of reason" that contained the prohibition against tasting the fruit of the tree from which must come all our evils was replaced by the "distrust of the distrust," and God was expelled from the world that He had created while His power passed over entirely to reason. The latter, it is true, had not created the world, but it offered us in limitless number the very fruits against which the Creator had warned us. It is to be believed that it was precisely their "infinity" that seduced man: in the world where the fruits of the tree of knowledge became the principle not only of all philosophy but of being itself, thinking humanity dreamed of the possibility of the greatest victories and conquests. Whom should it distrust—the serpent who praised reason, or God who criticized reason? The answer could not be doubtful. It is necessary, according to Hegel, to oppose distrust to distrust. Hegel forgot only one thing, doubtless *bona fide*: if the serpent spoke the truth, if those who taste the fruit of the tree of knowledge really become "like God," if Pythia was also right and Socrates was indeed the wisest of men, then philosophy cannot be other than edifying; its essence, its meaning, is to edify. And not only among us on earth but in the other world also, if man is destined to live again after death, nothing will change in this respect: "The greatest good of man is to discourse daily about virtue."[4] To put it differently, according to the wisdom of Socrates, the greatest good for man is to feed on the fruits of the tree of knowledge.

It is not for nothing that Hegel recalled, in speaking of Socrates, the myth of the fall of man. It appears that the sin is hereditary: Socrates repeats Adam.

In Hegel's interpretation one finds again all the circumstances of the fall of the first man (and it may be that Hegel deliberately emphasized the parallels). The serpent is the Delphic god, and the woman intervenes this time also. Xanthippe could not play the role of Eve, it is true, but Pythia fills it perfectly; she gathers the fruits of the tree of knowledge and persuades Socrates that they are "the greatest good for man" and that, consequently, it is they and not the fruits of the tree of life that supply man with "the one thing necessary." Yet, though Hegel does not cease stubbornly repeating that knowledge is bound up with distrust of distrust, with the break with God and with faith in the serpent, his philosophy does not show us with the desired clarity and fullness what the fruits of the tree of knowledge have brought us.

If Hegel went with such enthusiasm to the serpent, it is doubtless because he did not suspect what could result from this commerce. The illuminations of Socrates were strange and incomprehensible to Hegel. As for Heraclitus, he pretended to have assimilated all his philosophic ideas, but he required them only in order to attain certain external purposes. Among the ancients it is Aristotle alone who was really close to him, and I believe that I am not exaggerating in saying that of all the philosophers of antiquity it was Aristotle who exercised a decisive influence over Hegel. Aristotle, who was "moderate to excess," who knew with such inimitable art to stop in time and who was so deeply persuaded that he had to seek truth and authentic reality in the middle zones of being, seeing that the limits of life present no interest for us—Aristotle appeared to Hegel as the model of the philosophic mind. The caution of the Stagyrite was, in his eyes, the best guarantee of what he considered his ideal—scientific rigor. The "best" must be sought between the "too much" and the "not enough." It is there also that the truth must be sought. Limitation, Aristotle taught, is the sign of perfection; and it was in this doctrine that Hegel found a sure refuge against the waves of the "bad infinity" that threaten to drown men.

When Socrates heard the serpent's words (let me be allowed, following Hegel, to hold on to the biblical image) "you shall be like God," and, turning away from God, tasted the fruits of the tree of knowledge—he went to the end: these fruits alone give life to men. Aristotle, however, stopped in time. Throughout his *Ethics* one finds remarks of this kind: "those who say that a man on the rack . . . can be happy, provided only that he be a virtuous man, speak—whether they mean to or not—an absurdity."[5] Such remarks, thrown out in passing, constitute the very foundation of Aristotle's ethics; they are obviously directed against Socrates whose ardent thought and life bear a quite different testimony. His conviction that nothing bad can happen to a good man and that knowledge is virtue, a conviction that appears to many people as the expression of a naive optimism, hid in itself the most terrible and cruel "truth" that the human soul has ever accepted.

When the schools deriving from Socrates declared solemnly that the virtuous man would be happy even in the bull of Phalaris, they contented themselves with expressing under a new form what constituted the meaning, the very essence, of the Socratic ethic. And, on the contrary, when Aristotle insisted that virtue alone did not suffice for happiness and that the latter demanded a certain minimum of temporal goods, he was defending himself against Socrates. Aristotle refused to admit that the fruits of the tree of knowledge could end by pushing man into the belly of the bull of Phalaris and make him taste that happiness of which not only the Stoics but also the Epicureans speak and which constitutes the foundation of the ethics of the last of the great philosophers of antiquity, Plotinus. The dishonoring of his daughters, the murder of his sons, the destruction of his fatherland—nothing troubles the happiness of the wise man, teaches Plotinus.[6] The meaning and the importance of ethics lies precisely in the fact that its "good" is autonomous, that is to say, completely independent of "things that are not in our power." The ethics that is afraid and therefore turns aside, as in Aristotle, from the bull of Phalaris renounces in the end its essential task.

Socrates saw this; he knew what the fruits of the tree of knowledge bring to men; he had tasted of them as Adam had once tasted of them. For Aristotle, however—as well as for Hegel in our day—these fruits were only "a mental perception" (*theôria*); he was content with contemplating them and did not even suspect the terrible poison with which they were permeated. So it is not to Socrates that one should go to seek naivete and unconcern but to those who have betrayed Socrates "willingly or unwillingly." Aristotle had recourse to a minimum of temporal goods in order to escape the bull of Phalaris. But the bull is not a fiction, it is reality itself. And knowledge does not have the right to deny its existence; it must even cut short every attempt to drive the bull of Phalaris outside the limits of the real. Everything that is real must be recognized as rational. That is what Hegel said. That is also what Aristotle said two thousand years before Hegel: "There is something of the divine in the nature of everything."[7] Thus one can find traces of the divine even in the bull of Phalaris, and reason, consequently, has not the right to refuse its benediction to it. Finally, wisdom brings man not "happiness" (*eudaimonia*) but something quite different; or, to put it more accurately, the happiness promised by wisdom is worse than the worst misfortunes that strike mortal men.

But how could the wisdom that leads men to the bull of Phalaris seduce them? Being a practical man Aristotle felt the danger; he understood that

Socrates' wisdom could not find in the world the "selflessness," the "spirit of sacrifice" on which his ethic relied. And the same practical sense whispered to Aristotle that the scorn which the philosophers ordinarily bear to the mob, *hoi polloi*, is simulated. Philosophy cannot get along without general agreement; in this respect it strives for the goodwill of *hoi polloi* or mob that it rejects in words. But if this is so, there is no place in ethics for the bull of Phalaris. Ethics must keep at its disposal a certain minimum of temporal goods. When such a minimum is guaranteed—or even when one succeeds at least in convincing men that what terrifies them and consequently appears to them eternally problematic is pushed to a sufficient distance, so that every direct threat is avoided— then only can one set about philosophizing in all tranquility. In that case one can accept from the hands of Socrates his truth that virtue and knowledge are one and the same thing; this truth then acquires, to be sure, another significance than that conferred upon it by the wisest of men, but this is precisely what is required. Philosophy becomes at the same time *vera* and *optima* (the true and the best), but it is not obliged to demand of men the impossible.

It was all the easier for Aristotle to escape the bull of Phalaris since Socrates himself had suggested to him (perhaps intentionally) how he should go about doing this. It would seem that the knowledge with which Socrates had promised to enrich humanity should have led it to entirely new sources that had been ignored up until then, and that the good discovered by this knowledge could have nothing in common with the good which men had previously obtained. But, as I have already indicated, Socrates, in setting out on the search for knowledge and the good, turned precisely to men of whom he himself said that they knew nothing, that they had no relationship with the good, and that they boasted of their knowledge only because they had lost all shame; Socrates turned to doctors, cooks, carpenters, politicians, etc.

The historians of philosophy have often asked how the wisest of men could confuse what is useful in daily life with what is morally good; they have seen here one of those inconsequences which the greatest minds do not succeed in avoiding. But it is to be believed that if there is inconsequence here it was intended. It would not have been difficult for Socrates himself to expose the *metabasis eis alio genos* (passing over into another realm) of which he was guilty. And, alone by himself, not surrounded by anxious disciples who wished to obtain answers to all questions and sharp-eyed opponents who threatened to call by its true name the source whence he drew his truths, Socrates doubtless saw clearly that the "useful" of the doctors and the cooks did not at all resemble the "good" with which he was called to endow men. It was in this probably that Socrates' "secret," which he concealed with so much care under the mask of irony and of dialectic, consisted: since the gods do not exist, it is necessary to accept the wisdom of the serpent. The serpent, however, has no power over the tree of life, over *res quae in nostra potestate non sunt* [things which are not in our power]; it has power only over the tree of knowledge. From the moment the gods left the world, the tree of knowledge forever hid the tree of life.

V

We know Socrates, who left no writings, only through the accounts of his disciples, Plato and Xenophon, and through second-hand pieces of information. But everything that seems unclear to us, debatable and incomplete in Socrates' doctrine can be completed and clarified from Spinoza's works. It would not be exaggerated, I think, to say that Socrates was resurrected in Spinoza or even that Spinoza was the second incarnation of Socrates. "Let us sacrifice with reverence to the shade of the holy, rejected Spinoza," says Schleiermacher, who was, according to Dilthey, the greatest of the German theologians after Luther. It was in the same tone the ancients spoke of Socrates—the best of men, the righteous one, the holy one. If recourse could be had to the oracle in modern times, it would certainly have called Spinoza, as it once did Socrates, the wisest of men.

Kierkegaard reproaches philosophers for not living in accordance with the categories in which they think. This reproach perhaps contains some truth, but it is certainly not applicable either to Socrates or to Spinoza. What makes both of them so remarkable is precisely the fact that they did live in the categories in which they thought, thus miraculously transforming the "true philosophy" into the "best philosophy," to use Spinoza's terms, or incarnating knowledge in virtue, to speak as Socrates did. In Socrates, universal and necessary truth led to the "highest good"; in Spinoza, his *tertium genus cognitionis, cognitio intuitiva* (third kind of knowledge, intuitive knowledge), ended in the *amor Dei intellectualis* (intellectual love of God) and the supreme *beatitudo* (blessedness) that is connected with it. But it is an error to brush aside, as people too often do, the fundamental idea of Socrates and Spinoza by invoking their "intellectualism." One can thus rid himself of them, but it is then impossible to understand the problem on which the thought of the wisest among men, both in his first and second incarnations, was entirely concentrated. To this the subsequent development of philosophy clearly bears witness. "All knowledge starts with experience"—so begins the *Critique of Pure Reason;* but Kant adds immediately that it does not follow from this that it comes entirely from experience. And, indeed, there is in our knowledge something that we never find in experience, a certain *Zutat* (seasoning) according to Hegel's expression, or, to speak as Leibniz did, "there is nothing in the intellect that was not in the senses, except the intellect itself." Our knowledge reduces itself entirely to this mysterious *Zutat,* and in the end experience plays hardly any role in the act of knowing.

It is true that those who sought knowledge were always interested in not detaching it from experience and also often substituted experience for knowledge. Scarcely had Aristotle said "all men desire by nature to know"[8] than he hastened to add: "this is seen in the pleasure that sensible perception gives us." But Aristotle knew perfectly well that knowledge is distinguished *toto coelo* from sensible perception. We recall with what insistence he emphasized that knowledge is knowledge of the universal and the necessary and that it is such knowledge alone that science seeks. We ought then to say: knowledge begins with experience and ends by completely brushing it aside. There is not, there must not be, any place in science for "pleasure in sensible perception." The purpose of knowledge is to detach itself from the sensible given, to overcome it. The sensible given is something that arises and disappears continually and never abides, something that one cannot take hold of and must consequently rid himself of, or, as the philosophers say, that one must raise himself above.

This is what Socrates taught; and such was also the meaning of Spinoza's philosophic "conversion." The unstable and transitory character of everything terrestrial filled his soul with disquietude and anxiety, as he himself admits in his *Tractatus de intellectus emendation* (The Treatise Concerning the Amendment of the Intellect). The attachment to the sensible given which, as Aristotle rightly remarked, is proper to all men, and which Spinoza also experienced, constitutes at first blush a very natural human aptitude, but in reality it is laden with threats and prepares for us the worst catastrophes. How can one attach himself to that which has a beginning and must, consequently, have an end? How can one admit such a dependence? The more passionately we attach ourselves to the temporal, to the passing, the more grievous will be the pain of parting when the moment comes for the object of our attachment to return into that nothingness from whence it arose for a brief moment.

Even though pleasure in sensible perception be proper to all men, it does not constitute a common virtue, a principle of power, but rather a common defect, a principle of weakness. And if Aristotle approximated it to knowledge, this was only thanks to a misunderstanding, perhaps intentional. Aristotle took his departure from Socrates and Plato and, as we know, always emphasized that knowledge is of the universal and that if everything were reduced to sensible perceptions (*ta aisthêta*) there would be no knowledge. Knowledge thus presupposes a certain transformation of man: he denies what he loved, what he. was attached to, and devotes himself to something quite new that differs entirely from the object of his former attachment. Even though he despised the Bible and so never took the trouble to reflect on the philosophic import of the myth of the fall, Hegel saw correctly when he said that the fruit of the tree of knowledge is what in modern language is called reason, which draws everything out of itself and which since Socrates has become the principle of philosophy for all time. But Hegel could never decide to draw from this idea the conclusions that follow from it and to say, as did Spinoza: "We may therefore conclude absolutely that Scripture must neither be accommodated to reason nor reason to Scripture."[9] Just like Aristotle, Hegel possessed a safety valve in case the tension should become too dangerous. That is why, like Aristotle, he did not discern the bull of Phalaris hidden behind the wisdom of Socrates. That is also why he did not suspect that the words of the God of the Bible could be true, that is to say, that knowledge would poison the joy of existence and lead man, through terrible and loathsome trials, to the threshold of nothingness. Why did Aristotle and Hegel remain blind to what Socrates and Spinoza saw? I do not know. But everything leads me to believe that neither Aristotle nor Hegel learned anything from the Socratic-Spinozist vision.

From the pieces of information we possess it is difficult to determine how Socrates resolved the problem of free will. But Spinoza knew that men were as little free as inanimate objects. Had the stone been endowed with consciousness it would imagine that it falls freely (*se liberrimum esse*). In the same letter (LVIII) Spinoza further says: "Without, I hope, contradicting my consciousness, that is, my reason and experience, and without cherishing ignorance and misconception, I deny that I can by any absolute power of thought think that I wish or do not wish to write." And immediately afterwards, to remove all doubt from the reader, he explains: "I appeal to the consciousness, which he has doubtless experienced, that in dreams he has not the power of thinking that he wishes or does not wish to write; and that, when he dreams that he wishes to write, he has not the power not to dream that he wishes to write."

How are we to understand these puzzling words? It would seem less proper for the clear-headed Spinoza than for anyone else to seek in dreams the explanation of what happens in reality. No one denies that sleep fetters the human will. But sleep is followed by awakening, which consists precisely in the fact that man breaks the fetters which paralyze his will. It often happens to us, even before we awaken, to feel that everything that is occurring belongs not to true reality but to dream-reality, which, at the cost of a certain effort, we can brush aside and cast away from ourselves. To be sure, if the sleeper had preserved that capacity for clear and contradiction-free thought, of which Spinoza and his teacher Descartes speak so much to us, he would have to say that his judgment that he is sleeping and that his reality is a dream-reality conceals within itself a contradiction and must therefore be considered false: it is in the dream-state, indeed, that it seems to him that he is sleeping and dreaming. Besides, the sleeper, like the awakened person, does not feel himself, generally speaking, bound or deprived in any sense of his liberty; in dreaming we no more feel ourselves in the power of a strange force than in the state of waking. A suspicion penetrates into us only when we begin to feel that the force which dominates us is hostile to us, when the dream becomes a nightmare. It is then only that there suddenly comes to our minds the absurd, inept idea—one recognizes the absurd, the inept, by the fact that it contains an inner contradiction—that this reality is not the true reality but a dream, a lie, an illusion.

At the same time we suddenly find ourselves before a dilemma: what shall we choose—the reality of the nightmare or the absurd assumption? The reality of the nightmare offends our entire being; to admit the absurd is an offence against reason. It is impossible not to choose, for if one does not himself decide, someone or something will decide for him. In dreaming, as is known, man chooses the absurd assumption: before the horror of the nightmare the fear of offending reason loses all power over us—we awaken. In the state of waking a different "order" prevails. We "accept" everything—no matter how shameful, how repugnant, how frightening that which we must accept appears—provided only that reason, as well as the principle of contradiction which protects it, be not outraged. For, *Quam aram parabit sibi qui majestatem rationis laedit?* (What altar will he build for himself who insults the majesty of reason?), as Spinoza, who denied the freedom of man, wrote.

Or was Nicolas of Cusa closer to the truth in affirming that God lives "inside the wall of the coincidence of opposites" and that this wall "is guarded by an angel stationed at the entrance to Paradise"? It is true that it is obviously not given man to drive this angel away; and besides, not only Spinoza, who did not believe, but still more the believer will shudder with horror at the idea that he should raise his hand against the guardian posted by God Himself at the gate of Paradise. For what altar will the man who violates the commandment of God build for himself? There cannot even be a question, it seems, of "free" decision here. To pass from the nightmarish dream to the beneficent reality of the waking state is not forbidden to man, but to pass from the nightmare of reality to the God who lives inside the wall of contradiction—this is not given to us; God Himself here sets a bound to our freedom.

Spinoza, of course, would not have admitted the formula of Nicolas of Cusa; for Spinoza, the God of Nicolas of Cusa, his paradise, his angel stationed at the entrance to Paradise—all these were only the images of a naive mind which still had not freed itself from traditions and prejudices. But the thought of Nicolas of Cusa expresses the pathos of the Spinozist philosophy more completely than Spinoza's own words—*quam aram parabit sibi* [what altar will he build for himself]. . . And further, *quam aram parabit sibi* is also an image in which can be found traces of that very tradition which had inspired Nicolas of Cusa with the idea of the angel posted at the door of Paradise. But the chief thing is that both Nicolas of Cusa and Spinoza were firmly "convinced" that it is not given mortal men to overcome the bounds established by the "law" of contradiction and that, consequently, one cannot escape the nightmare of reality. The philosopher is obliged, like everyone else, to accept reality; before reality the philosopher finds himself as impotent as anyone. The only thing then that the philosopher can and must do is to teach men how they should live in the midst of this nightmarish reality from which one cannot awaken because it is the only reality. What this means is that the aim of philosophy is not truth but edification, or, to put it differently, not the fruits of the tree of life but the fruits of the tree of knowledge. It is thus that Socrates understood the task of philosophy in antiquity, and it is thus that Spinoza understood it in modern times.

We have already heard Socrates. Let us now listen to Spinoza who completed what Socrates had begun. Spinoza's task consisted in uprooting from the human soul the ancient idea of God. As long as this persists in man, we live not in the light of truth but in the darkness of falsehood. All prejudices, writes Spinoza, "spring from the notion, commonly entertained, that all things in nature act as men themselves act, namely, with an end in view. It is accepted as certain that God Himself directs all things to a definite end, for it is said that God made all things for man, and man that he might worship Him."[10] All prejudices have for their source the conviction that God sets up purposes or goals. Now in reality, "God . . . has no principle or goal of action."[11]

When one reads this, one asks himself before everything else: "Is Spinoza right or not? Do the people who believe that God sets Himself certain purposes know the truth, while those who affirm that every purpose is alien to God deceive themselves? Or is the contrary the case?" Such is the first question that arises quite naturally, or of itself, before us. But given what Spinoza has previously said to us, we must raise another question before this one: "Is man free to choose this or that answer when it is a question of knowing whether God does or does not set Himself purposes? Or is the answer to this question already prepared in advance, before man poses the question, before man who asks it has even risen from nothingness into being?" We recall that Spinoza has openly admitted to us that he was not free to write or not to write. Is he then free to choose between this or that solution to the question that presented itself to him? A hundred years later Kant fell into the same snare. Metaphysics, he says, must decide whether God exists, whether the soul is immortal, whether the will is free. But if the will is not free or if its freedom is doubtful, then it is not given man to choose when it is a question of God's existence and the soul's immortality. Someone or something has already decided, without him, the question of God's existence and the soul's immortality; whether he wishes it or not, he is obliged to accept the answer that will be presented to him.

VI

The problem of free will is usually connected with ethical questions. But as was already brought out in part in the preceding chapter, the problem is still more closely connected with that of knowledge. More precisely: freedom, on one side, and our ideas of good and evil, on the other, are intertwined to such a degree with our theories of knowledge that every attempt to treat the problems outside their mutual relationships leads inevitably to partial or even false conclusions. When Leibniz stated with assurance that a man with his hands tied can still be free, his assurance was based on the conviction that it is given to "knowledge" to answer the question of freedom and that we must accept the answer furnished by knowledge as final and without appeal. Such was also Spinoza's conviction. But "knowledge" furnished Spinoza an answer completely different from what it furnished Leibniz. Leibniz "knew" that our will was free, Spinoza that it was not free.

The celebrated debate between Erasmus of Rotterdam and Luther turned around the same question. Erasmus wrote *Diatribae de libero arbitrio* [Discourses on Free Will]; Luther answered him with his *De servo arbitrio* [On the Bondage of the Will]. And if we ask ourselves how it was that Erasmus and Leibniz knew that the will is free while Luther and Spinoza discovered that it is not free, we shall find ourselves in a very difficult situation from which we shall not be able to escape in the ordinary way, that is to say, by checking the arguments of the two parties. It is certain that they were both equally honest and correctly reported their personal experience. But how is one to know which of these personal experiences testifies to the truth? The problem appears even more complex if one takes account of the fact that there is a conflict not only between different individuals, but also between the experiences of one and the same individual, who sometimes feels himself free and sometimes unfree. Spinoza is an example: when he was young he affirmed free will, but when he was older he denied it. "Freedom is a mystery," said Malebranche, and like everything that bears the mark of mystery, freedom hides within itself an inner contradiction. Every attempt to rid oneself of it always leads to the same result: one rids oneself not of the contradiction but of the problem.

Is it necessary to show this in the case of Spinoza? An ass placed at an equal distance between two bales of hay will die of hunger, he says, but it will not turn towards the one or the other unless an external force intervenes. And man is in a similar situation: he goes to his ruin, he knows that death lies in wait for him, but even the consciousness of the greatest dangers will not draw him out of the lethargy to which he has been condemned by the "order and connection of things" that has always existed and remains forever unchangeable—just as the bird hypnotized by the serpent throws itself, on its own, into the monster's jaws. If Spinoza's thought is translated into simpler language, it appears that his reflections have finally the same meaning as Luther's words: by nature man is free, but his freedom is paralyzed by someone or something. Hence this puzzling contradiction, so sad and so torturing: man, who above all others in the world prizes his freedom, feels that it has been taken away from him and sees no possibility of recovering it. Everything that he does, everything that he undertakes, not only does not deliver him but makes him still more a slave. He acts, he writes, he reflects, he perfects himself in all sorts of ways, but the more he strains his powers, the more he perfects himself and reflects, the more he becomes conscious of his complete incapacity to bring about, by his own power and on his own initiative, any change whatsoever in the conditions of his existence. And what most weakens and paralyses his will is thought, that precisely on which men ordinarily base all their hopes of deliverance. As long as man did not "think," he believed that "God directs everything to a definite end." But when he began to reason, he suddenly discovered that this was only a prejudice, an error, born of the free will to which he so eagerly aspires and which once perhaps had the power of transforming his desires into realities but which today, enfeebled and impotent, can only torment man by recalling to him a past forever lost. When it was still itself, it inculcated in man the conviction that high and important purposes are realized in the universe, that the good, the evil, the ugly, the beautiful, etc., exist. But "knowledge" has disarmed the will and deprived it of its decisive voice when it is a question of truth and of being. God does not set Himself any purpose. The will and the intellect of God as little resemble the will and the intellect of man as the constellation called the Dog resembles the dog, the barking animal. Let us turn our gaze toward the ideal science, toward mathematics, and we shall know where and how truth is to be found. We shall then become convinced that truth is one thing and that the "best" is another. There is no "best" for God, and those who "maintain that God does everything with a view to the good" are still more in error than those who suppose that "everything depends on His (God's) discretion." Necessity reigns over everything: "God does not act out of freedom of the will."

Spinoza does not cease repeating to us that Necessity is the essence and foundation of being: "things could not have been brought into being by God in any manner or in any order different from that which has in fact obtained."[12] For him, *sub specie aeternitatis* (in the perspective of eternity) has the same meaning as *sub specie necessitatis* (in the perspective of necessity). In all the history of thought probably no other philosopher developed with such obstinacy, with such passion, the theme of the omnipotence of Necessity. And he assures us, along with this, that he has "demonstrated" his theses *luce meridiana clarius* (clear as day light). That he has expressed *luce meridiana clarius* the conviction that has seized hold of the human mind is indisputable, but can this pass for a demonstration? When he affirms, on the one hand, that "God acts solely by the laws of His own nature and is not constrained by anyone,"[13] and, on the other hand, is indignant at those who admit that God can act *sub ratione boni* (with a view to the good), the question quite naturally arises: whence does he know that the *sub ratione boni* does not constitute one of the "laws of His (God's) nature," and perhaps even the supreme law? If Spinoza had affirmed that God is outside and beyond all laws, that He is Himself the source and creator of laws— very well! But this thought is far from Spinoza. Human reason can renounce everything, but it will not consent to free either the highest or the lowest being, either the Creator or the creatures, from obedience to laws. So, even though Spinoza affirms that "if men were born free, they would form no conception of good and evil," it is no more given him to realize the ideal of the man who stands beyond good and evil than the ideal of freedom.

The end of the fourth part and all of the fifth part of the *Ethics* testify clearly to this: the man whom Spinoza calls free is not at all free, and the happiness that the philosopher brings has for its primary condition the distinction between good and evil. If we wish to decipher the profound meaning of the Socratic doctrine that knowledge is identical with virtue and that nothing bad can happen to a good man, we must address ourselves, not to the historians who show how naive and superficial was the wisest of men, but to Spinoza who, two thousand years later, took upon himself the burden of the problems raised by Socrates. We even find in Spinoza Socrates' irony, but it is hidden under the *more geometrico* (according to the geometric method). The mathematical method—is it not indeed an irony in the mouth of the man who affirmed that *summum mentis bonum est Dei cognitio* (the mind's highest good is the knowledge of God) and that *summa mentis virtus Deum cognoscere* (the mind's highest virtue is to know God)? Since when is mathematics interested in things like *summum bonum* [highest good] or *summa virtus* [highest virtue]? And how does it happen that God who has bound Himself "not to act with a view to the good" has yet brought the summum bonum?

It is clear that Spinoza's *summum bonum* [the highest good] was of a very special kind. Like Socrates, Spinoza plucked the fruits of the tree of knowledge, which became for him the principle of philosophy for all time. His *summum bonum* and his *beatitudines,* like Socrates' "happiness" and "highest good," have absolutely nothing in common either with happiness or with the good. That is why he demands so insistently of men that they renounce the beautiful, the good, all "purposes," desires and instincts. It is on this condition alone that men will obtain the "contentment with oneself" which "understanding" brings and become "like God, knowing good and evil." All human attachments must be replaced by "love for the eternal and infinite" which is none other than the "intellectual love of God," of which Spinoza says that it "necessarily springs from the third kind of knowledge." The noblest part of man is his *mens* (mind), *ratio* (reason), *intellectus* (understanding). And Spinoza knows firmly that "the human mind is eternal, the human mind cannot be completely destroyed with the body," and again, "we feel and experience that we are eternal."

At first reading it may seem that Spinoza contradicts himself when he says, on the one hand, "properly speaking, God neither loves nor hates anyone" and proclaims, on the other hand, "hence it follows that God, insofar as He loves Himself, loves men, and, consequently, that the love of God towards men and the intellectual love of the mind towards God are one and the same."[14] But there is no contradiction here. The God of Spinoza "knows no passions"; joys and sorrows are alien to him, and "love" in the first instance has a meaning quite different from what it has in the second. It is here that the spiritual relationship between Socrates and Spinoza becomes especially clear. Both of them, like the first man, allowed themselves to be seduced by the promises of the tempter, "you shall be like God, knowing good and evil." Both of them, like the first man, exchanged the fruits of the tree of life for those of the tree of knowledge, that is to say, "the things that are not in our power" for those that are in our power. Did they decide to do this freely or did they, as the Bible says, act under the influence of a mysterious enchanter? We shall return again to this question. What is certain is that, having stretched forth their hands toward the tree of knowledge, men have forever lost their freedom. To put it differently, they have preserved only the freedom to choose between "good" and "evil."

It is not for nothing that Spinoza, who denied freedom, entitled the two last parts of his *Ethics* "of human freedom" and "of human bondage." Not only is there no contradiction here, but rather a strict relationship, one of immense metaphysical significance. Men have completely forgotten that at some distant, perhaps mythical, time of their existence, they had the possibility not of choosing between good and evil but of deciding whether evil should exist or not exist. They have forgotten this to such a degree that we are all convinced that man never had such freedom, that such freedom is an impossibility not only for man but for a higher being as well.

In his remarkable study "On the Essence of Human Freedom," a study certainly inspired by the fourth and fifth parts of Spinoza's *Ethics*, Schelling brings us testimony of touching candor on this matter. "The real and living concept, however, consists in the fact that it (freedom) is a capacity for good and evil. This is the point of greatest difficulty in the whole doctrine of freedom, and it has always been felt as such." And indeed, according to our conception, freedom is the freedom to choose between good and evil: if we wish, we choose the good; if this does not suit us, we choose the evil. But evil might not have existed in the universe at all. Whence did it come? Do not Necessity and the capacity for choosing between good and evil testify, not to our freedom—as Spinoza and Hegel thought and as all of us also think—but to our enslavement, to our loss of freedom? The free being possesses the sovereign right to give names to all things, and they will bear the names that he confers on them. The free man might not have authorized evil to enter the world, but now man must be content with "choosing" between the evil that is not subordinated to him and the good that is likewise no longer in his power. But for Socrates already it was evident that man had never possessed such power and such possibilities. Names were given to things neither by man nor even by the Being in whose image man was created, and evil entered the world without demanding authorization of anyone. In his first incarnation Socrates did not even try to struggle against this self-evidence; in any case, he says not a word of his attempts, perhaps because they always ended in shameful failure. But in his second incarnation, when he appeared to men in Spinoza's form he showed himself a little more candid. He allowed us to have a glimpse of his fruitless struggles and even admitted to us, as we recall, that his situation, that is to say, the situation of a man "who is led by reason alone," was no better than that of Buridan's ass who dies of starvation between two bales of hay.

In his youth he could not admit this idea. In the *Cogitata metaphysica* he still maintained human freedom, and added that if we were not free, "man would have to be regarded not as a thinking being but as a most infamous ass." But the years passed, and with a terror to which the first pages of his *Tractatus de intellectus emmendatione* [Treatise concerning the Amendment of the Intellect] bear witness, Spinoza declared that there is no difference between man and Buridan's ass: they are both deprived of freedom, their will is similarly paralyzed. It was long ago that the choice was once and for all made for them: "God has no principle or end of action." This is reality—the final and definitive reality. And the philosopher is as little capable of changing anything in it as the man in the street or "the ass, the most infamous of animals." These are "things that are not in our power." The philosopher has at his disposal only the *docet* (teaching) how "to bear with equanimity" what fate brings us. And man must be content with this: "happiness is not the reward of virtue but virtue itself."

VII

The idea of finality, the idea of an omnipotent God who created man and blessed him—this idea runs through and animates the entire Bible. But the Middle Ages already could not without difficulty accept the Bible's logic, which constantly offends the habits of rational thought. I shall not exaggerate, I think, in saying that the Scholastics, who called Aristotle to rule over all the domains of theology, themselves thought what Spinoza was later to proclaim openly: "God did not wish to teach the Israelites the absolute attributes of His essence, but to break down their hardness of heart and draw them to obedience; therefore He did not appeal to them with reasons but with the sound of trumpets, thunder and lightnings."[15] And indeed, the God of the Bible in no way resembles Aristotle: instead of arguments there are sounds of trumpets, rolls of thunder, lightnings. And so throughout Scripture, beginning with Genesis and ending with the Apocalypse: over against the logic of human reason are set the omnipotent *fiat* and the thunder.

With the conscientiousness and determination that are especially his, Spinoza concludes that "between faith and theology or philosophy there is no connection or affinity . . . Philosophy has no end in view but truth, faith looks for nothing but obedience and piety."[16] To be sure, philosophy and theology cannot and do not wish to have anything in common. The philosopher and the theologian must recognize this if they have enough courage to express in words the profoundest human experience, or, to put it better, if it has been given them to know, through their own experience, the illuminations that are produced when the different orders of being and of human thought strike up against and contradict each other.

Luther is infinitely distant from Spinoza, and yet in his doctrine of faith and free will we encounter the very thoughts that we find in Spinoza and expressed in almost the same words. Spinoza refers to Exodus 20:20; Luther to Jeremiah 23:29, "is not my word like . . . a hammer that breaketh the rock in pieces?", and to I Kings 10:11–13. He says: "The law is a hammer that breaks rocks, a fire, a wind, and that great and mighty shaking that overthrows mountains."[17] There is, it is true, an essential difference between Luther and Spinoza, a difference that we must state as precisely as possible in order to clarify the problem of the relationship between knowledge and freedom. Both Luther and Spinoza drew from their extraordinary inner experience the profound conviction that the human will is not free. And both of them were equally convinced that "there is no connection between faith and philosophy." But while Spinoza affirms that philosophy has no end other than truth and that the goal of theology is piety and obedience, Luther says, or rather cries out with all the force and ardor of which a man is capable when he struggles for his most precious good, that the source of truth is not knowledge, the knowledge that reason brings to man, but faith, faith alone. Strange as it may seem, Luther was convinced that the goal of philosophy is not truth but obedience and piety, while truth is obtained only through faith, *sola fide.* Inspired as he was by Scripture, Luther could not finally speak otherwise. Hegel himself, let us recall, saw in the fruits of the tree of knowledge the principle of philosophy for all time. Now it is thanks to these fruits that man acquired the faculty of distinguishing between good and evil and became bound to submit to the laws of the good. Thus, if Socrates in antiquity and Spinoza in modern times tasted of these fruits, by this very fact they denied truth and replaced it with something quite different. Instead of truth humanity received "obedience and piety." The world found itself subordinated to a law that is impersonal and indifferent to everything, and it is in voluntary obedience to this law that both mortal men and the immortal gods must find their greatest contentment.

To be sure, as I have already indicated, despite their intellectual honesty which is unparalleled in the history of philosophy, Socrates and Spinoza were obliged in this case to put a good face on a bad situation. Socrates did not succeed (and basically he recognized it) in constructing a bridge between knowledge and virtue; Spinoza no more succeeded in keeping himself on the heights of the mathematical method. He could never forget that, having lost his freedom, man has been changed from *res cogitans* (a thinking being) to *asinus turpissimus* (a most infamous ass), and this thought tormented him to the end of his life. But both of them were enthralled to such a degree by the idea of Necessity and of the eternal order that every manifestation of human freedom appeared to them both foolish and sacrilegious. Seduced, as Adam had been, by the magic "you shall be like God," they agreed to everything, even though their agreement was no longer a free act but a forced adaptation to the conditions determined in advance by being. The man *qui sola ratione ducitur* (who is led by reason alone) finds himself obliged sooner or later forever to renounce his freedom and to make others renounce theirs. Suppressing his revolt into the deepest part of himself and swallowing the outrage (*asinus turpissimus*), he must glorify the God who knows no purpose and man who, in harmony with his God, is prepared "to endure both faces of fortune with equanimity" and to find there *acquiescentiam in se ipso* (contentment with oneself) or *beatitudinem* (happiness).

Of course, if Socrates or Spinoza had wished to realize fully the ideal of the man *qui sola ratione ducitur*, they would not have had to make the least allusion to *acquiescentia* and *beatitudo*. Why choose *acquiescentia*? Why not prefer for oneself anxiety? There is not, there cannot be, place in philosophy for any preference whatever. Philosophy, like mathematics, seeks not the best but the true. Its basic principle is *non ridere, non lugere, neque detestari, sed intelligere* (not to laugh, not to lament, not to curse, but to understand). And, as it is a question only of "understanding," *acquiescentia in se ipso*, the calm and balanced mind enjoys no right or special privilege over the disturbed and agitated mind. The *tertium genus cognitionis* (third kind of knowledge), which reveals the necessary relationships of things, will find for all states of the mind and body the place that is appropriate to them.

It is thus, I say, that the man who is led by reason alone should have thought. In his eyes the difference between *res cogitans* [a thinking thing] and *asinus turpissimus* [a most infamous ass] ought not to be clothed with any particular importance. Human beings imagine that they constitute in the universe a kind of state within a state and that it matters greatly to someone or to something that they be *res cogitantes* [thinking things] and not *asini turpissimi* [most infamous asses]. But we know that these are only prejudices of the ignorant and churlish mob, prejudices of which the philosopher wishes to rid himself and can do so. Yet neither Socrates nor Spinoza could resolve to do this: the sacrifice was too hard, even for them. Before his judges, who held his life in their hands, Socrates continued to repeat that he would not renounce his "good," even if the gods did not exist, even if the soul were not immortal. And Spinoza—as if it had been decreed that he should follow Socrates in everything and reveal what Socrates had left unsaid—declared in the next to the last theorem of the *Ethics* (before saying: "Happiness is not the reward of virtue, but virtue itself"): "even if we did not know that our mind is eternal, we should still consider of primary importance piety and religion, and generally all things that in Part IV we showed to be attributable to courage and high-mindedness." The mob, says Spinoza in the explanation of this theorem, judges otherwise: if men knew that no reward awaits them after death no one would do his duty, for people believe that in following the way of the good they are renouncing their rights and imposing heavy burdens on themselves.

But we ask once again: why does Spinoza consider the mob's judgment low and contemptible and his own noble and elevated? For him who has understood "through the third kind of knowledge" that everything happens in the world necessarily, the mob's judgment and Spinoza's are only links in an infinite series of events. Neither the one nor the other can lay claim to any special qualification. One person, after discovering that the soul passes and disappears along with the body, will renounce morality and religion and say, with St. Paul, "let us eat and drink." The other, on the contrary, will say, like Socrates, "I shall not deny the good; I shall not eat nor drink, and I shall continue to seek happiness in the good." And neither the one nor the other has a right to expect the approval of others and to consider their judgments and valuations universal and necessary. But neither Socrates nor Spinoza will renounce universality and necessity for anything in the world: all humanity must think and speak as they do.

It is in the "must" that the meaning of Spinoza's geometrical method and Socrates' dialectical method lies. Indeed, if, like a stone or an *asinus turpissimus,* man is subject to the law of necessity, if neither man nor God Himself acts in view of some purpose but "only according to the laws of their nature," then philosophy has nothing more to do: everything has already been done before it and without it, everything will continue to be done without it. The life of the universe follows the course determined for it in advance, and there exists no power in the., world which can change or wishes to change in any way whatsoever the established "order and connection of things." But if the structure of being can not be changed in any way, if what is must be accepted as much by the philosopher as by the mob (i.e., *asinus turpissimus*)—for we know that in the face of reality all are equally impotent—what difference is there between the wise man and the imbecile? Yet there is a difference, there must be, or else Socrates and Spinoza have nothing to do in the world, or else they have no reason for being. One understands now why the wisest among men allowed himself to be seduced by the craftiest of animals. The serpent offered him, in place of the fruits of the tree of life, that is to say, in place of the "things that are not in our power" the fruits of the tree of knowledge, that is to say, reason which draws everything out of itself. This substitution promised man complete independence: "you shall be like God." But all that reason could draw out of itself was happiness in the bull of Phalaris. No matter what Spinoza may say, it is philosophy and not religion that demands *obedientiam et pietatem* [obedience and piety]. The wise man must "endure and await with equanimity both faces of fortune," even when, like his humble companion, he dies of hunger between two bales of hay.

VIII

Thus, reason teaches piety and obedience. If, then, faith also taught piety and obedience, there would be no distinction between reason and faith. Why then does Spinoza affirm so insistently that "there is no connection between philosophy and faith" and that they "are totally different"? And why did Luther, for his part, attack reason so violently? I recall that Luther—who in all things followed Scripture and particularly St. Paul, who in turn relied on Isaiah—every time he pronounced judgments that were particularly audacious and offensive to reason was convinced, like Spinoza, that man's will is not free. And I would add to this that the source of their conviction, in both cases, was their inward experience. Finally—and this is the most important thing—these "immediate deliverances of consciousness" caused them a mad terror. Both of them experienced something akin to what a man buried alive feels: he feels that he is living, but he knows that he can do nothing to save himself, and that all that remains to him is to envy the dead who do not have to be concerned with saving themselves. Not only *De servo arbitrio* [On the Bondage of the Will] and *De votis Monasticis judicium* [On Monastic Vows] but all of Luther's works speak to us of the boundless despair that seized him when he discovered that his will was paralyzed and that it was impossible for him to escape his downfall. Spinoza does not speak freely of what takes place inside himself, and yet, calm and reserved as he appears, he at times allows confessions to escape that permit us to catch a glimpse of what his philosophical "happiness" cost him. Spinoza never succeeded in forgetting—how can one forget such things?—that a man deprived of freedom *non pro re cogitante, sed pro asino turpissimo habendus est* (would have to be regarded not as a thinking thing but as a most infamous ass).

But it is here that Spinoza and Luther part company. Since our direct consciousness tells us that freedom does not exist, it does not exist. It may be that this is terrifying, it may be that the man deprived of freedom is indeed no more than an *asinus turpissimus*, but this in no way changes the situation. Terrors and horrors, whatever they may be, are not arguments against truth, just as happiness and joy do not bear witness to truth. By virtue of its discretionary power, reason commands: *non ridere, non lugere, neque detestari* (not to laugh, not to lament, not to curse). Why must one obey reason? Why may one not oppose to the immediate deliverances of consciousness *lugere et detestari*? "Experience" itself, the "immediate deliverances of consciousness" contain no such prohibition; "experience" is not at all interested that men should not weep and curse. "The true is the index of itself and of the false" can no longer justify reason's pretensions to omnipotence. The immediate deliverances of consciousness, so long as they do not go beyond their proper limits, bear witness both that man's will is not free and that man weeps and curses the fate that has taken away his freedom. And he who allows himself to be guided by experience and experience alone permits himself to weep and curse when he discovers that an invisible power has deprived him of his most precious good—freedom. But to him who takes reason for his guide, *qui sola ratione ducitur* [who is guided by reason alone], it is strictly forbidden to weep and curse. He must be content with understanding, *intelligere*. To put it differently, one takes away from him the last vestiges—not merely the vestiges, but the very memory (Plato's *anamnêsis*) or, if you prefer, the very idea—of freedom. *Ratio* (reason) brings with it the *tertium genus cognitionis—cognitio intuitiva* (third kind of knowledge—intuitive knowledge), the knowledge that by virtue of its power—acquired no one knows where—transforms purely empirical judgments, statements of fact, into universal and necessary judgments, that is, confers on the "real" immutability and definitively fixes it in *saecula saeculorum*.

Whence comes this dreadful power of reason? By what magic does it bring it about that the real becomes necessary? I think you will not find any answer to this question in any philosopher. But I know definitely that men do everything in their power to turn this question aside. Spinoza, who wished to reason "according to the geometric method," permits himself to defend rational knowledge with "theological" arguments. He calls reason "our better part" and even "the divine light," and is not afraid, when necessary, to write that phrase that I have already quoted and that one would expect to find in a catechism rather than in a philosophic treatise: "what altar can he build for himself who offends the majesty of reason?" It is true that there was no other way out for Spinoza: there, where man learns that the sum of the angles of a triangle is equal to two right angles, one can only learn that we have never had and never shall have free will, or that it is forbidden us to weep and curse when we discover that our will is not free, or that our curses and tears, our despair and rage, will never be able to overcome the "true philosophy" that knowledge furnishes us and regain our lost freedom. But if this is so, then Spinoza's statement that I have already quoted and that appears indisputable—"the goal of philosophy is only truth, while the goal of faith is only obedience and piety"—appears to be a false and dangerous auto-suggestion. Philosophy, and precisely that philosophy which found its most complete expression in Spinoza's work, with the *intelligere* and the *tertium genus cognitionis* that crown it, is not at all concerned with truth and seeks only "obedience and piety" which, in order to turn aside all suspicion from itself, it attributes to faith.

Spinoza states—and here again we approach Luther—that the God of the Bible did not in any way dream of making known to men His absolute attributes but wished simply to break their obstinacy and their wicked will; wherefore he had recourse not to arguments but to trumpets, thunder and lightning. But if the arguments in which Spinoza put his trust led him to the conviction that everything happens in the universe by virtue of Necessity, which condemns man to the fate of the stupid animal who dies of hunger between two bales of hay, does this not indicate that "arguments," by paralyzing man, do not at all lead him to the truth? That they do not awaken but rather still more stupefy our slumbering thought? And that if God had recourse to thunder and to lightning, it is because it was impossible otherwise to return to the human soul, in its lethargy and semi-death, its ancient freedom, impossible to deliver it from obedience and make it escape the limits of the piety into which the power of reason had forced it, impossible to make it participate in the truth? *Verbum Dei malleus est conterens petras* (the word of God is a hammer, breaking the rocks), says Luther, following the prophet; this "word" alone is capable of breaking the walls with which reason has surrounded itself. And it is in this that the function and meaning of "God's hammer" consist. This wall is nothing other than the *acquiescentia in se ipso* (contentment with oneself) and that *virtus* (virtue) which expects and demands no reward, for it is itself the supreme reward, the summum bonum, or the *beatitudo* (blessedness/happiness) proclaimed by Socrates in his first and second incarnation. The thunderbolts of the prophets, of the apostles, and of Luther himself were directed against the altars erected by human wisdom. "Because man is presumptuous and imagines himself to be wise, righteous and holy, it is necessary that he be humbled by the law, that thus that beast—his supposed righteousness—without whose killing man cannot live, be put to death." In all his works Luther speaks again and again of the *malleus Dei*, the hammer of God, which breaks the trust that man puts in his own knowledge and in the virtue founded on the truths furnished by this knowledge.

A page further he says again, with still more power and passion: "Therefore God must have a strong hammer to break the rocks, and a fire blazing to the middle of the heavens to overthrow the mountains, that is, to subdue that stubborn and impenitent beast—presumption—in order that man, reduced to nothing through this contrition, should despair of his power, his righteousness and his works," which means, translating Luther into the language of Spinoza, *non intelligere, sed lugere et detestari* [not to understand, but to lament and to curse]. To put it differently, having discovered by his own experience to what abyss the "divine light" of which the wise men have spoken so much led him, the man who has lost his freedom and has been transformed from a *res cogitans* into an *asinus turpissimus* begins to make absurd, mad attempts to struggle against the force that has bewitched him. *Acquiescentia in se ipso* [contentment with oneself] and the *beatitudines* [blessings] that are strictly bound to this *acquiescentia*, as well as *virtus*, the virtue that finds its supreme reward in itself, all the "consolations" given by the fruits of the tree of knowledge, to use the biblical image, or by reason which draws everything from itself, to speak as Hegel did— all these things suddenly allow their true nature to appear, and we discover that they bring us not eternal salvation but eternal death. And our first answer is the *lugere et detestari* which is forbidden by the philosophers but which testifies to the persistence in man of certain vestiges of life. Man himself then calls upon the terrible *malleus Dei* [God's hammer] and joyously welcomes the sound of trumpets, thunder and lightning. For only the thunderbolt from heaven that breaks the rocks can break "that obstinate and impenitent beast, presumption" which has so seized hold of man that he is prepared to accept everything that fate sends him *aequo animo* (calmly/with equanimity) and has even learned to find in this total acceptance his *summum bonum. . . .*

Where Socrates, in his first and second incarnation, saw man's salvation, Luther saw his destruction. *Intelligere* and *tertium genus cognitionis* deliver man over into the hands of his worst enemy. He "who is led by reason alone" cannot recover his lost freedom; it remains for him only to learn and teach others to find the "best" in the inevitable. One must consider himself happy even in the bull of Phalaris. One must allow himself to die quietly of hunger between two bales of hay in the conviction that the world is ruled by a law from which no one can escape. Reason avidly seeks universal and necessary judgments. Men must see in reason their "better part" and, in submitting to it, find their good in these very universal and necessary truths. Placed at equal distance between the idea of God and immortality on the one hand, and the idea of Fate, on the other—both of which attract him—man will not turn to God: he cannot decide freely; he knows that decision does not depend on him and he will go where Necessity propels him, being accustomed *aequo animo ferre et expectare utramque faciem* (to await and endure calmly both faces) of omnipotent fate. All the *docet* (teaching) of philosophy, all of philosophy itself in which the search for truth has been replaced by edification, lead us inevitably to this.

Luther knew this, quite like Socrates and Spinoza. He also spoke *de servo arbitrio* (of the unfree will). But his *docet* appears to be something quite different. More exactly, his *de servo arbitrio* led him to a hatred of *docet* of every kind and, consequently, of the reason that is the source of all *docet*. Leaving to philosophy the glorification "of obedience and piety," he concentrated all his thoughts on the struggle against the idea of Necessity. The *malleus Dei* in Luther strikes not man but that *bellua* (monster) or *bestia obstinax* (obstinate beast) which makes man believe that, in perfecting himself morally, he can attain to the virtue which requires no reward, for it is already happiness itself or, as Luther said, "man presumptuously claims to be holy and righteous." The virtue and happiness of the man who by his own powers can turn neither to God nor to immortality, for reason has enchained his will and obliged him to go where Necessity pushes him, appeared to Luther as the fall of man, as original sin. The idea of law and order, on which all our thought is based, is also for him the worst of errors. The source of truth is found where human reason least expects it; and it is there also that one can attain the good which we have exchanged for philosophical happiness.

Luther calls this source "faith." Let us then for the present give it the same name, if only to indicate that there can be another source of truth than that of which Socrates spoke and that the truth in no way resembles the universal and necessary judgments of Aristotle, Spinoza and Kant, that the truth has nothing in common with Necessity. "Nothing is more inimical to faith than law and reason, and these two cannot be overcome without great effort and labor, yet they must be overcome if you wish to be saved. When, therefore, conscience frightens you with the law . . . conduct yourself as if you had never heard anything of the law but rather as if you are ascending into darkness, where neither law nor reason give light but only the riddle of faith . . . Thus the gospel leads us beyond and above the light of law and of reason into the darkness of faith, where light and reason have nothing to do. Moses on the mountain, where he speaks with God face to face, has, makes and employs no law; only when he comes down from the mountain is he a law-giver and does he rule the people through law. So let the conscience be free from the law, but let the body obey it."

What Socrates and Spinoza glorified as "our better part" and "the divine light" appear to Luther to be *bellua qua non occisa homo non potest vivere* (the monster without whose killing man cannot live). When Moses on the mountain saw truth face to face, the chains that bound his consciousness immediately fell away and he obtained the most precious of gifts—freedom. But when he descended from the mountain and mingled with men, he found himself again under the domination of the law; as it did to Socrates and Spinoza, eternal, immutable law appeared to him as belonging to the very nature of being, as constituting the universal and necessary truths of which it is always the question here. Such a "metamorphosis" is incomprehensible to "reason." Reason is convinced that law is always law, for him who keeps to the mountain-top as well as for him who has descended into the valley. Its power cannot undergo any diminution. As for Luther, he throws himself into the darkness and abyss of faith in order to find there the power to struggle against the monster that the wise adore. Or, to put it better: he attains that extreme tension of the soul wherein it ceases to calculate in advance, to measure, to weigh, to adapt itself. *Malleus Dei*, the trumpets, the thunder, the lightnings of which Spinoza spoke with so much scorn, awakened in Luther's soul all the *ridere, lugere et detestari* [to laugh, lament and curse] that reason had lulled to sleep. Luther forgets the *obedientiam et pietatem* [obedience and piety] under the domination of which he had long lived—had he not been a monk, had he not sworn obedience to the good and pronounced vows as solemn as those with which Spinoza's works are filled?—but now he thinks of only one thing; he must kill this abominable "monster without whose killing man cannot live."

Which road leads to the truth? Is it the road of reason, of obedience and piety that brings us into the kingdom of Necessity, or is it the road of "faith" which declares an implacable war against Necessity? Behind Socrates' autonomous ethics and reason we have discovered the bull of Phalaris; Spinoza's *sub specie aeternitatis* has changed man under our eyes from *res cogitans* [a thinking thing] into *asinus turpissimus* [a most infamous ass]. May it be that Luther's thunderbolts and audacity, born of tears and despair, will bring us something else, and that out of the "darkness of faith" the freedom that man lost in entrusting himself to knowledge may be won again?

IX

It is usually held that German idealist philosophy sprang entirely from Luther. How this opinion arose is difficult to say. Perhaps the historians of philosophy have allowed themselves to be led astray by a very simple train of reasoning: all the representatives of German idealism—Kant, Fichte, Schelling, Hegel—were Lutherans, *ergo* German idealism sprang from Luther. But it suffices to recall what Hegel said about original sin, or Kant's "I ought, therefore I can," or Schelling's famous essay "On the Essence of Human Freedom" (even if it be only the quotation from it cited above), or Fichte's ethical idealism to realize that Luther remained entirely outside German philosophical thought. "I ought, therefore I can," says Kant, while Luther's entire doctrine rests on the opposite assertion: "I ought, I wish even, yet I can not." The law is not given man to guide him but only to make him aware of his weakness and impotence; "the law accuses, terrifies and condemns." After the fall, man lost both his freedom of will and his freedom of thought; he cannot go where he wishes to go and he takes appearances and illusions for truths. In Luther's lifetime his doctrine seemed unacceptable and absurd both to the learned Erasmus and to the Catholic theologians nurtured on the Bible. According to Luther, God is beyond good and evil, beyond truth and falsehood. How could philosophy or even theology accept this—especially philosophy? At bottom Kant, Fichte and Schelling thought as did Hegel: the serpent did not deceive Adam, Socrates repeated Adam's act, and the fruits of the tree of knowledge have become the principle of philosophy for all time.

The only exception to this was Nietzsche. He alone saw in Socrates a fallen man. Socrates "appeared to be a healer, a deliverer. Is it still necessary to show the error in his belief in "reason" at all costs? It is self-deception on the part of philosophers and moralists to think that they are leaving *décadence* by making war against it. To escape it is beyond their power; what they choose as a remedy, as a means of deliverance, is only another expression of *décadence*. They merely *change* its expression; they do not destroy it . . . To be *forced* to fight against the instincts—this is the formula of *décadence; as long as* life *is on the ascendant*, happiness and instinct are identical." And again: "The morality of the Greek philosophers since Plato is pathologically conditioned, just as is their lofty estimate of dialectic. Reason = virtue = happiness only means: We must imitate Socrates and establish forever against the dark instincts a *daylight*—the daylight of reason. We must be intelligent, clear, lucid at all costs; every surrender to the instincts or to the unconscious leads downward."

In general Nietzsche treats Luther very cavalierly; many a time he calls him a coarse and brutal peasant. But in the papers found after his death we read: "Luther's language and the Bible's poetic form as the foundation of the new German poesy—this is my discovery." And, indeed, Nietzsche is the first of the German philosophers who turned to Luther and the Bible. The subtitle of the work from which I have quoted his remarks on Socrates is already sufficiently revelatory in this respect: "How one philosophizes with the hammer." We recall the role that the "hammer of God" plays in Luther and in the prophets. Furthermore, in his reflections on Socrates, Nietzsche basically only repeats what Luther had said about the fallen man. The fallen man is entirely in the power of an alien force and can do nothing more to save himself.

Such precisely is Nietzsche's Socrates; the more he struggles, the more desperately he strains his forces, the more surely he marches to his ruin. He has lost his freedom and does not choose, though he is persuaded to the contrary; he is pushed and dragged and does not even feel that he is in chains. Socrates went to reason, to the good, as the first man stretched out his hand to the fruit of the tree of knowledge; but where they expected to attain resurrection and life they found only corruption and death. This is the meaning of Luther's terrible words: "Man must distrust his own works and, like a cripple with slack arms and legs, implore grace as the effector of works." This is also the meaning of his doctrine of "the law" and of his *de servo arbitrio* [on the bondage of the will].

Luther's as well as Nietzsche's "experience" correspond so little to what men ordinarily find in experience that they appear to them fantastic; they have been brought, it seems, from another world, completely foreign to our own. Luther and Nietzsche were not the only ones, however, to have such experiences. In Kierkegaard's *Thorn in the Flesh* we find a similar testimony: "You wish to run faster than ever, but you feel that you cannot even lift your feet from the ground; you are prepared to sacrifice everything in the world to buy even only an instant and you learn that it is not for sale for 'it does not lie in any one's will or power but only in God's mercy.'" All this is so much outside the field of our vision that it seems to us to have passed beyond the limits of all possible and actual human interests. If, after the fall, our will is so weakened that we can do nothing for our own salvation—Nietzsche does not hide the fact that he, like Socrates, is a fallen man—and we are forced to go, arms dangling, to our ruin without even trying to fight, what interests can still be in question? All interests have vanished; it remains for us only to look straight before us, with heart frozen. It remains for us only to renounce forever *ridere, lugere et detestari* to learn to find "the highest good" in *intelligere*.

Luther could still "implore grace as the effector of works." But for Nietzsche, judging by what he says in his books, prayers as well as He to whom Luther addressed his prayers had ceased to exist. How pray when there is no one to hear us? How beseech God when "knowledge" brings us the "universal and necessary truth" that God does not exist or, as Nietzsche said, that men have killed God?

But, strangely enough, in Nietzsche as in Luther, the moment of the deepest fall was followed by an entirely new revelation. When Nietzsche felt that Socrates' "wisdom" was only the expression of his "fall" and that man, like a bird bewitched by a serpent, does not go where he wishes but is dragged against his will by an incomprehensible force into the abyss of physical and spiritual annihilation, there suddenly rose before him the idea of the Eternal Return, an idea completely alien to his thought as well as our own. It was as if he had suddenly been transported, like Moses, to that peak where "he speaks with God face to face." He discovered that there—face to face with the primordial mystery, "law and reason have nothing to do," and he began to speak of the will to power, of the morality of masters, and of all that he had found "beyond good and evil."

I repeat that Nietzsche felt himself, quite like Socrates, a fallen man. The laws of reason and morality were deeply embedded in him, they had somehow become part of his spiritual being; to tear them out without killing his soul seemed to him as impossible as to extract the skeleton of a man without first killing the man. In his view, just as in ours, these laws express our deepest nature; beyond good and evil, beyond the truth, there is only the void, nothingness, where everything disappears. Nevertheless, it is there that one can, one must, seek omnipotence, the power that will save man from death! Luther's *sola fide* led him to Him of whom he said, "for God is the Almighty who creates everything out of nothing." But does not then Nietzsche's "Will to Power" express under another form Luther's *sola fide*? Luther relied on the authority of the Bible, on the prophets and apostles, while Nietzsche's leap to the heights of Sinai began at the moment when the Bible had lost all authority in his eyes. On the contrary, everything that still retained any authority for him warned him imperiously that the "Will to Power" was the worst of follies and that there was no salvation, no refuge for a thinking man other than the *beatitudines* brought by Socrates and Spinoza.

These lines are taken from *Dawn of Day*, a book which belongs—as is commonly held—to Nietzsche's "positivist" period. And yet we find here, expressed with perhaps even greater force, what Luther had already said about the law. Luther could, despite everything, still rely on the authority of the Bible. He admits openly: "I would not have dared so to call the law but would have considered it to be the greatest blasphemy against God, if Paul had not done it before." Nietzsche, however, could not appeal to anyone; he was abandoned to himself and his "madness." When the modern man, educated by Hegel, who has inoculated him with the wisdom of the Biblical serpent, hears or reads Luther's discourses, he calms himself with the thought that these are only the visions of a medieval monk who has rid himself of his cowl but not of his prejudices and his foolish fears. Nietzsche, however, was never a monk and was familiar with all the conquests of science. Furthermore, we must not forget that everything Luther said about "the law" was directed especially against the monks, who felt the hair rise on their heads when they read his writings. Their life was in fact founded on the conviction that "to him who does what is in his power God does not deny grace." (Luther even says, "God unfailingly gives grace.") Luther's thought, however, was born out of his profound conviction that the more the fallen man struggles to save himself, the more surely (like Socrates in Nietzsche) does he go to his ruin, and that only he who *remissis manibus et pedibus* (with slack arms and legs) surrenders himself to the will of God, who is beyond all the laws dictated by morality and reason, can participate in the supreme truth. There can be no doubt about it: from the human point of view, Luther's doctrine, in its harshness and cruelty, surpasses anything that the most pitiless human mind could ever imagine. The God of the Bible, if He is in fact such as Luther represents Him, deserves not our love but our eternal hatred (as, by the way, Luther himself several times says).

There is another objection that, from our modern point of view, is still more decisive. The monks declared that "to him who does what is in his power God does not deny grace"; Luther proclaimed that "man must distrust his own works and implore grace as the effector of works." But both the monks and Luther spoke of what does not exist. *There is in the universe neither God nor grace, and real being develops entirely on a level that Luther's ideas do not even touch.* Man's task consists, then, in recognizing the conditions of his existence and in adapting himself to them in such a way that his wants and needs are satisfied to the highest possible degree. There are, of course, many terrible and frightening things in life, but wisdom teaches us not to demand the impossible. Socrates was right when he concealed the bull of Phalaris by affirming that no evil could befall a good man. Spinoza was also right when he erected over his *asinus turpissimus* the beautiful altar of ethics with the inscription, "Happiness is virtue itself." But, to tell all, Aristotle and Hegel were more truthful and more perceptive than all the others: "the highest good" presupposes a certain minimum of temporal goods, and he alone can attain the happiness of contemplation who possesses the skill and the resolution necessary to keep himself far away from those realms of being where bulls of Phalaris and *asini turpissimi* haunt man's imagination.

Now both Luther and Nietzsche knew all this. Yet it is precisely against this presumptuousness, against this "stubborn and obdurate beast who imagines himself to be wise, righteous and holy" that their thunderbolts were directed. It is in his faith in his own "knowledge" and his own "morality" that they saw the "fall" of man. "The freedom of thought of our scientists," says Nietzsche, "is in my eyes only a jest—they lack in these things my suffering, my passion." Now this is a variation on Luther's theme—"the monster without whose killing man cannot live." It is an objection, Nietzsche's objection, against what we commonly call free and objective inquiry, against what Spinoza called true philosophy and what Socrates proclaimed as universal and necessary truth. But can suffering, even if it be measureless, or passion, even if it be the most ardent and powerful, be set in opposition to universal and necessary truth? And where shall we go to seek an answer to this question? In experience? But we have already seen that experience gives us neither true philosophy nor universal and necessary truths. Experience brings only "conviction" or "belief." But conviction inspires in Nietzsche no confidence. "In every philosophy," he writes, "there comes a moment when the conviction of the philosopher appears on the scene or, to use the language of an ancient mystery: *adventavit asinus pulcher et fortissimus.*" Again the *asinus*, and apparently the same one that we have met in Spinoza and the one from which Socrates' "irony" once sprang. But its power is so great that the most daring minds submit to it. We remember Kant's sentence, "Reason aspires avidly to universal and necessary truths"; we remember also Aristotle's reflections on the same theme. Who, then, inspired men with this "conviction" thanks to which experience is transformed into "knowledge"? And how is it that this conviction has come to rule despotically over our world? Whatever the answer to these questions may be, one thing remains indubitable: it is impossible to fight against this conviction by means of arguments and objections. It is outside of, and precedes, all objections; it takes the place of arguments. To it can be opposed only "passion," hatred, the raging desire to be freed from it at all costs. Hence Luther's *malleus Dei,* hence Nietzsche's *Wie man mit dem Hammer philosophiert* (How one philosophizes with the hammer). It is impossible otherwise to break the enchantment which has—God knows when and how taken possession of men. . . .

X

Just as did Nietzsche, Luther discovered with horror that where Socrates and Spinoza had found the supreme and only possible consolation there opened up the abyss of eternal death. Luther writes: *Deus est . . . creator omnipotens ex nihilo faciens omnia . . .* "God is . . . the almighty creator who makes everything out of nothing. . . . But that most noxious pest, the illusion of righteousness—which does not wish to be sinful, impure, miserable and damned but rather righteous and holy—does not allow him to come to this, his natural and proper work. Therefore God must use this hammer, namely, the law, in order that he may break, crush, grind down and completely destroy this monster with its self-confidence, its wisdom, its righteousness, its power, etc. . . ." As if he were replying to Luther across the centuries, Nietzsche cries with an almost demented passion: "In man creature and creator are united: in man there is matter, shred, excess, clay, mire, folly, chaos; but there is also the creator, the sculptor, the hardness of the hammer, the divinity of the spectator, and the seventh day:—do you understand this contrast? And that your sympathy for the "creature in man" applies to that which has to be fashioned, broken, forged, stretched, roasted, annealed, refined—to that which must necessarily suffer and is meant to suffer?"[18]

These lines are basically only a repetition of Luther's words; the expressions, the tone, even the thought are identical. But Luther had heard them from the prophets. All that the prophets say is animated by a single desire, permeated by a single thought: *Deus est creator omnipotens* [God is the allpowerful creator] (in Nietzsche—"Will to Power"). And it is to Him, the *creator omnipotens*, that both Luther and Nietzsche rush headlong, smashing without regret all obstacles in their way. Luther says: *frangere, contundere, prorsus ad nihil redigere* (to break, to crush, completely to destroy); Nietzsche in no way yields to him in this respect—he also tears, breaks, burns, completely destroys precisely that to which men hold fast above all, that which they esteem and love more than all, that which they worship. On the altars erected by Socrates and Spinoza, Luther and Nietzsche see that *bellua nocentissima qua non occisa homo non potest vivere* (most noxious monster without whose killing man cannot live).

But how did it happen that Luther and Nietzsche saw a monster where the wisest of men, a righteous and saintly man, saw and worshipped a divinity? How could Socrates' *summum bonum*, his "knowledge," which was for him the source of his saintliness, be changed in Luther's eyes into the "illusion of righteousness," into sin, corruption, death? We must not deceive ourselves: the thunderbolts of Luther and Nietzsche are directed against the god of Socrates and of Spinoza. Luther constantly curses both Socrates' good and his truth, while Spinoza was convinced, let us remember, that he who has offended reason would no longer have the right to pray and that all altars would be forbidden to him.

It will be said that the *Deus omnipotens ex nihilo faciens omnia* [the allpowerful God makes all things out of nothing] still existed for Luther, while Nietzsche had denied God. That is so—and it is here that we touch upon the most difficult of problems.

I have said that Luther's *Creator omnipotens* [allpowerful creator] was transformed by Nietzsche into the "Will to Power," which he set in opposition to the Socratic "good." Socrates' ethics was the doctrine of a fallen man concerning the ways to salvation; but a fallen man—Scripture tells us and Nietzsche also suggests to us—is a man condemned to a punishment whose horror surpasses the cruelest imagination: from *res cogitans* (a thinking thing) he is transformed into *asinus turpissimus* (a most infamous ass) and dies of hunger between two bales of hay, since his will is paralyzed and he is incapable of moving on his own initiative any of his limbs or making the slightest motion. Perhaps he remembers at times that there exists or existed somewhere a *Macht* [power] capable of breaking the spell. But he cannot turn toward it; he "aspires eagerly" to knowledge, to universal and necessary truths. The "knowledge" on which he counts or, rather, on which he is forced to count, is, however, of no help to him; not only does it not dissipate the spell, it causes it.

Socrates was a fallen man, Spinoza was a fallen man—but Nietzsche also, like all of us, is descended from Adam. When, in Engadine, at an elevation of six thousand feet, he had that sudden illumination that he later called the idea of the "Eternal Return," he submitted his "revelation," as each of us would have done in his place, to the judgment of reason. He wished to prove it, establish its truth, transform it into knowledge. And it was to the same tribunal that he submitted his "transvaluation of all values," his "Will to Power," his "beyond good and evil" and even his "morality of masters." And, of course, after reason had pronounced its judgment and the verification had been completed, Nietzsche returned with empty hands; only the Socratic-Spinozist "virtue" was left to him. For even Moses himself could speak face to face with God only as long as he held to the heights of Sinai; as soon as he descended into the valley the truth that had been revealed to him was transformed into law. "To see the creator and the master of the universe is difficult, but to show him to others is impossible," says Plato. It is doubtless because of this that Nietzsche has told us almost nothing of the idea of the "Eternal Return" which, by his own confession, he felt himself called to reveal to the world; and what he does tell of it shows only that it was not given to him to bring such a thing to men. What he offered them is something completely far as can judge, in his *Beyond Good and Evil*, did he succeed in expressing this idea in an adequate way: "'This I have done,' says my memory. 'This I cannot have done,' says my pride, and remains inexorable. Finally it is my memory that yields."[19]

It is in these words, almost devoid—by human reckoning—of all meaning, that we must seek the explanation of the inner struggles that nourished Nietzsche's thought. The memory, that is to say, the exact representation of reality in thought, says to man: "You have done this, it was so."—"No, I could not have done this, it was not so" replies that which Nietzsche calls, not with complete precision, his "pride." (In *Thus Spake Zarathustra*, after the conversation with the dwarf about the Eternal Return, Nietzsche expresses himself better when, characterizing "this something" in himself that refuses to accept the real, he says: "*Mein Grauen, mein Ekel, mein Erbarmen, all mein Gutes und Schlimmes schrie mit einem Schrei aus mir.*" [My horror, my hatred, my loathing, my pity, all my good and my bad cried with one voice out of me.] And the memory yields: that which was becomes that which has never been.

In *Thus Spake Zarathustra*, in the chapter entitled "Of the Redemption," Nietzsche returns to this theme: "to redeem the past and to transform every 'it was' to 'thus would I have it'" And he returns to it again in the third part of the chapter "Of Old and New Tablets." All that has accumulated in the soul of man during the course of long years of suffering and trial and that, by the decree of our reason which has seized the right of final decision, cannot even raise its voice when it is a question of truth and error, is suddenly permitted to proclaim its rights. And it even realizes them: that which has been, says Nietzsche, becomes that which has not been. It is probably impossible to "explain" how these rights are realized, for they are realized precisely because and insofar as man learns or, rather, decides to do without all explanations, to disregard them, to despise them. For this there is also required that mysterious and sudden illumination through which there arose in Nietzsche the idea of the Eternal Return. Man refuses obedience to reason which, until now, has dictated its laws to nature itself. What Descartes called "eternal truths" and Leibniz *vérités de raison* and what, according to Socrates and Spinoza, is revealed to the "eyes of the mind" loses all power over man. "When, however, we admit that it is impossible that something should be made out of nothing, then the proposition 'out of nothing is nothing made' . . . is considered an eternal truth . . . Of the same kind are the following propositions: it is impossible that the same thing should simultaneously be and not be; that which has happened cannot become something which has not happened; he who thinks must, while he thinks, exist . . . and innumerable others."[20]

So Descartes speaks. One cannot argue with these innumerable eternal truths. Disgust, horror, hatred, scorn—no matter how powerful they may be—cannot overthrow them. These truths are eternal; they are before being, before man, before God. But when Nietzsche was transported six thousand feet high and higher still above all human thoughts, he felt suddenly that the eternal truths had lost their power and no longer dictated their laws either to the world or to him. I repeat: he did not find the words he needed to designate what had appeared to him and began to speak of the Eternal Return. But here was something infinitely more important than the Eternal Return. He discovered that, despite the eternal law *quod factum est, infectum nequit esse* (what has happened cannot become something that has not happened), not memory, which exactly reproduces the past, but a certain will ("pride," I say again, is not the proper word here) has by its own authority rendered the past non-existent; and he discovered that it was this will that brought him the truth. He who so violently attacked the Bible dares to speak of "redemption." Redemption from the past, from the enslavement of the law and laws thanks to which alone the past remains unshakable. These laws, which reason draws out of itself, are precisely that bellua (monster), that *bestia, qua non occisa homo non potest vivere* (beast without whose killing man cannot live).

Behind Nietzsche's Eternal Return is hidden, it seems, a force of infinite power that is also prepared to crush the horrible monster who rules over human life and over all being: Luther's *Creator omnipotens ex nihilo faciens Omnia* [the allpowerful creator makes all things out of nothing]. The omnipotent Creator is not only beyond good and evil but also beyond truth and falsehood. Before His face (*faces in faciem*) both evil and falsehood cease to exist and are changed into nothingness, not only in the present but also in the past. They no longer are and never have been, despite all the testimonies of the human memory. In opposition to Hegel who, drawing up the balance of all that he had learned from his predecessors ("Socrates produced the principle of philosophy for all future times"), hoped to find God such as He was before the creation of the world and the finite spirit in logic, that is, in the system of eternal and unchangeable truths—Nietzsche longed only to escape from the domination of these truths. Explaining his idea of the Eternal Return, he writes: "A great struggle awaits us. For it is required a new weapon, the hammer: to bring on a terrible decision."[21] And again: "The philosophy presently on the throne does not cease remembering that all things are perishable in order not to consider them too important and to live peacefully in their midst. But for me, on the contrary, everything seems too important to be so transitory; I seek eternity for everything."

It is not to be doubted that Nietzsche clung to the idea of the Eternal Return because—in opposition not to Marcus Aurelius but to Marcus Aurelius' master, the master of all those who philosophize, Socrates—he was seeking to obtain eternity for the things which, according to our conception of truth, are condemned to annihilation. But does this mean that he wished eternity for "everything"? He himself has just told us that his "pride" condemned to death certain things to which eternity was guaranteed without any intervention on his part. Nietzsche even obtains in this way results that are quasi-miraculous: that which was, the past which enjoys the omnipotent protection of the truth of reason—*quod factum est, infectum esse nequit* [what is done cannot be undone]—is transformed by his will into that which has never been. Why, then, does he suddenly demand eternity for "everything"? Does he wish to satisfy reason, which aspires eagerly to universal and necessary truth? But this would mean that when memory says to a man, "you have done this," no discussion, no protest, is any longer possible, for the memory reproduces exactly the past to which eternal existence in truth is guaranteed. To put it differently, he must renounce the "Will to Power" and adopt the attitude of the common man who accepts everything that fate brings him, or even the attitude of the sage who not only accepts everything but sees in this disposition *aequo animo utramque faciem fortunae ferre* (to bear both faces of fortune calmly) a virtue and considers this virtue his supreme good. It is impossible to escape the stone that calls itself "it was," and "redemption" becomes a word devoid of meaning.

Nietzsche allowed himself to be ensnared by Socrates' logic, the logic of the fallen man. The "stubborn and impenitent monster" was not killed, it only seemed to be dead. Nietzsche's hammer did not break the pretensions of reason, which entrenched itself behind universal and necessary judgments. We must return to Luther whose hammer struck more powerfully and more accurately than Nietzsche's. Let us forget that Luther was a theologian. Let us forget that he repeated the prophets and the apostles. We are not bound by any authority. Authority, indeed, is only a residue of the pretensions of reason, which aspires eagerly to universal and necessary judgments. But where truth is, there is not, there cannot be, any constraint. There is freedom. Let us listen to Luther. Let us listen to the prophets and the apostles such as they were in the sight of their contemporaries—simple, despised, even persecuted men. Now, when these men speak of redemption, it does not even occur to them that anyone or anything could place them before the dilemma: either accept everything that has been, or make everything that has been not to have been. Among the things that have been there are some that one can save and others that one can annihilate. God came down on earth, He became man, He suffered, but not in order to realize one of those universal and necessary truths that reason draws out of itself. He came to save men.

Luther writes: "God sent His only begotten son into the world and laid upon him all the sins of all men, saying: Be thou Peter, that denier; Paul, that persecutor, blasphemer and doer of violence; David, that adulterer; that sinner who ate the apple in paradise; that thief on the cross—in sum, be thou the person who committed the sins of all men." The form is different, in keeping with Luther's epoch and environment, but the profound thought of these lines is identical with that which appeared to Nietzsche under the aspect of the idea of the Eternal Return: it is necessary to deliver oneself from the past, to transform that which once was into that which has never been. Peter, Paul, King David, the thief on the cross, Adam who tasted the apple—these are all "fallen men," like Socrates, Wagner and Nietzsche. They cannot save themselves by their own powers. The more they struggle, the more they sink. But Luther was not enchained by the eternal truths of reason. He sees in them, on the contrary, "the monster without whose killing man cannot live." If these truths are destined to triumph, there is no salvation for men. To put it differently, in philosophic language, in absolutizing truth we relativize being.

Luther decides to hand truth over to the power "of the omnipotent Creator, who makes everything out of nothing." If truth is in the hands of the Creator, the Creator can abrogate it, entirely or in part. He can bring it about that Peter's denial, Paul's persecutions and blasphemies, David's adultery never existed but that certain other things among those that have been are preserved forever. God, indeed, is not rational truth, which, itself deprived of will, can yet paralyze the human will. And God does not fear anything, for everything is in His power. He is not even afraid of transferring to His son all the sins of the world, or, more exactly, to make of him the greatest of sinners. "All the prophets," writes Luther, "saw this in the spirit: that Christ would be the greatest robber, thief, defiler of the temple, murderer, adulterer, etc., such that no greater will ever be in the world."

The Christ, the consubstantial son of the Father, that is to say, God Himself, is, then, the greatest sinner who ever lived on earth! But this means that God is the source and creator of evil; one cannot suspect Luther of Docetism. The prophets "saw" and proclaimed this just as they saw and declared that God had hardened, that is, made wicked, Pharaoh's heart. Such visions and proclamations, even though they come from the prophets, appear to human reason, bound by universal and necessary truths, blasphemous and sacrilegious; they outrage God, reason tells us, and they deserve the worst tortures in the hells both of this world and the other. God responsible for evil? God the Creator of evil? *Absit*—this be far from us—cried the Fathers of the Church as well as the simple monks. Evil exists on earth, yet it is not God who is its author but man; otherwise it is impossible to justify and save God's goodness. And indeed, if the eternal truths are before God and above God, if *quod factum est, infectum esse nequit* [what is done cannot be undone], then we have no choice: we must set against God, the creator of good, man, the creator of evil. Man becomes *creator omnipotens, ex nihilo omnia faciens* [allpowerful creator who makes all things out of nothing]. And then redemption, deliverance from the past, from the nightmare of death and the horrors of death, is impossible. There remains only one way out: to recognize that the universal and necessary truths and that reason which brings us these truths constitute precisely that *bellua, qua non occisa homo non potest vivere* [the monster without whose killing man cannot live].

Luther felt that man would recover freedom only when reason and the knowledge that reason gives us will have lost their power. And Nietzsche, as we have seen, felt this also. He refused to accept the testimony of fact and tried to break the self-evidences with the hammer of his will. But when Zarathustra came down from his heights to men, he was obliged to come to terms with his terrible enemy. We read in *Ecce homo*, Nietzsche's last work, "My formula for the greatness of man is *amor fati* [love of what is fated]—to change nothing, neither before nor after, throughout all eternity. Not only to bear Necessity, and still less to hide it—all idealism is a lie in the face of Necessity—but to love it."[22] But such was precisely the teaching of the decadent, the fallen man, Socrates! Such were the fruits of the tree of knowledge which, according to Hegel, were to be the principle of philosophy for all time. It was this also that Spinoza, who assimilated Socrates' wisdom and saw happiness in virtue, proclaimed.

Instead of engaging in supreme combat with Necessity, Nietzsche, *velut paralyticus, manibus et pedibus omissis* (like a cripple, with slack arms and legs), abandons himself to his adversary and hands over his soul to it; he promises not only to obey and venerate but to love it. And he does not make this promise only in his own name; all must submit to Necessity, venerate and love it, or else they will be excommunicated. Excommunicated by whom? *Amor fati*, says Nietzsche, is the formula for greatness, and he who refuses to accept everything that *fatum* [fate] imposes upon him will be deprived of the praise, the encouragement, the approbation that the idea of "greatness" contains in itself. The old "you will be like God" arose anew, one knows not whence, and cast a spell upon Nietzsche who, before our very eyes, had made such heroic efforts to pass beyond good and evil, that is, beyond all praises, encouragements and approbations.

How could this happen? Must we believe in the intervention of the biblical serpent who had once seduced Adam? Indeed, translated into the language of Luther, *amor fati* means that Nietzsche sees "the monster without whose killing man cannot live" not in the chains which bind the human will but in the human will itself, in its drive to power. Accordingly, he strains all of his forces not to destroy or at least weaken his enemy but to kill in himself every desire for battle, to learn to see his essential task in uncomplaining, joyous even, and loving submission to all that comes to him from outside without his knowing whence or how. And this is the same Nietzsche who spoke so much of the morality of masters and railed so scornfully against the morality of slaves, who refused to stoop or bow down before any authority whatsoever! But when he looked Necessity in the face, his powers betrayed him and he built for it an altar of which the most exacting of the inhabitants of Olympus could have been jealous.

Thus was everything that Luther had said in *De servo arbitrio* [On the Bondage of the Will] and in *De votis monachorum* [On Monastic Vows], and what Nietzsche himself had glimpsed in Socrates' fate but never succeeded in discovering in his own, confirmed: the fallen man cannot do anything for his own salvation, his choice is no longer free, everything that he undertakes brings him closer to death, and the more he "does" the weaker he becomes and the deeper his fall. And then there is still this point that is no less important: the fallen man—and we know that Nietzsche realized this when he thought about Socrates—puts all his trust in knowledge, while it is precisely knowledge that paralyses his will and leads him inexorably to his downfall.

This Necessity of which Nietzsche tells us—whence, indeed, does it come? Who or what is it that has brought it to us? If one had put this question to Nietzsche he would probably have replied "experience." But we have already seen that one cannot discover Necessity in experience. Knowledge draws the idea of Necessity from a source quite other than experience. Moreover, without the idea of Necessity knowledge would immediately collapse. But where Necessity is, there is not, there cannot be, freedom; consequently where knowledge is, there is no freedom. It seems that Nietzsche was very near throwing down the gauntlet before knowledge and going to seek the truth elsewhere. And not only because Socrates' example had put him on guard against the consequences of an exaggerated trust in knowledge. Nietzsche knew certain experiences which show that he aspired with all his being to rid himself of knowledge and to penetrate into those realms of being where the enchantment of knowledge would no longer weigh upon man, would no longer enchain him. He tells us of this in the same *Ecce homo.* I hope that the reader will excuse this rather long quotation, considering the importance of the question for us: "Can anyone at the end of this Nineteenth Century possibly have any distinct notion of what poets of a more vigorous period mean by inspiration? If not, I should like to describe it. Provided one has the slightest remnant of superstition left, one can hardly reject completely the idea that one is the mere incarnation, or mouthpiece, or medium of some almighty power. The notion of revelation describes the condition quite simply; by which I mean that something profoundly convulsive and disturbing suddenly becomes visible and audible with indescribable definiteness and exactness. One hears—one does not seek; one takes—one does not ask who gives; a thought flashes out like lightning, inevitably without hesitation—I have never had any choice about it . . . Everything occurs quite without volition, as if in an eruption of freedom, independence, power and divinity. . . ."

How little the necessity of which Nietzsche here tells us resembles the Necessity that had led the ancients to the conception of fate indifferent to everything! And the question rises for us: when was Nietzsche in the power of "prejudices"—when he glorified *amor fati* in the conviction that fate is invincible, or when he declared that everything "occurs quite without volition" but nevertheless "as if in an eruption of freedom, independence, power and divinity?"

He ends thus: "This is my experience of inspiration. I have no doubt that I should have to go back millennia to find someone who would have the right to tell me: 'such is also my experience.'" I think these words provide a reply to the question we have just raised: at moments the "prejudices" of men who lived thousands of years earlier were much closer to Nietzsche than the "truths" of his contemporaries. Nevertheless, in the end he brought his illuminations to the tribunal not of those "prejudices" on which the ancient freedom that had no fear of anything was nourished, but to that of knowledge, which has begotten the indifference, passivity and dreary submissiveness of modern thought. The idea of the Eternal Return wished to be "based" on something, and it was always to this very fate that it turned to obtain its right to existence. For it cannot maintain itself by its own will, it has no will; and it can no longer maintain itself by the will of any living being, the living being has no power. Everything depends on fate: will it or will it not agree to concede to this idea some place in the structure of being? For the decisions of fate are unchangeable and without appeal, whether it be the existence of the individual or all of humanity or even of the universe that is in question, and the virtue of the simple mortal as well as of the wise man consists not only in accepting the decisions of fate but in revering them, even loving them.

It is unnecessary to describe here in detail how Nietzsche tried to obtain from fate the right to existence for his idea of the Eternal Return. Nietzsche says that fate granted his prayers, but it is hardly probable that he himself seriously believed that one could "demonstrate" the idea of the Eternal Return and give it a solid foundation and that the considerations on which he established it were capable of convincing anyone whomsoever. And yet he did not fail to reason honestly and scrupulously on the subject, not like his distant ancestors with whom he carried on a dialogue in *Thus Spake Zarathustra*, but as a learned man, that is, one who sets out from the idea of submission to Necessity and not from the idea of power, must reason. From the point of view of "demonstration," the idea of the Eternal Return, even under the modest form which Nietzsche gave it in order to bring it before the supreme judge, is greatly inferior to the majority of the modern ideas which Nietzsche had so mordantly mocked. The idea of the Eternal Return or, more exactly, what was revealed to Nietzsche under this form, can maintain itself only when the throne or seat of Necessity is destroyed. And it is precisely against this throne that Nietzsche had to raise his hammer. The sufferings, the horror, the despair, the hatred, the disgust, the joys and hopes that it was given Nietzsche to know—all these he would have to throw at the monster's head to destroy it.

It seems that Nietzsche himself thought that such was precisely his life's task and that he made truly super-human efforts to fulfill it. He weighed himself down with an enormous burden and was ready to take on even more. In one of his letters he says that he would gladly experience the worst sufferings that any human being had ever known, for it is only on this condition that he could believe he had really seen the truth. And his wish was fulfilled. Except for Kierkegaard, perhaps, not one of the thinkers of the nineteenth century knew the horrifying experiences through which Nietzsche passed. But he found that this was still not enough; he did not have the daring to rise up against Necessity and defy it. When he stood before Necessity and looked it straight in the eye, his powers betrayed him and he became paralyzed, like Socrates, like Spinoza. "The necessary does not offend me, *amor fati* is my innermost nature," he says in *Ecce Homo* as if he had forgotten all that he had said so many times about the morality of masters and slaves, the "Will to Power," the freedom that lies "beyond good and evil." Instead of fighting against the monster he becomes its ally, its slave, and directs his hammer not, to be sure, against those who refuse obedience to Necessity (all submit to Necessity, the wise as well as the foolish) but against those who refuse to consider submission to Necessity as *summum bonum* and *beatitudo*. Nietzsche sets his pride in *amor fati* and bases all his hopes on "you shall be like God, knowing good and evil." His philosophy, like Socrates' and Spinoza's, is changed into edification: man must "endure both faces of fortune with equanimity;" no evil can come to a good man, for he must find happiness even in the bull of Phalaris.

Nietzsche's "cruelty," which frightened so many people, did not originate with Nietzsche. It had already been introduced into the soul of the first man, who let himself be tempted by the fruits of the tree of knowledge. It had already been proclaimed by the wisest among men, who had discovered the universal and necessary truths. Original sin weighs heavily on fallen humanity, and all the efforts that it makes to deliver itself break, like waves on a rock, against the invisible wall of prejudices that we venerate as eternal truths. And Nietzsche could not escape the fate of all; the idea of Necessity succeeded in seducing him also. He bowed his own head, and called all men to prostrate themselves, before the altar or throne of the "monster without whose killing man cannot live."

XI

Even more clearly than in Nietzsche does the strict bond that exists between knowledge and freedom or rather, the loss of freedom, appear in the shattering fate of Kierkegaard. Nietzsche called himself the anti-Christ and deliberately fought against Socrates. Kierkegaard regarded himself as a Christian, considered the Bible revelation, and said that he had nothing to learn from Socrates since Socrates was a pagan. In reality, however, he never succeeded in escaping from the power of the Socratic ideas. I should even say that the more he fought against Socrates, the more he became entangled in his nets. Strange as it may appear, something drove this Lutheran, this candidate in theology, away from Luther. By his own admission Kierkegaard had read almost nothing of Luther. "I have never read anything of Luther," he notes in his Journal. And this is certainly no accident: the modern man cannot help but seek *lux legis* (the light of law) and he fears above all else *tenebrae fidei* (the darkness of faith).

It must be said frankly at the risk of arousing the indignation of many of Kierkegaard's admirers: Kierkegaard's Christianity brings us what Socrates, in his first and second incarnation, had already offered—the virtuous man will be happy even in the bull of Phalaris. In a discourse entitled "To Suffer Once, To Live Forever" Kierkegaard compares men to criminals from whom one cannot wrest an admission of their crimes by sweetness and good words and whom it is therefore necessary to submit to torture; and he declares, "Hope, in the eternal sense, is conditioned by a horribly painful interior tension, and the natural man will never resolve to take this on himself of his own free will." Also, "the Christian consolation leads, by human reckoning, to a despair more terrible than the worst terrestrial sufferings, than the worst temporal misfortunes. And it is here alone that edification, Christian edification, begins."

Anyone who has read Kierkegaard must recognize that all his writings, all his thoughts, reflect the same spirit as the lines I have just quoted. The very titles of his works—*Fear and Trembling, The Concept of Dread, The Sickness Unto Death, The Thorn in the Flesh*—testify to the sufferings and anxieties with which his life was filled to the brim. In his *Journal* he writes: "When I am dead, *Fear and Trembling* alone will suffice to make my name immortal. People will read the book, they will translate it into foreign languages. Men will shudder at the frightful pathos with which it is permeated" (II, 89). A year previously he had already noted, "It seems to me that I have written things that must move the very stones to tears" (I, 389). And again, "Can men imagine how much I have suffered, how much I constantly suffer, and with what atrocious suffering my existence is bound up" (II, 142). Near this we find the following testimony: "In eleven months I finished *Either/Or*. If anyone in the world knew what provoked the appearance of this book! My God, a work so immense! Everyone imagines that I was impelled to write this book by some deep sentiment, but in reality it

relates entirely to my private life. And my purpose—if people kn⸢ ⸥
purpose was, they would declare me stark mad" (I, 183).

Such confessions—and the *Journal* is filled with them—give u⸤ ⸥
a key not only to Kierkegaard himself but also to the extremely com⸤ ⸥
sophic problems bound up with his work, which is unique in the o ⸏⸏⸏ᴧᴧᴏn
of its thought. It is beyond doubt that what Kierkegaard lived through, and
of which he tells us in his books, was so horrible that the very stones would
have had to pity him. But it is no less certain, on the other hand, that if men
had known for what reason Kierkegaard raised such a storm, they would have
laughed at him or shut him up in a madhouse. Moreover, despite the many passages of the *Journal* which permit us to divine what it was that made Kierkegaard
suffer, he himself remains persuaded that no one will ever know the cause of his
torments and where the "thorn in the flesh" of which he speaks so insistently
was driven in.

Furthermore, he solemnly forbids anyone to try to discover the concrete
circumstances that broke his life and informs us that, for his part, he has taken
all necessary measures to bewilder and confound the curious who would gain
possession of his secret. In this he partly succeeded. Some believe that the
wishes of a dead man must be respected; others recoil before the complexity
of the Gordian knot in which Kierkegaard deliberately interwove truth and
falsehood. It seems, then, that we shall never succeed in determining exactly
what it was that happened to Kierkegaard, even if we believe that the wish he
expressed while still living in our world no longer binds anyone now that he
has left this world almost a century ago. One may, indeed, assume that what
torments Kierkegaard in the other world is the thought that he did not have the
courage while alive to proclaim his secret openly in the face of all, and that if
there were now someone to pierce his secret and reveal it, he would deliver the
dead man's soul from a great burden and at the same time render an immense
service to all who seek and think.

Kierkegaard is neither the first nor the last among men who carried with
him to the grave a secret that he would have done better to leave on earth and
for the earth. I shall mention, for example, Nietzsche. Nietzsche talks to us
incessantly of the "masks" under which human beings hide their *innere Be-
sudelung* (inward soiling). And, quite like Kierkegaard, he is afraid to call that
which torments him by its true name. Socrates likewise had his secret which
remained inviolate, and Spinoza also, and even great saints like Bernard of
Clairvaux whose *perdita vita* (wasted life) troubled Luther so much. One can,
of course, speak of ideas without touching the life of the men in whose soul
the ideas arose. Setting out from Spinoza's maxim "the true is the index both of

..self and of the false," we can assume that for the verification of any philosophic conceptions proposed to us there are available principles that are immanent in them. But here is one of the worst *petitio principii* that reason, which aspires avidly to universal and necessary judgments, has ever forged. If it is given to men to realize the critique of reason not by means of reason and the principles immanent in reason, we must be prepared before everything else to renounce Spinoza's principle. We must have the courage to tell ourselves that the secret of Kierkegaard, of Socrates, of Spinoza or of Nietzsche must not fear men and hide itself like a thief in the night, that the secret which was so mocked and slandered that it ended up by being ashamed of itself must occupy the first place among the truths.

Kierkegaard reproached the philosophers for not living in the categories in which they thought. Would it not be more correct to reproach them for not having the daring to think in the categories in which they lived? Kierkegaard himself wishes to believe that he lives in the categories in which he thinks, and it is in this that he sees his "merit." "The explanation that I hide in my inmost being, the more concrete explanation that includes my dread still more precisely—this I do not write down." But, despite his efforts to bewilder us, it is beyond doubt that the "concrete" is his breaking off with his fiancée, Regine Olsen. He could not, of course, hide the breaking off itself. But he did hide the fact that he had broken with the young girl not of his own volition but because he was obliged to do so, obliged not internally by some "higher" consideration but externally— because of a circumstance that was banal, offensive to him, shameful even, and utterly repugnant. This is what he wished to hide, and he did all in his power to make people believe that he had broken with Regine Olsen voluntarily, that it was on his part a freely offered sacrifice to God. Even more, not only did he succeed in making others believe this, he *almost* succeeded in persuading himself of it. But this was false. It was a "suggestion," not even—it seems—an auto-suggestion. Kierkegaard had not sacrificed Regine; Regine had been taken away from him by force. And it was not God who had taken her away but the obscure powers that had once taken away Eurydice from Orpheus. Not only was Regine taken away from him, everything that God gives to man was taken away from him. What is, then, most terrible, most shaking in Kierkegaard's fate (and also in Nietzsche's), is that *he had nothing more to sacrifice.* To offer a sacrifice one must have something, but Kierkegaard (quite like Nietzsche) possessed nothing. He was a poet, a thinker. He even believed that he was extraordinarily endowed in this respect. But he had no use for these talents. If at least, he had been capable, like Orpheus, of moving the stones! But we know that when he spoke men laughed and the stones were silent, as they always remain silent.

Besides, did Orpheus himself possess this power? Has there ever been a man on earth to whom it has been given to conquer the inertia and silence of this immense universe of which, according to the teaching of the wise, we are all only links? To put it differently, has there ever been a man audacious enough to think in the categories in which he lives and to descend, despite "eternal laws," into the Hades forbidden to mortals?

Be that as it may, Kierkegaard appears to us now as, in a way, "Orpheus come back to life"; what he loved was taken away from him and since he no longer possessed the power of his prototype, who made himself understood by stones and animals, he had to turn to men. Now men are worse than stones; stones are content to keep silent, while men know how to laugh. Therefore one can tell stones the truth, but from men it is preferable to hide it. It is impossible to tell men that hell must violate the eternal laws of its hellish being for a Soren Kierkegaard and a Regine Olsen (in other words to take account of a particular and consequently insignificant circumstance). Furthermore, one cannot speak to men of hell, especially to the educated men of our time; the word "hell" does not exist for them. They know that there are immutable principles which determine the structure of being, that these principles admit of no exception and make no distinction between an Orpheus inspired by the gods and the least of beggars. It is useless to speak to men of Kierkegaard's "sufferings" when he learned that hell would not restore Regine Olsen to him. In general, it is useless to speak of sufferings: no matter how terrifying they may be, can they shake the "order and connection of things" and the "order and connection of ideas," that is, our thought, that is based on it? Spinoza's *non ridere, non lugere neque detestari, sed intelligere* (not to laugh, not to lament, not to curse, but to understand) is as unpitying as the laws of hell. All argument is here vain; we must obey. Nietzsche himself, who "had killed the law," ended with *amor fati*. What can Kierkegaard do? It is impossible for him to accept the idea that his torments will pass without leaving any traces and will change nothing in the general economy of the universe. But one cannot speak of this; it is "shameful," and one must hide it and act as if it never were. Why is it "shameful"? Why must Kierkegaard not speak of what Orpheus once sang? It will be objected that Orpheus is an imaginary or, in any case, mythical person. Orpheus in the flesh and bone would not have dared fight against hell and would have been content with "justifying" his submission through lofty considerations, i.e., through thoughts about sacrifice, etc.

Whence shame came into the world no one knows. In Plato's *Symposium* Alcibiades says that Socrates taught him shame. According to the Bible shame is the consequence of sin: when Adam had eaten the fruit of the tree of knowledge he was ashamed of his nakedness which heretofore had not seemed shameful to him. In both cases shame is bound up with knowledge and placed in dependence on it. Not knowledge as "pleasure in sensible perception" but the knowledge of universal and necessary truths. Knowledge obliges man to accept the real, that is, "things that are not in our power." And it is knowledge, likewise, which suggests to him that there is at times something shameful in this acceptance. When Kierkegaard speaks of voluntary sacrifice and has nothing to sacrifice—for he has been stripped of everything—he does not even suspect that, following Adam's example, he is hiding his nakedness under a fig leaf. He believes, on the contrary, that he is accomplishing a sublime work, that he is "saving" his soul and helping others save theirs. But it is then precisely that that happens against which both Luther and Nietzsche warned us, the first in saying "for man must distrust his works," and the second "everything that the fallen man undertakes to save himself does nothing but hasten his fall." Kierkegaard concludes that we must live in the categories in which we think—and stretches forth his hand to the tree of the knowledge of good and evil whose fruits, as Hegel has explained to us, became the principle of philosophy for all time. Kierkegaard detested and despised Hegel. A few months before his death he made the following entry in his *Journal:* "Hegel! Would that I were permitted to think like the Greeks: how the gods must have laughed! A poor professor who grasped the necessity of everything that exists and transformed the universe into a plaything. Ye gods!" (II, 351). But Kierkegaard could never bring himself to renounce the idea that our life must be determined by our thought, to break with Socrates. Even in his moments of highest spiritual tension, as we shall see, he could not resolve to exchange the "light of reason" for "the darkness of faith," to use Luther's language, and turned to Socrates.

In *The Thorn in the Flesh* he writes: " . . . and when mortal dread takes hold of a man, time stands still. To wish to run faster than ever before and not be able to move a limb, to be ready to sacrifice everything else just to purchase an instant and then to learn that it is not for sale, because 'it depends on no man's will or permission but only on God's compassion.'" One would think that anyone who had passed through such an experience must forever lose all trust in his "works." What works can a man for whom time has come to a stop accomplish—a man who, like Spinoza's *asinus turpissimus* (most infamous ass) that is hypnotized by a hostile power, is incapable of making the least movement? But precisely in such moments Kierkegaard always remembers Socrates: nothing bad can happen to a good man, the good man will be happy even in the bull of Phalaris. Even if his will is paralyzed, even if he is condemned to die of hunger between two bales of hay, there still remains to him one "work": he can still

ATHENS AND JERUSALEM

"endure both faces of fortune with equanimity," he can still glorify *fatum*, he can still demand of himself and of all men that they find supreme happiness in the horrors of life. It is not only philosophy, indeed, but all of Christianity that is reduced to *Erbauung,* to edification.

XII

Two books are particularly revelatory in this respect—*Fear and Trembling* (along with *Repetition*) and *The Concept of Dread.* The first is devoted to Abraham and his sacrifice, that is, to the problem of faith; the second deals with original sin. I recall once more that Kierkegaard was born and grew up in a strict Lutheran environment. Even though he had not read Luther's works, he could not but profess Luther's *sola fide.* With age, however, he moved further and further away from Luther and his *sola fide* in order to regain "free will," thus approaching that conception of faith as "faith formed by love" that Luther attacked so violently in Catholicism. In 1844, when he wrote *The Concept of Dread,* he already understood faith quite differently than in 1843 when he wrote *Fear and Trembling;* between these two works one of those events which are unimportant in other people's eyes but which determined Kierkegaard's fate happened: Regine Olsen, his former fiancée, became engaged to Schlegel. For everyone else this was only another engagement like all others and could furnish no material for profound meditation. For Kierkegaard, however, this meant: Socrates was the wisest of men, and Abraham, the father of faith, must and could be accepted only insofar as his faith confirmed and expressed Socrates' wisdom.

As everyone knows, God turned Abraham's hand away at the moment he raised the knife over his son and Isaac remained alive. Regarding this, Kierkegaard says in *Fear and Trembling,* "Let us go further. Let us assume that Isaac had really been slaughtered. Abraham *believed*. He had faith, not in some future happiness in another world but that he would be happy here *in this world*. God could return to him Isaac whom he had killed. Abraham had faith in the power of the Absurd;[23] all human calculation had long ceased to exist for him." A page further Kierkegaard adds, " . . . the movement of faith must always be made by virtue of the Absurd, but it must be noted that the finite is not lost thus but won in its totality." And further on, to make his conception of faith clearer for us, Kierkegaard tells us the "invented" story of the poor young man who fell in love with a princess. It is obvious to everyone that the young man will never obtain the princess as his wife. But "the knight of faith," who knows as well as "everyone" how mighty is the power of the "everyday" over men, makes the "movement of faith," and a miracle happens: "I believe," says he, "that she will be mine; I have faith by virtue of the Absurd, for to God everything is possible."

Yet at the same time Kierkegaard several times admits to us, "As for myself, I do not believe; I lack the courage for that." Instead of saying, "I lack the courage," perhaps Kierkegaard should have repeated what he had written in the *Thorn in the Flesh,* "to wish to run faster than ever before and not be able to move a limb" and recalled Luther's *De servo arbitrio. What is it that prevents him from believing?* Faith is what he needs most in the world. Faith means that God can give Abraham a new son, recall the slaughtered Isaac to life, unite the poor young man with the princess, force hell to violate its laws and return Regine Olsen to Kierkegaard.

It is clear that it is not courage that is involved here—on the contrary, if courage is needed it is rather to renounce faith. And, in general, anyone who knows Kierkegaard's life will not be able to deny him courage, just as he cannot deny it to Socrates or Spinoza. This is why the road to "faith" for Kierkegaard passes inevitably through "infinite resignation": "This resignation is that shirt of which an old folk-tale speaks; its thread is woven in tears, the shirt is sewn in tears. . . . The mystery of life consists in the fact that every man must sew for himself such a shirt." And in this "infinite resignation lies rest and peace." It is not difficult to discover behind this infinite resignation Socrates' bull of Phalaris, Spinoza's *beatitudines,* or Nietzsche's *amor fati.* Kierkegaard passed through all this; but while Socrates' wisdom stopped here, considered this the final end and blessed this end as the supreme goal of man, Kierkegaard could not stop here when he wrote *Fear and Trembling.* Or, to put it better, he could still not stop here. He called upon himself all the horrors of existence—by the way these, as we know, did not wait for his summons to visit him—not in order to appear a model of virtue and astonish people by his resistance and heroism. He expected from these horrors something different: God could return to Abraham his slaughtered son. Kierkegaard hoped that his sufferings would finally break in him that trust in the given, in experience, which reason inspires in men and by virtue of which they "accept" the real as inevitable.

Kierkegaard in a way gathered and concentrated all his powers, all his capacities for despair—the beginning of philosophy, he said, is not wonder, as the Greeks taught, but despair—to obtain the right "to weep and curse" and to oppose his tears and curses to the limitless demands of the reason which has enchained the human will through universal and necessary truths. The "knight of resignation" must become the "knight of faith." Kierkegaard writes: "Reason is right: in our vale of tears where reason reigns as master it is impossible (that for God everything be possible). Of this the knight of faith feels as certain as the knight of resignation. The only thing that can save him is the Absurd, and this he acquires through faith. He sees the impossibilities and at the same moment has faith in the Absurd." Here is still another confession—the moment in question is so important that we must concentrate all our attention on it: "If I renounce everything, this is still not faith—it is only resignation. *This movement I make by my own efforts,*[24] and draw from it as a prize myself in my eternal consciousness, in blessed agreement with my love for the eternal Being. *Through faith I renounce nothing;*[25] on the contrary, through faith I acquire everything—even in the sense in which it is said that he who has faith as a grain of mustard can move mountains." And not only move mountains; infinitely more is promised to one who has faith: "Nothing will be impossible for you." In other words, reason with its universal and necessary truths, reason which rules autocratically over our world, will forever lose its power. "Beyond reason and knowledge"—these words of Plotinus express the same thought. Plotinus also began with an apotheosis of resignation: if your sons are killed, your daughters dishonored, your fatherland destroyed, it must all—he declared—be "accepted." But he ends up with a demand for the impossible: Beyond reason and knowledge lies the impossible. When Kierkegaard opposes to the knight of resignation, i.e., Socrates, the knight of faith, i.e., Abraham, he expresses basically the same thought as Plotinus, whom he probably knew hardly at all. But he uses the term "faith," which is foreign to Plotinus.

"My intention," says Kierkegaard at the end of his introduction to *Fear and Trembling,* "is to draw out in the form of problematics the dialectical in the story of Abraham in order to show what a monstrous paradox faith is, a paradox that transforms murder into a holy action, pleasing to God; a paradox that returns Isaac to Abraham; a paradox that no thought can master for faith begins precisely where thought ends." This is Kierkegaard's basic idea which he never stops repeating throughout all his works. Six years after *Fear and Trembling* he writes in *The Sickness Unto Death:* "To believe means to lose reason in order to find God." This formula, recalling Pascal's *s'abêtir* (to humble oneself) which has given rise to so many commentaries, carries Kierkegaard, it seems, beyond the limits of philosophic problems: if thought is brought to a halt, if reason is lost, does this not mean that philosophy also ends and is lost? But it is precisely on this account that I have recalled Plotinus' words "beyond reason and knowledge." Indeed, though he never says anything of Abraham and Isaac and perhaps never even thought of them, having attained the limit beyond which Socrates' bull of Phalaris is found and where man must accept passively everything that is real according to the testimony of reason, so that "he is no longer to be held a thinking thing but rather a most infamous ass," Plotinus made what Kierkegaard recommended—a leap into the unknown, where the competence and power of reason come to an end. Did philosophy then end for Plotinus? Or did it, rather, only begin, for it was only then that the critique of pure reason was attempted, that critique without which there cannot be any philosophy? I say "attempted" for it has been realized only once since humanity has been in existence, when God said to Adam, "The day you eat the fruit of the tree of the knowledge of good and of evil, you shall die." And indeed, the critique of pure reason is the greatest paradox, which saps the very foundations of thought. "It requires no support, as though it could not carry itself."[26] This idea which appeared to Plotinus in connection with the bull of Phalaris appeared to Kierkegaard in connection with the biblical story of Abraham's sacrifice. If man is really *res cogitans* and not *asinus turpissimus* he will never accept the reality where reason reigns and where human *beatitudo* consists in putting oneself joyfully under the protection of universal and necessary truths—Isaac slaughtered by his father, man thrown by a tyrant into the bull of Phalaris.

Abraham raised his knife against his son, Abraham was a child murderer, that is, the greatest of criminals. According to the Bible, however, Abraham was a righteous man, the father of faith. What then remains of the Socratic-Spinozist edification, and the *beatitudines* promised by it, for the man who has decided to kill his son? Is there any peace of soul possible for him? Such a man is condemned forever. As long as reason reigns over the universe it is as impossible to save him as to make that which has been not to have been. Kierkegaard sees as clearly as Descartes saw that "what has happened cannot be made not to have happened" Kierkegaard sees, then, that it is necessary to choose between Abraham and Socrates, between him whom Scripture declared a righteous man and him whom the pagan god proclaimed the wisest of men. And Kierkegaard, conscious of the heavy responsibility with which he was charged, took the part of Abraham and began to speak of the "suspension of the ethical" with a daring that reminds one of Luther and the prophets. He notes in his Journal: "He who succeeds in resolving this enigma (the suspension of the ethical) will explain my life." Nietzsche's "beyond good and evil," which differs from the suspension of the ethical in form only, was also for Nietzsche not the solution of a theoretical problem, as he himself in several places admits, but a way out of the impasse into which the universal and necessary truths had pushed him.

To make clearer what Kierkegaard meant when he spoke of "the suspension of the ethical," I shall quote again one of his almost involuntary confessions; when it is a question of the relationships between lovers, Kierkegaard's confessions are always against his will. He tells the love story of the young man and young woman and ends it thus: "The ethical could not come to their help, for they have a secret which they hide from it, a secret which they take upon themselves, for which they accept responsibility." What is this secret? Kierkegaard proceeds to explain it to us. "The ethical as such is the universal. . . . As soon as the particular man opposes the universal he has sinned and can reconcile himself with the universal only in acknowledging his sin. . . . If this is the highest that can be said of man and his existence, then the ethical has the same meaning as eternal happiness which for all eternity and at every instant constitutes the end (*telos*) of man." It is easy to recognize in these words the deepest and dearest thought of Socrates and Spinoza. The ethical was them not only the supreme but the essential value. You may possess all terrestrial goods, but if you lack the "ethical" you have nothing. And, on the contrary, if everything is taken away from you and you have saved the "ethical" only, you have the one thing necessary—you have "everything." The "ethical" is a value *sui generis* [of a unique kind] which is distinguished *toto coelo* [by the whole extent of the heavens] from all other values. The goods which the "ethical" has at its disposal differ as much from the goods which the man who does not participate in wisdom seeks and finds as the constellation called the Dog differs from the dog, the barking animal. It is with deliberate intent, of course, that I use Spinoza's image, and it is with intent also that I do not quote the end of the sentence, to the effect that they have in common only the name. For even their names are different: on the one hand a constellation, on the other a dog, an animal that not only barks but is despised. It would have been more logical on Spinoza's part to say not *animal latrans* (a barking animal) but *animal turpissimum* (a most infamous animal). It is beyond doubt that the source of the Socratic-Spinozist ethic was a profound metaphysical shaking, if one may so express oneself. In Kierkegaard's terms, the *beatitudo* [supreme happiness] brought by the Socratic ethic is worse—if one evaluates it by human standards—than the worst calamities.

Kierkegaard felt Socrates' problem, which is the basic problem not only of ethics but of all philosophy, no less deeply than Nietzsche. And, like Nietzsche, he strained all his powers to overcome Socrates' enchantment. It was for this reason alone that he turned to the Bible; it was only to deliver himself from the temptation of the *beatitudines* [blessings] promised by the wisest of men that he remembered Abraham. But, unlike Nietzsche, Kierkegaard never thought of considering Socrates a "fallen man" who, as Hegel tells us, transformed the fruits of the tree of knowledge into the principle of philosophy for all future time. Socrates is, for Kierkegaard, a pagan, but the most perfect man who lived on earth before the truth of the Bible was revealed to the world. At the very moment when, carried beyond good and evil, he finds himself face to face with Abraham, dares to proclaim his "suspension of the ethical," and sees that man is forced to hide from the "ethical" his final secret, he continues to cling compulsively to Socrates. He compares Socrates to the Christian mystics and declares with assurance, "The system begins with nothingness, and it is with nothingness that mysticism always ends. The latter is the divine nothingness, as Socrates' ignorance, with which he not only began but also always finished, or to which he returned, was piety."

As I have indicated, Socrates' ignorance was not ignorance; Socrates knew that he did not know, and aspired eagerly to the knowledge that appeared to him the only means possessed by man for avoiding the fatal consequences of the fall. Nietzsche felt that "man must distrust his works" and that death awaits the fallen man precisely where he believes himself to see the road to salvation. But Kierkegaard does not even dream that Socrates is the fallen man *par excellence* and that "knowledge" is not a remedy for the "fall" and that the need, the hunger for knowledge is already the expression and confirmation of the fall. That is why in the *Concept of Dread* Kierkegaard attributes to Adam before his fall the same "ignorance of nothingness" which he had found in Socrates and which, having reached the extreme degree of tension, is realized in the act of disobedience to the divine command. To put it differently, Socrates, for Kierkegaard, is man as he was before tasting the fruit of the tree of knowledge. That is why in *Fear and Trembling* he dares turn to Abraham only after having obtained the favorable disposition of the universal and necessary truths. At the very beginning of this book, as if to excuse himself before the "ethical" for the offence that he is about to perpetrate against it, he declares: "In the world of the spirit an eternal divine order rules; here the rain does not fall equally on the good and the wicked, here the sun does not shine indifferently on the good and the wicked. Here there is only one law: he who does not work does not eat."

What is this "world of the spirit?" How did Kierkegaard know it? It is not from the Bible surely that he learned it, for in the Bible it is said that the sun rises equally on the good and the wicked. But this Kierkegaard could not endure: in "the world of the spirit" there must be another "order," another "law"; in the world of the spirit the sun rises only on the just and only he who works eats. Why must there be another law here? No answer to this question is found either in *Fear and Trembling* or in *The Concept of Dread*. But *The Thorn in the Flesh* contains a confession which sheds light on Kierkegaard's "suspension of the ethical" as well as on his attitude toward Abraham's sacrifice: "In the world of the spirit," he says, "luck and accident do not make one a king and another a beggar, one more beautiful than the queen of the Orient and another more miserable than Lazarus; he only is excluded from the world of the spirit who has excluded himself. In the world of the spirit all are invited."[27]

At the last moment, Kierkegaard returns to the "ethical." It is only in it that he hopes to find protection. And, indeed, here in our world the sun rises indifferently on the just and on the wicked. Still worse, it sometimes happens that the just never see the smallest ray of the sun. The sun is among the "things that are not in our power." No, neither in our power nor in the power of God. Can one attach himself to what caprice and chance bring and take away? Can one love it? By virtue of the Absurd, Kierkegaard has told us, he believed that God returned Isaac to Abraham, that the princess would belong to the poor young man. As long as he hid from the "ethical" his faith in the Absurd he could maintain his faith. But when he resolved to reveal his "secret" in order to obtain the blessing of the ethical, the secret lost its magic power, and from the world where the sun shines on both the just and the wicked Kierkegaard entered the world of Socrates, the world of necessary truths, where—to be sure—there are no sinners but only just men, but where the sun has never risen and will never rise.

XIII

Kierkegaard felt himself irresistibly drawn to Abraham, but he "understood" in Abraham only what recalled to him Socrates in his first and second incarnations. He tried in every way to make Abraham pass into a "new" category but did not succeed in this at all. The most extraordinary thing is that, quite like Nietzsche, Kierkegaard comes to the boundary beyond which Socrates' enchantment no longer acts on man and where the freedom for which we passionately long awaits us, but it is impossible for him to pass beyond this boundary and follow Abraham.

Above all, Abraham is for Kierkegaard a man driven out of the "universal" and deprived, therefore, of the protection of universal and necessary truths. Kierkegaard dares to say, "Faith is the paradox that the individual as individual is above the universal." He even repeats this a page further. But both times he makes a reservation: "He only, however, is as an individual man above the universal who has first submitted to the universal and has become a man, an individual, through the universal."

This reservation is extremely characteristic of Kierkegaard's thought. He, who so violently attacked and mocked Hegel, nevertheless does not cease seeking everywhere the dialectical movement, the natural development. Hardly does he glorify the Absurd and proclaim that he who wishes to possess faith must renounce reason and thought than it appears that one cannot renounce it, that it is necessary to observe a certain order and rigorous progression. And this at the very moment when reason, which has established all "orders" and all "rigors" no longer has any power over us. "God is the friend of order," he writes, without suspecting that this is equivalent to saying God is the slave of order. In

Plato, in those brief moments when he succeeds at the cost of an extreme tension of all the faculties of his soul in delivering himself from the reason which crushes him, there arises always the "sudden" (*exaiphnês*), as proclaimer of the wished for but far removed freedom. Kierkegaard fears the "sudden" and does not trust freedom, even when it comes from God. Comparing Abraham to the tragic hero, he is ready to envy the latter. "The tragic hero renounces himself in order to permit the universal to express itself; the knight of faith renounces the universal in order to become a particular man. . . . He who imagines that it is quite comfortable to be a particular man can be sure that he is not a knight of faith. The knight of faith knows, on the contrary, that it is a glorious thing to belong to the universal. . . . He knows how pleasant it is to be a man who has his fatherland in the universal, who finds in the universal a sweet refuge where he is gathered with open arms when the desire to enter it takes hold of him. But he knows that above the universal rises a solitary, narrow and abrupt path; he knows how fearful it is to be born solitary, to follow an always empty road without ever encountering a living soul. He knows very well where he is and how men regard him. Humanly speaking, he is a madman and can make no one understand him. "A madman"—the expression is too weak. If people refuse to consider him mad, then he is a hypocrite and the higher he ascends on the path the more frightful a hypocrite he is. The knight of faith knows that it is good to hand oneself over to the universal. This demands courage but brings with it peace, precisely because it is done for the sake of the universal."

"It is a glorious thing to belong to the universal!" We recognize this thought: Socrates and Spinoza not only proclaimed it, they actualized it in their lives. But we recall also something else: the universal and necessary truths demand of man that he accept *aequo animo* [calmly] everything, including the bull of Phalaris, that fate brings him; they demand that he be ready to transform himself from a *res cogitans* [thinking thing] into an *asinus turpissimus* [most infamous ass]. Aristotle did not suspect this, but Socrates and Spinoza knew it perfectly well. When Kierkegaard speaks of the tragic, he holds to the Aristotelian point of view: one can envy the tragic hero—the universal and necessary truths take his side. And Kierkegaard even refers to the Aristotelian conception of tragedy. He also quotes, with an indulgence that seems hardly compatible with his character, Aristotle's corrective to Socrates' ethic of which we have already spoken, i.e., that it is necessary for the virtuous man to have a certain minimum of temporal goods. Kierkegaard's indulgence is, of course, explainable. He makes every possible effort to introduce Abraham into another "category" than that which he marked out for Socrates. Thus, when it is a question of the "ethical" or of the "tragic hero," he tends to separate himself in the sharpest possible way from Socrates and, to accomplish this more easily, substitutes Aristotle for Socrates.

Abraham, as I have already said, is above all, for Kierkegaard, a man driven out of the universal and therefore deprived of the protection of universal and necessary truths. "The knight of faith is completely abandoned to himself, and it is in this that the horror of his situation consists." He decides everything himself and always at his own risk and peril. He cannot take counsel of anyone. He cannot even find any support in the church. "The hero of the church expresses the universal by his acts. . . . There is no one in the church who does not understand him. The hero of faith is deprived of this. . . . Even if a man were timorous and cowardly enough to wish to become a hero of faith at others' risk, he would not succeed. For only the individual man as such can become a knight of faith. It is in this that his greatness, which I understand even though I cannot myself attain it, consists; but it is in this likewise that the horror of the situation, which I understand even better, consists."

These confessions contain an extremely important truth. We recall that Nietzsche said the same thing but in other terms: when he saw himself obliged to leave the universal, or, as he himself put it, "to kill the law," he almost became mad with horror. But there is in Kierkegaard's case a particularity that is at first sight negligible but produces the effect of a dissonance and is significant. Kierkegaard speaks not only of the horror but also of the greatness of the situation of the knight of faith. The very term "knight of faith" sounds rather strange: one could say that faith implores the benediction of the very universal that it has fled. Is not the "knightly," indeed, one of the categories that belongs, so to speak, to the "ethical"? But the tribute paid to the "ethical" is still more manifest in the "greatness" imputed to the knight of faith and in Kierkegaard's efforts to place the knight of faith at a level above the tragic hero in the hierarchy of human values. This also is a tribute to the "universal": Kierkegaard could not resolve to break once and for all with the habits of thought that men had adopted after Socrates, who provided the principle of philosophy for all time. If Kierkegaard had wished and been able to speak all of the truth, he would have had to root out from his soul all the ideas of "greatness" and of "knightliness" that his memory suggested to him. To one who has dedicated himself to faith there remains only "horror," and he must renounce forever all "consolations" that the "universal," by raising some to the dignity of "knight" and according to others "greatness," has distributed. Aristotle could speak of the greatness and beauty of the tragic: he saw it on the stage. But for the man who has lived tragedy in his own soul these terms have no meaning. Tragedy is the absence of any way out. There is nothing beautiful in this, nothing great; it is only ugliness and misery.

The universal and necessary truths not only do not support the man fallen into a situation with no way out but do everything, on the contrary, to crush him once and for all. Man sees every way cut off precisely at the moment when the universal and necessary truths, which promised to sustain and console him in all circumstances, suddenly reveal their true face and demand imperiously of man that he transform himself from *res cogitans* into *asinus turpissimus*.

Should not Kierkegaard, who had been drawn by the Absurd because it was the Absurd precisely that promised to deliver him from universal and necessary truths, have known this? God can give Abraham another son, God can bring Isaac back to life, nothing is impossible for God. . . . But as I have indicated, neither in his books nor in his *Journal* did Kierkegaard ever dare say that his Isaac was none other than Regine Olsen and that it was because of Regine Olsen that he had had the audacity to proclaim his "suspension of the ethical." This was his "secret" that he hid from the "ethical," that he hid from the Absurd, that he was unwilling even to admit to himself. For scarcely would he have called it by its true name than the universal and necessary truths would have deprived him not only of the title "knight of faith" but also that of "tragic hero." The worst thing for Kierkegaard is that he was aware that everything that had happened to him had happened "naturally," without God or the devil or even pagan fate having intervened in any way. This Kierkegaard, who was prepared to bear everything, could not accept. But he could no longer destroy this nightmare. It is for this reason that it was necessary for him to persuade himself that his break with Regine was a voluntary sacrifice—the repetition, in a way, of Abraham's sacrifice, who had agreed with God only because his was also a voluntary sacrifice. But whence does Kierkegaard know that God is more pleased with voluntary sacrifices than with others? We cannot put such a question to Socrates. His "ignorance" furnished him a definite answer; but had not Kierkegaard repeated many times that Socrates was a pagan and that he, Kierkegaard, had nothing to learn from Socrates? Now it appears that the Christian also cannot do without Socrates, just as he cannot do without universal and necessary truths.

At the same time that he wrote *Fear and Trembling* Kierkegaard wrote his *Repetition*, the subject of which is not Abraham but Job. Job, as is known, did not voluntarily kill his sons nor dissipate his wealth. All these misfortunes broke upon him suddenly without his expecting them. He has not even the right to claim the high dignity of the tragic hero. He is quite simply a miserable old man, like many—a burden on himself and on others. In our time of war and social upheaval one meets such Jobs at almost every corner of the street. Yesterday a king, today only a beggar lying on an ash-heap, scratching his boils with a shard. And yet, the biblical Job, who was neither a knight nor a tragic hero, succeeds in drawing Kierkegaard's attention and "merits" that the philosopher should devote to him, as to Abraham, an entire book—*Repetition*. One can say of this book what Kierkegaard himself said of *Fear and Trembling*: "if men felt the somber pathos that animates it, they would be seized with horror." *Repetition* is also written in "fear and trembling" by a man upon whom has fallen the terrible hammer and who asks himself in his terror whence the blow came to him: is it the *malleus Dei,* the hammer of God, or simply the "natural" power of the universal and necessary truths? According to the Bible, it was God who tested Job as He tested Abraham. But we cannot "know" this: "what is the knowledge that can be so constructed that a place is found for testing, which, in the infinite perspective of thought, does not exist, for it exists only for the individual? Such a knowledge does not exist, such a knowledge cannot exist."

But to what purpose does Kierkegaard invoke Job's memory and raise all these terrible questions? The hero of *Repetition,* just like Kierkegaard, was a man who was obliged to break with his fiancée. "Oh, my unforgettable benefactor," he says, "O martyred Job! May I join you, may I be with you? Do not push me away I have not possessed your wealth, I have not had seven sons and three daughters. But he also can lose everything who has not had much, and he also can lose son and daughter who has lost that which he loved, and he also can find himself covered with boils who has lost his honor and pride and at the same time the power and meaning of his life." What is it that Kierkegaard expects of Job? Why does he wish "to join him"? "Instead of seeking help from a *professor publicus ordinarius* [well-renowned professor] celebrated throughout the entire world, my friend [that is, Kierkegaard] runs to a private thinker, Job." The celebrated professor is obviously Hegel. Long before Hegel, however, Spinoza had already seen the "necessity of everything," and Hegel in this respect only repeated Spinoza. Why, then, did Kierkegaard not even once dare to think that the Olympic gods had burst out laughing on hearing Spinoza? Socrates had also taught the universal and necessary truth, but the god of Delphos did not mock him; on the contrary, he proclaimed him the wisest of men.

What would Job have answered Socrates and Spinoza if they had come to offer him their wisdom and their consolations? Kierkegaard never raised this question, neither at the time that he wrote *Fear and Trembling* and *The Concept of Dread* nor in the last years of his life when he so violently attacked the Protestant church and the married pastors. In his *Either/Or* Kierkegaard permits himself to set Job against Hegel, at whom the gods laughed so gaily. But the gods respected Socrates, and Spinoza was Socrates' second incarnation. Kierkegaard could never overcome the anxiety that he felt before Greek wisdom. We shall see that, according to Kierkegaard, man left the hands of the Creator with his soul filled with anxiety, that anxiety is—in a certain sense—a fundamental trait or even the essential faculty of man. But when he wrote *Fear and Trembling* and *Repetition*, Kierkegaard still refused to think thus. He went to Abraham and Job because he saw in them beings who had had the power and audacity to overcome all their anxieties and to rise above the "edification" of Socrates and the Delphic god who had blessed Socrates. Abraham did not know fear; God was with him, God to whom nothing is impossible. And in Job "daily experience" had still not completely destroyed the memory of the time when reason did not rule as master over the earth. Or, more exactly, the misfortunes which fell upon Job reawakened in him this memory.

Kierkegaard writes: "The importance of Job does not consist in the fact that he said, 'The Lord hath given, the Lord hath taken away, blessed be the name of the Lord.' This he said only at the beginning, he did not repeat it later. The importance of Job consists in the fact that he fights through the boundary disputes to faith, that here that terrible revolt of the wild and pugnacious powers of passion takes place." To put it differently, daily experience or the immediate data of consciousness constitute for men the supreme tribunal in the question of truth: whatever "experience" brings us, whatever the "data" show us, we accept it all and consider it true. In a world where reason rules it is madness to fight against the given. Man can weep and curse the truths that experience reveals to him, but he knows that it is in no one's power to overcome them, that they must be accepted. Philosophy goes even further: the data must not only be accepted, they must be blessed. Nietzsche even tells us that "Necessity does not offend him." Also, Job, a righteous man, begins by completely repressing to the depths of his soul all *lugere et detestari* (weeping and cursing): "the Lord hath given, the Lord hath taken away, blessed be the name of the Lord." But as his misfortunes multiply and grow, the tension of the repressed *lugere et detestari* increases, and this tension finally bursts the hard shell of the self-evidences that paralyze his freedom. "The meaning of Job consists precisely in the fact that he does not diminish the passion of freedom with false consolations."

Good will and wisdom speak through the mouth of Job's friends; and yet not only do they not succeed in calming him, they only irritate him more. If Socrates or Spinoza had come to console Job, they would not have been able to tell him anything other than what Eliphaz, Zophar and Bildad said. They are men and, like all men, they are in the power of the "given." And not only are they in the power of the given, they are condemned to think that everything that exists in the universe, living and dead, powerful and miserable, low and high, shares their fate, that is, is a slave to these truths. Job's friends look at him in silence for seven days. But one cannot look and remain silent forever.

One must speak. And hardly do their lips open than they begin, as if obeying Spinoza's precept, to say what they could not refuse to say. Perhaps they realized that a man who speaks thus no longer *pro re cogitante sed asino turpissimo habendus* (is to be regarded as a thinking thing but rather as a most infamous ass), but they continue to speak, themselves afraid of what they have said. What can be more shameful, what can be more outrageous than the necessity to think and say not what we desire to say but what we are forced to say "by the laws of our nature"? If, at the time of his prosperity and happiness, Job had found himself before a being "fallen from the lap of the universal" and had tried to console him, it is certain that he would have had to tell him only what his friends later had to tell him. Does he not also begin with "the Lord hath given, the Lord hath taken away, blessed be the name of the Lord"? And it appears that it is piety that dictated these words to him. Yet it is not piety but wickedness—and even that deepest wickedness, that *pietas et obedientia* which had permeated the flesh and blood of man after he tasted the fruits of the tree of knowledge—that speaks through his mouth. It seems that Kierkegaard felt this: herein lay the secret that he hid so carefully from the "ethical," herein only lay the meaning of his "suspension of the ethical." But he can only temporarily push aside the "ethical." Not only does he never connect the "ethical" with the fall of man, but the "ethical" appears to him always a necessary dialectical moment in the development of man toward the religious, and—as if he were an orthodox Hegelian—a moment that can only be suspended (*aufgehoben*) but not once for all abrogated.

Shortly before his death in 1854, he wrote in his *Journal:* " . . . when Christ cried out 'My God, my God, why hast Thou forsaken me?' it was terrible for Christ, and so it is ordinarily presented. But it seems to me that it was still more terrible for God to hear this cry. To be so immutable is horrifying! But no, the most terrible thing is not this, it is to be immutable and at the same time to be Love: infinite, deep, inexpressible suffering! Oh, what have I, a miserable man, suffered in this respect: not to be able to change anything whatever and at the same time to love. I have experienced this, and it helps me to understand even though only a little, from afar, the sufferings of the divine love."

I think that, after everything that has already been said, these lines need no commentary. The universal and necessary truth has conquered not only Kierkegaard but God Himself. Not everything is possible for God, many things are impossible for Him; and what is impossible is the principal, the most important, the most necessary. God's situation is worse even than Kierkegaard's or Nietzsche's into whose soul has crept "the most fearful, the blackest, the most terrifying." It is with such an "experience" that Kierkegaard approached the biblical story of the original sin. One can say in advance: for man as for God there is only one solution, only one possibility of salvation: the fruits of the tree of knowledge which, after Socrates, became the principle of philosophy for all time and transformed themselves almost under our eyes into Spinoza's *beatitudines*. The outraged "ethical" will receive complete satisfaction: man will reveal to it all his secrets. Hegel, whom Kierkegaard had offended still more than the "ethical," will perhaps forget all the cruel words that the rabid author of *Either/Or* had directed at him. And then the Olympic gods will no longer laugh at Hegel, but it will be Hegel's turn to laugh at the Olympic gods.

XIV

God must learn from Socrates and seek help from him whose truth has become the principle of philosophy for all time. All the *lugere et detestari* of God Himself break against His "immutability," just as Kierkegaard's *lugere et detestari* break against the immutable laws of being, of that order into which he was plunged by his birth. And it remains to God only "to endure both faces of fortune with equanimity" and "through the third kind of knowledge" to arrive at the conviction that "happiness is not the reward of virtue but virtue itself." According to Socrates, a virtuous man will be happy even in the bull of Phalaris; according to Kierkegaard, "Christianity" does not reveal to us a new truth but brings us an edification which, like the edification brought by Socrates, is worse, by human reckoning, than any calamity. Luther said of God that he was "the omnipotent God who creates everything out of nothing." For Kierkegaard, God's will is paralyzed by His immutability, as man's will is by Necessity—and, indeed, in even greater measure. Before His beloved son who agonized on the cross, God feels the horror of His impotence, as does Kierkegaard before Regine Olsen whom he tortures; he feels that he must run, do something, but at the same time he is aware that he is wholly in the power of "the categories of his thought" and cannot move any of his limbs.

Luther, it is known, spoke also of *de servo arbitrio*—of the bound will, but his *de servo arbitrio* was concerned only with man. For Kierkegaard, as for Socrates and Spinoza, *de servo arbitrio* extends likewise to God. There was one moment, however, when Kierkegaard resolved to seek salvation in the Absurd. By virtue of the Absurd, he tells us, God could decide for the "suspension of the ethical," could return Isaac to Abraham, could recall a dead man to life, etc.—that is, overcome His immutability. But even when he proclaimed the omnipotence of God, Kierkegaard did not succeed in ridding himself of the thought that "in the world of the spirit" there is, there must be, a certain order—different from what we observe here on earth, yet a strict, eternal order: there the sun does not rise equally on the good and the wicked, there only he who works eats, etc. Accordingly, Abraham's faith, no matter what Kierkegaard says, was not at all a "suspension of the ethical." On the contrary, in the final analysis it appears that Abraham's faith obeyed the demands of the "ethical." Despite what he has told us, Kierkegaard did not perceive in Abraham the free fearlessness of a man behind whom stands the omnipotent God; Abraham was in his eyes a "knight of resignation" (to use his own language), just as God, who abandoned His son, was only a "knight of resignation." Abraham's faith, for Kierkegaard, is not God's gift, it is his own desert. Man must believe, Kierkegaard endlessly repeats, and he who accomplishes this duty "works" and acquires by his work the right to the goods laid up for the just in the kingdom of the spirit where the sun rises only on the "just." Virtue, like faith, consists in living in the categories in which we think. God must be immutable—and He sacrifices His son: Abraham must obey God—and he raises his knife over Isaac. The life of the spirit begins beyond the boundary of the "you must" from which God is no more free than man.

From where did Kierkegaard take this truth? The Bible does not at all represent God as immutable, and in the Bible the father of faith, Abraham, does not always obey God. When God, inflamed with anger against men, decides to make them perish through the flood, the righteous Noah does not enter into dispute with Him but locks himself in his ark, happy to save his own life and that of his dear ones. But Abraham argued with God about Sodom and Gomorrah, and God forgot that He is immutable and gave in to his "servant." It is obvious that biblical "faith" has nothing in common with obedience, and that every "you must" is located in regions where the rays of faith do not penetrate. Kierkegaard himself writes in the *Sickness Unto Death* about the mysterious words of St. Paul—"all that does not come of faith is sin" (Romans 14, 23): "that the opposite of sin is not virtue but faith constitutes one of the most decisive definitions of Christianity." And he repeats this several times in the course of the book. In *The Concept of Dread* he writes: "The opposite of freedom is guilt." But if this is so, if to sin and guilt faith and freedom are opposed, then do not Kierkegaard's reflections on the order and laws that rule in the world of the spirit show that man has neither faith nor freedom and that he knows only guilt and impotent virtue? Does it not appear that Kierkegaard has drawn his Christian edification not from the Absurd that he glorified, not from the Bible that he considered as the revelation of truth, but from the "knowledge" that the wisest among men brought us after eating from the fruits of the tree of knowledge?

Speaking of the first man, Kierkegaard declares with assurance in *The Concept of Dread*: "Innocence is ignorance. In the state of innocence man is determined not as mind but as soul, in unmediated union with his nature. The mind is still dormant in man. This idea is in harmony with the Bible which denies to man in the state of innocence knowledge of the difference between good and evil." Indeed, the Bible says that in the state of innocence man did not know the difference between good and evil. But this was not a weakness, a defect; on the contrary, it was a power, a tremendous advantage. Man as he left the hands of the Creator did not know shame, and this also constituted a great advantage. The knowledge of good and evil, as well as of shame, came to him only after he had tasted the fruits of the forbidden tree. This is incomprehensible to us, just as we do not understand how these fruits could bring him death. And relying on the infallibility of our reason, we wish with all our powers that the mind should be dormant in the man who does not know the difference between good and evil. But the Bible does not say this. The Bible says, on the contrary, that all the misfortunes of man come from knowledge. This is also the meaning of the words of St. Paul quoted by Kierkegaard: "all that does not come of faith is sin." In its very essence knowledge, according to the Bible, excludes faith and is the sin *par excellence* or the original sin.

Contrary to what Kierkegaard asserts, it must be said that it was precisely the fruits of the tree of knowledge which lulled the human mind to sleep. This is why God forbade Adam to eat of them. The words that God addressed to Adam, "As for the tree of knowledge of good and of evil, you shall not eat of it, for on the day that you eat thereof you shall surely die," are in complete disagreement with our conception of knowledge as well as our conception of good and evil. But their meaning is perfectly clear and admits of no tortured interpretation. I repeat once more: they constitute the only true critique of pure reason that has ever been formulated here on earth. God clearly said to man that he must not put his trust in the fruits of the tree of knowledge, for they carry with them the most terrible dangers. But Adam, like Hegel later, "opposed distrust to distrust." And when the serpent assured him that the fruits were good to eat, that having eaten of them men would become like God, Adam and Eve succumbed to the temptation. This is what the Bible tell us. This is how St. Paul understood the biblical account, it is also how Luther understood it. St. Paul says that when Abraham went to the Promised Land he departed without knowing where he was going. This signifies that only he attains the Promised Land who takes no account of knowledge, who is free of knowledge and of its truths: where he arrives will be the Promised Land.

The serpent said to the first man: "You shall be like God, knowing good and evil." But God does not know good and evil. God does not *know* anything, God *creates* everything. And Adam, before his fall, participated in the divine omnipotence. It was only after the fall that he fell under the power of knowledge and at that same moment lost the most precious of God's gifts—freedom. For freedom does not consist in the possibility of choosing between good and evil, as we today are condemned to think. Freedom consists in the force and power not to admit evil into the world. God, the freest being, does not choose between good and evil. And the man whom He had created did not choose either, for there was nothing there to choose: evil did not exist in paradise. Only when man, obeying the suggestion of a force hostile and incomprehensible to us, held forth his hand towards the tree did his mind fall asleep and did he become that feeble being, subject to alien principles, that we now see. This is the meaning of the "fall" according to the Bible. This appears to us so highly fantastic that even men who considered the Bible an inspired book attempted by every means to attach to it commentaries that would modify its meaning. Kierkegaard in this respect was, as we have seen, no exception. According to him, following the sin man, having learned to distinguish good and evil, awoke from his sleeping state. But then what kind of sin would this be? Would we not in that case have to admit—as Hegel thought—that it was not the serpent but God who had deceived man?

Kierkegaard could not resolve to acknowledge this openly, but it is to this conclusion precisely that his commentaries in fact lead. He declares: "I shall say frankly that I cannot form any precise idea of the serpent. Above all, the serpent places us before the difficulty that the temptation comes from outside." No doubt, according to the Bible, the temptation came from without. And it is likewise beyond doubt that there is here something monstrous for our reason and still more so for our morality. But did not Kierkegaard himself invoke the Absurd, did he not speak to us in an inspired tone of the "suspension of the ethical?" Why then, in the face of the most troubling enigma that the Bible poses to us, does he turn again to reason and morality? Whence did this "temptation" come to him? From without or from within? And is there not here something more terrible, infinitely more terrible, that temptation? Kierkegaard could not form any precise idea of the serpent, and yet he himself has told us of the fearful anxiety experienced by the man who feels that he must run as quickly as possible but that a mysterious force paralyses him and prevents him from making the slightest movement! And not only Kierkegaard but God also is in the power of this force that has paralyzed His will. What then is this force? Is the biblical serpent, perhaps, merely a symbol, merely an image of that which determined Kierkegaard's fate, which determines all men's fate? Is not to forget the serpent under the pretext that it is impossible to bring it into our thought equivalent to renouncing that truth that the biblical account of the fall reveals to us by substituting for it theories drawn from our own "experience?"

Kierkegaard does not raise such a question. He wishes unconditionally to "understand," to "explain" the fall, and yet he never stops repeating that it is inexplicable, that it does not admit of explanation. Accordingly he tries in every way to discover some lack, some defect in the state of innocence. This state, he says, "includes peace and calmness, and yet there is in it something else still; this is not disturbance nor struggle—there is nothing for which one could struggle! What then is it?—Nothingness! What result does this nothingness produce? It produces anxiety. The profoundest mystery of innocence is that it is at the same time anxiety. . . . Psychology has never concerned itself with the concept of anxiety, wherefore I must draw attention to the fact that it is necessary to sharply distinguish anxiety from fear and other similar states; the latter always relate to something definite, while anxiety is the reality of freedom as possibility before all other possibility." Again we ask ourselves: "whence did Kierkegaard take this? Who revealed to him the secret of innocence?" The Bible says not a word of it. According to the Bible, shame and anxiety came only after the fall and proceed not from innocence but from knowledge. Thus anxiety is not the reality of freedom but the manifestation of the loss of freedom. Even more: in the Bible the anxiety that was born after the fall is strictly bound up with the threat of numerous calamities—you shall eat your bread in the sweat of your brow, you shall bear children in pain, sicknesses, privations, death, all the sufferings that came to the afflicted Job, the no less afflicted Kierkegaard and Abraham himself, at least potentially, for Abraham stood to lose what was dearest to him in the world.

But Kierkegaard felt that if he admitted that anxiety was born after the fall and that it is the expression not of the reality of freedom but of the loss of freedom, he would have had to agree to something the very idea of which appeared to him unbearable: he would have had to speak aloud his "secret" and, ignoring the judgment of the "ethical," call it by its true name or at least admit in general terms that he had broken with Regine Olsen not by virtue of the "immutability" of his nature but by virtue of the "necessity" that had enchained him. This he could not resolve to do. If Kierkegaard had had a son who was as dear to him as Isaac was to Abraham, he would have had the courage to offer him up as a sacrifice. But to cover himself with shame in the eyes of the "ethical"—no, this he would not have consented to do, even if God Himself had demanded it. I think that one can say the same of Nietzsche. He accepted all the sufferings to which he was condemned but, put to the torture, he continued to repeat that necessity did not offend him, that he even loved it. Just as in Kierkegaard, the ontological category of necessity "changes itself" in him into the ethical category of "immutability" from which God can escape no more than man.

It is in this that the result of the fruits of the tree of knowledge consists, here is the meaning of the "fall of man." In what is only an empty phantom, in nothingness, man suddenly perceives omnipotent necessity. That is why everything that the fallen man undertakes to save himself only brings him closer to the abyss. He wishes to flee "necessity," and he changes it into an immutability from which it is impossible to escape. Certainly he cannot fight against necessity, but he can hate it, curse it. But immutability must be adored, for it leads him to the kingdom of the "spirit," it gives him the "eyes of the mind" and thanks to the "third kind of knowledge" it brings to birth in him "love for what is eternal and infinite, the intellectual love of God." Kierkegaard began by perceiving in innocence and ignorance anxiety before nothingness. In order to understand and explain this anxiety, he recalled the fear that is aroused in children by frightening fairy tales. From anxiety before nothingness and from childish terror he passed abruptly to the horrors of real life with which his own existence was filled.

We recall what Kierkegaard has told us of the horrors he underwent. One would think that he would have concentrated all his powers on rooting out of his life the principle that had introduced these horrors into it. But, on the contrary, he wishes to justify, to legitimize, to confer eternity on this principle. The anxiety before nothingness, from which have sprung all the evils of existence, he discovers in man in the state of innocence. No great perspicacity is required to perceive in this nothingness not that ordinary and impotent nothingness which is incapable of putting an obstacle to the slightest human interests, but the omnipotent Necessity before which human thought has throughout all time bowed. But if this is so, if nothingness possesses this tremendous, even though negative and destructive, power—what makes Kierkegaard say that he does not understand the role of the serpent in the account of the fall? For the serpent was just that terrible nothingness, that "monster without whose killing man cannot live," to speak as Luther did.

Should Kierkegaard not have known this? Was it not the anxiety before nothingness that had risen between him and Regine Olsen, between God and His beloved son? It is here only that the profound meaning of the apostle's words, "everything that does not come of faith is sin," appears. Knowledge did not liberate Kierkegaard but bound him, just as it binds all of us. Nothingness is not a nothing, it is a something, and it is not given anyone to kill it, to deprive it of its annihilating power. But if this is so, the ignorance of the first man could not last forever: at a certain moment his eyes had to be "opened," he had to "learn." And this moment, despite what the Bible says, was not a fall but the birth of mind in man, the birth of mind in God Himself. The biblical revelation leads to the same result as the pagan wisdom: there is no force that can deliver men from the power of necessity, of nothingness, of the sufferings and evils they bring. We must accept all this, we must live with all this. Religion and philosophy, as well as ordinary good sense, are completely in accord here. The only thing religion and philosophy can offer us is an edification which, by human reckoning, is worse than the most frightful calamities. But we have no choice. The choice has already been made for man as well as for God. Both man and God act "solely out of the laws of their own nature and are not coerced by any one." The law of human nature is necessity. The law of God's nature is immutability or, to put it differently, necessity transformed into an ethical category. Had Kierkegaard not perceived in his relationships with Regine Olsen that very necessity which condemned God to remain a powerless spectator of the sufferings of His beloved son on the cross?

XV

Kierkegaard declared that before Abraham raising his knife over Isaac we feel a *horror religiosus*. But that is not so. We feel horror, and that extreme form of horror which is worthy of the epithet *religiosus*, when we see that the monster named necessity, that is, nothingness, approaches man while he, as if under the influence of a supernatural spell, not only cannot make the least movement, not only does not permit himself to express his despair and his protest through an anguished cry—as happens in nightmares—but, on the contrary, strains all the faculties of his soul to justify and to "understand," that is, to transform into an eternal truth what is given to him in experience merely as a fact. Kierkegaard does not stop repeating: "the possibility of freedom does not consist in the power to choose between good and evil. Such an interpretation conforms as little to the Bible as to thought. Possibility consists in the fact that man 'can.'" He says, "original sin takes place in impotence," and "anxiety is the dizziness of freedom." But to overcome his impotence, to leave his dizziness, to conquer anxiety, to realize the power that promises him freedom is infinitely more difficult for man than to choose between good and evil.

Kierkegaard began by declaring that God can return Isaac to Abraham, restore his children and wealth to Job, and unite the poor young man with the princess, but ended by taking away from God His beloved son, that is, reduced God's freedom to the possibility of choosing between good and evil: the immediately given must be accepted by all—by God as well as men. This "truth," that did not exist for the first man, became on the day Adam tasted the fruits of the tree of knowledge the principle of thought for all times. And it is only by accepting this truth that man can enter into the "kingdom of the spirit." Kierkegaard's "kingdom of the spirit" means: the immediate deliverances of consciousness are invincible, it is impossible to escape them, the salvation of man lies in "you shall be like God, knowing good and evil."

Towards the end of his life Kierkegaard became enraged when he heard a pastor console a mother who had lost her child by recalling to her how God had tried Abraham and Job. Christianity brings not consolation but an edification which, like Socrates', is worse than all evils. As can be seen from certain "indirect" confessions, Kierkegaard tried to arouse anxiety and horror of life in the soul of the young Regine Olsen. He did not succeed, it is true, in "raising" her to himself. Despite all his cleverness, he did not even suspect, it seems, what he was doing in the soul of the young woman; this trial he was spared. When he related that his beloved was seventeen years old and he seven hundred, he imagined that, at the cost of an apparently innocent exaggeration, he had justified himself before the "ethical." But this was not an exaggeration, it was a lie and a by no means innocent lie. He was not seven hundred years old, he was seventy; an old man of seventy was engaged to a girl of seventeen and, seeing that he could not recover his youth, that God Himself could not return it to him, he threw himself desperately toward the tree of the knowledge of good and evil and wished to force Regine Olsen to follow him. Necessity is transformed under our eyes into immutability. Bewitched by anxiety before the primordial nothingness that rises between Himself and His son, as it arose between Kierkegaard and Regine, God Himself loses His omnipotence and becomes as weak as man whom He created. This means: when knowledge destroyed our freedom, sin took possession of our soul. Not only do we not dare to return to the state of ignorance, but ignorance seems to us a slumber of the spirit.

Kierkegaard appeals to the Absurd, but in vain: he appeals to it but is incapable of realizing it. He speaks to us constantly of the existential philosophy; he rails at speculation and the speculators with their "objective" truths but, like Socrates and Spinoza, he himself aspires to live and oblige others to live in the categories in which they think. He refers incessantly to Scripture, but in the depths of his soul he is convinced, he "knows" that "God did not wish to teach the Israelites the absolute attributes of His essence. . . . Therefore He did not appeal to them with reasons but with the sound of trumpets, thunders and lightnings." All of us, furthermore, are persuaded that only "grounds or reasons" lead us to the truth; as for celestial thunder, it is only an empty sound. The "you shall be like God" has seduced us and that "enchantment and supernatural slumber" of which Pascal spoke has taken possession of us. And the more we try to subordinate our life to our thought, the heavier our slumber becomes. Socrates' "I know that I know nothing," Spinoza's "third kind of knowledge,"

Kant's reason that "aspires eagerly to universal and necessary judgments"—all these cannot deliver man from his somnolence, cannot restore to him the freedom that he has lost, the freedom of ignorance, the freedom not to know. We "accept" the dishonoring of our daughters, the killing of our sons, the destruction of our fatherland, that "God has neither purpose nor end," that it belongs to metaphysics (which this does not at all concern) to decide whether God exists, whether our soul is immortal, whether our will is free, while we, to whom this is more important than anything else in the world, are forced to crush in ourselves all the *lugere et detestari*, to submit in advance "with equanimity" to the decisions of metaphysics, whatever these may be, and even to consider this submission a virtue and to see in virtue the supreme happiness.

The philosophy which begins with necessary truths can only end in a sublime edification. And the religion which, to obtain the approval of philosophy, sees in the ignorance of the first man a slumbering of the spirit can only conclude with a no less sublime edification. Socrates and Spinoza spoke of the bull of Phalaris, Kierkegaard, of the happiness that is more terrible than the worst human torments. And, indeed, there is no other way out. As long as we submit to the domination of the Socratic knowledge, as long as we do not find the freedom of ignorance, we shall remain prisoners of that enchantment which transforms man from *res cogitans* (a thinking thing) into *asinus turpissimus* (a most infamous ass).

But can man by his own efforts escape from the magic circle into which Necessity has pushed him? The horror of the fall, the horror of the original sin of which Nietzsche and Luther have told us, consists precisely in the fact that man seeks his salvation just where his ruin awaits him. Necessity does not offend the fallen man. He loves it, he venerates it, and this veneration is in his eyes the testimony of his own grandeur and virtue, as Nietzsche who reproved Socrates' decadence has himself confessed. And Spinoza, following the thought of the wisest of men, sings the glory of Necessity. The capacity "to endure with equanimity" everything that fate decrees no longer offends him, it even rejoices him. It brings to men, as the most precious *docet* (teaching), the commandment *non ridere, non lugere, neque detestari, sed intelligere* (not to laugh, not to weep nor curse, but understand), and the indifference to "things that are not in our power"—the raping of daughters, the murdering of sons, etc. Kierkegaard hands God Himself over to the power of Necessity, upon which he confers the nobler name immutability, in order to redeem the offences that he had committed against the "ethical." The "ethical," that is, the fruits of the tree of the knowledge of good and evil, of which Aristotle tried to rid himself by means of his minimum of temporal goods, has destroyed everything and has led man to the abyss of nothingness.

It is thus alone that one can understand the "cruelty" that Kierkegaard and Nietzsche openly taught and that was already present in Socrates' and Spinoza's doctrine, hidden behind their *beatitudines*. This "cruelty" reveals the true meaning, the hidden meaning of the words "you will be like God." Behind Socrates' and Spinoza's apparent calmness one senses the same horror of the rejected *lugere et detestari* that one hears in the flaming words of Kierkegaard and Nietzsche: it is not given the fallen man to reconquer his lost freedom by his own "works." Knowledge and virtue have paralyzed our will and have plunged our spirit into a somnolence such that we see our perfection in impotence and submission. But if it is not given us to break the circle "by our own works" and attain true being, perhaps what "happens" to us independently of our will, contrary almost to our will, will transport us beyond the limits of the enchanted kingdom where we are condemned to draw out our existence. Besides virtue and knowledge there are still in man's life the horrors of which Kierkegaard and Nietzsche spoke so much and with which Socrates' and Spinoza's *docet* and edification are permeated. Whatever they may do, the knowledge that suggests to us that Necessity is invincible and the wisdom that assures us that the virtuous man will enjoy happiness even in the bull of Phalaris never succeed in extinguishing in us the *lugere et detestari* [weeping and cursing]. And it is out of these *lugere et detestari,* these horrors of life, that the terrible hammer of God, the *malleus Dei* of the prophets and Luther, is forged. But the hammer is not directed against the living man, as Nietzsche and Kierkegaard, who followed the way traced by Socrates and Spinoza, believed. "Because man is presumptuous and imagines himself to be wise, righteous and holy, it is necessary that he be humbled by the law, that thus that beast—the illusion of righteousness—without whose killing man cannot live, be put to death."

Put into modern language, we find that man must awake from his millennial sleep and decide to think in the categories in which he lives. Knowledge has transformed the real into the necessary and taught us to accept everything that fate decrees. And here precisely is the dizziness, the impotence, the paralysis, the death even—it sometimes seems—of freedom; to speak as Spinoza did, man is changed from a *res cogitans* into an *asinus turpissimus*. Can a living man, a free man, accept the dishonoring of his daughters, the murder of his sons, the destruction of his fatherland? Not only men but the very stones would have wept, Kierkegaard tells us, if they had known the sufferings with which his life was filled, but men laughed when they listened to him. If the word "sin," which today is forgotten, still has any meaning whatsoever, then the most terrible, the mortal, unpardonable sin consists in this acceptance and still more in the edification, in the equanimity, which "true philosophy" offers us and on which it rests. It is here that we must seek that "monster without whose killing man cannot live." Hypnotized by the false "you shall be like God, knowing good and evil," which since Socrates has become the principle of thought for all times, Kierkegaard and Nietzsche themselves directed all their powers to convincing man that he must renounce "the things that are not in our power" and that "happiness is not the reward of virtue but virtue itself." "Arguments," whatever they may be, are incapable of shaking man's conviction regarding the omnipotence of Necessity. But under the blows of the *malleus Dei,* the so greatly scorned *lugere et detestari* are transformed into a new power that awakes us from our slumber and gives us the audacity to enter into a struggle against the monster. The horrors on which Necessity established itself are then turned against it. And in this supreme, mortal combat man perhaps succeeds in delivering himself from knowledge and reconquering true freedom, the freedom from knowledge which the first man had lost.

III

On the Philosophy of the Middle Ages

[Concupiscentia Irresistibilis]

"If you wish to subject everything to yourself,
subject yourself to reason."

—Seneca

" . . . all these things will I give thee, if thou wilt fall
down and worship me . . . Get thee hence, Satan:
for it is written, Thou shalt worship the Lord
thy God, and Him only shalt thou serve."

—Matthew 4:9–10

I

One of the latest works of Etienne Gilson, the eminent historian of the philosophy of the Middle Ages, is entitled *L'esprit de la philosophic medievale*. Its subject, however, is much more comprehensive than one would assume from the
title. Here, indeed, he speaks not only as a historian of philosophy but as a philosopher. Utilizing the rich historical and philosophical materials gathered in
the course of long years of fruitful work, he raises with rare mastery and solves
one of the fundamental and most difficult of philosophical questions: Was there
a Judeo-Christian philosophy and—this is particularly important—how was
such a philosophy possible and what novelty did it bring to human thought?

At first glance it seems that the expression "Judeo-Christian philosophy"
contains an inner contradiction, especially in the sense that Gilson confers upon
it. According to Gilson, the Judeo-Christian philosophy is a philosophy which
has as its source the biblical revelation. At the same time he believes that every
philosophy worthy of the name is a rational philosophy which is based on evidence and leads, or at least tends to lead, to demonstrable, indisputable truths.
But all revealed truths, Gilson insistently and even, one might say, joyously emphasizes, have disdained demonstrations. "Greek thought," he says, "did not attain the essential truth that the biblical word 'Hear, O Israel, the Lord our God,
the Lord is one' with one blow *and without a shadow of proof*[1] proclaims."[2] And
further, "Here again not a word of metaphysics, but God has spoken, the matter
is settled, and it is the Book of Exodus that sets up the principle on which the
whole Christian philosophy will henceforth be suspended."[3] And for the third
time: "Nothing is better known than the first verse of the Bible, 'In the beginning
God created the heavens and the earth.' Here again not a trace of philosophy.
God no more justifies in a metaphysical way the statement of what He does than
the definition of what He is."[4] And so it is throughout Scripture: God does not
justify Himself, does not prove, does not argue, that is, He delivers His truths
quite otherwise than does metaphysics. Nevertheless the truths that He proclaims are as convincing as those that our natural reason succeeds in producing
and, above all, they are self-evident. Gilson repeats this with the same insistence
when he declares that the biblical truths are not at all concerned about their
demonstrability. "The first of all the commandments is this: 'Hear, O Israel,'" he
quotes Mark 12:29 and adds immediately, "But this 'I believe in one God' of the
Christians, the first article of their faith, appeared at the same time as a rational,
irrefutable self-evidence."[5] And then also: "In delivering in this simple formula—'in the beginning God created the heavens and the earth'—the secret of His

creative action, it seems that God gives to men one of those puzzling words long sought, of which one is sure in advance that they exist, that one will never find them unless they are given to us, and whose self-evidence nevertheless forces itself upon us with an invincible power as soon as they are given to us."[6] He quotes Lessing: "Without doubt, as Lessing profoundly said, when the religious truths were revealed they were not rational, but they were revealed in order to become rational." To be sure, he has to restrict Lessing's thought, and this is extremely significant: "Not all, perhaps, but at least certain ones—and here lies the meaning of the question to which the chapters that follow will try to find the answer." It is with this sentence that he finishes the first chapter of the first book.

I could multiply quotations on this matter from Gilson's book, but this seems to me unnecessary. The sentences that I have already quoted show the reader in what direction Gilson tries to orient our thought: the revealed truth is founded on nothing, proves nothing, is justified before nothing and—despite this—is transformed in our mind into a justified, demonstrated, self-evident truth. Metaphysics wishes to possess the revealed truth and it succeeds in doing so: this idea, which constitutes in a way the *leitmotif* of Gilson's beautiful book, permits the author to establish a strict bond between medieval philosophy, on the one hand, and ancient and modern philosophy, on the other. Just as in Hegel, philosophy, in the course of its millennial history, remains one: the Greeks sought what the scholastics sought and what the father of modern philosophy, Descartes, sought; and all who followed Descartes never could and never even wished to escape the influence of the philosophy of the Middle Ages. Gilson quotes the phrase of Clement of Alexandria which shows that Christian thought in its beginnings already admitted two "Old Testaments"—the Bible and Greek philosophy;[7] he indicates that the philosophers of the Middle Ages believed that the Delphic "know thyself" had "fallen from heaven." It is therefore wrong, according to him, to believe with Hamelin that Descartes reasoned as if nothing had been done in the domain of philosophy after the Greeks. Not only Descartes but all of his successors, up to the most eminent representatives of modern philosophy, were strictly bound to the scholastics: Leibniz, Spinoza, Kant and all the German idealists followed the way traced by scholastic thought; they also considered Greek philosophy as a kind of second "Old Testament."

But modern philosophy could not have accomplished what it did without the scholastics, who succeeded in joining to the Bible and to the truths revealed by the Bible the self-evident truths discovered by the Greeks. The very title of Descartes' basic work, "Meditations on metaphysics, wherein the existence of God and the immortality of the soul are demonstrated" and "the kinship of his proofs for the existence of God with those of St. Augustine and even those of St.

Thomas" are already sufficiently persuasive in this respect. It is especially important to indicate that all the Cartesian system "rests on the idea of one omnipotent God who somehow created Himself, even more naturally created eternal truths—including those of mathematics—, who created the universe *ex nihilo*." No less significant is the conclusion of Leibniz's *Discours métaphysique* that Gilson quotes in its entirety and of which he says: "These are not the words of a man who believed himself to have come after the Greeks as if nothing had been between them and himself." According to Gilson, one could say the same of Kant, "if people did not so often forget to complete his *Critique of Pure Reason* with his *Critique of Practical Reason*. One could even say as much of our contemporaries." So he finishes his introductory remarks on the role of medieval philosophy in the history of the development of modern philosophical thought. And he declares no less categorically in the final chapter of the second volume of his work, "It will not suffice for a metaphysical thesis to have forgotten its religious origin to become rational. It would then be necessary to expel from philosophy as well as from its history—along with the God of Descartes—the God of Leibniz, of Malebranche, of Spinoza and of Kant, for no more than the God of St. Thomas would these have existed without the God of the Bible and the Evangelist."

At the same time Gilson is not at all inclined to minimize the importance of the influence Greek philosophy exercised on medieval philosophy, as a less learned historian and one more preoccupied with apologetic than with the philosophical problems he has raised would have tried to do. I do not mean by this that Gilson does not have his own clear and determinate conception of the meaning and importance of the work accomplished by the Judeo-Christian philosophy and that, under the cover of historical questions, he tries to avoid the heavy responsibility that falls necessarily on one who must express himself openly on the very essence of the matter. On the contrary, I repeat, he attacks with noble audacity questions of principle and, if for this he utilizes historical materials, it is only insofar as he can count on finding in history data that will permit us to bring into clarity an extremely complex and confused situation— the situation in which European thought found itself when it recognized the necessity of incorporating into the truths drawn at the price of long and painful effort by the ancient world the "revelations" which suddenly fell on the world from the heavens when the Bible was disclosed to it. Gilson declares unhesitatingly, "Philosophy, in making itself more truly philosophy, becomes more Christian." Here finally is the basic thought of his work and, far from hiding it, he sets it in the foreground. "The conclusion which results from this study or, rather, the axis that traverses it from end to end, is that everything happens as if the Judeo-Christian revelation had been a religious source of philosophical development, the Latin Middle Ages being, in the past, the testimony *par ex-cellence* of this development."[8] And yet he shows himself so objective and at the same time so convinced of the correctness of the conception he defends that he declares with the same assurance: "One could legitimately ask if there would ever have been a Christian philosophy if Greek philosophy had not existed."[9] And again: "If it is to the Bible that we owe a philosophy that is Christian, it is to the Greek tradition that Christianity owes the fact that it has a philosophy."[10] Whereas Plato and Aristotle have sunk into the past of history, "Platonism and Aristotelianism continued to live in a new way by collaborating in a work for which they did not know themselves destined. It is thanks to them that the Middle Ages could have a philosophy. It was they who taught the idea of 'the perfect work of reason'; they pointed out, along with the master problems, the rational principles which govern their solution and the techniques through which they are justified. The debt of the Middle Ages to Greece is immense. . . . "[11]

Such, in a few words, are the essential ideas of Gilson's remarkable work. Without the ancient philosophy which set out from self-evident truths discovered by natural reason, medieval philosophy would not have existed; and without the medieval philosophy, which assimilated to itself the Bible's revelations, there would not have been any modern philosophy. It is clear that the problems raised and resolved by Gilson transcend the limits indicated by the relatively modest title of his book. It is not a matter of the spirit of medieval philosophy— in other words, of determining and characterizing in a more or less complete and detailed fashion what the most remarkable and influential thinkers of the Middle Ages did. To be sure, such a subject would have presented exceptional interest, especially treated by a specialist in the material and a writer like Gilson; his work would have been valuable even if he had held simply to the promises of his title. But the question the author has actually raised excites us even more. Revelation, he himself has told us, never proves anything, is founded on nothing, and is never justified. Now rationalism consists essentially in the fact that it founds, proves and justifies each of its assertions. How, then, could medieval philosophy discover a metaphysics in the Book of Exodus? The essential thing for metaphysics is not only to present us with truths but to do it in such a way that these truths are irrefutable and that there be no place beside them for other truths contradicting them. Can there, then, be a metaphysics where all proofs, on principle and once for all, are rejected? All the fundamental truths of revelation have come to man without "a shadow, without a trace of proof," as Gilson has told us, speaking in his own name and in the name of medieval philosophy. Even more, we read at the end of the third chapter of the second volume: "The metaphysics of the Book of Exodus penetrates to the very heart of epistemology, in that it makes the intellect and its subject dependent on God, from whom both draw their existence. What it brings us here that is new is the notion, unknown to the ancients, of a created truth, spontaneously ordained to the Being who is at the same time the end and the beginning, for it is by Him alone that it exists, as He alone can perfect and fulfill it."

That the metaphysics of the Book of Exodus is precisely such is beyond doubt: the God of Scripture is above the truth as well as the good. When Descartes says this he is only expressing what every line of the Bible asserts. But can this "new thing" which the Bible brought find any place in that conception of metaphysics that the ancient world had elaborated? And can Greek philosophy help the medieval thinker participate in such a truth? Greek philosophy set as its task the searching out of self-evident truths which, being self-evident, are also irrefutable. When Kant wrote at the beginning of his *Critique of Pure Reason* (First Edition), "Experience indeed teaches us what is but it does not say that what is must be precisely so and not otherwise; that is why experience does not give us true universality, and reason, which aspires avidly to this kind of knowledge, is irritated rather than satisfied by experience," he was only summing up in a few words what modern philosophy had inherited from ancient philosophy. Aristotle expresses himself similarly in his *Metaphysics:* "For the practical man well knows the 'that' but not the 'why'; but the theoretical man knows the why and the causal relationship."[12] Empirical knowledge consists in knowing how things happen in reality (*to hoti*) but it is not yet the knowledge why (*to dioti kai hê aitia*) what happens must happen precisely so and could not happen otherwise.[13]

Among the Greeks the idea of knowledge was indissolubly bound to the idea of necessity and constraint. And this is also true in the case of St. Thomas Aquinas: "The meaning of knowledge is that, of what is known, it is believed impossible for it to be otherwise."[14] Is it to be assumed that one can succeed in subjecting to the fundamental principles of Greek thought, or to reconciling with them, the metaphysics of the Book of Exodus which makes truth dependent on the will (the Greeks would have said—and rightly—the arbitrariness) of God? And then, how does one know to whom it is given to resolve this question: must we submit to the metaphysics of the Book of Exodus and accept its epistemology or, on the contrary, must we verify and correct the epistemology of the Book of Exodus by making use of the rational principles that Greek philosophy has transmitted to us? Descartes, we know, wholly accepted the "new thing" that the Bible had brought men: he declared that the self-evident truths had been created by God.

I shall return to this later, but I believe that it is well to recall in this connection now that Leibniz, who had quite as much right as Descartes to the title

"Christian philosopher" and whose philosophic genius was no smaller than that of Descartes, was horrified to see Descartes abandoning truth to "arbitrariness" even if it were the arbitrariness of God. This fact alone shows us the tremendous difficulties that are met by every attempt to force on the Biblical philosophy the principles on which the rational philosophy of the Greeks was founded and on which the rational philosophy of modern times is still founded. Who will settle the argument between Leibniz and Descartes? The philosophy of the Book of Exodus tells us that truth, like everything that exists, was created by God, that it is always in His power and that it is in this precisely that its high value and its superiority in relation to the uncreated truths of the Greeks consists. Descartes acknowledged this, Leibniz was indignant over it. The situation seems to have no way out and we, it seems, are then obliged forever to renounce any Judeo-Christian philosophy. No one can settle the argument between Descartes and Leibniz. For Leibniz, who all his life tried to reconcile reason and revelation, it was absolutely clear that the Cartesian solution radically denied the rights of reason: Descartes, however, who was no less perceptive than Leibniz, did not even suspect that he was ruining the sovereign rights of reason.

The situation becomes still more complicated by the fact that when medieval philosophy—which tried to draw from Scripture, according to the principles elaborated in Greece, the metaphysics of which it had need—found itself faced with the epistemological problem (I prefer to say, the metaphysics of knowledge), it appeared completely to have forgotten the passages of the Book of Genesis which relate directly to this problem. I am thinking about the story of the fall of the first man and the fruit of the tree of the knowledge of good and evil. If we wish to participate in the biblical epistemology or, to speak more exactly, in the metaphysics of knowledge, we must above all else realize as precisely as possible the meaning of this story.

II

This task is much more difficult than might appear at first blush. Gilson is certainly right: like the men of the Middle Ages we have inherited from the Greeks both the fundamental philosophical problems and the rational principles for their solution, and also the entire technique of our thought. How shall we succeed in reading and understanding Scripture not according to the teaching of the great Greek masters, but as they who have transmitted to us, by means of the Book of Books, that which they called the word of God wished and demanded of their readers? As long as the Bible was exclusively in the hands of the "chosen people," this question did not arise: it could at all events be assumed that men, when they listened to the words of Scripture, did not always find themselves under the dominion of rational principles and of that technique of thought which has somehow become our second nature, which we consider—without even realizing it—as the immutable conditions for the grasping and possession of truth. Gilson sees correctly also when he says that the medieval thinkers always tried to retain the spirit and letter of Scripture. But is good intention sufficient in this instance? Is a man educated by the Greeks capable of preserving that freedom which is the condition of the right understanding of what the Bible says?

When Philo of Alexandria undertook to present the Bible to the cultivated world of the Greeks, he found himself obliged to have recourse to the allegorical method: it was thus only that he could hope to persuade his listeners. Impossible indeed to contradict before educated people the principles of rational thought and the great truths that Greek philosophy, in the person of its most remarkable representatives, had brought to mankind! Furthermore, Philo himself, who had assimilated Greek culture, could not accept the Bible without first verifying it through the criteria which the Greeks had provided him for distinguishing truth from error. The result of this was that the Bible was "raised" to such a philosophic plane that it could amply satisfy the demands posed by the Hellenistic culture. Clement of Alexandria assumed the same role as Philo; it is not for nothing that Harnack calls him the Christian Philo. He set Greek philosophy on the same plane as the Old Testament and not only obtained the right to affirm (as we recall) that knowledge (*gnôsis*) is inseparable from eternal salvation but that if they were separable and if he, Clement, were offered the choice, he would have given the preference not to salvation but to *gnosis*. If one takes account even only of Philo and of Clement of Alexandria, it is clear in advance that neither the Fathers of the Church nor the philosophers of the Middle Ages could accept the account of original sin as it is found in Genesis, and that, in the face of this account, the thought of believers was placed before the fateful dilemma: either the Bible or the Greek "knowledge" and the wisdom founded on this knowledge.

Indeed, what is the content of these chapters of Genesis that concern the fall of the first man? God planted in paradise the tree of life and the tree of the knowledge of good and evil, and He said to man: "From every tree of paradise you may eat; however, from the tree of the knowledge of good and evil you shall not eat, for on the day that you eat thereof you shall surely die." While God ordinarily proclaims His truths "without any trace of proof," this time His prohibition is accompanied not by His sanction, as we have tried to believe in order to simplify the problem, but by His motivation: the day you taste the fruits of the tree of knowledge you shall surely die. A relationship is thus established between the fruits of the tree of knowledge and death. God's words do not mean that man will be punished for having disobeyed, but that knowledge hides in itself death. This appears beyond doubt if we recall the circumstances in which the fall took place. The serpent, craftiest of the animals created by God, asks the woman, "Why has God forbidden you to eat of the fruit of all the trees of paradise?" And when the woman replies to him that God had forbidden them only to eat of the fruits of a single tree that they might not die, the serpent answers, "You shall not die, but God knows that the day you eat of these fruits your eyes will be opened and you will be like God, knowing good and evil." "Your eyes will be opened," says the serpent. "You shall die," says God. The metaphysics of knowledge in Genesis is strictly tied to the metaphysics of being. If God has spoken truly, knowledge leads to death; if the serpent has spoken truly, knowledge makes man like God. This was the question posed before the first man, and the one posed before us now.

It is not necessary to say that the pious thinkers of the Middle Ages could not even for a moment admit the thought that truth was on the side of the tempting serpent. But the Gnostics declared openly that it was God and not the serpent who had deceived man. In our age Hegel was not at all embarrassed to say that the serpent had spoken the truth to the first man and that the fruits of the tree of knowledge became the source of philosophy for all time. If we ask on what side the truth is, and if we admit in advance that our reason is called to pronounce the final judgment in the argument between God and the serpent, no doubt is possible: it is the serpent who triumphs. And as long as reason remains "prince and judge of all," we cannot expect any other decision. Reason is the source of knowledge: how can it then condemn knowledge? On the other hand—we must not forget this—the first man possessed a certain knowledge. In the same book of Genesis it is said that when God created all the animals, He led them to the man in order that he might give a name to each.

But the man, seduced by the serpent, was not content with this knowledge: the "that" (*hoti*) did not suffice for him; he desired the "why" (*dioti*); the "that" irritated him just as it irritated Kant. His reason aspired avidly to universal and necessary judgments; he could not feel satisfied as long as he had not succeeded in transforming the truth that was "revealed" and situated above both the universal and the necessary into a self-evident truth that certainly deprives him of his freedom but protects him against the arbitrariness of God. Certain conscientious theologians, concerned no doubt with defending man against the arbitrariness of God, have tried to derive the Greek word *alêtheia* (truth) from *a-lan-thanô* (to open up, to reveal). In this way revelation was inwardly related to truth: revelation consisted in opening up the truth, and so there was no reason to fear that God could have abused His limitless freedom: the universal and necessary truth dominates God as well as man. It came finally to the same result as in Hegel: the serpent did not deceive the man. But it ended there not *explicite* but *implicite*. The theologians avoided Hegel's frankness.

The situation of the medieval philosophers who found themselves placed before the obligation of transforming the truths received from God "without any shadow of proof" into proven truths, into self-evident truths—as the principles of the Greeks demanded of them—differed in no way basically from that in which the first man found himself standing before the tree of knowledge. Gilson admirably shows us the almost superhuman efforts made by the philosophers of the Middle Ages to overcome the seduction of "knowledge" and also how this seduction took stronger and stronger hold on their minds. The thought of Anselm, he writes, "was long obsessed by the desire to find a direct proof of the existence of God, one that was based on the single principle of contradiction."[15] In another place he speaks of the emotion of the same Anselm, of St. Augustine and St. Thomas at the memory of these moments when "the opacity of faith suddenly gave way in them to the transparency of intelligence."[16] And the "most subtle intellect" of Duns Scotus himself who, with an incomparable daring, declared the total independence of God in relation to the highest and most immutable principles was even for him incapable of tearing out of his soul the *concupiscentia irresistibilis* (irresistible desire) which impelled him to replace faith with knowledge. Gilson quotes from his *De rerum prima principia* the following confession that is truly worthy of being reproduced in full: "Lord our God, when Moses asked you, as of a very truthful teacher, what name he should give you before the children of Israel, you replied: 'I am who I am.' You are then the true being, you are the total being. This is what I believe but it is this also—if possible—that I would wish to know."

One could, in this connection, reproduce still many other passages from scholastic thinkers quoted or not quoted by Gilson: the "knowledge" by means of which the serpent succeeded in seducing the first man continued to attract them with an irresistible force. "Experience" does not satisfy but rather irritates them, just as it was later to irritate Kant; they wish to know—in other words, to be convinced that what is not only is but cannot be other than it is and must necessarily be what it is. And they seek guarantees not from the prophet who brought God's word to them from Sinai nor even in God's word itself: their intellectual longing will be satisfied only when the word of God brought by the prophet will have obtained the blessing of the principle of contradiction or some other principle that is as immutable and impassive as the principle of contradiction. Now this is precisely what the first man wished when he stretched forth his hand to the tree of knowledge; it is this by which he let himself be tempted. He also wished "to know," not "to believe"; he saw in faith a kind of diminution, an injury to his human dignity, and he was certain of this when the serpent told him that after he had eaten of the fruits of the forbidden tree he would become like God—knowing.

I repeat: The medieval philosophers who aspired to transform faith into knowledge were far from suspecting that they were committing once again the act of the first man. Nevertheless it is impossible not to agree with Gilson when he writes, regarding the attitude of the Scholastics toward faith: "Faith as such suffices for itself, but it aspires to transmute itself in the understanding of its own content; it does not depend on the evidence of reason but, on the contrary, it is faith that engenders reason." And further, "This effort of the truth that is believed to change itself into the truth that is known is truly the life of Christian wisdom; and the body of rational truths that this effort gives us is the Christian philosophy itself."[17]

It may be supposed that the first man, when he heard the tempter's words, thought likewise: it seemed to him, too, that there was nothing dangerous or condemnable in his desire to know, that this desire was good. It is a remarkable thing: most of the great scholastic thinkers (there were, however, some exceptions: Peter Damian and his followers of whom we shall speak later) never wished to see and never came to understand that the original sin consisted in the fact that man had tasted of the fruits of the tree of knowledge. In this respect the mystics hardly distinguished themselves from the philosophers. The unknown author of the famous *Theologia deutsch* declares openly: Adam could have eaten twenty apples—no evil would have come of it; the evil was in his disobedience to God. St. Augustine says the same thing but in a less trenchant way: "For in that place of so much happiness God did not wish to create and plant evil. But obedience was inculcated by the commandment—a virtue that in the rational creature is, so to speak, the mother and keeper of all virtues, for the creature was so made that it is useful for it to be subjected to God but injurious for it to do its own will and not the will of Him by Whom it was created."[18] And so perceptive an eye as that of Duns Scotus did not succeed in distinguishing (or perhaps did not dare to distinguish) the true significance of the biblical account. "The first sin of man . . . according to what Augustine said, was an immoderate love of union with his wife." In itself Adam's act, the eating of the fruits of the tree of knowledge, was not evil.

Gilson very finely characterizes the attitude of the Middle Ages toward the biblical account of the fall: "This is why the first moral evil receives in the Christian philosophy a special name which extends to all the faults engendered by the first: sin. In using this word a Christian means always to signify that—as he understands it—moral evil, introduced by free will into a created universe, puts directly at stake the fundamental relationship of dependence which unites the creature with God. *The prohibition, so light and—so to speak—gratuitous, which God imposes on the perfectly useless use by man of one of the goods placed at his disposal*[19] was only the sensible sign of this radical dependence of the creature. To accept the prohibition was to recognize the dependence; to break the prohibition was to deny it and to proclaim that what is good for the creature is better than the divine good itself."[20]

The medieval philosophers never stopped reflecting on sin; moreover, they were not content with reflecting on it, they suffered from it. But they could never resolve to connect the fall of man with the fruits of the tree of the knowledge of good and evil. How could they resolve to do this since all—and we also, for that matter—have at the bottom of our hearts only one thought, only one care: "I believe, Lord, but if it is also possible, it is this that I would wish to know." They knew well that "obedience is the mother and keeper of all virtues," but they did not for an instant admit that the knowledge to which they aspired so eagerly could conceal sin within itself and were only astonished that the first man should have been incapable of submitting himself to a prohibition so insignificant, so easy, as not eating the fruit of one of the trees that grew in Eden. Yet the biblical story spoke to them clearly and distinctly of the fruit of the tree of knowledge, while only the truths that had come to them from the Greeks testified to *obedientia*.

The Greeks, indeed, placed obedience above everything else. Seneca's phrase is well known: "The Creator and Ruler of the world Himself once commanded, always obeys." For the Greeks there was always something suspicious in the *jubere* (commanding): it contained, in their eyes, the germ of limitless freedom, that is, a detestable arbitrariness, while the *parere* (obedience) was the principle and promise of the good. And they established on the parere the knowledge that puts an end to unbridled freedom.[21] It is enough to recall the dispute between Callicles and Socrates in Plato's *Gorgias,* which passed on to St. Augustine, the Fathers of the Church, Duns Scotus, and to all medieval philosophy the extraordinary, exclusive value that they accorded to the *parere* as well as to the knowledge that is based on the *parere,* and from which they also drew, along with this knowledge, the opposition between good and evil which, as Gilson has just told us, could not exist even for a moment without the idea of obedience. A breach occurred in the central or fundamental idea of the philosophy of the Middle Ages which aspired so passionately, so violently, to become Judeo-Christian: the Bible warned man of the horrible danger involved in tasting the fruits of the tree of knowledge, Greek philosophy considered *gnôsis* (knowledge) as the spiritual nourishment *par excellence* and saw the supreme dignity of man in his faculty of distinguishing between good and evil. Medieval philosophy was incapable of renouncing the Greek heritage and found itself obliged in the face of the fundamental problem of philosophy, the problem of the metaphysics of knowledge, to ignore the Bible.

III

It was not only the biblical account of the fall which put man on guard against the "knowledge" of the ancient world. The prophets and the apostles had risen with extreme force against the Graeco-Roman "wisdom." The medieval philosophers certainly knew this. Gilson cites in full the famous verses of the first chapter of the first letter of St. Paul to the Corinthians (19–25) on the impossibility of reconciling the truth of revelation with human truth, and I think it well to recall the passage here: "For it is written (Isaiah 29,14): 'I shall destroy the wisdom of the wise and I shall bring to nothing the prudence of the prudent.' Where is the wise? where is the scribe? where is the disputer of this world? Hath not God made foolish the wisdom of this world? For after that, in the wisdom of God, the world by wisdom knew not God, it pleased God by the foolishness of preaching to save them that believe . . . the foolishness of God is wiser than men; and the weakness of God is stronger than men."

Gilson indicates in a footnote that these words always inspired the enemies of the "Christian philosophy," among whom the first place is occupied by Tertullian who opposes, as is known, Jerusalem to Athens (*quid ergo Athenis et Hierosolymis?*—what has Athens to do with Jerusalem?). Yet the eminent historian does not believe that they could and should have stopped the medieval philosophers from their efforts to transform the truths of revelation into truths of rational knowledge. According to him, those who denied that a rational Judeo-Christian philosophy is possible could not base themselves either on the prophet Isaiah or on St. Paul. Indeed, to understand the true meaning of these words it is necessary, above all, to remember that for St. Paul the gospel is the way to salvation and not the way to knowledge. And then: "At the very moment that St. Paul proclaims the bankruptcy of Greek wisdom, he proposes to substitute for it something else, which is the person of Jesus Christ himself. What he intends to do is to eliminate the seeming Greek wisdom, which, in reality, is only foolishness, in the name of the seeming Christian foolishness, which is nothing but wisdom." All this is correct, but it is a commentary on Tertullian's opposition of Athens to Jerusalem rather than an objection to his position, for the Apostle still "proclaims the bankruptcy of Greek wisdom." What for Athens is wisdom is for

Jerusalem foolishness: Tertullian said nothing else. One cannot even say that Tertullian had denied the possibility of a Judeo-Christian philosophy. He wished only to secure freedom and independence for it, believing that it had to have its own source of truth, its own principles, its own problems—that were not those of the Greeks. According to him, if the revealed truth seeks to justify itself before our reason by means of the same procedures that the Greeks used to justify their truths, it will never succeed in arriving at this justification, or it will succeed only by denying itself, for what is foolishness for Athens is wisdom for Jerusalem and what is truth for Jerusalem is for Athens a lie. This is the meaning of the famous passage of his *De carne Christi* [On the Incarnation] which has long been quoted under the abbreviated and consequently weakened form *credo quia absurdum* (I believe because it is absurd), which even the mob repeats. In Tertullian we read: *Crucifixus est Dei filius: non pudet quia pudendum est; et mortuus est Dei filius: prorsus credibile quia ineptum est; et sepultus resurrexit: certum est quia impossible* (The son of God was crucified: it does not shame because it is shameful; and the son of God died: it is absolutely credible because it is absurd; and having been buried, he rose from the dead; it is certain because it is impossible).

Here is the same thought as in Isaiah and St. Paul but adapted to the Scholastic philosophical terminology. And yet it rebels to such a degree against the wisdom of the world that Leibniz, who reproduced these words, did not believe it necessary to stop and examine them; they are only a "religious phrase," says he. And he drops completely the beginning clause which ends with the words *non pudet, quia pudendum est* [it does not shame because it is shameful]. His hand, one may believe, did not have the power to reproduce words so immoral. Yet if Isaiah and St. Paul are right, Tertullian's declaration must serve as the introduction or *prolegomenato* the organon of the Judeo-Christian philosophy, which was called to proclaim to the world the new notion, completely ignored up until then, of "created truth." We must, before everything else, reject the basic categories of Greek thought, tear out from our being all the postulates of our "natural knowledge" and our "natural morality." Where the educated Greek opposes to us his imperious *pudet*, we shall say it is precisely for this reason that it is not shameful. Where reason proclaims *ineptum* (absurd), we shall say that it is precisely this that preferentially deserves our complete trust. And finally where it raises its *impossible*, we shall oppose our "it is certain." And when reason and morality will call before their tribunal the prophets and the apostles and along with them Him in whose name they dare defy the Greek philosophy, do you think that Tertullian will be afraid of the judgment, as Leibniz was?

I have already more than once had occasion to speak of Tertullian and of his violent attacks on Greek philosophy. But before passing on to an examination of the results to which the attempt of the medieval philosophers to establish a symbiosis between Greek knowledge and the revealed truth led, I would wish to dwell on two moments of the history of the development of European thought. I believe this will permit us to see more clearly into the question that concerns us here: what the essence of the Judeo-Christian philosophy was.

The history of philosophy is ordinarily divided into three periods: the ancient which ends with Plotinus, the philosophy of the Middle Ages which ends with Duns Scotus and William of Occam (after whom comes "the decay of Scholasticism"), and the modern which begins with Descartes and continues up to our own time and of which it is impossible to know where it will lead us. Now there is here an extraordinary fact: the philosophy of Plotinus is not only the culmination of the almost thousand-year development of Greek thought; it is also a defiance of this thought. Zeller was right: Plotinus lost confidence in philosophic thought; the fundamental principles and eternal truths of his predecessors ceased to satisfy him, and it seemed to him that these principles and these truths do not liberate the human spirit but enslave it. And this after he had held to them all his life and had taught others to follow them. His *Enneads* present, indeed, a puzzling mixture of two divergent streams of thought. If Zeller is right that Plotinus had lost confidence in thought, then this modern historian of philosophy is also right in greatly valuing Plotinus precisely because the latter, as the Greek tradition demanded of him, based all of his searchings for truth on the *dei* (must) and on *ex anankês* (necessarily); or in other words, he tried to obtain judgments rigorously proven and controlled, judgments that constrain. But he tried to obtain them, obviously, only to reject them despite himself. The "knowledge" which his predecessors had transmitted to him and which was founded on the necessity that constrains became unbearable to him precisely because it constrained him. He perceived in knowledge chains from which he had, at all costs, to escape. Knowledge does not liberate; it enslaves.

Plotinus seeks, then, a way out; he seeks salvation outside of knowledge. And he who had taught "the beginning was the logos, and everything is *logos,*" felt suddenly that the meaning of philosophy—"the most important thing," as he put it—consisted in the fact that it delivered from "knowledge": this was the meaning of his "ecstasy." Above all, one must "soar above knowledge" and awaken from the enchantment of all the *dei* (you must) and *ex anankês* (necessarily). Whence came this "must," whence came this "necessary" that has permeated human thought? On what does their force and power rest? The supreme principle—what Plotinus calls "the One"—knows neither the "must" nor the "necessary" and has no need of their support. "It requires no support, as though it could not carry itself" (*ou gar deitai hidryseôs, hôsper auto pherein ou dynamenon*). It lies "beyond reason and thought." It is free of all the limitations which the *nous* that "came after us" has invented.[22] And just as the One has need neither of support nor of foundation, likewise the man "awakened to himself no longer feels the need of any support, of any foundation whatsoever. He feels himself to belong to a higher fate (*praestantioris sortis*), throws far from himself all, the heavy "musts" and "of necessity," and like the gods of Greece does not touch the earth with his feet. It is hardly necessary to say that Plotinus, insofar as he tried "to soar above knowledge," did not leave any trace in history. The "to soar above knowledge" and the "it requires no support" were a break with the tradition of ancient thought which always sought knowledge and solid foundations. Rare are those who have had the courage to repeat after Zeller that Plotinus had lost confidence in thought. Most historians are interested in Plotinus only so long as they find in him the customary argumentation which convinces everyone and which rests on the omnipotence of Necessity. St. Augustine himself, who was constantly inspired by Plotinus (some pages of his work appear almost translated from the *Enneads*) did not wish, or did not dare, to follow Plotinus in rootlessness and took from Plotinus only what he could assimilate without denying the fundamental principles of Greek thought.

But the development of Greek philosophy stopped after Plotinus or, to put it more accurately, Greek philosophy decayed after Plotinus, just as Scholastic philosophy began to decay after Duns Scotus and Occam. Human thought then congealed into immobility and sank into endless commentaries on what had already been done, instead of going forward at its own risk and peril towards the puzzling unknown of which Plotinus had spoken. It is not for nothing, furthermore, that Plotinus himself says that when the soul approaches the limits of being it stops: "it is afraid that it has nothing." It is afraid to rid itself of the constraining "must" and "of necessity." It has so long borne their yoke that it seems to it that freedom is a principle of destruction, of annihilation. No one, then, follows the path indicated by Plotinus. History succeeded in turning the attention of later generations away from what had been most original and most daring in him—his cultivation of rootlessness (people ordinarily speak of Asiatic influences; it would perhaps be better to remember the "Asiatic" *ex auditu*). But the fact that the last of the great Greek philosophers allowed himself to shake the foundations upon which the ancient thought rested is impossible to deny; and even Zeller, always so prudent and objective, is obliged, as we have seen, to confirm this.

The second period of European philosophy ended in a similar fashion. Almost immediately after the brilliant Thomas Aquinas (and as if in response to him) the last great Scholastics rose with unheard of violence against all the "musts" and "of necessity" through the help of which thought subsisted and developed and to which were bound the goods promised by reason to man. Here finally is the meaning of what is ordinarily called their "voluntarism." Most of the historians of theology (particularly the Protestants) and most of the historians of philosophy have tried to weaken in one way or another the violence of the challenge thrown by the last great Scholastics to their predecessors, insofar as the latter tried to connect the truths of the Bible with the truths obtained by reason. And from their point of view these historians are right, just as they are when they try to "defend" Plotinus against the reproach that some people have made against him, to the effect that he exercised, through his doctrine, a destructive influence. History is bound to consider only those things to which it is given to determine future development. But the judgment of history is not the only judgment and it is not the final judgment.

If one wished to reduce to a brief formula the ideas that mankind received from ancient thought, I think it would be difficult to find anything better than what Plato says in the *Phaedo* and in the *Euthyphro* about reason and morality. There is no greater misfortune for a man, we read in the *Phaedo*, than to become a hater of reason, a *misologos*. The holy is not holy because the gods love it, but it is precisely because the holy is holy that the gods love it, says Socrates in the *Euthyphro*.

One could say without exaggeration that these words contain the two principal commandments of Greek philosophy, its *alpha* and *omega*. When we today still aspire so eagerly to truths that are universal and obligatory upon all, we are fulfilling the demands made by the "wisest of men." It is certain indeed that it was the "righteous" Socrates who inspired in his pupil Plato the worship that gods as well as mortals must render to reason and morality. And I would add that if Socrates had had to choose between reason and morality, and if he had agreed to admit even hypothetically that reason can be separated from morality—be it only for God—he would have renounced reason but would not have denied morality for anything in the world. Above all, he would not have agreed to free the gods from morality. That the gods in a pinch may soar with Plotinus above knowledge—this may be! But a god who is beyond morality is not a god but a monster. One could have wrested this conviction away from Socrates only with his life. And I think that one can say the same thing of all of us: it is a great misfortune to become a hater of reason but to be deprived of the protection of morality, to abandon morality to anyone's power—this is equivalent in our eyes to destroying the world, to condemning it to death.

When Clement of Alexandria teaches that knowledge and eternal salvation are inseparable from each other but that if it were not so and if he had to choose between them, it is knowledge that he would choose, he is only repeating the dearest thought of Socrates and all of Greek philosophy. When Anselm seeks to deduce the existence of God from the principle of contradiction, he tries to obtain what Socrates attempted—to blend knowledge and virtus into one—and in this he sees the essential task of life. It is easy for us today to criticize Socrates. According to us, knowledge is one thing and virtue is another. But the ancients, "those ancient and blessed men" who were better than we and closer to the gods, built a "truth" that is not afraid of our critiques and is not even concerned with them. And, to tell all, let us recognize this: even though we criticize Socrates we are still not delivered from his enchantment. A "postulate" of our thought, like that of ancient thought, is always the conviction that knowledge = virtue = eternal salvation. I am not speaking only of the philosophers of the Middle Ages. Hugo of St. Victor declared openly that the Socratic "know thyself" fell from heaven, just like the Bible. We shall have more than once to allude to the strange attraction that the ancient wisdom exercises over medieval and modern thought. For the moment, I shall content myself with indicating that the Scholastic philosophy not only did not wish to fight, but was even incapable of fighting, against the magic spell of the Greek wisdom, as we also do not wish and are incapable of doing. For us, too, Socrates remains the best of men, the wisest of men, a righteous man. For us, too, the judgment of the Delphic oracle remains final.

Once only—and aside, moreover, from the great highway followed by philosophy—someone appeared to express doubt on the oracle's and history's judgment about Socrates: Nietzsche found in Socrates the *décadent*, that is to say, the fallen man *kat' exochên [par excellence]*. And as if he were recalling the story of Genesis, Nietzsche called a "fall" precisely that in which the oracle and history and Socrates himself saw Socrates' greatest merit—his worship of knowledge, to which he was prepared to sacrifice not only his life but also his soul. Up until Nietzsche everyone assumed that "know thyself" had fallen from heaven. But no one believed that the prohibition against tasting of the fruits of the tree of knowledge had fallen from heaven. The "know thyself" was a truth; the tree of knowledge a metaphor, an allegory of which one had to rid oneself, like many other allegories of the Bible, by filtering it carefully through Greek reason. The fundamental truths that had fallen from heaven even before the Graeco-Roman world encountered the Bible were the principles expressed by Plato in the phrases from the *Phaedo* and the *Euthyphro* that I have quoted above. Everything that the Middle Ages read in the Bible was refracted through these truths, which thus purified inadmissible elements for cultivated minds. And then suddenly Duns Scotus and Occam impetuously attacked these unshakable truths. As if defending themselves in advance against the conformity of the peace-loving Lessing, they strained all the forces of their marvellous dialectic to remove from the jurisdiction of reason and transport into the domain of *credibilia* (things to be believed) almost everything that the Bible tells us of God: that "God is living, wise and well-disposed," that He is "efficient cause," that He is immovable, unchangeable, and did not cease to exist after creating the world. Duns Scotus says, "On theories rest the *credibilia,* through which or to the assumption of which reason is compelled, but which are more certain for the Catholic through the fact that they do not rely on our blinking and—in most things—vacillating understanding but firmly on Thy most solid truth."

Thus could Duns Scotus speak—the very Duns Scotus who, as we recall, had replaced the "I believe, Lord, help thou my unbelief" brought by Jerusalem with the "I believe, Lord, but if it is possible, I would wish to know" derived from Athens. *Intellectus* for him is no longer "ruler and judge of all" but a blinking and vacillating guide of the blind. And Occam expresses himself no less categorically: "And so the articles of faith are not principles of proof or conclusion, and they are not probable, because to all or to most or to the wise they appear false, and in accepting this they become wise for the wise of the world and especially adherents of the natural reason." Duns Scotus and Occam do not seek of reason any justification of what the revealed truth has brought. They go even further. They attack what was for the Greeks, as well as for us, the most unshakable of principles: the autonomy of morality proclaimed by Socrates. *Dico quad omne aliud a Deo est bonum quia a Deo volitum et non ex converso* (I say that everything other than God is good because it is willed by God and not vice versa). Or: "As God therefore can act otherwise, so can he also give another law as right which becomes right if it is given by God, for no law is right except insofar as it is accepted by the divine will." For "God cannot wish anything with whose wishing He could be in the wrong, for His will is the highest rule."

If one still recalls that, according to Duns Scotus, "there is no cause why His will willed this except that His will is His will," it is difficult to assume that the theologians and historians who tried to save Scotus' reputation by seeking to show that his God is not at all "arbitrary" could attain their goal. Perhaps the hair on our head rises at the thought but he who, like Scotus, declares that *omne est bonum quia a Deo volitum est et non ex converso* or, like Occam, that "God can be obliged to nothing and therefore the occurrence of what God wishes is just" affirms in God "*schlechthinnige und regellose Willkur*" (wicked and lawless arbitrariness), no matter how much the theologians may protest.[23] There is no rule above God, no law limits His will; on the contrary, He is the source and master of all laws and rules. Just as in Plotinus: "it requires no support, as though it could not carry itself." It is the same "groundlessness" but it is a still more terrible one, and for the rational man a still less acceptable one. Can one trust such a God, no matter how often the Bible repeats: "Hear, O Israel!"? And if the God of the Bible is such, a God who creates and destroys everything—including the eternal laws—what has He then in common with the rational and moral principles of the ancient wisdom? Is a symbiosis still possible between the Greek and the Judeo-Christian philosophies?

It is clear that a break between them is inevitable, and that this break must be the end of medieval philosophy if the latter has not sufficient power and daring to continue its way at its own risk and peril without letting itself be guided by the ancients. It did not have the courage: it wished at all costs to preserve its bond with the "fatherland of human thought," with Greece. "It died of its own dissensions," writes Gilson, "and its dissensions multiplied from the time it took itself as an end instead of ordering itself toward that wisdom which was at the same time its end and its origin. Albertists, Thomists, Scotists, Occamists contributed to the ruin of medieval philosophy in the exact measure that they neglected the search for the truth by exhausting themselves in sterile battles. . . . Medieval thought became only an inanimate corpse, a dead weight, under which the ground that it had prepared and on which alone it could build collapsed."

After Duns Scotus and Occam, who had withdrawn the base elaborated by centuries, medieval philosophy died, as Greek philosophy, incapable of bearing Plotinus' "it requires no support" died, of terror. It could not bear the "limitless and lawless arbitrariness" which shone through the *omne est bonum quia a Deo volitum et non ex converso* [everything is good because God wills it and not the other way around] of Scotus, that is, what constituted the very essence of "the metaphysics of the Book of Exodus" and what it was called precisely to proclaim: "the notion, unknown to the ancients, of a created truth, spontaneously ordered towards the Being who is at the same time the end and the origin," as Gilson so well expresses it.[24]

It was not in vain that the Scholastics lived for so many centuries under the shadow of the Greek wisdom and its eternal, uncreated truths. Duns Scotus himself wished with all his powers "to know," and when his successors had to choose between the revealed truth and the self-evident truth, they turned away from the former and held out their hand toward the tree of knowledge, enchanted by the always seductive *eritis scientes* (you will know). And what was written came about: "medieval philosophy became an inanimate corpse, a dead weight." What then will be the end of modern philosophy? It is difficult to foresee this. But if it continues to see in the fruits of the tree of knowledge, as Hegel taught, the sole source that makes us participate in the truth, and if what is written is destined to be fulfilled, then we must believe that it also will not be able to avoid the fate of Greek philosophy and medieval philosophy. Or is Gilson deceived and is the "created truth" a *contradictio in adjecto*, just like the revealed truth of which the Fathers of the Church and the Scholastics have spoken to us so much and with such great enthusiasm?

IV

We have now arrived at the greatest of the temptations that lay in wait for medieval thought, which set as its goal to support and ground—through rational argument—the revealed truth. With his customary perceptiveness, Gilson has very well discerned and masterfully described all the vicissitudes of that intense struggle which developed in the course of the Middle Ages between the Greek idea of an uncreated and eternal truth and the Judeo-Christian idea of God, the sole creator and source of everything that exists. As might be expected, this struggle was concentrated principally around the question of the relationship between faith and reason.

Already in St. Augustine it is clearly established that faith is subject to the control of reason, that it almost seeks this control. Before one believes, it is necessary to determine whom one believes, *cui est credendum*. From this point of view, "reason precedes faith." Hence, the conclusion: *intellige ut credas, crede ut intelligas* (understand in order to believe, believe in order to understand). Speaking of himself, St. Augustine says more than once: "I should not have believed in the truth of the Gospel unless the authority of the Catholic Church moved me to it."[25]

Always true to historical reality, Gilson characterizes the mutual relationships between faith and reason of the scholastic philosophy in the following terms: "It is not at all a question of maintaining that faith is a type of knowledge superior to rational knowledge. No one has ever claimed this. *It is, on the contrary, self-evident that faith is a simple substitute for knowledge*[26] and that, wherever the thing is possible, the substitution of knowledge for faith is always a positive gain for the mind. The traditional hierarchy of modes of knowledge, among the Christian thinkers, is always faith, understanding, seeing God face to face. 'The intellect which we have in this life,' writes St. Anselm, 'I take to be the middle between faith and seeing.'"[27] Indeed, the great majority of the medieval thinkers shared the judgment of Anselm of Canterbury. Saint Thomas Aquinas writes: "For faith holds itself in the middle (between knowledge and opinion), going beyond opinion insofar as it has a firm assent but falling short of knowledge insofar as it does not have vision."

As Gilson indicates, from St. Augustine on the study of the relationship between faith and knowledge had for its point of departure Isaiah VII, 9, in the Septuagint translation: *Si non credideritis, non intelligetis* (If you will not believe, you will not understand). St. Augustine "repeats these words endlessly." They represent "the exact formula of his personal experience." St. Thomas Aquinas repeats them also, though he knows not only that they translate the text of Isaiah incorrectly but quotes next to them[28] the correct translation: *Si non credideritis, non permanebitis* (if you will not believe, you will not endure). However, reason seeks evidence so avidly, aspires to universal and necessary judgments so passionately, that the Hellenized—that is to say, transformed into its opposite—strophe of the prophet speaks more to the soul of the Scholastic philosopher than the original text. Anselm of Canterbury joyously took up St. Augustine's reflections. "It is known from St. Anselm himself," Gilson recalls, "that the original title of his *Monologium* was 'Meditations on the rationality of faith,' and that the title of his *Prosologion* was none other than the famous formula: a faith which seeks understanding."

Fides quaerens intellectum (faith seeking understanding), like *credo ut intelligam* (I believe that I may understand), were at the base of all of St. Anselm's reflections. "As soon as a Christian reflects on the obtaining of grace, he becomes a philosopher," says Gilson in another place.[29] But to what did this "reflection," according to the Scholastics, lead? Gilson answers thus: "If it is true that to possess religion is to have everything else, it is necessary to *show* it. An apostle like St. Paul *can be content* with preaching it, a philosopher would like to be sure of it."[30] Here, then, is how medieval philosophy understood its task, here is how it conceived the relationship between faith and knowledge. The apostle "contented himself with faith, but the philosopher wished more—he could not be content with what preaching brings him ("the foolishness of preaching," as St. Paul himself puts it). The philosopher seeks and finds "proofs," convinced in advance that the proven truth has much more value than the truth that is not proven, indeed that only the proven truth has any value at all. Faith is then only a "substitute" for knowledge, an imperfect knowledge, a knowledge—in a way—on credit and which must sooner or later present the promised proofs if it wishes to justify the credit that has been accorded to it.

It is beyond doubt that Gilson expounds correctly the position of medieval philosophy on the relationship between faith and knowledge. The principles for seeking truth that it had received from the Greeks demanded imperiously that it not accept any judgment without having first verified it according to the rules by which all truths are verified: the truths of revelation do not enjoy any special privilege in this respect. Defending himself against Luther who calls down the fire of heaven on reason, Denifle, one of the best specialists in the history of medieval philosophy, cites in his book, *Luther and Lutheranism,* these remarkable words of St. Bonaventura: "The truth of our faith is in no worse situation than other truths, but in the case of other truths every truth that can be attacked by reason can and must also be defended by reason; so similarly the truth of our faith." And immediately afterwards, Denifle reproduces a no less characteristic sentence of Matthew of Aquasparta: "To believe against reason is blameworthy."[31] And Denifle was right; such indeed was the goal that medieval philosophy set for itself: the truths of faith can and must be defended by the same means that are employed to defend all truths, otherwise they would find themselves in "a worse situation." And St. Thomas Aquinas from his side warned us: "No one should decidedly adhere to an exposition of Scripture that with sure reason is ascertained to be false . . . in order that, from this, Scripture not be derided by the infidels."

Harnack then was in error when he declared that "one of the heaviest consequences of the doctrine of Athanasius the Great was that, after him, people forever renounced clear and rigorous concepts and accustomed themselves to contradictions. What contradicts reason became—not immediately, it is true, but little by little—the distinctive character of the sacred."[32] Certainly the Fathers of the Church, like the medieval philosophers, could not avoid contradictions, just as Plato and Aristotle did not succeed in ridding themselves of them in their systems; but these contradictions were never exposed to the light of day and no one ever boasted of them. On the contrary, people always tried to shade and hide them more or less cleverly by having recourse to a rigorous, though apparent, logic. Contradictions were admitted only in a very limited number, and it was not permitted anyone to multiply them according to his arbitrariness and fancy. A small number of contradictory but unchanging notions which always repeated themselves were accepted by all the world not, however, as contradictory but as rigorously logical, and it is for this reason precisely that they were recognized as true. In his polemic against the Arians, St. Athanasius himself carefully avoided everything that might permit his adversaries to reproach him with lack of logic and especially, of course, *boulêsis* (desire or willing): "Just as opposed to desire is that which is reasonably chosen, so what exists by nature precedes and is superior to free choice." It is obvious that one for whom, as for St. Athanasius, God's nature is anterior to and independent of His will, not only cannot seek but still less will admit anything that troubles the eternal and immutable order of being. If despite this, Harnack perceives contradictions in St. Athanasius' doctrine, this does not at all prove the indifference of the latter to the principles and technique of thought of the Greeks.

ATHENS AND JERUSALEM

Still less do we have the right to suppose that the medieval philosophers tried to rid themselves of the principle of contradiction. On the contrary, almost all (there were some exceptions but they were very rare) were deeply convinced that "it is blameworthy to believe against reason." In addition to what Gilson and Denifle have reported to us, one could quote many other texts which show that the Scholastics were deeply concerned to safeguard the rights of the principle of contradiction, even going to the point of limiting the divine omnipotence for its sake. St. Thomas Aquinas Writes: "Only that is excluded from the divine omnipotence which contradicts the reason or essence of being, that is, that something at the same time be and not be; and something that is of a similar nature is that something not have been that has been."[33] And again: "That which contains a contradiction does not fall under God's omnipotence." And in Article 4 of the same question he repeats: "that that which has been should not have been—with the contradiction that it implies—is not subject to the divine power," and relies on St. Augustine and Aristotle: "and the philosopher says: this only God is powerless to do—to make that which has been not to have been." Even in Duns Scotus, who defended so passionately the omnipotence of God against all limitations, we read the following: "It is firmly to be held that for God everything—except what is manifestly impossible *ex terminis*, or the impossibility or contradictoriness of which is self-evidently deduced—is possible."[34] Even the impetuous Occam humbles himself before the principle of contradiction and seeks to obtain its approval and protection for his judgments that are of such provocative daring: "It is an article of faith that God assumed human nature; it involves no contradiction for God to assume the nature of an ass, and with equal reason He could take on the nature of stone or wood."

From where does the Judeo-Christian philosophy draw this unshakable conviction that the principle of contradiction cannot be overcome? Not from the Bible, surely. The Bible takes no account of the principle of contradiction, just as it takes no account of any principle, of any law, for it is the source, the sole source, and master of all laws. But if the principle of contradiction "is not subject to the divine omnipotence," then it exists of itself and is independent of God. And we must be prepared to admit that the truth of revelation is quite different from the truth of natural reason. So it is that we read, for example, in Duns Scotus: "With absolute power God can save Judas; on the other hand, with ordered power He can save this or that sinner, though he may also never be saved; but He cannot make stone or wood blessed, with neither absolute nor with ordered power." But in the Gospel it is written: "For I say unto you that God is able of these stones to raise up children to Abraham."[35] One can find in the Bible many statements of this kind that have broken through the Chinese wall of impossibilities raised by the principle of contradiction; and every time the medieval thinkers found themselves face to face with them, they were obliged to retreat before the invincible logic of the natural reason. "In St. Augustine's thought the work of creation was an instantaneous *fiat*, which means not only that the six days of which the account of the Book of Genesis speaks are an allegory and are in fact reduced to a moment, but also that from that moment on the work of creation was really finished."[36] The six days of creation are an allegory—here is a very seductive idea, one of those bridges constructed by Philo of Alexandria thanks to which we can pass so easily above the abyss that separates Athens from Jerusalem. But this idea, which at first blush is so completely innocent, gives the victory to the serpent whose venom, if it did not forever kill, at least for centuries paralyzed, the revealed truth. It means, indeed, that everything that does not agree with Greek thought, everything that can resist a verification effectuated according to the criteria established by this thought, must be rejected as false.

One cannot but remember, writes Gilson, "the innumerable biblical expressions that picture God as offended, irritated, vengeful or appeased. No one is unaware that such images do not authorize us to ascribe human passions to Him. Assuredly the Judeo-Christian God is not similar to the gods of the Greek mythology. He does not feel anger or regret; His inner life is no more troubled by our insults than gladdened by our praises. In this sense it is not Homer but Aristotle who is right."[37] Once more we must agree with Gilson. When the philosophers of the Middle Ages read in the Bible that God became angry or was glad or that He intervened in the daily affairs of men (the miracle of the marriage at Cana which Hegel later mocked), in the depths of their souls there was doubtless born the very same thought that the reading of Homer aroused in Aristotle: "the poets lie a great deal." To be sure, none of them ever, like the pious Philo, dared to pronounce these blasphemous words even to himself. They did not say "they lie a great deal" but "it is an allegory." I repeat, however, that this word "allegory" was only the egg from which was to be hatched the scorn of European thought for revealed truth.

By means of the allegorical method of interpretation modern thought ended by completely "purifying" philosophy of the "gross prejudices" that the old book had introduced into the sublime kingdom of wisdom. Hegel already was not afraid to recall, in connection with the exodus of the Jews from Egypt and the miracle of the marriage at Cana, Voltaire's cynical sarcasms about the God who concerned himself with the establishment of places for easing oneself. The Aristotelian "the poets lie" or, to put it better, the fundamental principles of the Greeks and the Greek technique of thought had done their work. These principles wished themselves to judge, to teach, to be really the "first principles" and admitted no power above themselves. "The mark of the philosopher is that he can judge about everything," Aristotle firmly declares.[38] Or again: "The wise man must know not only what follows from the first principles but also the first principles themselves in order to possess true knowledge."[39] One can believe only what is acceptable to these principles. Faith must obtain the blessing of the first principles, and the faith that has not obtained this blessing has no right to existence.

The first educated Greek who rose up against the Judeo-Christian doctrine (at the time of Celsus Judaism and Christianity were still hardly distinguished from each other but rather almost identified) showed himself particularly indignant over the fact that the new doctrine constantly and exclusively insisted on a faith which not only had not succeeded in justifying itself before reason but even pretended insolently to do without this justification. In the eyes of Celsus this was a sin against the holy spirit; everything will be forgiven but this. For, before believing, the reasonable man must first take account of whom it is he believes. We have seen that this question, which did not exist not only for the first Christians but also for the Jews, always troubled the Fathers of the Church. They wished, as St. Bonaventura was later to say, that the truth of their doctrine not be in a worse situation than all other truths; they wished that it be founded on unchanging and indisputable first principles. We recall that Anselm of Canterbury was "possessed," following Gilson's expression, by the idea of finding a proof for the existence of God which rests only on the principle of contradiction.

If we ask ourselves whence this "possession" came, why the philosophers of the Middle Ages aspired so eagerly to the "demonstrated" truth, we shall find no other answer than that already given by Gilson: the principles of the Hellenic philosophy and the technique of Hellenic thought held them in their power and bewitched their minds. For Aristotle, who had in a way drawn up the balance of all his predecessors' work, the principle of contradiction was not only a principle (*archê*) but "the most unshakeable of all principles," as he more than once says. Some people judge, he declares in several places of his *Metaphysics,* that Heraclitus did not admit the principle of contradiction. Aristotle tries to prove that such a judgment is absurd, as Protagoras' "against every reason stands another reason" is absurd. It is true that his objections come down to the statement that he who denies the principle of contradiction recognizes it in this very denial. It is true also that one can turn his objections around and say that, in arguing with Heraclitus and Protagoras who deny the principle of contradiction, Aristotle argues as if they recognized the principle. But he holds in reserve still another argument (if one can call it an argument) that is, in his opinion, invincible: "For what a man says, he does not necessarily believe."[40] That is, Heraclitus and Protagoras themselves did not take what they said seriously. Aristotle declared with the same assurance—and let us recall that St. Thomas Aquinas refers to him in this connection—that what had once been could not not have been and that this principle puts a limit to the omnipotence of the gods. No one dreams of denying that these "first principles" are the condition of the possibility of knowledge; everyone is likewise agreed, that they did not "fall from the heavens," that Aristotle obtained them by his own powers here on this earth, and that not only do they not demand "revelation" but that all revelation must justify itself before them, for the gods themselves are subject to them. The discovery of truths independent of God's will—*veritates emancipatae a Deo*—was for Aristotle the greatest of victories; so he realized his ideal, the idea of the philosopher who can think "freely," and obtained autonomy for knowledge, just as the Pelagians, thanks to their *homo emancipatus a Deo,* realized the ideal of ethical autonomy. We shall see later that Leibniz also welcomed with enthusiasm "the eternal truths that are in the mind of God independently of His will."

One would think that the religious philosophers of the Middle Ages should have seen that it was precisely this question of the eternal truths, the truths independent of God, that hid in itself the greatest dangers, and that they should consequently have strained all their powers to defend Jerusalem against Athens and recalled in this connection the warning of the Bible against the fruits of the tree of knowledge. Some of them did remember it. Gilson quotes in a footnote Peter Damian who affirmed that *cupiditas scientiae* (lust for knowledge) was for men "leader of the flock of all vices," but Gilson realizes that no one listened to Peter Damian; Bonaventura himself found these words strange. The enchantment of the fruits of the tree of knowledge always persists: we today aspire as eagerly to the eternal truths as the first man. But what is it that seduces us in these truths that depend neither on ourselves nor on God, and why is it that we base our best hopes on the principle of contradiction or on the idea that what has once been cannot not have been? We do not even raise this question—as if the independence of the eternal rational and moral truths were the guarantee of our own independence. But it is just the opposite: these truths condemn us to the most repugnant slavery. Being independent of God's will, they themselves have neither will nor desire. They are indifferent to everything. They are not at all concerned with what they will bring to the world and to men, and automatically actualize their limitless power with which they themselves have nothing to do and which comes to them one knows not whence nor why. From the "law"—what has once been cannot not have been—may flow for us a good but also an evil—a horrible, insupportable evil; but the law will accomplish its work without caring about this. One cannot persuade the eternal truths, one cannot move them to pity. They are like the Necessity of which Aristotle said that "it does not allow itself to be persuaded." And despite this—or precisely because of this—men love the eternal truths and prostrate themselves before them. We can obtain nothing from them, consequently we must obey them. We have not the power to escape them, we see in our impotence an "impossibility," consequently we must worship them. This is the true meaning of the *cupiditas scientiae:* a puzzling *concupiscentia irresistibilis* [invincible desire] carries us toward the impersonal, indifferent to everything, truth that we raise above the will of all living beings.

Is it not clear that we are in the power of that terrible, hostile force of which the Book of Genesis speaks to us? We have seen that all the commentators believed that the sin of the first man consisted in an act of disobedience: Adam wished "to be free," he refused to submit. In reality it is just the opposite that happened: having tasted of the fruits of the tree of knowledge, man lost the freedom that he possessed on leaving the hands of the Creator and became the slave of "the eternal truths." And he does not even suspect that the *eritis scientes* (you shall know) by means of which the tempter bewitched his soul led to his "fall." He continues to the present day, indeed, to identify his eternal salvation with knowledge. And when he hears the apostle's word, "for the creature was made subject to vanity not willingly, but by reason of him who hath subjected him," and that a day will come when he will be delivered from the "bondage of corruption into the glorious liberty of the children of God,"[41] he takes refuge in Aristotle who declares, "One can say this but one cannot think it" or even "the poets lie a great deal." The principles of the Greek philosophy have accomplished their work: we all prefer the peace of submission to the dangers and uncertainties of struggle. The work of Boethius, *De consolatione philosophiae* [On the Consolation of Philosophy], which was so attractive to the Middle Ages, is particularly characteristic in this respect.

De consolatione philosophiae is the Book of Job written by a man who, though a Christian, belonged to the Graeco-Roman culture. Hardly had philosophy approached Boethius' bed than it set itself the duty of chasing away "the Muses who stand at my bed dictating words to my weeping. Who, says philosophy, let these stage prostitutes, who not only do not alleviate his pains through any remedy but further nourish them with sweet poisons, come to this sick man?" Before offering its help, philosophy, like Job's friends, demands that the man who suffers be silent and cease to complain and call for help: *Non ridere, non lugere, neque detestari, sed intelligere* (not to laugh, not to lament, not to curse, but to understand) as Spinoza was later to put it. It is only on this condition, that is, that man renounce everything, that philosophy can come to his aid by conferring upon him its *intelligere* (understanding). *De profundis ad te, Domine, clamavi* (out of the depths I cried unto thee, O Lord) must be rejected, forgotten forever. It obstructs the road that leads to the wisdom founded on rigorous knowledge. Philosophy certainly acts honestly: "the most beautiful maiden in the world cannot give more than it has given." It can only "explain" to Boethius that what happened to him happened because it could not be otherwise. As for saving him from prison and the torture that awaits him, this philosophy cannot, as it assuredly knows (Zeus himself says this to Chrysippus), do; no one in the world can do more.

Job's friends said the same thing to Job that Boethius' philosophy said to him; knowing well that they could not help him, they also proposed to him that he seek consolation in "wisdom" or, to put it differently, in submitting to the inevitable. Philosophy succeeded in convincing Boethius; he accepted its "consolations." As for Job, he did not chase away the Muses, he drove out his friends—"You are miserable comforters"—and resolved to oppose his *lugere et detestari* [weeping and cursing] to the *intelligere* [understanding] that philosophy offered him. There can surely be no doubt on the matter: the principles of the ancient philosophy and of the Greek thought would have taken the side of Boethius and not of Job, and rigorous logic does not permit human sorrow to raise its voice when it is a question of the truth. Job demanded that what had been should not have been, that his murdered children should not be murdered, that his burnt up wealth should be intact, that his lost health should not be lost, etc. . . . In other words, he demanded what "does not fall under God's omnipotence," what God Himself cannot accomplish because the principle of contradiction, "the most unshakeable of all principles," will not authorize it. It is true that in the Bible something else is said: according to the Bible, philosophy was covered with shame while the Muses, with their *lugere et detestari* and the *De profundis ad te, Domine, clamavi* (out of the depths I cried unto thee, O Lord) triumphed over the *intelligere* and over all the eternal uncreated truths obtained by the *intelligere*. God returned to Job his flocks, his health, his children. God brought it about that *quod fuit non fuisse* (what had been had not been), without concerning Himself with any laws whatsoever. But, of course, one cannot demand of a learned man that he believe all these stories, just as one cannot demand of him that he accept the God of the Bible who rejoices, becomes angry, regrets what He has done, transforms water into wine, multiplies loaves of bread, leads the Jews across the Red Sea, etc. All this must be understood allegorically or metaphorically. More exactly, as long as the "the most unshakeable of all principles," the principle of contradiction, will not have been overthrown, as long as it commands God rather than obeys Him, and as long as man will not resist the temptation to transform the revealed truth into a self-evident truth, it will be necessary to protect oneself against all these stories by means of the words (or exorcism?) *del maestro di coloro che sanno* (of the master of all those who know): "the poets lie a great deal." Human groans, curses and supplication must be silent before the unchangeable principles of being.[42]

V

Under the aegis of the eternal truths there was introduced into medieval philosophy a profound distrust precisely toward the "notion, unknown to the ancients, of a created truth" that this philosophy, as Gilson so well says, was called by the very content of the Bible to proclaim to men. On the road that led to the created truth the principle of contradiction arose and opposed its veto. Gilson declares, it is true, that the notion of a created truth was preserved in Scholasticism and even stimulated modern philosophy: "The entire Cartesian system rests on the idea of an omnipotent God who somehow creates Himself and even more naturally creates the eternal truths, including those of mathematics!"[43] We shall return further on to the question of deciding whether we have or have not the right to affirm that the entire Cartesian system is founded on the idea of an omnipotent God who creates the eternal truths. But it is beyond doubt that Descartes did not recoil before such "paradoxes." He writes to Arnauld (29 July 1648): "But it does not appear to me that it is to be said of anything whatsoever that it cannot be done by God; since every ground of the true and the good depends on His omnipotence, I would not even be able to say that God cannot bring it about that there be a mountain without a valley or that one and two not make three; but I say only that He has given me a mind such that a mountain without a valley or a sum of one and two that does not make three cannot be conceived by me, etc."

So Descartes spoke in his letters[44]; but in speaking so he departed from the medieval philosophy as well as from the rules of the Greek philosophy by means of which the Middle Ages tried to understand and justify the truth of the biblical revelation. We recall what Aristotle said about those who denied the principle of contradiction: one can say this but one cannot think it. We remember that St. Thomas Aquinas, Duns Scotus and even Occam said that "what includes in itself a contradiction does not fall under God's omnipotence." But to assume that God can create a mountain without a valley, or bring it about that one and two not be equal to three, etc., is to recognize the independence of God in relation to the principle of contradiction. If Descartes really thought what he wrote to Arnauld and Mersenne, we are obliged to confess that the greatest rationalist of modern times broke with the ancient philosophy and took the road opened up by Tertullian and Peter Damian! Gilson quotes in a footnote a text of Peter Damian's that I believe is necessary to reproduce *in extenso*:[45] "Can God bring it about that what has been shall not have been? If, for example, it is firmly established that a virgin was corrupted, would it be impossible that she become again unspotted? This, as far as nature is concerned, is certainly true, and the judgment stands. . . . For contraries in one and the same subject cannot agree. This will further rightly be characterized as impossible if reference is made to the impotence of nature. Yet far be it that this be applied to the divine majesty. For He who gave nature its origin can, if He wishes, easily take away the necessity of nature. For He who rules over the created things does not stand under the laws of the Creator, and He who created nature turns the natural order according to His own creative will."

What difference is there between Damian and Descartes? In view of Aristotle's first principles, both affirm self-evident absurdities: one can say this but one cannot think it. The principle of contradiction is the "most unshakable of principles." If it is overthrown, the idea of knowledge no longer has any meaning. Damian, it is true, cites examples other than Descartes', examples that are more concrete and closer to real life.[46] Can God create a mountain without a valley or bring it about that one and two not be three—these, it seems, are theoretical, abstract questions which touch neither the fate of the world nor of man. But when Damian demands "if it is firmly established that a virgin was corrupted, would it be possible that she become again unspotted?," our interest is concentrated not on theoretical propositions but on what has immense, decisive importance for men. A *virgo corrupta* is a woman who has fallen, sinned, or been dishonored. As long as the principle of contradiction rules undividedly, as long as it remains "an eternal truth, a truth not subject to God," once the sin or dishonor has come into the world, it remains there finally and forever. No one in the world can return to the woman her honor and deliver her from the shame or sin of her voluntary or involuntary fall, for it is not given to anyone "to take away the necessity of nature." We must say the same of Job: the divine omnipotence itself cannot return to him his murdered children. And if the Bible tells us the opposite, the believing philosopher, like the unbelieving Greek, is obliged to see in these stories only a metaphor or allegory.

Then, another question: Descartes affirms that judgments such as "one and two do not make three" or ideas such as "a mountain without a valley" appear contradictory to us only because God has given us an understanding incapable of thinking otherwise. But he himself admitted, at least as a hypothesis, that a powerful but malevolent and hostile spirit can deceive man through the self-evidences. One would think that such an assumption would have held the attention of a man who knew the Bible and considered it an inspired book once he was endowed, by some unknown miracle, with the thought that the self-evidences by themselves still do not bear witness to the truth. But this idea did nothing more than brush his consciousness and vanished without leaving any traces. He wished at all costs to preserve the self-evidences and the reason that is the source of the self-evidences. And he connected the "eternal truths" not with the malevolent spirit who deceives man but with God who, as he tried to prove to us, never deceives. St. Thomas Aquinas did the same thing: in order to save Aristotle's "first principles" from all attacks, he asserts that "the knowledge of the principles known naturally is inspired in us by God, for God Himself is the author of our nature."[47] The thought of Peter Damian follows a different route. Gilson expresses it briefly thus: "The life of a Christian has only one goal—to bring about his salvation. Salvation is achieved through faith. To apply reason to faith is to dissolve it. . . . In sum, it is the devil who has inspired men with the desire for knowledge and it is this desire that has caused the original sin, the source of all our evils."[48] And he quotes immediately afterwards these few lines of Damian's work *De sancta simplicita:* "Furthermore, he who wished to introduce the hosts of all vices installed the lust for knowledge as commander and so, through it, let loose on the unhappy world all the hosts of iniquities."

The difference between Descartes and Damian appears clearly: Descartes is afraid, even in his letters, to offend reason: "What altar will he who offends the majesty of reason build for himself?" as Spinoza was later to say. But for Damian there is not, there cannot be, any place for other majesties besides the "divine majesty," and he is prepared to rise up against anyone who would dare to limit the omnipotence of God. He remembers the "you will be like God" that the Middle Ages had completely forgotten, and he is not afraid to refer to the Book of Genesis at the risk of provoking the mockery of the unbelieving and hearing Aristotle's ironic "the poets lie." But from the *philosophic* point of view, Damian and Descartes finally say the same thing: the "first principles" inherited from the Greeks are not at all principles, for in the world created by God there are not and cannot be any first principles, that is, principles absolutely independent and sufficient by themselves. As for our certainty that there cannot be a mountain without a valley and that one and two cannot but make three, we must see here only temporary suggestions: if they come from the Creator they are not dangerous and can even be beneficial; if they come from the enemy of the human species they are doubtless deadly. But in any case, as conditioned and relative, they have no right to the predicate of eternity and must sooner or later disappear. And then the metaphysics of knowledge that is in harmony with the Judeo-Christian revelation will show that the reason that aspires eagerly to universal and necessary judgments is not at all worthy of having altars built to it.

Such is the meaning of Damian's thought, and this is what Descartes also tells us in his letters. Both of them destroy the foundations of the Socratic thought that one must not disdain reason, one must put nothing above the good, not even God. Both of them, if you wish, realize the synthesis of Plotinus' "soaring above knowledge" with Duns Scotus' "*schlechthinnige und regellose Willkur*" [wicked and lawless arbitrariness]. To be sure, it is impossible to defend this thesis through the methods that are used to defend other truths. It is a truth of "revelation." Like David in the Bible before the gigantic Goliath armed from head to foot, it remains invisible even to the "eyes of the mind," unarmed and defenseless before the innumerable army of all historic philosophy's arguments. It does not even have the sling possessed by the young shepherd, the future great king and psalmist. And yet, weak as it was, it entered into combat with "the wisdom of the century." "The unlearned rise and storm heaven," as Saint Augustine with amazement exclaimed. And Saint Thomas Aquinas echoed him: "But it would be more wonderful than all signs if the world were brought to believing such hard things, executing such difficult things, and hoping for such exalted things by simple and unlearned men without miraculous signs." And indeed, the Bible was brought to the world by simple, ignorant people who were absolutely incapable of defending it by the methods which learned people use to attack it.

But this Bible did not satisfy the philosophers. Even Saint Bonaventura, whose "Adam, as Brother Alexander of Hales said of him, did not seem to have sinned," wished to obtain "demonstrated" truth. Even the saints no longer escaped the consequences of the original sin: the *doctor seraphicus* (angelic doctor), the spiritual heir of Saint Francis of Assisi, who had overcome all earthly passions, is nevertheless possessed, like all of us, with the *cupiditas scientiae* (lust for knowledge) and cannot overcome this passion. He wishes to "defend" the truth of revelation, to make it self-evident. Temptation lies in wait for us just where we least expect it. Our Greek teachers put our vigilance to sleep by suggesting to us the conviction that the fruits of the tree of knowledge were and must be the principle of philosophy for all time. Even the *doctor subtilis* allowed himself to be tempted, as we have seen. He believes, but faith is not enough for him. He asks of God permission to taste the fruits of the tree of knowledge. All the most remarkable and influential representatives of the philosophy of the Middle Ages repeat endlessly: *credo ut intelligam.*

It is here that the consequences to which the symbiosis of Greek philosophy with the truths of the Bible had to lead appear most clearly. The principles and technique of the ancient philosophy wrapped themselves around the Judeo-Christian revelation and choked it, as the ivy chokes the tree. Faith became a substitute for knowledge. The whole world openly admitted it, all the more so in that thus the mocking of the unbelievers was avoided. Scripture, it is true, was opposed to this conception of faith, but it is always possible to "interpret" Scripture. And as every interpretation presupposes a technique of thought, and this technique as well as the principles of thought were sought and discovered among the Greeks, it was clear in advance that the Bible, interpreted, would locate faith in the place suitable to it, below knowledge. The efforts of Duns Scotus and Occam to protect the domain of the *credibilia* against the invasion of reason did not turn medieval philosophy away from its effort to transform the revealed truths into self-evident truths. And such a transformation appeared and still appears the essential work of the Judeo-Christian thought.

We recall that Lessing affirmed that sooner or later all the truths of revelation would become truths of reason, and that Gilson was obliged to check his pious ardor. Not all, he says in the name of medieval philosophy, but only some. Here is something very significant. Why only some? And what shall we do with those that will never succeed in justifying themselves before reason? Will we not be forced to hide them in order to avoid railleries and wounding reproaches? Will we not even be obliged finally to renounce them if it appears at last that not only can they not count on the protection of reason but that their very existence is a defiance of reason? The prophet Isaiah and St. Paul have warned us that human wisdom is foolishness before God and that God's wisdom is foolishness in the eyes of men. And this, above all, because the source of the revealed truth is faith, which is not located on the level of rational comprehension. Faith cannot be changed and does not even wish to be changed into knowledge. The faith of which the Bible speaks to us delivers man, in an incomprehensible way, from the chains of knowledge, and it is only through faith that it is possible to overcome the knowledge that is bound to the fall of man. So that when we transform a truth given by faith into a self-evident truth or understand it as such, it is a sign that we have lost this truth of faith. "I know that God is one" means something other than "I believe in one God" and than that *Audi Israel* of the Bible that has found its expression in *credo in unum Deum*.

Gilson declares that monotheism was alien to the Greek philosophers. I cannot here examine this question and will content myself with recalling that, from its beginnings, Greek philosophy always sought to discover the single principle of the universe, beginning with Thales who proclaimed that the principle of everything was water. Aristotle ends the twelfth book of his *Metaphysics* (which Gilson uses precisely to prove that monotheism was strange to him) with this verse of Homer: "the rule of many is not good, let there be one master only." And Saint Thomas Aquinas, citing this passage, writes: . . . "Aristotle concludes from the unity of order in existing things the unity of the ruling God."[49] I do not at all mean by this that Aristotle's God is the God of the Bible. On the contrary, it is proper here to recall Pascal's words: "the God of Abraham, the God of Isaac, the God of Jacob, and not the God of the philosophers." If one could demonstrate clearly that the Greek philosophers were monotheists, this would not at all mean that they had had a premonition of the biblical revelation. The one God whose existence appears evident in the ordering of the universe resembles as little the God of the Bible as the dog, the barking animal, resembles the constellation called the Dog. Reason perceives a single principle. It must find him who, according to Pascal's expression regarding Descartes, gives the first fillip. Reason wishes to understand. It is not for nothing that Hegel so ardently defended the ontological argument against Kant. The God who seeks and obtains the protection of the principle of contradiction is certainly not the God of Abraham, Isaac and of Jacob. Of course, Hegel could admit such a God in all tranquility. A "proven" God could defend himself against Aristotle's logic as well as Voltaire's sarcasms.

But "faith"—again, naturally, the faith of the Bible—concerns itself neither with understanding nor with proofs. It requires something else, something completely different—something, as we shall see, that excludes once for all "understanding" and "proofs."

VI

When it is a question of biblical faith, we must above all recall the words of the prophet Habakkuk (II, 4), "the righteous shall live by faith," words which St. Paul repeats in the Epistle to the Romans (I, 17) and in the Epistle to the Hebrews (X, 38). How little these resemble the *credo ut intelligam* [I believe in order to understand] and the *si non credideritis, non intelligetis* [if you do not believe, you will not understand] of the Septuagint! Faith, in the prophets and apostles, is the source of life; faith, in the philosophers of the Middle Ages educated by the Greeks, is the source of the knowledge that understands. How can one not recall in this connection the two trees planted by God in the Garden of Eden? And as if he did not wish to allow any doubt to exist about the respective place of faith and knowledge in the scale of values, the apostle says almost immediately after citing Isaiah's words: "By faith Abraham, when he was called to go out unto a place which he should after receive for an inheritance, obeyed; and he went out, not knowing whither he went (Hebrews XI, 8.)." Here is something that unconditionally contradicts the teaching of the Greeks. Plato opposed to those who "know not where they are going" the philosophers who, being convinced that one cannot do what philosophy forbids, follow it wherever it leads them.[50]

It would be too easy to multiply quotations to prove that what St. Paul said of Abraham, who went he knew not where, would have appeared to the Greek thinkers the height of folly. And even if Abraham had arrived at the Promised Land, his act, in the judgment of the Greeks, would have been as absurd as if he had not arrived anywhere. What vitiates his act, in their eyes, is precisely what confers its immense value upon it, according to the apostle and the Bible: Abraham does not ask reason, he refuses to admit the legitimacy of the pretensions of knowledge. With what scorn Socrates in the *Apology* expresses himself concerning the poets, the prophets, the diviners: "those who do what they do not by reason but in obedience to nature or in enthusiasm." "I have left them," he concludes, "believing that I have over them the same advantage as over the politicians."[51] And in the *Timaeus* (the well-known passage 71E) and in his other dialogues, Plato turns away always from the "divine fate without reason," e.g., *Meno*, 99C or again the *Phaedo* (*aneu philosophiâs te kai nou*). What strikes and charms the apostle in Abraham, what he sees in him as the highest virtue, appears to Plato as a truly criminal frivolity. How indignant he and Socrates would have been if it had been given them to read what St. Paul writes in the Epistle to the Romans: "For what saith the Scripture? Abraham believed God and this was imputed unto him for righteousness." (Romans IV, 3.)

Celsus reflects very precisely the attitude of the Graeco-Roman world toward the fundamental principles of the new doctrine that irrupted into the world. The Greek wisdom could admit neither Abraham, the father of faith, nor St. Paul, nor the prophets of the Bible to whom the apostle constantly refers. The indifference, the "proud" scorn of knowledge, would be pardoned neither in this world nor in the other. St. Paul and his Abraham are only pitiful "haters of reason," who must be fled like the plague. It is impossible, on the other hand, to try to console oneself by saying that St. Paul was not a "thinker" and that he was concerned only with saving his soul. For the Greek philosophy (and Clement of Alexandria along with it, as we recall) believed that knowledge was the only way to salvation: "To him who has not philosophized, who has not purified himself through philosophy and who has not loved knowledge, it is not given to unite himself with the race of the gods."[52] If Abraham and St. Paul are not "thinkers," if they do not love and seek knowledge, they will never obtain salvation. The Greeks knew this well and they would never have agreed to grant anyone the right to raise and resolve the question of knowledge and the salvation of the soul: Aristotle has told us that philosophy itself resolves all questions. But St. Paul, for his part, would not have given in to the Greeks. The Greek philosophy was for him foolishness and he proclaimed, as Gilson says, "the bankruptcy of the Greek wisdom." In the Epistle to the Romans (XIV, 23) he expresses himself with still greater power: "All that does not come of faith is sin." And in the Second Epistle to the Corinthians (V, 7) he says: "For it is by faith that we walk and not by sight."

It is no longer a question only of the bankruptcy of the Greek wisdom but of a terrible danger. The Greeks await salvation from their wisdom founded on knowledge, but they are going to their ruin, for salvation comes from faith, from nothing but faith.[53] It is difficult not to see that there is a direct connection between the discourse of the apostle, the words of the prophets and the acts of the patriarchs, on the one side, and the story of the fall of Adam in the Book of Genesis, on the other side. It is still more difficult to assume that the relationship between faith and knowledge established by the medieval philosophy was borrowed from the Bible. On the contrary, it is clear that the "first principles" of the Greeks choked the essential truth of the biblical "revelation." Not only is not faith a lower form of knowledge, but faith abrogates knowledge. The father of faith went out without knowing where he was going. He had no need to know: where he would arrive, and because he would there arrive, would be the Promised Land. Obviously there could not be any greater folly as far as the Greeks were concerned. This is Tertullian's *certum est quia impossibile* (it is certain because it is impossible). All the definitions of truth given by Aristotle (and those which later were expressed in the formula of Isaac Israeli, accepted by the Middle Ages, that truth is *adaequatio rei et intellectus* [agreement between things and intellect]) are overthrown. It is not man who adapts himself to things and submits to them; it is things that adapt themselves to man and submit to him. Things will bear the name that man gives them: the *veritates aeternae, veritates emancipatae a Deo* (including the principle of contradiction), on which are founded and which guarantee the solidity and stability of the "knowledge" apotheosized by the ancient world, let man escape from their clutch.

It is to be assumed that the ancients would have been amazed (and perhaps even indignant) if they had read in the Bible that the Son of Man proclaims himself master of the Sabbath. No one can call himself master of the law. And still less has anyone the right to say that the Sabbath is made for man and not man for the Sabbath. This is even worse than Protagoras' statement "man is the measure of all things." It is destruction of the eternal and immutable order of the universe, of that *ordo* which is dear to the Greek heart. The Sabbath is not holy because God so ordained it, but it is because the Sabbath is holy that God ordained the commandment "Remember the Sabbath day." The holy is uncreated and exists from all eternity, just like the true; the eternal truths are the uncreated Sabbaths and the uncreated Sabbaths are the eternal truths. But what would particularly have revolted the Greeks is that Jesus permitted himself to transgress the commandment for a reason so completely insignificant—his disciples were hungry. Now, for a philosophic Greek—and it is in this that his wisdom and the good news that reason brought into the world consisted—the joys and sufferings of men belong entirely to the domain of being independent of, and consequently indifferent to, us of which the Stoics have spoken so much, or to the afflictions and passions from which Plato's *catharsis* has delivered us.

Epictetus was convinced that if Socrates had found himself in the situation of Priam or Oedipus, his customary calm would not have abandoned him. He would have uttered the words that he spoke in prison: if the gods wish it, let it be so! Socrates would certainly have spoken in the same way to Job if he had been among his friends (furthermore, Job's friends themselves realized what they had to say to him). But the Bible speaks quite otherwise: "the very hairs of your head are all numbered." (Matthew X, 30.) This does not mean that God is a good accountant who keeps his books carefully but that God comes to man's help and does so precisely in situations of which, according to the teachings of the Greeks, neither God nor men have even the right to dream. A woman approaches him. He heals her and adds, "Be of good comfort, my daughter, thy faith hath made thee whole." (Matthew IX, 22.) And we read again, "Oh, woman, great is thy faith: be it unto thee even as thou wilt. And from that very hour her daughter was made whole." (Matthew XV, 28.) To the blind who had come to him, he addresses these puzzling words: "According to your faith be it unto you." (Matthew IX, 29.) All these quotations, which could be multiplied many times, assuredly show that man acquires through faith something that is as far removed from the *catharsis* of the Greeks as from their *gnosis*. And these words of Jesus express this with special power (Matthew XVII, 20, Mark XI, 23, and Luke XVII, 6.): "For verily I say unto you, if ye have faith as a grain of mustard seed, ye shall say to this mountain 'Remove hence to yonder place'; and it shall remove and nothing shall be impossible for you."

It is easy to imagine the indignation that such words aroused among minds imbued with Greek culture; the calmest among them were not content with the Aristotelian "the poets lie a great deal." Even in our age Hegel, the "Christian" philosopher, was not ashamed to repeat in a less important context the cynical sarcasms of Voltaire. But it is not this aspect of the question that interests us here. Let us leave some to mock the Bible while others ask with admiration,

Who is he who speaks as one who has power? What is important for us is that the faith of Scripture has absolutely nothing in common with faith as the Greeks understood it and as we now understand it. The faith of the Bible is not the trust that we put in a teacher, in parents, in superiors, in a doctor, etc., which is really only a substitute for knowledge, a knowledge on credit, a knowledge not guaranteed by proofs. When one says to a man, "according to your faith be it unto you" or "if you have faith as a grain of mustard seed, nothing will be impossible for you," it is clear that this faith is a mysterious, creative power, an incomparable gift, the greatest of all gifts. And if furthermore, as in the examples already cited, the gift relates not to the domain that the Greeks called *ta eph' hêmin*, that is, what depends on us, but to what is outside our power (*ta ouk eph' hêmin*)— faith being capable of healing the sick, opening the eyes of the blind, even of moving mountains—then there cannot be any doubt that the faith of the Bible determines and forms being and thus abolishes knowledge with its "possible" and "impossible."

Socrates was right to demand of men knowledge for, like Aristotle,[54] like the Stoics, like all the Greek philosophers, he was dominated by the conviction that there exists an immense realm of being which is subject neither to men nor to the gods themselves—"that which is not in our power." And if this conviction really came to him from heaven, like his "know thyself," and was not inspired by a hostile force ("you shall be like God knowing"), then not only is it "blameworthy to believe contrary to reason" but it is also scandalous to believe "without philosophy and understanding," and everything that the Bible tells us about faith must be rejected. As for the teaching of St. Paul, who says that "a man is justified by faith without the deeds of the law" (Romans III, 28), this is immoral and revolting. And, in general, most of the ideas that he develops in his epistles and the quotations from the Old Testament with which his reflections are interspersed can awaken in educated people only feelings of irritation and revulsion. One could even say that he seeks deliberately to provoke the ancient wisdom as well as the traditional piety. He quotes (Romans IX, 15) the words addressed by God to Moses: "I will have mercy on whom I will have mercy, and I will have compassion on whom I will have compassion," and adds, "so then it is not of him that willeth, nor of him that runneth, but of God that showeth mercy." And again: "Therefore hath He mercy on whom He will have mercy, and him whom He will He hardeneth."[55] To all the "objections" that might be made against him, he opposes only Jeremiah's words: "Nay, but who art thou, O man, that repliest against God?" (Romans IX, 20.) Referring to the patriarchs and the prophets, St. Paul dares to say, "the law entered that the offence might abound." (Romans V, 20.) Or still again (Romans IV, 15): "Because the law worketh wrath; for where no law is, there is no transgression." And finally (Romans X, 20) : "But Isaiah is very bold and saith: 'I was found of them that sought me not; I was made manifest to them that asked not after me.'"

For the Greeks and the medieval thinkers who followed them, the words of Isaiah resounded like a terrible condemnation: vain are all our searchings, all our demands! God reveals Himself, God will reveal Himself, to him who does not seek, to him who does not ask. What more terrible thing can there be? What good, then, is Plato's *catharsis,* the Stoics' struggle, the monks' *exercitia spiritualia,* and the rigorous *itineraria* of the martyrs, ascetics and mystics? Will all these tremendous, superhuman and glorious works then have served for nothing? Is it possible to "defend," through rational arguments, the God of the Bible against these accusations that are so well founded on rational thought? Obviously not. One can only try to rid oneself of reason and its arguments as Pascal did: "humble yourself, impotent reason." Our conviction that self-evidence guarantees the truth appears to Pascal an *enchantment et assoupisse-ment surnaturel* [supernatural enchantment and slumber] into which our thirst for knowledge has plunged us. "If you wish to subject everything to yourself, subject yourself to reason," says Seneca in the name of the ancient philosophy. And it seems to us that this is the supreme wisdom: we submit joyously to the obligation that is imposed on us. But the Bible speaks quite differently. To the offer—"All these things will I give thee if thou wilt fall down and worship me"— it is answered: "Get thee hence, Satan! For it is written (Deut. VI, 13): 'Thou shalt worship the Lord thy God, and Him only shalt thou serve.'" (Matthew IV, 10.) It is in this that the essential opposition between the "truth" of the Greeks and the "revelation" of the Bible consists. For the Greeks the fruits of the tree of knowledge were the source of philosophy for all time, and by this very fact they brought men freedom. For the Bible, on the contrary, they were the beginning of enslavement and signified the fall of man.

Considering the difficulties that the biblical conception of the role and meaning of this *cupiditas scientiae* that lives in us presents, this is the time, it seems to me, to recall what Dostoevsky wrote on this matter. Dostoevsky certainly did not possess the erudition of a Pascal, and he was not very learned in theology and philosophy. But in the course of the four years that he spent in prison he read only the Bible, for he had no other book. And he drew from this reading the same hatred, the same scorn that Pascal had for "rational argu-ments." He also sees in the self-evidences of our thought only an enchantment, only a stupefaction of the spirit.

"The impossible," he writes, "is a stone wall. What kind of stone wall? But, of course, the laws of nature, the deductions of the natural sciences, mathematics.

The moment that it is demonstrated to you, for example, that you are descended from an ape, it is useless to make any grimace, admit the thing as it is. . . . Permit me if you will, someone will cry to you: it is impossible to debate the matter—it is two times two make four! Nature does not consult you, it has no concern for your desires. And what does it matter to it whether these laws please you or not? A wall is a wall, etc. But, good Lord! What do the laws of nature and of arithmetic matter to me when, for some reason or another, they do not please me? Of course, I shall not break the wall with my head, if I really have not the power to break it, but I shall not accept it, I shall not resign myself to it, merely because it is a stone wall and I lack the power. As if such a stone wall were *an appeasement and contained but a word of peace merely because it is two times two makes four.*"[56]

Translated into philosophic language, these overwhelming words constitute a defense that is decisive and unique of its kind against those universal and necessary judgments to which, according to Kant, our reason so avidly aspires, or against those "wherefore" (*dioti*) which are for the Stagyrite the very essence of knowledge (in Spinoza, *tertium genus cognitionis* or *intelligere*) and because of which St. Augustine and the Scholastics agreed to believe. With an audacity and clear-headedness that we seek in vain in the author of the *Critique of Pure Reason* and in the *maestro di coloro che sanno* (the master of all those who know), Dostoevsky hurls himself in an attack on the "eternal truths." And he attacks them precisely from the side which seemed "naturally" defended and consequently inaccessible. Before the wall, he says, men who are philosophically cultivated, that is, schooled by the Greeks, "bow down in all sincerity. . . . A wall for them has something calming, final, perhaps even mystical about it." Dostoevsky did not know Aristotle's metaphysics, he did not know his "Necessity does not allow itself to be convinced" and his "cry halt before Necessity"; but, if he had known them, he could not have better revealed and appreciated the meaning and content of the Stagyrite's philosophical endeavors. How did it happen that the greatest of the philosophers saw in the stone wall and in "two times two makes four" the final and supreme power and, what is more, prostrating himself before them, worshipped them?

Dostoevsky raises a question which must be considered as the basic question of the critique of pure reason but from which Kant, following the example of his predecessors, turned aside: the question of the conclusive value of proofs, of the source of that constraint which the self-evidences exercise. From where does this constraint come? Dostoevsky discovered in the Bible what, according to Gilson, the medieval philosophers had discovered there: "The divine law exercises no constraint on the will of man. . . . It is established that freedom is an absolute absence of constraint, even in relation to the divine law."[57] God does not constrain, but "two times two makes four" and the stone walls do constrain, and they constrain not only man but also the Creator. We have already heard enough about what "does not fall under God's omnipotence." Precisely because Necessity constrains, that is, is deaf to persuasion, men have seen in it something "calming, final, mystical even." Indeed, it is difficult for us to admit that an *indoctus* (unlearned man) should have been able to show such penetration and raise the basic problem of the metaphysics of knowledge. When Kant speaks of reason that aspires avidly to universal and necessary truths, when Aristotle writes at the beginning of his *Metaphysics* the famous phrase "by nature all men desire to know," they admit in advance and bless the constraint that flows from knowledge. The *doctor subtilis* himself—whose doctrine of freedom amounts almost to admitting the existence in the very bosom of being of a lawless, limitless arbitrariness—cannot prevent himself from adoring that constraining truth that is the condition *sine qua non* [indispensable] of knowledge. He defends his "freedom" by having recourse to the same means that are used for defending other truths: it cannot be found in *pejoris conditionis* (a worse condition). He writes: "Those who deny a contingent being are to be exposed to torture until they concede that it is possible not to be tortured." When Epictetus, to rid himself of those who dispute the principle of contradiction, is not content with referring to the self-evidences and appeals to more energetic means, to threats of violence, this is still understandable. One lets him pass, for he is considered only one of the *dei minores* [lesser gods] of philosophy. But Duns Scotus is not Epictetus, neither is Saint Thomas Aquinas. Duns Scotus is an extraordinarily keen and perceptive philosophical mind, a dialectician of genius. And yet, he also is obliged to have recourse to brutal physical constraint. If the truths did not possess for their defense anything but ideal proofs, if it were not given them to realize their rights through constraint and violence, there would not be much left of our so apparently solid knowledge. The God of the Bible constrains no one, but the truths of rational knowledge do not resemble the God of the Bible and do not even wish to resemble him: they constrain, and how they constrain! Self-evidence is only a hypocritical *sine effusione sanguinis* (without bloodshed) behind which pyres and tortures are hidden. And, let it be said by the way, this is what explains for us the paradoxical fact that the Christianity of the Middle Ages could have given birth to the Inquisition. If one can, if one must, defend the revealed truth by the same means as those employed to defend the truths obtained by natural reason, it is impossible to do without tortures, for the self-evident truths also rest, in the final analysis, on constraint.

The Greek philosophy stops here, as does the *Critique of Pure Reason*. But Dostoevsky feels that one cannot stop, that it is precisely here that the critique begins. "Two times two makes four (that is, the self-evident truths)," he writes, "is no longer life, gentlemen, but the beginning of death. In any case, man has always been afraid of the two times two makes four and I also am still afraid of it now." And suddenly he allows this to escape: "Two times two makes four is an insolence, two times two makes four rises across your way with hands on its hips and spits at you." The self-evidences and the reason which aspire so eagerly to self-evidence do not "satisfy" Dostoevsky, they "irritate" him. When he finds himself before the self-evident truths, he insults them, mocks them, sticks out his tongue at them. He wishes to live not according to rational freedom but according to his own "foolish" freedom. Such a pretension appears to us, to speak politely, absolutely paradoxical: we cannot admit such objections. Before reason and the truths that it reveals our teachers stood as if petrified, and they have taught us the same attitude. Bewitched by the fruits of the tree of knowledge which the Bible agrees were pleasant to the eyes and desirable to look at, not only Plato, that poetic and enthusiastic mind, but even the sober Aristotle, "moderate to excess," composed incomparable hymns to the glory of reason.

I cannot stop at length on this matter, but to show to what a degree the great representatives of the Attic genius found themselves dominated by the metaphysics of being that they had discovered, I shall recall to the reader these lines of the *Ethica Nicomachea* which, along with other passages of the same *Ethics* and the *Metaphysics,* express what determined the searchings of the Greek philosophy: "The activity of God, the blessedness of which surpasses everything, is purely contemplative, and among human activities the most blessed of all is that which most nearly approaches the divine activity."[58] If, as Gilson indicates,[59] the words "this is the perfection of man-likeness to God" express St. Thomas Aquinas' thought, then Plato's *catharsis* ends in "making oneself as like God as possible."[60] *Aletheia*—the truth which was opened up to the Greeks (*a-lanthanein*), is the immutable essence of being behind the changing appearances of the world accessible to all, and the contemplation of this essence dominated all their thoughts and desires. But even though he belonged to these *simplices* and *indocti* of which St. Augustine and St. Thomas Aquinas spoke, or, to put it better, precisely because he had conversed for so many years with the *simplices* and *indocti* who brought the Bible to the world, Dostoevsky discovered that the contemplation glorified by the Greeks consisted in the worship of the stone wall and of the petrifying "two times two makes four" and that under the much-vaunted freedom of philosophical search there was hidden an *enchantement et assoupissement surnaturel* [supernatural enchantment and slumber].

Yet what could Dostoevsky do? It is impossible to argue. Aristotle stops him cleanly with his "one can say this, but one cannot think it"; and Duns Scotus himself is not ashamed to declare "he is not to be argued with, but told that he is irrational." But in the final analysis, it is not others that Dostoevsky mocks, it is not with others—with Socrates, Plato and Aristotle—that he argues; it is with himself that he enters into battle, in himself that he tries painfully to overcome the fallen man and that *cupiditas scientiae* which Adam, who tasted the fruits of the forbidden tree, transmitted to us. This is why he had to say— no, not to say, but to cry: "I insist on my caprice and that it be guaranteed to me!" Or again: "I wish to live according to my foolish will and not according to the rational will." He sought to escape from the temptation "you will be like God, knowing" and the "all these things will I give thee if thou wilt fall down and worship me," as well as from that unconquerable fear before the "lawless and limitless arbitrariness of God" which was, it seems, inspired by the tempter in the first man and which became our second nature after the fall. "Hear, O Israel" signifies precisely that everything depends on the will of God—*omnis ratio veri et boni a Deo dependet* [everything which is true and good depends on God]. This is why it is written: "thou shalt worship the Lord thy God and Him only shalt thou serve." And he only will be able to free himself "from the bondage of corruption" (Romans VIII, 21.) who will overcome the fear before the boundless arbitrariness of God which our reason inspires in us and dissipate the enchantment of the eternal, uncreated truths. He only will be able to cry with the prophet: "Death, where is thy sting? Hell, where is thy victory?"

VII

The violence and frenzy of Dostoevsky's speech when he talks of the self-evident truths sufficiently show that he felt the deep, indissoluble bond that exists, as the Bible tells us, between knowledge and the evil that rules in the world. Insofar as and for as long as the truth is bound to knowledge, the evil is indestructible, the evil appears to be inherent in being as such. Medieval philosophy, which indifferently passed by Tertullian and Peter Damian but piously preserved the "first principles" of the Greeks, excluded from its field of vision the very possibility of the problematic of the book of Genesis, the problematic of knowledge. So it was obliged—like all the wise men of antiquity—not only to reconcile itself to the evil but to justify it. The philosophers of the Middle Ages were as little sensitive to the Apocalypse and its storms, to the book of Job and its cries, as to the story of Genesis about the fall of man. And, indeed, is it possible to oppose thunder and cries to reason? Thunder as well as cries come before reason: reason will calm the storm and suppress the cries. Even if he is a Christian, the philosopher will find more in Boethius' *De Consolatione* than in the Bible; or, in any case, with the help of Boethius' wisdom, he will succeed in calming the anxiety that the passionate words of Job and the rolls of thunder of the Revelation of St. John arouse in him. The "out of the depths I cried unto Thee, O Lord" likewise passes to the second level in the philosophy of the Middle Ages. The Psalmist's word does not, indeed, at all harmonize with the general spirit of the ancient philosophy, which was born "out of wonder" according to the teaching of Plato and Aristotle, and which has always warned men against despair and measureless sorrow.

Kierkegaard declared that the essential opposition between the Greek philosophy and the Christian philosophy comes from the fact that the former has for its source wonder and the latter despair. This is why the Greek philosophy, according to Kierkegaard, leads to reason and knowledge,[61] while the Christian philosophy begins where for the former all possibilities are ended, and puts all its hopes in the Absurd. Man no longer seeks to "know" and "understand"; he has become convinced that not only is knowledge impotent to help him but that it will demand that man worship it and see in its impotence something final, calming, mystical even. Kierkegaard returns to faith the position that the Bible had conferred upon it. It is only on the wings of faith that one can fly over all "stone walls" and the "two times two makes four" erected and apotheosized by reason and rational knowledge. Faith does not examine, it does not look around.

The Middle Ages, for which the Greek philosophy was a second "Old Testament" and which believed that Socrates' "know thy-self" had fallen from the heavens just like the *Audi Israel*, regarded thought as a looking around. The thought of Abraham, of the prophets and the apostles did not appear sufficient to it but had to be completed and corrected. To tell all, it was not really thought. Of course, this was not openly expressed thus, but everything that could be done was done to bring the structure and content of the truths of the Bible as close as possible to the ideal of the truth which the Greeks had worked out and in which, from the very beginnings of Hellenic philosophy, the Aristotelian assurance "intellect is a substance completely separated from the soul and is one in all men," was transparent. The Scholastics fought desperately against Aristotle's *intellectus separatus* (remember the polemic of Albertus Magnus and St. Thomas Aquinas against Siger of Brabant!)[62]; but even in fighting it they allowed themselves to be seduced by it. The ideal of the "reason that is separated from everything, impassive, and constitutes activity by its very essence"[63] (in the newer German philosophy *Bewusstsein überhaupt* [consciousness in general]) responded to the deepest needs of the soul that aspires to knowledge and finds in it calmness and peace.[64]

For God Himself one can find no greater praise than to represent Him under the aspect in which the *intellectus separatus* [intellect which is separate/ emancipated from God] appears in Aristotle. By means of the Aristotelian "the poets lie," medieval philosophy pushed aside the stories of the Bible which show us God rejoicing, being angry, regretting, etc., only for the purpose of "raising" God to the *intellectus separatus*. What is best in us, "what alone is immortal and eternal in us,"[65] is that by means of which we participate in reason. All of the Scholastics' thoughts reflect the deep conviction that the divine in the universe and in man is finally only "the separable, impassive and pure reason." This is never said *explicite*, but *implicite* this conviction persists in all the philosophic constructions. All that the Scholastics have told us of the principle of contradiction and of the other principles of our thought (more exactly, of being) permit us to realize the role that Aristotle's *intellectus separatus* (intellect which is separate from God) was destined to play in the development of the philosophy of the Middle Ages (and also of the new philosophy).

"It does not fall under God's omnipotence" is the decisive argument to which appeal is always made when it is a question of fundamental problems. Gilson's work testifies clearly to this. We have already seen how the Middle Ages interpreted the story of the fall. Having quoted the words of St. Paul which "echo the story of the book of Genesis"—"through one man sin entered the world"—Gilson writes, "Once more, in revealing to man a fact which by nature escapes him, revelation opens the way to the enterprises of reason."[66] But what does reason, placed before the truth that has been revealed to it about the fall of man, seek to achieve when it proposes to "understand" what it has learned from the Bible? Above everything, it must turn suspicion away from itself: it had, and still has, no part in the fall of the first man. Medieval philosophy, says Gilson, proposed "the most optimistic interpretation conceivable of a universe where evil is a fact whose reality cannot be denied."[67] The interpretation consists in the following: "Created *ex nihilo*, things are and are good because they are created, but their *changeability* is *inscribed* in their essence precisely because they are *ex nihilo*. Thus if one persists in calling the change to which nature is subjected as to an *ineluctable law* 'evil,' he must see that the possibility of change is a necessity that *God Himself could not eliminate* from what He had created, because the fact of being created is the deepest sign of this possibility itself."[68] And again: "It is not a question of knowing whether God could have made unchangeable creatures, *for this would be more impossible than to create square circles*. It has been seen that mutability is as co-essential to the nature of a contingent creature as immutability is co-essential to the nature of the necessary Being."[69]

Where did medieval philosophy find all this? Certainly not in the Bible. In the same chapter, "Christian Optimism," Gilson indicates that the optimism of medieval philosophy has for its point of departure the words of the Creator at the end of each day of creation, "and God saw that it was good," and the words spoken when, contemplating His work at the end of the sixth day, He declared Himself fully satisfied: "And God saw everything that He had made and it was very good." The story of the Bible does not make the least reference to the presence, in the act of creation, of any defect or fault which would have made possible the appearance of evil in the world. On the contrary, according to the Bible, the act of creation guarantees us that the created can and must be good, and only good. The idea that the created as created already bears in itself the possibility of evil was found by medieval philosophy not in the Bible but in the Greeks. Having created the world, the Demiurge of the *Timaeus* sees that the world is very far from perfection and tries, as much as is in his power, to correct his work, even if only partially. Epictetus relates, always rather naively but frankly and honestly, what he had learned from his teachers. We read in him that Zeus admits to Chrysippus that his power is limited: it was not in his power to give men full possession of the world and their bodies. He could give all this to them only for a certain time, for everything that is created, having had a beginning, must have an end (such is the law of being, ineluctable even for the gods: birth (*genesis*) is necessarily bound to death (*phthora*); so he made them participants in the divine reason (*intellectus separatus*), thanks to which they would somehow manage to adapt themselves and live in the created world.

So the Greeks thought: God, even for Plato, shares His power with Necessity. The act of creation inevitably introduced into the world imperfection and evil. But the position of the Bible is quite different: all possible perfections have for their single source the creative act of God. The Bible knows no power of Necessity and no insurmountable laws. It introduced into the world a new, unheard of idea—the idea of the created truth, the truth which the Creator rules as He wishes and which docilely accomplishes the desires of its master. How then could this truth change itself into an omnipotent law—this truth that was made to obey? Or must we admit that the Greek Demiurge was simply more perceptive than the Judeo-Christian Creator? The Demiurge realized immediately that there was something wrong in the universe, while the God of the Bible was content to repeat "very good" without suspecting that, by virtue of certain ineluctable laws which a mysterious hand had inscribed in the very essence of being, everything that is created cannot be "very good." In the final analysis, medieval philosophy discredited the creative act and admitted at the same time that God was not capable of estimating at its true value the world He had created.

It cannot be assumed, of course, that the medieval philosophers would have risen deliberately against the testimony of the Bible, just as it cannot be assumed that they would have used, in regard to the Bible, the expression "the poets lie" which Aristotle used concerning Homer. But the fundamental principles that they had accepted from the Greeks did their work for them. The Scholastics were ready to discredit the act of creation and to doubt the omniscience of God, rather than admit that there could be a defect in reason. They spoke, as if it were nothing, of the "ineluctable law" inscribed in the being of the created, of the impossibility for God Himself to get rid of this law, risen one knows not whence and imposed one knows not why—just as it is not given Him to create a round square. Every time they were convinced that they stood before an impossibility insurmountable even for God, it might truly be said that they felt, following Dostoevsky's expression, an almost mystical sense of satisfaction and inward peace: an impossibility, a stone wall, "two times two makes four"—consequently, one can and must stop.[70] That a round square is impossible—this truth, as irrefutable for God as for man, seems to be a gift fallen from heaven like the "know thyself" and other indisputable truths which, as also fallen from heaven, were gathered in ancient times by the Greeks: they guaranteed "knowledge."

But what difference is there between a round square and that mountain without a valley of which Descartes spoke? The mountain without a valley sets a bound only to human thought and does not in any way limit the divine omnipotence; why, then, should the round square enjoy such a privilege? Or must we consider what Descartes said merely a metaphor? He also did not believe that God was capable of creating a mountain without a valley and did not grant that the medieval philosophy, from which he had received the Bible that proclaims the possibility of mountains without valleys and round squares, had ever admitted any such thing: one can say this but one cannot think it, as the *maestro edi coloro che sanno* [the master of all those who knew] expressed it. The eternal truths are not created by God, they are drawn both for men and God from the *intellectus separatus*. It is Aristotle who judges the Bible and not the Bible that judges Aristotle: the principle of contradiction is "the most unshakable of principles." Without demanding authorization from anyone whomsoever, it inscribes whatever it pleases in the book of being and the Creator Himself is incapable of opposing it. We shall be obliged to return to this, but I would here cite the testimony of Leibniz who says that evil which, according to the doctrine of the Greeks, had its origin in matter flows, according to the "Christian doctrine," from the ideal, uncreated principles, from the eternal truths which, as we already know, were introduced into the mind of God without taking any account of His will.

We are convinced that, in the problem which was central for it, the philosophy of the Middle Ages rejected its task, which consisted in bringing to the world the idea, unknown to the ancients, of a created truth. It could still be assumed that God had created the universe—this Plato had also taught. But the truths are not created by God, they exist before Him and without Him and do not depend on Him. It is true that we meet also among the philosophers of the Middle Ages the idea of eternal, created truth. They thus acquired, in a way, the right to speak of conditions of being and existence that are "invincible" and "insurmountable" even for God. But they bought this right at the cost of an inner contradiction: for, if the truth is created, then, as we have just heard, it cannot be eternal and immutable—even if God wishes it. Yet to the created truth an indulgence is shown that the living man seeks in vain to obtain. The created man is necessarily imperfect and cannot pretend to eternal existence. But when it is a question of truth, the principle of contradiction shows itself disposed to renounce its sovereign rights: it grants to the created truth that immutability which is refused to living beings, without taking account of the precept "to believe against reason is blame-worthy."

And it was with the same heedlessness that medieval philosophy accepted the doctrine of the Greeks which affirmed that evil is only *privatio boni* (the privation of good). To him who wishes to "understand" evil, such an explanation appears satisfactory, for it more or less attains its goal. Evil arose "naturally" in the world; what other explanation can one then demand? All honor to the philosophy which could make the ineluctability of evil self-evident! Does not "to understand" and "to explain" consist in establishing that what is cannot be other than it is? In the knowledge that what is is inevitable ("everything that is real is rational," according to Hegel's formula), Greek philosophy succeeded in finding a solution, "something pacifying and even mystical." Yet the Judeo-Christian philosophy, insofar as it participated in the revealed truth, had as its task not to strengthen but finally to overcome the idea of inevitability. Gilson speaks to us of this many times. Evil explained does not cease to be evil. Evil as *privatio boni* [the privation of good] is quite as repugnant and inadmissible as evil that has received no explanation. And the attitude of the Bible towards evil is quite different. It does not wish to explain evil but to destroy it, to tear it out of being by the roots: before the face of the God of the Bible evil is changed into nothingness.

One can say that the very essence of the God of the Bible consists precisely in the fact that in "a world where evil is a given fact whose reality cannot be denied" there arises before Him in a mysterious way the possibility of what Gilson calls a "radical optimism": the metaphysics of knowledge of the Book of

Genesis refuses, contrary to the Greeks, to see in the "given fact" a reality that it is impossible to deny. It raises in its own way the question of what is a "fact," a "given," "reality" and, recalling "God saw everything that He had made and it was very good," it asks audaciously whether the "fact," the "given," the "real" actually possess the "final" character that we, not daring to dispute with reason and the principle of contradiction produced by reason, attribute to them. For Aristotle this is pure madness. He knows with certainty that the given is "the first and the beginning."[71] We today also say: one cannot argue with facts. And indeed, he who "knows" does not argue; he prostrates himself before facts. Knowledge paralyses his will, and he accepts everything that it brings him, convinced in advance that knowledge will make him like the gods (*eritis sicut dei scientes*). But the Bible says something else. God does not do this or that because it is good, but this or that is good because it was created by God. We know that this doctrine of Duns Scotus was rejected by medieval philosophy just as by modern philosophy. For our intelligence it is even more unacceptable than Plotinus' "beyond reason and knowledge"; or, to put it better, Plotinus' "beyond" frightens us because we feel that it hides within itself just that which Seeberg calls "arbitrary, lawless and boundless." Nevertheless, terrible as this may appear to us, the God of the Bible is not bound by any rule, by any law; He is the source of all rules and all laws just as He is master of the Sabbath. The tree of knowledge was planted by God near the tree of life, but not in order for man to feed on its fruits. The opposition of good and evil or, more exactly, the appearance of evil, bears no relation to the creation of the world; then everything was "very good," but only up to the moment of man's fall. Before then nothing limited the divine freedom and the human as well. Everything was good because it was made by God; everything was good because it was made by man, who was created in the image and likeness of God. This is precisely what this "very good" that is so mysterious to us means. Freedom as the possibility of choosing between good and evil, that freedom which the Greeks knew and which passed into medieval and modern philosophy, is only the freedom of the fallen man, freedom deformed by sin. It allowed evil to penetrate into the world and is powerless to drive it out. Thus, the more man clings to the idea that his salvation depends on "knowledge" and the possibility of distinguishing good and evil, the more deeply sin penetrates and roots itself in him. He turns away from the Bible's "very good," just as he turned away from the tree of life, and puts all his hopes in the fruits he gathers from the tree of knowledge.

"Good and evil by which we are praiseworthy or blameworthy"—so the Pelagians expressed themselves: praise or blame for good or evil actions become, in the eyes of man, not only the principal but the only spiritual value.

Thomas Aquinas—and in this he does not at all distinguish himself from the other philosophers of the Middle Ages—demands calmly, without apparently suspecting what he is doing, "whether to believe is meritorious." But is not faith a gift, the greatest gift that man can receive from the Creator? I recall once more "nothing shall be impossible for you." (Matthew XVII, 20) What can our merits and the praises of him who kept watch over the tree of knowledge do here? Is it not he who still suggests such questions to men today? To be sure, if freedom is only the possibility of choosing between good and evil and if faith is the result of such a choice when conditioned by the good, then one can speak of man's merits and even assume that our merits cannot but be recognized by God's judgment. But the judgment where our merits decide our fate or have even only a certain influence on the way in which our fate is decided, the judgment where virtues will be rewarded and vices punished, is not the "final judgment" of the Bible but the moral judgment of the Greeks that is perfectly understandable to man. In the Bible preference is given to the sinner who has repented over ten righteous men, there is more rejoicing over the return of the prodigal son than over the constancy of the faithful son, the publican takes precedence over the pious Pharisee. In the Bible the sun rises indifferently on the good and the evil. But even St. Augustine, who denounced Pelagius so unpityingly, can hardly bear the immorality of the Bible and allows a sigh of relief to escape when, dreaming of another world, he can allow himself to say: "there the sun does not rise over the good and evil, but the sun protects only the righteous."

VIII

The Pelagian *bonum et malum quo nos laudabiles vel vituperabiles sumus* (good and evil by which we are praiseworthy or blameworthy), in other words, the fruits of the tree of the knowledge of good and evil, became the spiritual nourishment *par excellence,* the "one thing necessary," for the medieval philosophers as it had been for the Greeks. "The greatest good of man is to discourse daily about virtue," says Socrates in Plato's *Apology.* And we shall hardly be mistaken if we see in this the *articulus stantis et cadentis* of the Greek wisdom. Gilson is certainly right when he urges us not to put too much trust in what is customarily called "the perfect serenity (*sérénité*) of the Greek world." Nietzsche was the first to discover many things which no one had suspected. He saw, we recall, and showed us in Socrates the *décadent,* the fallen man. And it was precisely in what the Delphic oracle regarded as his greatest merit and in what Socrates himself saw his difference from other men that his fall, in Nietzsche's eyes, consisted: Socrates esteemed and taught others to esteem in life only the praises of the good and feared and taught others to fear only the blame of the same good.

All of the Greek wisdom is based on this principle. The dialectic discovered by the Greeks had as its essential task to denigrate the fruits of the tree of life, to convince man of their uselessness and nothingness. The basic objection that the Greeks, as well as St. Augustine and later the Scholastics, made to the fruits of the tree of life was that these fruits are not in our power: the possibility of obtaining them, and still more of preserving them, does not depend on us. From this derives the very significant distinction made by the Stoics between "what is in our power" and "what is not in our power," and their no less famous doctrine that man must seek only that which is in his power, all the rest being relegated into the domain of the "indifferent."

We find in Epictetus the confession that the beginning of philosophy is the knowledge that man has of his own impotence before Necessity. To escape from the Necessity which rules in this world, there is no other means of salvation, the Greeks believed, than to turn toward the intelligible world. It is there that the wise man seeks a refuge against the sufferings, the horrors, the injustices of the real world. And since the intelligible world is accessible only to reason, to the spiritual vision, to the "eyes of the mind," the Greeks naturally put all their hope in reason and regarded it as the highest part of man. Furthermore, they had irrefutable arguments for doing so: man is a rational animal. Reason is his *differentia specifica* [specific difference] which distinguishes him from the genus of animals in general and, consequently, it is in this that his essence as man consists. For man to live according to nature, taught the Stoics, means to live according to reason. The Scholastic philosophy joyfully received this truth, among so many others, from the hands of the Greeks without even taking the trouble to look at what Scripture said on the matter or, to put it better, prepared in advance not assuredly to reject, but to be silent about, or interpret, everything in the Bible that could not be harmonized with the wisdom of the Greeks. It read in St. Paul that the principal and essential thing for man resides neither in reason nor in knowledge. Knowledge makes man presumptuous, and all the gifts of knowledge are nothing without love. The philosophers of the Middle Ages spoke constantly of love—Gilson devotes a remarkable chapter to their doctrine of love—but, as we shall see, the Scholastics were also obliged to proceed to a purification, a catharsis, of the love of the Bible in order not to offend in any way the ancient ideal. In the medieval philosophers love is transformed into what Spinoza later called *amor Dei intellectualis* [the intellectual love of God], so that Gilson's chapter could be applied quite as well to the philosophy of Spinoza as to that of the Middle Ages.

"When the so-called philosophers by chance speak what is true and corresponds to our faith, this is to be claimed for our use as from unjust possessors":

so St. Augustine defined his attitude towards Greek philosophy. Yet, as we have already had occasion to become convinced, in fact it was the opposite that happened: the Greek truth was not verified by means of the biblical truth but the biblical by means of the Greek. When trying to reconcile the Platonism of St. Augustine and of Dionysus the Areopagite with his own doctrine, St. Thomas Aquinas wrote: "For the intellectual light itself which is in us is none other than a certain similarity through participation with the uncreated light in which the eternal truths are contained."[72] It is difficult not to recognize here the idea of "the separated reason, the only immortal and eternal thing," the *intellectus separatus* of Aristotle. St. Thomas, it is true, refers to the text (Psalms IV, 7.): "There be many that say, Who will show us any good? Lord, lift Thou up the light of Thy countenance upon us." He also quotes the well-known text of St. Paul, Romans I, 20. But these quotations precisely make clear the goal that the medieval philosophers set themselves when they sought "metaphysical principles" in the Bible.

By means of the method of analogy, the most risky of methods imaginable, medieval philosophy passed from the empirical truths that the intelligence discovers in experience to the eternal and unchangeable truths that it called "metaphysical." Now when we examine it closely, it appears that the method of analogy is very little distinguished from the method of discovery of truth employed by Socrates and which hid in itself a secret defect. As has already been indicated, the latter inevitably led the last of the great Greek philosophers, Plotinus, to a distrust of the very essence of Greek thought. Socrates took for his point of departure what men ordinarily considered true and good; starting from this, he deduced that there is an eternal truth and an unchangeable good. He dealt always with men of action, practical men—smiths, carpenters, doctors, politicians, etc. He thus arrived at the conviction that the essence of the truth and the good consists in knowing the conditions in which man is born and in living in such a way as to submit to them and adapt one's activity to them. Up to this point he doubtless followed the right way. But when he concluded that the laws and conditions of human existence that he had observed reflected the truth *an sich* and that submission to these conditions was the good *an sich*, he committed a crying "leap into another realm." It is, indeed, just the contrary: the truth *an sich* and the good *an sich* cannot be perceived by him who, thanks to the conditions of his existence, finds himself placed in the necessity of "learning" and "adapting himself." The truth and the good live on a completely different level. How little the biblical words "lift Thou up the light of Thy countenance upon us" resembles those *rationes aeternae* (eternal reasons) for which the medieval philosophy, hypnotized by the Greek wisdom, had exchanged them! Here again we are forced to remember the tree of knowledge and the tree of life. The tree of knowledge bore the eternal truths and the "good and evil by which we are praiseworthy and blameworthy," that is, worthy of the praise and blame of him who, with his "you will be like God" reduced the human soul to slavery. Can one imagine anything which less resembles the living God of biblical thought than the eternal truths, incapable of changing anything whatsoever that they bring to man, congealed, petrified and petrifying? It is true that the Scholastic philosophers could cite—and they did not fail to do so—"I am the Lord and I do not change." But it is here that Gilson's comment is justified: our concepts fall to pieces when we try to introduce into them the content of the Bible. The immutability of God has nothing in common with the immutability of the eternal truths. The latter do not change because they have not the power to change; God does not change because, and insofar as, He does not wish to change and does not judge it good to do so. When Abraham, the father of faith, intercedes on behalf of Sodom and Gomorrah, God listens calmly, takes what he says into consideration and changes his decision. Of such examples one can find as many as one wishes in the Bible, and if one is not afraid of Aristotle and his "the poets lie," one would have to admit that the immutability of the biblical God has not even the most distant resemblance to that immutability which the Greek wisdom venerated, but even excludes it. Like the Sabbath, the immutability of which the Bible speaks exists for man and not man for the immutability. Immutability does not rule God, it serves Him, as do all the other truths which, insofar as they are created, possess only an executive power and only for as long as they are of some use.

All this clarifies, to a certain point, the relationship between the tree of knowledge and the fall of man. Enthralled by the tempter's words *eritis scientes,* Adam exchanged the freedom which determined his relationship to the Creator who hears and listens for a dependence on the indifferent and impersonal truths which do not hear and do not listen to anything and automatically actualize the power which they have seized. That is why it is incorrect to speak of the relationship of man to God as a relationship of dependence: the relationship of man to God is freedom. And it was precisely this that Dostoevsky had in mind when, face to face with "two times two makes four," with "the stone wall" and with other "impossibilities," he demanded that his "caprice" be guaranteed to him. He choked "in a universe where evil is a given fact whose reality cannot be denied," and he felt the necessity of submitting to the "given" as the consequence of the original sin. This is also the profound meaning of Nietzsche's doctrine concerning the morality of masters and slaves: behind Nietzsche's apparent atheism was hidden a desperate thrust towards the freedom of the innocent man who gave names to all things and ruled over all things. With still greater right Nietzsche could have spoken of the truths of masters and the truths of slaves, but he lacked the daring to do this.

We are so strictly bound by the fundamental principles of the ancient philosophy which we have imbibed with our mother's milk that every attempt to oppose to these principles the truth of the Bible appears to us not only mad but sacrilegious. The most remarkable representatives of the philosophy of the Middle Ages expected salvation from the fruits of the tree of knowledge and, despite his flights of genius, St. Augustine himself did not leave the eyes of the Greeks. He who so glorified the Bible nevertheless aspired to self-evidences; he who rose with such violence against Pelagius and his friends nevertheless believed that freedom consisted in the liberty to choose between good and evil and made man's salvation dependent on his merits and works. Thus when one compares St. Augustine's own writings with those fragments of the Psalms and other books of the Bible that he so joyfully interpolates in them, one cannot fail to notice, despite all the author's ingenuity, something artificial. It is not a free flight but a struggle against the all too human law of gravity: the arguments with which he abundantly sprinkles his reflections and a certain vehemence of tone remind us always that, even when it is a question of grace, the "mechanism" of understanding is not overcome.[73]

The "habit of reflecting on his faith," as well as the invincible need *die moralische Betrachtung der religiosen zu überordnen* (to set the moral point of view over the religious) permeate the whole medieval philosophy and particularly the doctrine of grace. When we are told "grace does not abolish nature,"[74] it may seem that this is a loving tribute to the Creator. But, on the contrary, we must see here a trick of reason which wishes at all costs to preserve its sovereignty. For reason the *potentia ordinata* (ordered power) of God is much more comprehensible and much more acceptable than his *potentia absoluta* (absolute power), which it fears at bottom more than everything in the world. Reason seeks and finds everywhere a well-defined order, an arrangement established once for all. It even goes so far as to oppose *potentia absoluta* to *potentia ordinata* as a supernatural to a natural order, thus brushing aside in advance every threat against the integrity of its sovereign rights. The following example is sufficiently eloquent in this connection, even though it concerns an unimportant question. We read in St. Thomas Aquinas: "Some say that the animals which are now wild and kill other animals were in that state (before the sin) tame, not only toward men but toward animals. But this is completely unreasonable. For the nature of animals was not changed through the sin of man so that those, for example lions and falcons, for whom it is now natural to eat the flesh of others then lived on plants."[75] Once more we must recognize that St. Thomas is right: "it is completely unreasonable" to assume that the carnivores fed on grass before the fall.

ATHENS AND JERUSALEM

But we read in Isaiah that God does not ask what must be according to the nature of things. The whole world knows the famous words: "the wolf and the lamb shall feed side by side and the lion will eat straw like the bullock." (Isaiah, LXV, 25.) St. Francis of Assisi even succeeded in changing the nature of the wolf merely by means of the soft words "brother wolf." And he succeeded in doing this only because, like Isaiah, he did not wish to "know" and did not aspire to transform the truth of revelation into self-evident and immutable metaphysical principles. For St. Francis of Assisi and Isaiah, unshakableness and immutability, the things that constitute the very essence of knowledge and that human reason seeks so avidly, offered nothing enticing: on the contrary, these terrified them. "'Two times two makes four' is already the beginning of death": every line of the Bible tells us this again and again. And if one had declared to the Apostle that "in a universe where evil is a given fact, its reality cannot be denied," he would have answered with the well known words: "The fool saith in his heart, 'there is no God.'" For the fact, the given, does not at all have the right to limit the divine omnipotence: the divine "very good" denies the fact as well as all "given," and only human reason sees in the "wherefore" (*hoti*) the "first and the beginning" (*to prôton kai archê*) which it has never been.

If one had proven to the Apostle with all the required evidence, like "two times two makes four," that man is descended from the ape, neither proofs nor evidence would have convinced him. He would perhaps have repeated Dostoevsky's words, "but what does it matter to me?" Probably, however, he would have recalled the Bible: " . . . as thou hast believed, so be it done unto thee." In other words, if you believe that you are of God, you are of God; if you believe that you come from an ape, you come from an ape: "the righteous shall live by faith." This is "entirely unreasonable," and it is beyond doubt that reason would direct the entire arsenal of its *vituperabilia* against the daring man who would have the audacity to affirm that among men some are descended from Adam who was created by God, and others from an ape that came naturally into the world and that no one created—and that this depends only on their faith.

For faith has nothing to do with this: it is knowledge and the eternal truths of the *intellectus* that rule in this domain. "For the intellectual light is nothing but a certain similarity through participation in the uncreated light." It is not given to any faith to overcome the self-evidence of the truths of reason. They are truths of reason precisely because no power in the world can overcome them. And if we attribute immutability to the Creator Himself it is only because we wish to see and can see in Him the "uncreated light": the method of analogy authorizes and obliges us to do so.

I have not here the space necessary to point out, like Gilson, all that the Scholastics accomplished in the domain of philosophy or, more exactly, the results at which they arrived in trying, and insofar as they tried, to draw from the Bible eternal and unshakable truths by using the principles and methods of research that they had inherited from the Greeks. Before the tree of life and the tree of knowledge they, like the first man, did not have the power to overcome the temptation *eritis scientes*. For the Scholastics, as for the Greeks, the final source of truth was reason with its immutable laws. That is why, as we have seen, they so carefully protected the principle of contradiction and were even ready to sacrifice to it the omnipotence of the Creator. That is why St. Augustine granted that the will of the fallen man was free, notwithstanding that it subjected itself without protest to that law by virtue of which "in our world where evil is a given fact whose reality cannot be denied" evil must be "explained" and accepted. To argue with the Greeks was to condemn oneself in advance to defeat or, to put it better, it was possible to argue with the Greeks only after having once for all taken the decision to renounce their principles as well as their technique of thought.

"If you wish to subject everything to yourself, subject yourself to reason." This was the summing up of the Greek wisdom, according to Seneca's formula. How could the Middle Ages reply to this maxim? Could they perceive here a temptation? Our entire experience of life and our entire reason are on the side of the Greeks. Philosophy in this respect is only the systematization and most complete expression of discoveries that each of us makes every day: one does not argue with facts, the fact is the final and definitive reality. The principle of contradiction and that law, just as unshakable, which holds itself under its protection and which says that what has been cannot not have been are inscribed in some way in the very structure of being, and the omnipotent Creator Himself is incapable of delivering being from their hold. It is only on condition of accepting and worshipping them that man, as Seneca, the disciple of the Greeks, tells us, can dominate the world. But in the Bible we hear something quite different. When the powerful and crafty spirit says, as if repeating Seneca: "All these things will I give thee if thou wilt fall down and worship me," he hears in reply: "Get thee hence, Satan, for it is written, 'Thou shalt worship the Lord thy God and Him only shalt thou serve.'" In other words, one does not even argue with reason, with its principle of contradiction, its "two times two makes four," its stone walls (that which has been cannot not have been; in the world where evil is a fact, its reality cannot be denied; man is descended naturally from the ape, etc.). One simply chases it away as a usurper—this reason to which he must submit in order to obtain any good.

Such is the teaching of the Bible. When Dostoevsky rudely mocked the pretensions of reason and its universal and necessary truths, he was only following the Bible. And though human, all too human, it was nevertheless an *imitatio Christi* (imitation of Christ). Reason does not have and cannot have a single universal and necessary truth, and it is not given to it, any more than to anyone except the Creator, to inscribe its laws in the structure of being. It is not in vain, however, that Kant said that experience only "irritates" the philosopher; experience does not contain what rational philosophy seeks to obtain. Experience does not at all prove that the principle of contradiction "does not fall under God's omnipotence" or what has been cannot not have been. All the "stone walls," all the "two times two makes four" already constitute a certain addition to experience, and it is from this addition that the tempter drew his *eritis scientes* [you will know].

Accordingly, the Bible sees in the eternal truths that are independent of the Creator only a lie, a suggestion, an enchantment. If the first man and all of us after him have not the power nor even the will to rid ourselves of these truths, this does not at all give us the right to consider them as something definitive and consequently calming, even mystical. On the contrary, this ought to be for us a source of unceasing, torturing, insurmountable anxiety. And it is certain that this anxiety has always persisted and persists still in the human soul, and that the Middle Ages knew it only too well. But it is no less certain that man fears anxiety above everything and makes every effort to choke it in himself. He is ready to accept anything whatsoever as definitive and forever insurmountable in fact and in right—matter, inertia, walls indifferent to everything—in order to be able to escape anxiety and cease struggling. *Non lugere neque detestari* [do not weep nor curse]—the Greek philosophy could never resolve to pass beyond the limits of this ideal. It is from this that the *credo ut intelligam* (I believe so that I may understand) of St. Augustine, of Anselm of Canterbury and of all those who followed them comes. From this comes Spinoza's *non ridere, non lugere, neque detestari, sed intelligere* [do not laugh, do not weep, nor curse, but understand]. Nietzsche himself, who overwhelmed minds with his "beyond good and evil" (which denied the fruits of the tree of knowledge though people did not realize it, any more than Nietzsche did), his morality of masters, his will to power (*Deus omnipotens, ex nihilo creans omnia*—allpowerful God who makes all things out of nothing), ended by glorifying the "love of fate." The supreme wisdom consists in loving the inevitable. He forgot that it was precisely this that Socrates, whom he recognized as the fallen man *par excellence,* had taught. But the Stoics are descended from Socrates, and when Seneca writes, "I do not obey God but I agree with Him in spirit, nor do I follow Him because it is necessary," he was only repeating Socrates.

On this point the Middle Ages could not and would not break with the tradition of Greek philosophy. It could not do this because it had borrowed from it the fundamental principles and technique of thought. It would not do it because this happens "not of him that willeth, nor of him that runneth, but of God that showeth mercy." (Romans IX, 16.) Certain chapters of the second volume of Gilson's work are particularly instructive in this respect: *L'Amour et son objet* (Love and Its Object), *Libre arbitre et liberté chretienne* (Free Will and Christian Freedom), *Loi et moralité chrétienne* (Christian Law and Morality). Medieval philosophy at times made extreme and desperate efforts to preserve the truth of revelation, while accepting the Greek wisdom. But all its efforts remained fruitless: the truth of revelation ended by completely resembling the natural truth. And this resemblance is expressed, above everything, in that it refuses to recognize its dependence on the Creator but wishes that the Creator obey it. From this comes the following unexpected and paradoxical result: when one reads the chapters mentioned above where, with his customary masterfulness, Gilson succeeds in giving an exposition in a relatively modest number of pages of the fundamental ideas of Scholasticism, it seems at times that it is not the medieval philosophy that is being discussed here but Spinoza's, and that the numerous quotations and references to the Bible must be taken in a figurative sense—or that there is to be seen here simply one of those annoying carelessnesses that even the greatest minds do not always succeed in avoiding. Be it a question of the peace of the soul, of the love of God, of virtue, of nature, of freedom—whatever be the theme of the medieval philosopher, one cannot fail to evoke the memory of the solitary Dutchman. There is the same aspiration towards a universal, rigorous and immutable order joined to an indifference, a scorn even, for all the goods of life (it is known that Spinoza reduced them to "wealth, honor and pleasures"); the same glorification of contemplation and of the spiritual joys which flow from it; the same freedom of the man *qui sola ratione ducitur*, who has adapted himself to the inescapable laws of the structure of being (*homo emancipatus a Deo* [man separate from God]); and finally the *amor Dei intellectualis* [the intellectual love of God] which dominates everything.

For medieval philosophy, says Gilson, "human love is only a finite participation in the love that God has for Himself."[76] And again, "God's love is only the generosity of the Being whose superabundant plenitude loves itself in itself and in its possible participations."[77] And in Spinoza we read: "For the mind's intellectual love of God is part of the infinite love with which God loves Himself"[78]; then, in the corollary, "hence it follows that, insofar as God loves Himself, He loves men, and consequently that God's love for men and the mind's intellectual love of God are one and the same." Whether Spinoza received his fundamental ideas directly from the Greeks or through the medium of the medieval philosophers is of no importance. What is important is that there is not and cannot be any trace in them of what animated and nourished the Judeo-Christian thought, no matter how we interpret the latter. The philosophy of Spinoza, as highly as we may value it, demands as *conditio sine qua non* [indispensable condition] that we renounce completely the truths of revelation. For Spinoza the Bible has nothing in common with the truth, just as the truth has nothing in common with the Bible. No one in the Seventeenth Century opposed to the stories of the Bible the Aristotelian "the poets lie" with so much frankness, rigor and courage as Spinoza. If it appears finally that the Scholastics were so close to Spinoza (one could show that the Scholastics' doctrine of being, founded on the Bible's "I am that I am" is not at all distinguished from Spinoza's doctrine of being), this would already entitle us to conclude that the Scholastics, *as philosophers,* were not inspired by the Bible, and that it was at the school of the *maestro di coloro che sanno* (master of all those who knew) that they learned to seek and find what they needed, not in the "foolishness of preaching" but in the self-evidences of reason.

Gilson opposes Luther to the Scholastic philosophy and, in emphasizing this opposition, says that many of the reproaches made against the Scholastics should have been addressed rather to Luther. It is beyond doubt, indeed, that Luther's doctrine is completely contrary to what the Scholastics sought and obtained. And Luther did not hide this. St. Thomas, he writes, "wrote many heretical things and is the originator of the now ruling pious doctrine of the awful Aristotle." Here, furthermore, is just one of his milder judgments on St. Thomas. Gilson is also right when he says that a consistent Lutheran is a *rara* (I would even say *rarissima*) *avis* [a rare or the rarest bird]. And yet Luther is strictly connected to the medieval philosophy, in the sense that the very possibility of his appearance presupposes the existence of a Judeo-Christian philosophy which, setting as its task to proclaim the idea—hitherto unknown—of a created truth, continued to cultivate the fundamental principles and technique of the ancient thought. Luther is ordinarily not even considered a philosopher by those, in any case, like M. de Wulf, who identify philosophy with rational philosophy. It would be more just, however, to place oneself on other grounds and to ask oneself: does not Luther belong to the small number of those who have daringly tried to realize the idea of philosophy that is not rational but Judeo-Christian, of a philosophy which permits itself to submit to a new examination precisely those fundamental principles and those methods of discovering the truth which, as "things known of themselves," the Middle Ages had accepted from their Greek masters docilely and without verifying them? Luther's *sola fide* (by faith alone) and *his tenebrae fidei, ubi nee lex, nee ratio lucet* (the darkness of faith, where neither law nor reason shines)—are these not an obvious reaction to the systematic attempt of the Scholastics to submit the truth of revelation to the control and guardianship of the truths that are obtained naturally?

For our reason faith is darkness, it is the lower degree which must be transcended in order to obtain clear and distinct knowledge. The apostles and the prophets were content with faith; the philosopher wishes more—he wishes to know. The apostles and the prophets awaited their salvation from on high; the philosopher finds his salvation through wisdom founded on stable knowledge, hopes to obtain the good will of the gods by means of his wise life, and wishes even that this wise life should guarantee him salvation: "God does not deny grace to him who does what is his." All this had been borrowed by the Scholastics from the Greeks. In the preceding chapters I have quoted many passages from Plato and Aristotle on this subject, and these quotations could be multiplied. But as for Luther, he fled from Athens. He feared, as Dostoevsky instinctively feared, the eternal truths; his entire being aspired to Jerusalem. Reason, which we consider our natural light, leads us to our ruin. The law, on which we rely as on an unshakable rock, in reality only multiplies the crimes. "Because man is presumptuous and imagines himself to be wise, righteous and holy, it is necessary that he be humbled by the law, that thus that monster—the illusion of his own righteousness—without whose killing man cannot live, be put to death." *Homo non potest vivere* is, in Luther, an objection against the self-evident truths that are revealed to us by the light of reason and the law. Similar objections were, for the Greeks, something completely new or, to put it better, simply could not find a place on the level of Greek thought. To obtain the truth, we must "kill" the self-evidences. "The righteous shall live by faith." This is the point of departure of what Kierkegaard was later to call "existential philosophy" and which he opposed to the speculative philosophy that we have inherited from the Greeks. Hence comes the implacable hatred that Luther had for Aristotle,[79] hence come Luther's *sola fide* and *servum arbitrium* (the bound will).

Luther's enslaved will is that *enchantement et assoupissement surnaturel* [supernatural enchantment and slumber] of which Pascal speaks. "Nothing is more strongly opposed to faith than law and reason, nor can these two be overcome without great effort and labor; yet they must be overcome if you wish to be saved." When and for as long as man puts his hope of salvation in them, our knowledge and our virtues are only "instruments and weapons of that infernal tyrant, i.e., sin, and through all these you are forced to serve the devil and to promote and augment his kingdom." Having tasted the fruits of the tree of knowledge, man has lost faith, and with faith freedom. Our will is bound by sin—it is paralyzed, plunged into a "deep dizziness" (Kierkegaard), almost dead. Knowledge has handed man over to the power of the truths that are uncreated or freed of God, and his virtues simply testify that he has exchanged God's "it was very good" for "the good and evil by which we are praiseworthy or blameworthy," that is, the fruits of the tree of knowledge. Such is the terrible and fateful consequence of the fall of the first man. He cannot escape from that slumber of the spirit which is altogether like death. The *eritis scientes* has enchained his intelligence as well as his consciousness; it has permeated and cast a spell over his entire being. Man aspires to knowledge, he is persuaded that knowledge is the same thing as salvation. Even more: if it appeared that knowledge is not salvation and that man had to choose between the two, he would prefer knowledge to salvation—as Clement of Alexandria said. This was, for Luther, the profound meaning of all the searchings of the Scholastic philosophy. But going further still, Luther had to recognize, terrified, that every man—and he himself before all—is in the power of that "infernal tyrant," i.e., sin, and that not only has he not the power to rid himself from this spell but that his fallen being continues to see in the *eritis scientes* and in the "walls of stone," the "two times two makes four," and the other self-evidences introduced by the *eritis scientes*, a solution—something calming and even mystical. Hence Luther's furious attacks against reason and its knowledge, against human wisdom and its virtues.

Gilson says: "To encounter *De servo arbitrio,* we must go to Luther. With the Reformation there appeared for the first time that radical conception of a grace which saves man without changing him, a justification which redeems corrupted nature without curing it."[80] Luther, indeed, was the first who spoke of the enslaved will; but he spoke of it precisely because he saw in our knowledge the original sin and became convinced that the Scholastic philosophy, instead of trying to deliver the will paralyzed by the sin of knowledge, followed the Greeks and did everything in its power to take away from man every possibility of regaining his original freedom. It taught, indeed, that knowledge is the highest degree of faith and that the wisdom founded on knowledge is the way to salvation. It concerned itself, then, with something quite other than restoring man and healing him from his frightful sickness. It declared that everything could still be put in order through good will and with the help of the Greek

m. But, in Luther's eyes, this was proof that not only is our will bound but it has even lost the memory of what freedom is. It loves its dependence on eternal truths emancipated from God with that love with which, according to the great commandment of the Bible, it should love God alone. From this *enchantement et assoupissement surnaturel*, to repeat once more Pascal's words, there is no salvation but through a help that is also supernatural. Our knowledge nourishes "that monster without whose killing man cannot live." Only the foolishness of faith, which does not ask anything of anyone, can awaken man from that torpor into which he sank after tasting the fruits of the tree of knowledge.

Luther's doctrine of the law and redemption is bound to *sola fide* and *de servo arbitrio*. We imagine that the law exists in order to direct man and to punish him: the Greeks always and everywhere sought, and taught us to seek, laws in order to submit to them. But the Bible tells us something else: when Moses was on the mountain face to face with God he had no law, but when he descended from the mountain he began to govern the people by means of law. Where God is there is no law, there is freedom. And where freedom is not, God is not. Redemption, according to Luther, consists in man's deliverance from the domination of sin, from the domination of the truths and laws that enslave him; the freedom of innocence, of ignorance, is returned to him. Sin not only does not exist in the present, it has also not existed in the past. "In a universe where evil is a given fact whose reality cannot be denied," *Deus omnipotens ex nihilo creans omnia* [the allpowerful God who makes all things out of nothing] shatters by His word the fundamental principle of the ancient thought: that which has been cannot not have been. "All the prophets saw this in the spirit," writes Luther, "that Christ would be the greatest robber, thief, blasphemer, murderer, adulterer, etc., such that no greater would ever be in the world."[81] Several pages further[82] Luther "explains" this shaking "truth" in a series of images that are even more terrible because they are more concrete: "God sent his only begotten son into the world and threw upon him all the sins of all men, saying, 'Be thou Peter, that denier; Paul, that persecutor, blasphemer and violent man; David, that adulterer; that sinner who ate the apple in paradise; that robber on the cross—in short, be thou the man who committed the sins of all men.'" These words of Luther's are for the Greek and medieval philosophy the worst of absurdities. God cannot overcome the principle of contradiction, for "it does not fall under God's omnipotence." God does not possess any magic word capable of rooting out of the past the sins of Peter, Paul and David and bringing it about somehow that the original sin, the sin of Adam, from which all the other sins flowed, never existed. The "eternal truths, truths emancipated from God" here automatically set a limit to the divine omnipotence. And it is still less possible and thinkable that the sins of David, of Peter, of Paul, and even of Adam should not be their sins but the sins of God—that God be a criminal "such that no greater has ever been in the world." To say such things is to defy and to outrage the Greek philosophy and the whole of the Greek wisdom.

Yet the task of the Scholastics, the task of the Judeo-Christian philosophy, consisted precisely in making all truths dependent on the Creator. Luther was not afraid to force "the most unshakable of principles," the principle of contradiction, as well as the self-evident truth that flows from it (what has been cannot not have been), to retreat before the divine omnipotence. It is only thus that one can radically heal man's fallen nature, it is only thus that one can destroy to the root the evil which entered the world along with sin and lead men back to the divine *valde bonum* (very good), to return to them that freedom which is not the freedom of choosing between good and evil with their praises and condemnations but the freedom to create the good, as He who made man in His own image creates it. Can one say that Luther speaks of the grace that saves man "without changing him, without curing him?" And does not the fallen man's complete and final *restitutio in integrum* [restitution to his state of health] consist precisely in the restoration of his freedom from the "eternal truths" and in the annihilation of sin not only in the present but also in the past (for as long as sin exists in the past it continues to rule in the present)?

So then Luther, with his *sola fide,* made a mad, desperate attempt to realize the very thing that the Judeo-Christian philosophy considered its essential task. History, it is true, has seen to it that men should not listen to Luther, as they have not listened to other thinkers who aspired to create a Judeo-Christian philosophy without taking account of the problems, principles or technique of the thought of the Greeks and who dared to oppose the "faith" of Jerusalem to the "knowledge" of Athens in order to overcome the latter through the former. But can history be considered the final court?

X

History pushed Luther into the background, just as it had pushed Plotinus, Tertullian, Peter Damian, and even Duns Scotus. Athens triumphed over Jerusalem. And if Descartes became the father of the new philosophy, it was only because he addressed himself to men—as he himself admitted—without taking any account of the faith to which they belonged. This is the meaning of Hamelin's statement that Descartes came after the ancients as if between them and him there had been no one except the physicists. In his letters we find such solemn declarations as "every ground of the true and the good depends on God's omnipotence." If this formula which united in itself the "soaring above knowledge" of Plotinus and the "everything else from God is good because it is willed by God and not *vice versa*" of Duns Scotus—had been completely realized in his philosophy, modern philosophy would have once and for all detached itself from that of the ancients and would have been obliged to set its own problems, completely different from those of the Greeks. It would have found "first principles" and would have radically modified the entire "technique of thought."

The created truth, the truth of which the son of man remains always master as he is of the Sabbath, as well as the good which has for its source the divine will that nothing limits—this, for the Greeks was only a *contradictio in adjecto,* consequently an impossibility and, further, an abomination of desolation. The idea of the created truth brings us back to that state of innocence and ignorance of which the Book of Genesis speaks and puts an end to rational philosophy. In his letters, Descartes had the daring to proclaim such a truth only because he was convinced in advance (*reservatio mentalis*) that it would oblige neither him nor anyone else to anything. One can say the same of the Scholastics who believed that they had as their mission to announce to the world the till then unheard of idea of a created truth. Descartes, like the Scholastics, could not help but understand that this was only an indispensable tribute paid by the believer to the Bible and that, having rendered this tribute in words, he then acquired the possibility and the right to "think" as his intellectual conscience demanded of him: *credo ut intelligam* (I believe that I may understand). It is enough to recognize the limitless will of the Creator only once; then nothing will prevent one from accepting the *potentia absoluta* [absolute power] which changed itself "willingly" and definitively into *potentia ordinate* [ordinate power] in order never again to be remembered. It is here that the power which Greek thought exercised over Descartes especially manifests itself. *Ipse creator et conditor mundi semel jussit, semper paret* (the Creator and Ruler of the world once commanded, always obeys), proclaims Seneca, repeating what he had been taught by Athens. The freedom to command was for the Greeks inconceivable and hateful; they recognized only the freedom to obey. The freedom to obey was and still remains the condition of rational thought and rational knowledge. God Himself was authorized to command only once, after which He obeys—just as do mortals.

Pascal, who was so perceptive, understood this: recall his famous words, "I cannot forgive Descartes . . . , etc." Like the Greek philosophers, Descartes carefully avoided the *jubere*—to command; he feared it instinctively, seeing in it—and certainly he was right to do so—the most dangerous threat to rational thought. And if the source of Descartes' philosophy is sought, it will be found not in the divine *jubere* but in the human or "metaphysical" *parere* [to obey]. *Apud me omnia fiunt mathematice in Natura* (For me everything in Nature occurs mathematically): this is the whole of Descartes. And that is why the condemnation of Galileo upset him so: "I am almost resolved to burn all my papers," he wrote to Mersenne. " . . . I confess that if the movement of the earth is false, all the foundations of my philosophy are also false." In his polemics against the unbelievers, St. Augustine could still refer to the Bible, where it is said that Joshua stopped the sun. And on the strength of this testimony the Church could also reject the Copernican theory. But it is no longer given Descartes to overcome Aristotle's "the poets lie." Joshua, who stopped the sun, completely destroys the foundations of his philosophy. To put it differently, in Descartes, as in the Greeks, God's *potentia absoluta* [absolute power] belongs to that *semel jussit* [once commanded] which, even if it did once take place, is treated by our thought as never having existed and as obliging us to nothing. Descartes could in all tranquility render unto God that which is God's for he knew definitely that Caesar would not suffer any harm from this and would fully receive that which is Caesar's. From this point of view it may be said without exaggeration that Descartes anticipated Kant. If one brings together his *omnis ratio veri et boni ab omnipotentia Dei dependsit* [everything which is true or good depends on God's omnipotence] with his *apud me omnia fiunt mathematice in Natura* [in my view, all things in nature occur in accordance with mathematics], one obtains a critique of pure reason: freedom is transferred to the intelligible world, while our world is handed over to the synthetic judgments *a priori* which no one can overcome and which no one even has the desire to overcome.

If you wish, the critique of reason is carried through in Descartes in a more radical fashion than in Kant. Awakened from his dogmatic slumber by Hume or by his own discovery of the antinomies of the pure reason, Kant was obliged to recognize that the idea of necessity, to which reason aspired so eagerly, has no root in experience and consequently in being, and that it is a phantom which has somehow taken hold of our consciousness. He concluded from this that the metaphysical ideas—the idea of God, of the immortality of the soul and of freedom—cannot be justified by means of those demonstrations which are used to prove the truths of mathematics and the natural sciences. But in *The Critique of Practical Reason,* reason attains an almost complete compensation: in place of the idea of necessity that has been taken away from it, it is offered the idea of the "should," of duty, of the imperative whose categorical character can compensate man for the heavy loss he has sustained. It is impossible to preserve *ratio veri* and to defend it against freedom but, thanks to the practical reason, *ratio boni* remains unshakable: Kant succeeded in maintaining it against all attacks, and "deduced" his famous ethical "law," the source and foundation of morality.

His successors, however, could not be content with this "almost" complete compensation and could not forget the losses that had been sustained. The harshest reproaches that Hegel made against Kant relate to *The Critique of Practical Reason*: the "ought" or duty does not replace the "necessary," even in the domain of the ethical. Only "the critique of reason," in the form that we find it in Descartes, can satisfy the man who thinks and furnish a solid base for philosophy. Just as in Kant, God, the immortality of the soul, and freedom are transferred into the intelligible world or, rather, unintelligible world, which has no relationship with us; the practical reason blends into the theoretical reason, and on our earth an unshakable order which assures "knowledge" with its eternal, irrevocable truths in *saecula saeculorum* is established. But neither Descartes nor Kant stopped before the question: whence comes the power of reason and its eternal truths? Still less did they think of what this power brings to men. They did not even believe it necessary to ask themselves—even if only to give their investigation formal perfection and desired fullness—whether metaphysics must really be a knowledge or science, whether the true goal of metaphysics and every prolegomena to it does not consist precisely in the testing of the pretensions of the eternal truths to reign over men and over all being. But it was with just this that the Judeo-Christian thought—the thought to which was revealed the truth of the one omnipotent God, Creator of heaven and earth—should have been concerned before everything else.

None of the influential "Christian philosophers" of modern times—neither the dogmatic Descartes nor the critical Kant—even tried to construct a philosophy having as its point of departure the revealed truth. On the contrary, I repeat, all of them applied themselves exclusively to driving out of our world the revealed truth, to relegating it to another world which has no relationship with ours. This tendency is expressed with particular force in the philosophy of Leibniz. Leibniz did not wish to awaken from his dogmatic slumber—not even later to go back, like Kant, to sleep more deeply. He was no longer willing to pay tribute to God, be it only in words, in order later to forget Him and to follow Caesar alone. It was not given Leibniz to debate with Kant but every time he recalled or there was recalled to him Descartes' *omnis ratio veri et boni*, Leibniz, ordinarily so reserved and calm, lost his self-control and was quite beside himself. We must assume that when he said "I despise almost nothing" the "almost" referred to the interpretation Descartes had given of the divine omnipotence. One can discuss everything in a calm and respectful tone, but limitless, unrestrained arbitrariness—even if it be the arbitrariness of God—is worthy only of scorn. Man, angels, God—all equally must recognize the power of reason. "For by what means will the true God be distinguished from the false god of

Zoroaster if all things depend on the caprice of an abstract power, without there being any rule or regard for anything whatsoever?" he asks in the *Treatise* which precedes the *Theodicy*.[83] And he repeats the same thing in the *New Essays*: "Faith must be grounded in reason . . . without this why should we prefer the Bible to the Koran or to the old books of the Brahmans?"[84] This argument appeared to him absolutely irresistible. Several pages further he declares: "Revelation cannot go contrary to clear evidence." And he immediately explains: "because even when revelation is immediate and original, we must know with evidence that we are not in error in attributing it to God."[85]

And indeed, who will guide us in our choice? Leibniz forgets only one thing: what if reason chooses not the Bible but the Koran or the old books of the Brahmans? But he should have thought of this possibility. Perhaps reason will reject the Koran but it is certain that if one gives it a choice between the Bible and the ancient books of the Brahmans, it will without hesitation prefer the latter, for the Bible is not afraid to contradict the self-evidences while the wisdom of the Brahmans is founded on these self-evidences. Yet Leibniz does not account for this. His argumentation, I repeat, appears to him absolutely irrefutable, as it doubtless does to most of those who read him. And he never loses an occasion to reproach Descartes for his attitude: "This is why I also find completely strange the expression of certain other philosophers who say that the eternal truths of metaphysics and geometry and, consequently, also the rules of goodness, justice and perfection are only the effects of God's will; it seems to me instead that they are only consequences of His understanding which assuredly does not at all depend on His will, no more than on His essence," he writes in the *Discourse on Metaphysics*. After reporting in the *Theodicy* both Bayle's reflections on Descartes and his disciples who believed that God is "the free cause of the truths and the essences" and Bayle's confession that despite all his efforts he had not succeeded in understanding this idea of Descartes but hoped that "time would resolve this beautiful paradox," Leibniz indignantly declares: "Is it possible that the pleasure of doubting can exercise so much influence over a clever man as to make him desire and hope to believe that two contradictories are never found together only because God has forbidden this to them, and that He could also have ordered them always to go together? What an excellent paradox this is!"

I hope that the reader will not reproach me for these long quotations from Leibniz: again, and for the last time, we are now before the basic question which the Middle Ages posed and which, from the Middle Ages, passed into modern and contemporary philosophy—the question of the created truth. Leibniz, who knew Scholasticism as well as Descartes and who, like Descartes, posed in all his writings as the faithful champion of Christianity, was organically incapable of "accepting" a truth created by God. Such a truth seemed to him the height of absurdity, and if it appeared that the Bible was called to proclaim it to men, he would have renounced the Bible as well as the God of the Bible without the least hesitation. Even Bayle, who had agreed with Descartes that *omnis ratio veri* depends on the will of God and that God could establish the principle of contradiction but that He could and can also suppress it, when he comes to the second part of Descartes' formula—*omnis ratio boni* [everything which is good]: depends on God—refuses to follow Descartes. He declares with genuine terror that it is impossible to accept or admit this. God Himself must be held in leash—otherwise what catastrophes He could unloose! But the eternal and uncreated truths are, of course, something else: they will never harm anyone.

Whence came this lack of trust in God in Bayle and in Leibniz, while they showed themselves quite disposed to confide their destiny to the eternal, uncreated truths? It is in vain that we shall await from them an answer to this question. Even more—Leibniz, who protects us with so much care against the arbitrariness of God, shows himself ready to accept in advance all that the eternal truths may bring with them. "The ancients," he writes, "attributed the cause of evil to matter, which they believed to be uncreated and independent of God. But where shall we, who derive all being from God, find the source of evil? The answer is that it must be sought in the ideal nature of the creature, insofar as this nature is contained in the eternal truths that are in the mind of God independently of His will." Can one say, after such a confession, that in the person of its most influential representatives modern philosophy has preserved any bond with the Judeo-Christian *Audi Israel?* What Leibniz tells us with such assurance leads us back to the *separatus intellectus* [the separate intellect] of Aristotle: Leibniz's thought continues to seek the truth as if between the Greeks and himself nothing important or significant had happened.

It must still be added: what we have just heard from Leibniz constitutes the point of departure of the philosophy of Descartes, who lived before Leibniz, and of Kant, who considered himself the destroyer of the dogmatism of Leibniz and Wolf. And all this had been prepared by the Scholastic philosophy. Quoting the well-known passage from St. Augustine's *Confessions:*[86] "Whence comes evil? Or was there an evil matter, out of which He made it? And did He form and order matter in such a way that He still left in it something that He did not change into good? Why now this?" Gilson asks: "But how could Augustine excuse a creator-God for having made matter evil or even only of having left it as how He found it?" And indeed, how could St. Augustine accept this? But with still greater justification it might be asked: how could Leibniz "excuse"

God for having created bad truths or, if He did not create them and found them ready-made, for having preserved them as He found them? However, neither St. Augustine nor the Scholastics nor Leibniz raised such questions. As far as matter is concerned, God can still manage it: Leibniz agrees to admit, as the Bible demands, that God created matter. But as for the ideal truths, this is something else: men and God Himself must submit to them; here begins the domain which *non cadit sub omnipotentia Dei.* At the same time Leibniz realizes clearly that these truths, which have entered into the mind of God without His will, show themselves to be precisely the source of all evil, of all the horrors of terrestrial existence. But this does not trouble him: he agrees to all, provided only that he can "understand," that he can "know."

Furthermore, and one cannot repeat this too often, when Leibniz expresses such judgments, he is expressing not only his own point of view. So thought the ancients, so thought the Scholastics, and so thought Descartes and all who came after him. No one has ever recognized Descartes' *omnis ratio veri et boni* [everything which is true and good]—Descartes himself no more than others. If historians of philosophy happen to recall it, this is only in passing (Schelling and Hegel even speak of it in their course on the history of philosophy); but most of the time they do not think of it. It is clear to everyone that the eternal truths entered the mind of God without asking permission of Him, and that Descartes himself could not think otherwise. No philosopher, however, permitted himself to state as candidly and as light-heartedly as Leibniz that the eternal truths or, as he puts it, the ideal principles, are the source of evil. Since the most ancient times it has been assumed that the responsibility for evil falls upon matter. But it appears that it is not matter, of which one can somehow or other rid oneself (in the Greeks catharsis led to "the delivery of the soul from the body"), but the ideal principles, from which one cannot escape, that are to blame. Leibniz and medieval philosophy taught, it is true, that amends for the evil which the ideal principles bring will be made by God in another world. With a truly puzzling "lightness," Leibniz develops at length the theme that if God, giving way to the demands of the eternal truths, was obliged to admit certain imperfections "here," "there" imperfections will no longer exist. Why? Will the eternal truths and the *intellectus separatus* that bore them and preserves them in its bosom ever renounce, in the other world, their power to do evil? Will the principle of contradiction and all that it brings with it cease "there" to be *noli me tangere* [do not touch me] and liberate the Creator?

It is difficult to believe that the perceptive Leibniz could have overlooked this question; but, enchanted by the ancient *eritis scientes* [you will know], he aspired to knowledge, nothing but knowledge which, for him, is eternal salvation.

Evil must be "explained"—that is all that is demanded of philosophy, whether it be Judeo-Christian or pagan: *credo ut intelligam* [I believe so that I understand]. The victim of a kind of enthusiasm, Leibniz proclaims in an inspired tone: "The eternal truths, the objects of wisdom, are more inviolable than the Styx. These laws do not constrain: they are stronger, for they persuade."[87] The eternal truths that entered the mind of God without His permission are forever inviolable, like the Styx, even more than the Styx: they have "persuaded" Leibniz, have persuaded all of us. How have they persuaded us? By their "constraint." No matter what they bring, we will not permit ourselves to argue with them, we will accept everything submissively and joyfully. If they proclaim that evil must exist in the world, that there must be more evil than good, we will accept it; how could we argue with them, since they are not content to constrain but also persuade us? If they brought it about that the good disappeared completely and only evil remained in the world, this also would have to be accepted; and if one day this happens, we shall submit: so boundless is their power.

Leibniz's theodicy reduces itself finally to this: basing himself on the ideal, uncreated principles, Leibniz shows that, insofar as and because they exist, evil must necessarily exist in the world. His theodicy, then, is not a justification of God but a justification or, more accurately, a voluntary perpetuation, of evil. How can we doubt after this that Leibniz's "will," the will of the man who knows, is enslaved and that it is a question here not *de libero* but *de servo arbitrio* [not free but unfree will], of an *enchantement et assoupissement surnaturel* [supernatural enchantment and slumber]?

If Hegel was wrong to declare that the biblical serpent did not deceive the man with his *eritis scientes*, he was perfectly right from a historical point of view. The fruits of the tree of knowledge became the source of philosophy for all time. Medieval philosophy, which was born and developed in the bosom of the most intense religious searching, was also incapable—and this despite the undeniable genius of its greatest representatives—of overcoming the temptation of rational knowledge. It sought the truth from the *intellectus separatus*, to which the entire universe and its Creator as well were subordinated. Modern philosophy merely continued and perfected the work of Scholasticism: the *intellectus separatus* (the *Bewusstsein überhaupt* [consciousness in general] of German idealism) was installed, in it, in the place of the biblical *Deus omnipotens, ex nihilo creans omnia* [the allpowerful God who makes all things out of nothing]. When Nietzsche proclaimed that we have killed God, he expressed briefly the conclusion to which the millennial development of European thought had led.

Can one, then, still speak, with Gilson, of a Judeo-Christian philosophy? I think we can. But to find it we must leave the high road that the development of European philosophy has followed. As we have already had occasion to become convinced, history has preserved the memory of a series of extremely remarkable and audacious attempts to oppose to the eternal truths discovered by reason the Bible's created truth. These broke completely with the ancient philosophy, and had for their origin the conviction that knowledge, and the wisdom of the Greeks founded on this knowledge, are the consequence of man's fall. Hence Luther's *De Servo Arbitrio,* hence Pascal's *enchantement et assoupissement surnaturel.* Knowledge does not free man but enslaves him by handing him over to the power of truths as invincible as the Styx but also, like the Styx, death–dealing; and the wisdom founded on this knowledge accustoms men to love and bless the truths of the Styx. It is only by overcoming in himself "presumptuousness" (not pride, but false pride), "the monster without whose killing man cannot live," that man acquires the faith which reawakens his slumbering spirit: this is what Luther's *sola fide* means. Luther and Pascal follow in the direct line of Tertullian who denied all our *pudet, ineptum, impossibile,* and of Peter Damian who, following the Bible, had the daring to see in the *cupiditas scientiae,* in the avidity with which our reason aspires to universal and necessary truths (that is, truths as inexorable as the Styx), the source of all the evils and horrors of terrestrial life.

But the distant past has no monopoly on these solitary thinkers. The scientific Nineteenth Century produced Nietzsche, Dostoevsky and Kierkegaard, who refuse to recognize the eternal truths of knowledge and the wisdom founded on them. Nietzsche's "will to power," his "beyond good and evil," his "morality of masters" which he opposes to the "morality of slaves" and through which already appeared the idea of the truth of masters (the truth over which the son of man rules as over the Sabbath)—these are only a desperate attempt to leave the tree of knowledge and return to the tree of life. And this is also the meaning of Dostoevsky's writings: where rational philosophy with its "two times two makes four," its "walls of stone" and other eternal truths discovers a source of peace, calmness, and even mystic satisfaction (the eternal truths not only constrain but persuade us, as Leibniz said), Dostoevsky sees the beginning of death. For Kierkegaard, the spiritual double of Dostoevsky, speculative philosophy is an abomination of desolation precisely because it disregards the omnipotence of God. Speculative philosophy bows down before the self-evidences: Kierkegaard proclaims the existential philosophy, the source of which is faith and which overcomes the self-evidences. He leaves Hegel, the famous *professor publicus* [well-renowned professor], to go to the private thinker Job; he opposes to the reason of the Greeks the Absurd. The beginning of philosophy is not wonder, as in Plato and Aristotle, but despair (*de profundis ad te, Domine, clamavi* [out of the depths I cried unto Thee, O Lord]). He replaces *credo ut intelligam* [I believe so that I may understand] with *credo ut vivam* [I believe so that I may live]. The model of the "thinker," in his eyes, is not Socrates who, as Kierkegaard himself admits, was the most remarkable of all men who lived before Europe received the Bible, but Abraham, the father of faith. In Abraham faith was a new dimension of thought that the world had not known before, that did not find any place on the level of ordinary consciousness, and that exploded all the "constraining truths" which our "experience" and our "reason" have whispered to us. Only such a philosophy can call itself Judeo-Christian, a philosophy which proposes not to accept but to overcome the self-evidences and which introduces into our thought a new dimension—faith. For it is only on these conditions that the idea of the Creator as the source and master not only of real but ideal being, for which the Judeo-Christian philosophy has striven and—according to Gilson—must strive, can be realized.

This is why the Judeo-Christian philosophy can accept neither the fundamental problems nor the principles nor the technique of thought of rational philosophy. When Athens proclaims *urbi et orbi*: "If you wish to subject everything to yourself, subject yourself to reason," Jerusalem hears through these words, "All these things will I give thee if thou wilt fall down and worship me," and answers, "Get thee hence, Satan, for it is written Thou shalt worship the Lord thy God and Him only shalt thou serve."

IV

On the Second Dimension of Thought

[Struggle and Reflection]

"The ancient and blessed wise
men who were better than we
and lived nearer to the gods."

—Plato, *Philebus*

"A great and final struggle
awaits souls."

—Plotinus, *Enneads* I, 6, 7

I: Ignava Ratio

Can reason be anything but lazy? Laziness is of its very essence, as is cowardice. Open any manual of philosophy and you will soon be convinced that reason even boasts of its submissiveness, its humility, its cowardice. Reason must "servilely" reproduce what is "given" to it, and it reproaches as the greatest of crimes every attempt at free creation. As for us human beings, we in turn must servilely obey all that reason dictates to us. And this is what is called "freedom." For he only is free who is "guided by reason alone." So Spinoza taught, so the ancients taught, so think all those who wish to learn and teach. And since almost everyone either learns or teaches, "lazy reason" (*ignava ratio*) becomes, in fact, the sole master of the world.

II: Two Measures

I irritate people, they say, because I am always repeating the same thing. This was also the reason for the Athenians' dissatisfaction with Socrates. One could rightly say that others are not always repeating the same thing. But no, it is clear that this irritation has another cause. No one would get angry if the things that I repeated were those to which people have become accustomed, which have always been admitted and are therefore comprehensible and agreeable to everyone. Then it would not seem that I am repeating "the same thing," that is, always the opposite of what people wish to hear. Everyone, for example, for centuries—ever since Aristotle—has repeated: the principle of contradiction is an unshakeable principle; science is essentially free examination; God Himself could not make that which has been not to have been; man must overcome his selfhood or particular being; everything must tend toward unity, etc. And no one gets angry, everyone is very happy and imagines that all this is new. But if you say that the principle of contradiction is not even a principle, that the self-evidences deceive us, that science is afraid of free examination—not only will people not permit you to repeat such things two or three times, but they will fly into a rage at your very first words.

We must believe that people become irritated for the same reason that a sleeper gets angry when one tries to awaken him. He would like to sleep, but they will not let him alone: "Wake up!" Why, however, should one get angry? One cannot, for all that, sleep forever. I certainly do not hope to succeed in waking sleepers (on this subject I have no illusions), but—no matter—the hour will come and someone else will wake them, not by discourses, but otherwise, quite otherwise. And then he who is called to awaken will awaken.

But, in that case, people will ask me, "Why do you struggle so?" Yes—it is true—I take pains, I struggle, knowing quite well that I shall arrive at nothing and that what I cannot do will be done without me. It is then easy to demonstrate that I contradict myself. And, indeed, for a long time now people would have demonstrated it to me if they had not felt that such a demonstration not only would not be disagreeable to me, but, on the contrary, give me great pleasure. Now one convinces people of error, however, only to annoy them.

III: The Fate of Socrates

Socrates was not poisoned because he invented new truths and new gods but because he annoyed and troubled everyone with his new truths and new gods. Had he remained quietly at home and written books or taught at the Academy, people would have left him in peace, as they left Plato in peace.

It is true that Plato also almost lost his life when he tried to interest the tyrant Dionysius in his ideas, but he succeeded in getting out of this bad situation. As for Plotinus, no one ever dreamed of laying a hand on him. Kings themselves venerated him, for he was not at all concerned with spreading his philosophy and even hid it from non-initiates.

What Hegel says about the "fate" of Socrates is, then, completely arbitrary. The death of Socrates did not by any means result from the clash of two orders of opposing ideas; Socrates perished because he did not know how, or did not wish, to be silent. Men are afraid not so much of truths, new or old, as of preachers of truths. For truth does not pursue or trouble anyone, while preachers are a very disagreeable lot, in perpetual disquietude and agitation, leaving no one in peace.

In brief, Socrates was condemned to death because he poisoned the existence of the Athenians (he himself, in the *Apology*, compares himself to a gadfly). Had he only been content to awaken himself or his friends, he would have been left in peace. People would even have repeated his words about the "true awakening."

And this is what happened at the end: no sooner had Socrates died than everyone began to sing his praises. It was known that he was no longer dangerous. Silent truths do not frighten anyone.

IV: Intellectual Honesty

Intellectual honesty led Spinoza and, after him, Leibniz, Kant and all the philosophers of modern times to the conviction that the Bible does not contain truth, that it is only morality, and that revelation is a fantastic imagination, while the postulates of practical reason have a high value and are very useful. Consequently? Consequently, you will say, it is necessary to forget the Bible and follow Spinoza and Kant. . . . But what if one should try for once to con-clude otherwise and say: "consequently," we must send intellectual honesty to the devil, in order to rid ourselves of Kant's postulates and learn to speak with God as our ancestors spoke with Him.

Intellectual honesty consists in submitting to reason not externally, through fear, but willingly, with all of one's heart. It is a virtue when the power of rea-son is legitimate. But what if reason has seized power illegally? Is not then our submission to its decrees a shameful slavery? No one wishes to speak of this or even to think of it. And people fly into a passion if anyone permits himself even to raise this question. At the very most we agree to interpret the Bible and to reconcile it with Spinoza and Kant. Hegel spoke readily of revelation, of the incarnation of God and of the absolute religion; and his intellectual honesty is beyond doubt. Hegel could betray Schelling, but he served reason with all his soul and heart.

V: The Intellectual Vision

Essentially the intellectual vision aspires to discover, behind living beings, the eternal and immutable principles which govern the universe. The "freest" human thought ceases to search and is satisfied when it thinks (or, as people prefer to say, when it is convinced) that, having transcended the limits of the individual, the arbitrary and the changing, it has penetrated into the domain of immutable laws. That is why all metaphysical systems begin with freedom and end with necessity.

But since necessity in general does not enjoy a very good reputation, one usually tries to demonstrate that this final and supreme necessity to which the intellectual vision aspires is in no way distinguishable from freedom or, to put it otherwise, that reasonable freedom and necessity are one and the same thing. Now, in reality, they are not at all the same. Reasonable or not, necessity is al-ways necessity. But people ordinarily call "reasonable" every necessity that can-not be overcome—a thing which they carefully dissimulate. And that is quite understandable. The indestructible need to live "according to one's own will" is inherent in the human soul; nothing will make it renounce its eternal dream. But a reasonable will, and what is more, a necessary will, is not "my own will"; the latter is something altogether different. What is more important to man than anything else in the world is to "act according to his own will," even if that will be unreasonable or foolish. And the most eloquent and convincing argu-ments remain useless in this matter.

Certainly it is not difficult to force man to silence, be it even by the blows of arguments (although there are much more powerful means); and, as history shows, reasonable arguments have always accepted all alliances. But silence is by no means a sign of acquiescence. It often happens that we are silent because we realize the uselessness of speech. Many people, moreover, are not at all lovers of argument. The philosophers (or at least the most intelligent of the philosophers) know this well. That is why they detest the mob so much (they "scorn" it, they say—this sounds more noble), although the mob only very rarely permits itself to contradict them. Men listen, nod in approval, and finally act as if they had heard nothing. Sometimes they even repeat what has been said to them. They repeat it continually, but they live and act as they please. "I see the better and approve of it, but I follow the worse."

Is it not strange? Freedom and necessity are identical; the systems which subordinate reality to ideal laws are true. Man recognizes all this, but when he passes on to action, one might truthfully say that the intellectual vision and its ideal essences never existed. Who, then, is right—the metaphysicians who seek ideal principles, or the simple mortals to whom their instinct whispers that ideal principles are of the devil, just as are all mechanistic explanations of the universe and of life?

VI: Inquiries

It appears to us that it is always good to inquire, and that the road which leads to truth is marked out by questions. We ask, What is the speed of sound? Into what sea does the Volga empty itself? How many years do ravens live? and so on, endlessly. To these questions we obtain precise answers which we consider true. And at once we conclude: since to thousands, to millions of questions of this kind we have obtained answers containing a certain truth, it follows that in order to find truth we must inquire. That is why we ask whether God exists, whether the soul is immortal, whether the will is free (to these three questions, according to Kant, all of metaphysics is reducible), convinced in advance that in this case, as in all others, we shall obtain the truth only by raising questions. Our reason thus anticipates what we have not yet verified, and we are finally quite satisfied: our "knowledge" has been broadened.

As daily experience proves, these kinds of burglary often remain unpunished— but not always. Sometimes someone does interfere in order to punish. Of course, it is not reason that will be punished (reason is too crafty or too ideal to assume any responsibility whatever), but rather the artless representatives of reason—men. Despite their insistence, men do not receive any answer to their questions, or rather, they obtain answers quite other than those which they expected. It serves them right. Why did they inquire? How can anyone hand over to anyone or to anything his right to God, to the soul, to immortality? For the fact is that, in inquiring, we renounce our right, we hand it over to someone. To whom? Who, then, is the someone or something that has stolen from us our soul and our God? And why has this something, to which our existence is perfectly indifferent, to which everything is indifferent, arrogated the right to pronounce final judgment on that which is more important to us than everything in the world?

VII: Unde Malum?

"Whence comes evil?" people ask. Many theodicies, very little different from each other, give answers to this question—answers which satisfy only their authors (do they satisfy them?) and the lovers of amusing literature. As for others, theodicies annoy them, and this annoyance is directly proportional to the intensity with which the question of evil pursues an individual. When this question acquires for us the importance that it had—for example—for Job, every theodicy appears sacrilegious. Every attempt to "explain" his misfortunes does nothing but aggravate them in the eyes of Job. He does not want explanations and answers. He does not want consolations. Job curses the friends who have come to see him precisely because they are his friends and because, in their condition as friends, they wish to "alleviate" his situation, insofar as any man can help another. And it is precisely this "insofar as" that is unbearable for Job. If it is impossible to help him, it is better not to console him.

To put the matter otherwise, one can ask (sometimes, as in the case of Job, the question is inevitable) "Whence comes evil?" but one cannot answer this question. And it is only when the philosophers recognize that one cannot answer this and many other questions that they will know that one does not always ask to obtain answers, that there are questions whose significance lies precisely in the fact that they do not admit of answers because answers kill them.

Is this not very understandable? What is to be done? Be patient. Man must resign himself to many things still more difficult.

VIII: On the Truth Which Constrains

One person asks how knowledge is possible, how it can be that something which differs essentially from us enters into us. Having put this question, he will be satisfied only when he will have proved, or imagine himself to have proved, that the subject and object of knowledge do not differ and are at bottom one and the same thing and that, consequently, the impossible does not exist. Why should the thought that the impossible exists trouble him so much, and why should he find so reassuring the thought that the impossible does not exist. And again, why should he yearn so strongly for tranquility, as if tranquility were the greatest of human goods? I do not undertake to answer these questions, and I am inclined to believe that he cannot answer them either.

Another person has other concerns. He would be very happy to learn that not only what is possible exists, but that it happens sometimes that the impossible also exists. But reality forces him to recognize, on the contrary, not only that the impossible does not exist, but that many things that are possible do not exist either. There would be nothing finally impossible in the fact that men should love one another; now, in reality, *homo homini lupus est* [man is wolf to man]. There would be nothing impossible either if men, like certain animals, lived for several centuries or if they died when they themselves wished and not on a day and at an hour fixed no one knows by whom or by what. Still many other things of this kind appear to experience unrealizable. And the thirst for absolute knowledge that torments mankind is also unrealizable: we know very little, and what we do know is relative. The final truth hides itself behind impenetrable darkness, though there would be nothing impossible if the truth did not remain hidden to men who long for it so greatly.

But it happens that the theorist of knowledge at times feels other disturbances as well: Why does that which *is* in no way correspond to that which we wish would be? I shall be told that this is not an appropriate question for the theory of knowledge. But, yes, it is, much more so than that of which we spoke above—how it is possible that what is not similar to us becomes the object of our knowledge. This question appears fundamental and essential only because we are superstitiously convinced that the possible alone exists. But that is a prejudice which daily experience contradicts. This experience shows us that if one combines in a certain proportion oxygen with hydrogen, one obtains water—oxygen with nitrogen, air. Now this is something that is clearly impossible. Why should oxygen and hydrogen produce water? Why should they combine and give birth to a new product, or rather, why is not the result of their combination air? All this is perfectly arbitrary; all this is groundless and, consequently, impossible. Chemistry is the science of the absolute arbitrariness that rules in nature. Chemistry takes its rise from the principle that anything one wishes may arise from anything else one wishes, but with this restriction—that it is not a question of our wish or that of other men who study chemistry, but of the wish of someone or of something that we are incapable even of naming. We are constrained, whether we will it or not, to study chemistry, that is, to recognize the wish of this someone or something which acts as it pleases.

But one is then justified in asking: Whence does it come that this someone or something (at bottom everyone is convinced that it is not a living being) commands and we are constrained to obey? To put the matter otherwise, whence comes the *constraining* power of knowledge? Why should oxygen and hydrogen combining produce water, and not bread, gold, or a musical symphony? Or why is water the product of oxygen and hydrogen, and not of sound and light? Whence comes the irresistible *force* of scientific truths or even of simple empirical truths? And how does it happen that men who are so disturbed at the idea that the least impossibility might steal into reality establish with indifference that that reality contains many things inadmissible to us? It is, for example, much easier to admit Pygmalion's statue, Joshua's sun, and all the rest, than to accept the fact that the Athenians poisoned Socrates. And yet we are *constrained* to affirm the opposite. Joshua did *not* stop the sun, Pygmalion did *not* animate his statue—but the Athenians *did* poison Socrates.

Now, to admit this would be only half a misfortune. But the most incomprehensible thing of all is that philosophers should glorify and bless this constraint which knowledge exercises and demand that everyone else do the same (the theory of knowledge is in fact nothing else than knowledge raised to the level of the ideal, identified with truth). Those who are so agitated at the thought that any impossibility might be introduced into reality consider the constraint which knowledge exercises perfectly reasonable and legitimate. Why? There is here something that is incomprehensible. Should not one ask himself, before everything else, whence this *constraint* comes? And who knows: if the philosophers were to make the impossible more of their business, if this constraint were to trouble them, if they were to resent it as an offence—perhaps many judgments considered today as necessary and consequently obligatory for everyone would appear absolutely foolish and ridiculous. And the greatest of absurdities would then be found to be this very idea of a truth which constrains.

IX: The Source of Metaphysical Truths

Ipse conditor et creator mundi semel jussit, semper paret. "The Master and Creator of the world Himself commanded once and obeys always," says Seneca—repeating, as is his custom, the words of others. But if this is so, if God commanded once in order thereafter to content Himself with obeying this single order, then, even in that case, the fact that He commanded, be it only once, is much more important for Him and for us than the obedience to which He has ever since kept.

It is not obedience that characterizes the power of God and His role in the universe. The weakest of beings, even the inanimate objects of the inorganic world, are also capable of obedience. And yet our knowledge is devoted exclusively to the study of the laws of phenomena, as if free creation were something criminal or shameful, so that men and God Himself must not think of it or, at the very least, must not speak of it any more. All truth for us flows from the *parere* [to obey], even metaphysical truth. And yet, the only source of metaphysical truth is the *jubere*; and as long as men will not participate in the *jubere* [to command] it will seem to them that metaphysics is impossible. Kant turned away from metaphysics only because he had caught in it a glimpse of the terrible *jubere*, that *jubere* which he translated (and rightly) by a term which everyone holds in horror—"the arbitrary."

X: THE ABSOLUTE

The mortal sin of the philosophers is not the pursuit of the absolute. Their great offence is that, as soon as they realize that they have not found the absolute, they are willing to recognize as absolute one of the products of human activity, such as science, the state, morality, religion, etc. Obviously the state, just like science, morality and religion, has very great value—but only so long as it does not pretend to occupy the throne of the absolute. Religion itself, no matter how profound and sublime it be, is, in the last analysis, only a vessel intended to contain the absolute—the vestment, so to speak, of the absolute. And it is necessary to know how to distinguish the sacred treasure from the vessel which contains it; otherwise one risks falling into idolatry. But men do not know how, or rather, do not wish, to make this distinction. Idols are to them—why, one does not know—nearer, more comprehensible, than God. Holy Scripture speaks much of these things. Idols seduced even the Jewish people, which was called to reveal God to half the human race, and it was only thanks to the prodigious efforts of its prophets that it succeeded in attaining the heights where eternal truth is discovered.

XI: NATURE AND MAN

Men, says Spinoza, imagine that they do not constitute merely one of the elements or links of the chain which is called nature and pretend to form, in the bosom of nature, a kind of state within a state. Is not rather the contrary true? Would it not be more exact to say that men have the feeling of being only tiny, powerless wheels of an enormous machine, and that they have completely forgotten that the world was created for their sakes?

XII: OF RADICAL DOUBT

And yet the *Deus malignus* [the malign Creator] did deceive Descartes! Descartes needed the *cogito ergo sum* [I think, therefore I am] for his theory of the *clare et distincte* as the sign of truth or, to put it in a different way, for his theory of truth; but the *cogito ergo sum* finally gave him nothing. Descartes' doubt was a sham. The philosopher pretended to doubt his own existence, then to admit it by relying on proofs that he himself had discovered. Hume is perfectly right: if Descartes had succeeded in pushing his "radical doubt" to the end, he would never have been able to get out of it. Had he doubted the existence of God, everything would have been finished and the "proofs" would have been of no help to him.

With a prudence which makes us think rather of a somnambulist than of a philosophic seeker, Descartes directs his doubts precisely to that truth which no one can deny. And over this he cries victory: proofs can conquer the most radical doubt; therefore, we have at our disposal sufficient means to attain truth. But he should have reasoned otherwise: I do not have at my disposal any proofs of my own existence, but I have no need of them; consequently, certain truths, very important truths, manage completely without proofs. Descartes would not then perhaps have become the "father of the new philosophy," but he would have attained something much more important than the right to take his place in the Pantheon of great men.

XIII: MIRACULOUS METAMORPHOSES

In the eye of others we see a straw, but in our own we do not even notice a beam. That is true. Every one of us has been in a position to verify it more than once. But let us raise another question: How does it happen that in the eye of our neighbor we see the smallest straw and that in our own we do not see even a beam? The simplest explanation is to allege our imperfection, our narrowness of mind. We are, indeed, imperfect and limited. But may there not be another, "better" explanation? Perhaps the straw which is in the eye of our neighbor is only a straw and will always remain a straw, while to us it is somehow miraculously given to transform the most horrible beam in our own eye into something useful, necessary, and even beautiful. And conversely, in a fashion quite as mysterious—that is, miraculous—the straw which is in our own eye may suddenly begin to grow and be transformed into a monstrous beam like that which is described in Scripture (in connection with the prophet Elijah). But people hardly like to speak of miraculous metamorphoses; they do not see them where they exist. And yet they would do well to notice them. They would also do well to read Holy Scripture more attentively.

XIV: DOGMATISM AND SKEPTICISM

Dogmatism is much closer to skepticism than we imagine who, versed in the history of philosophy, know with what violence these two schools have always struggled against each other. For the dogmatics, quite as much as for the skeptics, the essential thing is their *epochê* (suspension of judgment)—with this difference: that the skeptic, when he has had enough of trying to untie the Gordian knot of existence, declares, "We know nothing and can know nothing; it is useless to struggle," while the dogmatic says, "I already know all that is necessary to know; accept what I know and be content."

To put the matter in another way—if I may be permitted on this occasion to recall a popular Russian proverb—"that which the sensible man has in his head, the fool has on the tip of his tongue." Or, to speak philosophic language, it is the difference between *explicite* [explicit] and *implicite* [implicit]. That the dogmatics are cleverer than the skeptics—of this there is no doubt. Everything *explicite* is necessarily somewhat foolish: it is impossible, indeed, to say everything that one has in his heart and it is, moreover, not even necessary. How people would laugh if, instead of carefully hiding the source whence he draws his truths, the dogmatic led everyone to them! He knows quite well that his affirmations are perfectly arbitrary; perhaps he cherishes his right to the arbitrary more than anything else (Plato, for example, or Plotinus). But he knows equally well that he can keep this right only if he succeeds in hiding from the eyes of others that which is most important to him and never says a word about it to anyone. "The most important" is beyond the limits of the comprehensible and the explicable, that is to say, beyond the limits of that which can be communicated by words.

XV: The Minimum of Metaphysics

Philosophers today freely boast that their systems employ only a minimum of metaphysical postulates. The critiques of Kant have obviously done their work. People do not like metaphysics, they do not believe in it, they are ashamed of it and flee from it. And if it is impossible to flee from it, people try to justify themselves by explaining that they dealt with it only because they could not do otherwise and only so long as was absolutely necessary.

But is it really so improper to deal with metaphysics? The ancient metaphysicians were not at all ashamed of metaphysics, and they did not flee from it as from a person of questionable morals. The "minimum" of metaphysics would have been, in their eyes, a timid and ridiculous limitation. Moreover, it is probable that metaphysics itself hardly appreciates timid people and those who are too much concerned with their reputation. Plato and Plotinus, who were its favorites, aspired to the maximum of metaphysics. Also, while criticizing and refuting them, people continue, nonetheless, to listen to them.

XVI: The Maximum of Metaphysics

At first blush, knowledge seems to consist in the assimilation of something new, something which one did not know before. In reality, it is not at all a question of simple assimilation. Before assimilating man begins by "preparing" that which he is to assimilate, so that what he assimilates consists always of two elements: that which is given to him and that which he himself creates. Also, it is a mistake to consider the object of knowledge as "existing by itself" (*das Ansichseiende*); but a still greater mistake is to believe that this point of view is ontological.

"That which exists by itself," that is to say, independently of the knower, is not at all "that which truly exists." And when people try to convince us that "naturally," that is to say, before all theory, man stands opposite the object which is independent of him, and that natural knowledge consists in an effort to "grasp" this object as it exists by itself—this "description" of natural knowledge is incorrect.

Likewise, it is incorrect to believe that natural knowledge realizes that the image of the "object" which it creates is not the object itself, but only the symbol of the object, which is independent of our consciousness. "Natural knowledge" never dreamed of anything of the kind. If one should say—not even to a primitive man, but to a man little acquainted with philosophic conceptions—that the image that we make of an object is not the object itself but an ensemble of conventional signs which differ from the real object as much, for example, as the word differs from the thought that it expresses—if one should say this to him, he would be surprised and perhaps even shocked. And, of course, the idea that the objects that he knows are *not* independent of his knowledge would appear to him much more admissible than the theory that affirms that these objects differ completely from the image of them that his knowledge gives him.

Physics teaches us that sound is not sound, that color is not color; chemistry tells us that water is not water, etc. . . . Philosophy goes still further in its efforts to lift the veil of Maya which covers the universe, and in place of this universe it pretends to install as "really existing" something which does not resemble our universe, something which no longer resembles anything at all. But if we were to ask a man who thinks "naturally" (that is, who does not know theories and is not afraid of them): "Does "true being" belong to that denuded universe which philosophy sets up and which it declares to be independent of the subject who knows it, or rather to this other universe, filled with sounds and colors and forms and in the creation of which the subject who knows it has taken an active part?"—he would reply without the least hesitation that the essence of the world suffers not at all from the fact that it is given to man as the subject of knowledge to participate in its creation; but that if the objects of knowledge which exist independently of him or of anyone else are such as the philosophers represent them, then there would remain nothing of either "truth" or "being."

The role of the theory of knowledge, which wishes to be theory as little as possible, and aspires to penetrate "being," consists, then, not in trying to save or justify the independence of that which it calls *das Ansichseiende* (the denuded world) but in learning to see the essence of being in that universe which (though it is dependent on the subject or even precisely because it is dependent on him) has everything that it requires to be appreciated and loved. That which truly exists must be defined in terms of that which is truly important and truly valuable. The Greeks knew this, but we have forgotten it to such an extent that when people remind us of it we do not even understand what they are talking about. We have such great confidence in our thought, we are so deeply persuaded that our thought with its one dimension is the only one possible, that we consider the philosophy of the ancients, who still had the feeling of a second dimension, almost a superstition. It is true that we do not say this openly. We study the ancients and we have the greatest respect for them—verbally; but no one, I think, would repeat after Plato: "the ancient and blessed wise men who were better than we and lived closer to the gods. . . ."

We are convinced that the ancients were only "blessed" because they were ignorant, and that, consequently, we are superior to them and closer to God. The ancients set for themselves "practical" goals, while we seek truth in an entirely disinterested way. We wish our metaphysical thought to be scientific also. Now, science demands before everything else that one should renounce the second dimension of thought, and, as follows from this renunciation, that he should be prepared to seek truth in a purely theoretical way, that is to say, passively, with a perfect indifference toward anything which may arise and firmly resolved in advance to accept everything. For us, not only philosophic truth but also metaphysical truth is *adaequatio rei et intellectus* (the agreement between thing and intellect); we must accept with submission all the commandments of *res* [thing], no matter how monstrous they be. If a *res* commands us, we shall admit that people poisoned a mad dog, and we shall admit equally (we have, in fact, admitted it), at the command of another *res*, that the Athenians poisoned Socrates.

The greatest sin of man, in our eyes, is to set up his own demands and to express his own will; in letting his demands and his own will (as the second dimension of thought) intervene in thought, man, according to us, cannot attain the essence of being. The Greeks (not all, of course) saw things quite differently. They felt that submission, obedient acceptance of everything which happens, hides true being from man. To attain true reality, it is necessary to consider oneself the master of the world; it is necessary to learn to command and create. There where we distinguish only a criminal and impious caprice, there where there is lacking all "sufficient reason" and where, according to us, every possibility of thinking ends—*there* they saw the beginning of metaphysical truth. They spoke like those who "have power," that is to say, like beings to whom has been accorded a supreme power freely to express their own will, who have been called to transform this will into truth and to create a new reality.

For the ancients metaphysics was not the continuation of science. For them the final *archê* (source of truth) was to be found beyond the limits of knowledge; and this source has nothing in common with the principles upon which knowledge is founded. This seems to us absurd, completely mad. We desire metaphysics to be a science, and we believe that the Greeks deceived themselves, that they confused theoretical problems with practical goals. Was it the Greeks who deceived themselves by introducing free will into metaphysical thought, or is it rather we who are wrong in subordinating metaphysics to the idea of necessity? Who is worse? Who is closer to God? Be that as it may, among the Greek philosophers we accept and understand only Aristotle and the Stoics; the others we push away. And that is quite natural. In Aristotle and the Stoics we find a minimum of emphasis placed on metaphysics (i.e., the free will of which it is impossible for us to conceive), and a maximum on necessity (Aristotle was convinced that "necessity does not allow itself to be persuaded"), that is to say, on the order and the obedience to law which we understand so well. However, we correct even Aristotle and the Stoics and adapt them to our needs, though they themselves had already sufficiently corrected their own predecessors.

Plato, like Socrates, tried to penetrate into the regions where being is created and to participate in its creation. Such was, in their eyes, the task of metaphysics, the "preparation for death" which led them from the middle zones of human existence to the boundaries of life. Aristotle and the Stoics did not wish to go "so far." They accepted necessity and adapted themselves to it. We, also, refuse to penetrate into these regions. We are too lazy and too fearful to wish to approach God. It suffices for us to become organized after a fashion on earth. That is why we have such a fear of "our own will" and why necessity appears so lovable to us. That is why we consider the world which has been stripped by science as true being (minimum of metaphysics) and grant to it the right to an independent existence, while we call the real world a phenomenon, an appearance, and ban it from our ontology.

XVII: The Meaning of History

People seek the meaning of history and they find it. But why must history have a meaning? This question is never raised. And yet if someone raised it, he would begin, perhaps, by doubting that history must have a meaning, then continue by becoming convinced that history is not at all called to have a meaning, that history is one thing and meaning another. A candle worth a kopek set fire to Moscow. Rasputin and Lenin, themselves only kopek candles, set fire to all Russia.

XVIII: Freedom of Thought

According to Kant, our thought—our excellent and only guide in the labyrinth of existence—leads us finally to regions where it becomes powerless and useless, where the principle of contradiction, which never deceives and which always furnishes answers that have an unambiguous meaning, no longer rules but where, instead, antinomies which exclude all possibility of answer rule. What, then, is to be done? Kant says we must stop, for here there is nothing any longer to interest us. Where questions remain necessarily without answer, man has nothing more to do, nothing more to search.

Now, one obviously can stop, and the majority of people do stop. But is it really necessary to do so? What if it is not necessary? What if it is found, on the contrary, that man is capable of "re-learning," of transforming himself, of re-educating himself in such a way as to free himself from the need of obtaining unambiguous answers to all questions? What if man ever succeeded in coming to feel that such answers, though they had formerly consoled him and even made him rejoice, are in reality the curse of his existence, that vanity to which the creatures are subject, despite themselves, groaning and as in travail to this day? (Romans 8:20–22.)

Kant forgot Holy Scripture when he meditated on the relationships between science and metaphysics. That is a pity! If he had remembered, he would perhaps have been able to answer differently the questions he raised. Perhaps it would not have seemed to him that metaphysics loses its *raison d'être* if it does not lead us to general and necessary judgments. Perhaps he would even have been led to recognize that the *raison d'être* of metaphysics is precisely to return to man his primordial freedom and to break forever the bonds in which general and necessary truths have fettered us.

Kant, like his successors—Fichte, Schelling, Hegel—speaks of freedom often and enthusiastically. But when these men found themselves face to face with true freedom, they were terrified. They were petrified, as if they had seen not freedom but the head of Medusa surrounded by serpents. The scientist cannot get along without necessary judgments; how should metaphysics be able to renounce them? One can, in fact, neither discuss nor prove anything if there is not an obligatory norm. Even relationships between men become impossible if they do not submit to a single principle equally constraining for all. But all this only proves one thing: our thought has arrogated rights which do not belong to it. From the fact that, in the empirical domain, the idea of constraining truth is the condition of knowledge, one cannot in any way conclude that it must be the same in the domain of metaphysics—just as the fact that the possibility of communication between men presupposes, according to our observations in a great number of cases, the recognition of one or several fundamental principles that are common to all, does not at all justify the conclusion that communication between men is possible only if they agree to recognize the absolute power of a *single* truth.

Exactly the opposite is the truth. Such a demand often destroys all possibility of communication. The Eastern Church separated from the Western Church precisely because of *filioque*. Catholics have in fact no communication with Eastern Orthodox believers; they even hate them—even though Catholicism and Eastern Orthodoxy are both Christian religions. I do not even speak of the abyss which separates Christianity from Islam or Buddhism. Not only does communication become impossible, but the supposed necessity of bowing down before a single truth leads to an eternal hatred. The Crusades still exist in our day. Men who live side by side detest and despise each other. They do not dream of "communicating" with their neighbors, but each wishes to subordinate the other, to oblige him to forget himself, to renounce everything which he needs and is important to him. Obviously we can declare that there is no salvation outside our truth. But we cannot anticipate in any case that, armed with a single truth, we shall find the way to all human souls. Here again our thought deceives us with illusory promises. In this way, on the contrary, all avenues of approach are cut off and one obtains unity among men not by communication but by the destruction of all who think, feel, or desire differently than we.

It will be said that it is dangerous to grant "freedom" to men. Meister Eckhardt taught that he who has succeeded in entering into communion with God has no need of dogmas, but freedom proved to be fatal for Eckhardt. Without realizing it, he slipped from the summit that he had apparently succeeded in attaining to the plane of current thought and substituted an abstract idea for God. As for German idealism, which owes much to Eckhardt, it denied God completely. All this is perfectly correct. But if Eckhardt did not know how to stay at the altitude he had attained, if the German idealists slipped back to positivism, it was precisely because their ultimate aim was to attain a single truth for all and because they did not believe in freedom.

XIX: Abraham and Socrates

When God says to Abraham, "Leave your country, your friends and your father's house, and go to the land that I will show you," Abraham obeys and "leaves without knowing where he is going." And it is said in Scripture that Abraham believed God, Who imputed it to him for righteousness. All this is according to the Bible. But common sense judges quite otherwise. He who goes without knowing where he is going is a weak and frivolous man, and a faith which is founded on nothing (now faith is always founded on nothing, for it is faith itself that wishes to "found") cannot be in any way "imputed for righteousness." The same conviction, clearly and neatly formulated and raised to the level of method, reigns in science, which was born of common sense. Science, in fact, is science only so long as it does not admit faith and always demands of man that he realize what he is doing and know where he is going. Scientific philosophy, or to put it another way, the philosophy which utilizes in its search for its truths the same methods that science employs in its search for its truths also wishes to know where it is going and where it is leading its adherents. It follows from this that faith is distinguished from science, above everything else, by its methods.

The believer goes forward, without looking to the right or to the left, without asking where he is going, without calculating. The scientist will not take a step without looking around him, without asking, and is afraid to budge from his place. He wishes to know beforehand where he will arrive. Which of these two methods leads us to "truth?" One can discuss this matter, but it is beyond doubt that he alone will be able to attain the promised land who, like Abraham, decides to go forward without knowing where he is going. And if philosophy wishes to attain the promised land (Kant himself, you will recall, said that metaphysics must reveal for man God, freedom and the immortality of the soul), it must adopt the method of Abraham and not that of Socrates and teach men at all events to go forward without calculating, without seeing anything beforehand, without even knowing where they are going.

Is it possible that such a philosophy should become the philosophy of the future? Or is this rather the philosophy of a far-off, forever lost past—the philosophy of the ancient and blessed wise men who (to recall once more the terms of Plato) were better than we and lived closer to God?

XX: A Deception

It often happens that man deceives himself, that he believes he knows something when in fact he does not know. To guard himself from errors he has had to seek out "criteria" of truth. One of the surest criteria of truth that men have found is coherence among different pieces of knowledge, or, to put it differently, the absence of contradiction between these pieces of knowledge. Man seeks and finds relationships between phenomena, and the existence of these relationships is the guarantee of truth for him. Little by little he comes to imagine that his task is not to discover truth, but rather somehow to create around himself an atmosphere of agreement, an ensemble of coherences from which all contradiction will be banished. Finally he is ready to recognize as "truth" every coherence, even if it be imaginary or non-existent. And there is no way of making him let go of this idea. It is also impossible to make him remember that there was a time when he himself knew that truth has absolutely nothing to do with coherence. When Plato reminded himself of this, people accused him of foundering in dualism and mythology—others even say, of babbling (Hegel). At the very best, people try to interpret him in a modern fashion by reducing, for example, his *anamnesis* [recollection] to synthetic judgments *a priori*.

XXI: Teachers and Students

Reason is *judex et princeps omnium* [judge and principal of all things] according to St. Anselm of Canterbury. It would seem that reason should be satisfied with such a high token of respect. But no, this does not suffice for it. Reason wishes to be the creator, the sole creator, of everything that exists. There is room to believe that those who have fought against reason have basically always fought against its immoderate pretensions. It does not suffice for reason to be the prince and judge of the world. Like the old peasant woman of the Russian folk tale, it wishes that the golden fish itself should be under its command.

This is not a figure of speech nor an exaggeration. It is just so that things really happen. Over many minds the pretensions of reason work in an irresistible fashion: if reason demands our obedience, it must follow that it has the right to demand it. But there are others to whom these pretensions appear insupportable. In *The Life of St. Abraham of Smolensk* it is said that the teachers "weighed down" the students. And it is told also of St. Serge of Radonezh that he was "tormented" by his teacher. Indeed, teachers live only on the alms of reason, and the students whom they force to submit to a non existent omnipotence are thereby weighed down and tormented.

XXII: Truth and Mystery

The "initiate" is not a man who "knows," that is to say, one who has once and for all seized the "mystery." One cannot once and for all possess mystery, as one can truth. Mystery rises and disappears, and when it disappears the initiate is only the most insignificant of the insignificant children of the world. For the ordinary children of the world are completely ignorant that they are insignificant and even imagine that they are worth a great deal, while the initiate knows that he is lowly; and this knowledge makes him the most miserable of men, as Pushkin testifies. St. Bernard bears similar witness. "But for these years that I wasted on the enjoyment of life, for I lived in corruption, my contrite and humble heart, O God, thou wilt not despise."

But men do not believe Pushkin; they no longer believe the saints. They must, however, venerate great men and saints. Now he who wishes to venerate must learn, before everything else, the "great art" of not seeing.

XXIII: Clare et Distincte

The Cynics were convinced that reality aspires to light, and they were not afraid to demonstrate their conviction by the most repugnant of acts. Ham also sought clarity and distinctness, and he cast eyes on the nakedness of his father. But all the philosophers have been persuaded that light is always good. Why, then, did they call the Cynics dogs, and why did they scorn Ham? What was it that prevented them from putting everything into full light, as did Ham and the Cynics? It is not in vain, obviously, that Socrates himself asked his demon to protect him from clarity and distinctness. There are truths that do not wish to be truths for all; and they are drawn from a source which no one could call luminous, even by way of metaphor.

XXIV: Faith and Proofs

Heinrich Heine says that when he was a child he used to amuse himself by teasing his French teacher. When the latter, for example, asked him how one said "*la foi*" [faith] in German, Heine would answer: "*der Kredit.*" And still today many very serious people, without the least intention of amusing and in all sincerity, identify faith and credit. It seems to them, indeed, that faith is nothing other than knowledge—with this single difference: that he who has faith takes proofs on credit under the verbal promise that they will be presented in time. You cannot convince anyone that the essence of faith and its most admirable, its most miraculous, prerogative consists precisely in that it does not feel the need of proofs, that it lives "beyond" proofs. This privilege is sometimes considered a *privilegium odiosum* [hateful privilege], sometimes—still worse—as skepticism badly dissimulated. For what is a truth that cannot be imposed by means of proofs?

XXV: Truth and the Recognition of Truth

When a man tries to convince others of his truth, that is to say, when he tries to make what he has discovered obligatory for all, he usually believes that he is guided by the most exalted of motives—love of neighbor, the desire to dissipate the darkness of error, etc. The theory of knowledge maintains these pretensions as well as does ethics. Both, indeed, set it down that truth is one, that it is truth for all. But the theory of knowledge and ethics, like the humanitarian wise men, does not clearly discern whence the need comes which man feels to bring it about that all should recognize one truth.

No, he who tries to lead all men to his unique truth is not thinking of his fellow man. But he does not dare, he cannot himself, accept his truth as long as he has not obtained its recognition, real or fictional, by all others. For it is less important for him to possess truth than to obtain universal recognition. That is why the theories of knowledge and ethics occupy themselves so much with limiting as much as possible the rights of questioners. Aristotle already considered all "exaggerated" curiosity the sign of a defective education. This way of dealing with objectors would appear less convincing if men were not more concerned with the general recognition of their truth than with the truth itself.

XXVI: The Secret of Matter

The Aristotelian definition of matter as "that which exists only in potentiality," has played a very great role in the development of the sciences, and it seems that it still continues to direct our thought.

The potential existence of matter furnishes us a "natural" explanation of the innumerable and strange transformations that we observe in the universe. The atomic theory, the theory of the electron, and even pure energy—all rest on the idea that matter exists only potentially, or, to put it differently, that matter is "nothing," but a nothing whence there can arise, and do arise, the most extraordinary things. Neither Aristotle, of course, nor any of his pupils and disciples ever said anything of the kind. The idea that something, no matter how lowly or insignificant it may be, can be born of nothing, was unacceptable, insupportable even, to Aristotle and to all those who followed him (and who has not followed him?). The great merit of Aristotle lay precisely in having succeeded in a way in "domesticating" and "ennobling" this idea, which is mad and fantastic but which, nonetheless, gushes from all the pores of being. Instead of saying, "Matter does not exist; things are born capriciously of themselves despite all reasonable evidence," Aristotle says, "Matter is what exists only in potentiality." The term "in potentiality" swallowed up and perfectly digested, it seems, the capricious and the arbitrary and even the outraged self-evidences. Thanks to this magic formula, the enigma immediately ceased to be an enigma, the fantastic was transformed into the natural. Since matter exists only potentially, it is possible to make anything one wishes arise from it: for it is in this precisely that the meaning of the idea of potentiality resides. The enigma has disappeared, I say; it has apparently been buried forever. It is henceforth unnecessary to ask by virtue of what miracle all the extraordinary things that we see around us can arise from a non-existent matter, and how it happens that from this same matter there are born things as different from each other as, on the one hand, the dust of the earth or stinking mire, and, on the other hand, Alexander the

Great or the wise Socrates. The magic formula has been found: matter possesses being only in potentiality and consequently we are assured that we shall obtain all answers to all questions.

It is then correct to say that our thought owes everything to Aristotle. He knew, in fact, what it was necessary to do in order to kill mystery. And yet the mystery is not dead and never will die; it only seems to be dead. And, at the side of the "natural" thought which was satisfied with the simplified "explanations" of Aristotle, there will always persist in the human soul an unrest which seeks and finds its own truths.

XXVII: Knowledge and Treasures

According to Aristotle, as everyone knows, the "fortuitous" cannot not be the object of knowledge. In order to make himself perfectly clear, he cites the following example (*Met.* 1025–30 ff): In digging up the ground to plant a tree, a man falls on a treasure. It is clear that this event was not produced by necessity and it is clear, also, that such things do not happen constantly. Therefore the treasure is that "fortuitous" which cannot be an object of knowledge and awaken our scientific interest. Human reason, the human need to know, and science—the daughter of this need and this reason—have nothing to do here. However, the man *has* discovered a *treasure*. Aristotle himself says it. Should he not act to possess himself of it as quickly as possible? It is a question of a treasure, I repeat, and not of an earthworm or a decaying log.

It can happen to a man, it has at times happened to him, thus to put his hand, by accident, on some good that is still better than a treasure. He may be engaged in working his field and suddenly he discovers a source of "living water," or else the edge of his plough breaks open a Pandora's box deeply buried in the earth, and lo, all the evils this box contains escape and are dispersed throughout the world. That is a matter of chance also. And, since it is a matter of chance, science and thought have nothing to see in it. It is necessary for us "simply" to accept, in the first case, the advantages and, in the second case, the disadvantages which result, and to direct our attention to that which happens necessarily and constantly, or at least frequently.

One cannot raise questions about Pandora's box or the source of living water. One cannot even think of them, since one has found them by chance, that is to say, not by seeking them "methodically" but only because one has found them on his way. That which must determine our researches is not the importance of the object and its value, but the conditions under which it appears to us. If it has been discovered "regularly," if it repeats itself with a certain constancy, then we shall seek and study it. But if, like the treasure in Aristotle's example (what was it that moved Aristotle to speak of a "treasure"? Could he not as well have said a "stone"?) or the Pandora's box and living water of my examples, the object—no matter how important and how precious it may be—permits itself to rise before us capriciously without concern for any rules or even contrary to all rules, then for nothing in the world shall we admit that it may have any part in the stock of our truths.

Now, since treasures are always discovered "accidentally" and there is not, there cannot be, a theory for the methodical search and discovery of treasures, people draw from this a conclusion which is surprising but which appears indubitable to everyone: treasures do not exist and neither do wells of living water. So everyone reasons, and people are so completely habituated to this reasoning that they do not notice that it does not even satisfy the demands of elementary logic. From the fact that men discover "treasures" only "accidentally" it does not at all follow that treasures do not exist. One may "deduce" only one thing from this fact, and that is, that he to whom it has been given to discover a treasure must renounce methodical researches and entrust himself to chance. Men have, at times, had this audacity. I think that it has even happened to every man, at least once in his life, to have more confidence in chance than in reasonable necessity. But people guard themselves well against admitting this. It is impossible to draw from "chance" a theory, or, to put it otherwise, a proposition which is valid for everyone and always. So that whatever one does, whatever one says, men will continue, as in the past, to seek and to find only that which happens by necessity or at least frequently, and they will always hold that not only revelations but treasures also exist only in imagination.

XXVIII: On the Sources of "Conceptions of the World"

The appearance of man on earth is an impious audacity. God created man in His own image and likeness and, having created him, blessed him. If you accept the first of these two theses, your philosophical task will be *catharsis* (purification) or, to put it another way, you will try to kill in yourself your particular being, your so-called "ego," and aspire to be dissolved in the "supreme" idea. The fundamental problem for you will be the ethical problem, and ontology will be in a way a derivative of the ethical. Your ideal will become the kingdom of reason to which all who are prepared to renounce the primordial *jubere* (the right to command) and to see the destiny of man in the *parere* (obedience) free access.

If, on the other hand, you accept the second thesis, the fruits of the tree of knowledge of good and evil will cease to tempt you; you will aspire to that which is "beyond good and evil." The *anamnesis*, the remembrance of that which your ancestor Adam contemplated in paradise, will not stop troubling you. Hymns to the glory of reason will appear tiresome, and in the midst of your self-evidences you will feel yourself as if in prison. Plato felt himself shut up in a cave; Plotinus was ashamed of his body; the men of the Bible were ashamed and afraid of their reason.

There is every reason to believe that Nietzsche turned away from Christianity because the Christians, taught by Aristotle and the Stoics, completely forgot the primordial *jubere* [to command] and remembered only the *parere* [to obey] which follows it. That is why Nietzsche spoke of the morality of slaves and the morality of masters. He could have, he should have, spoken as well of the *truth* of masters (of men to whom it is given to command) and the *truth* of slaves (of those whose destiny is to obey).

I could also mention in this connection Dostoevsky, but no one will believe me. Everyone is convinced, in fact, that Dostoevsky wrote only the several dozen pages devoted to the starets Zossima, to Alyosha Karamazov, etc., and the articles in the *Journal of a Writer* where he explains the theories of the Slavophiles. As for *Notes from the Underground,* as for *The Idiot,* as for *The Dream of a Ridiculous Man,* as for the nine-tenths of all that constitutes the complete works of Dostoevsky—all that was not written by him but by a certain "personage with a regressive physiognomy" and only in order to permit Dostoevsky to cover him with shame.

So profound is our faith in the *parere* (that is what we express in affirming that everything happens "naturally"), so great is our fear of everything, no matter what it may be, that recalls even from afar the *jubere* (the miraculous, the supernatural)!

XXIX: Chance and Time

How strangely the great thinkers sometimes deceive themselves! The transiency of terrestrial things has always been a matter of trouble and anguish for men: everything that has a beginning has an end. Among the important philosophers of antiquity there were hardly any who did not reflect on the inevitable end of everything that is born. But all those who have meditated on this question have established (one hardly knows why) so strict a bond between the idea of death and the idea of change that the two ideas at present are only one. That which changes now appears as insignificant, as miserable, as that which is condemned to die.

Why? There is nothing evil in the capacity for change that things have. Why is it evil that Julius Caesar should first have been born an infant, then become an adolescent, then an adult man? Would it have been preferable that he had remained throughout his entire existence what he was when he left his mother's womb? It is clear that change in itself has nothing evil in it. What *is* evil is that things and men often change quite otherwise than we should wish them to. The years make wine better, but sometimes they also make it sour. Man also changes. He changes, and suddenly is transformed into an old man—weak, decrepit, dribbling.

That is why young people do not feel how strictly time is limited. They bathe in its infinity. Not only behind them, they believe, but before them also there extends a boundless immensity; one can then spend without counting. They even have the impression that time flows too slowly and seek to hasten its course. They feel that changes await them. They hope these changes will be beneficial, and would wish that they happen as quickly as possible. Old men, however, see things quite differently: time flies much too quickly for their liking. Each day that passes brings them new sorrows, it "calls and brings them closer to the grave" as the Russian poet Derzhavin "sang" at the end of his life. But old men, quite like young, have nothing against the changes and flow of time. What saddens the former and rejoices the latter is not the fact that they are subject to change; it is the character of the change. If life were even more in flux than it now is and hid within itself the possibility of still more unexpected surprises, but if these changes and surprises did not threaten man with diverse evils, there would never occur to anyone the idea of lamenting over the instability of existence and of seeking the permanent behind the changing.

Now, however, not only do people seek this, but they see in the stable and permanent the ideal, God Himself. For it was not Spinoza who invented amor erga rem aeternam (the love for the eternal). Philosophy has cultivated *res aeternae* since time immemorial. Men are so afraid of the possible evils which, they believe, lurk in change that they are ready to renounce everything which changes and finally to *deify* that which remains always equal to itself, that which never had any beginning and will never have an end, even though this should be only an inanimate, dead thing. And indeed, the dead, the inanimate, does not change. . . .

Now it may be that our terrors are in vain; it may be that our thought deceives us—this thought that is always incited by fear and nourished by dread. It may be that the bond between change and the end, or death, that we observe in the conditions of our existence and that our frightened thought has elevated to the rank of truth *a priori* and immutable—it may be, I say, that this bond does not in any way constitute a law or a general rule having absolute power over men. Under other conditions, perhaps, when there will be men who will make themselves obeyed by the laws and there will no longer be laws which oblige men to obey them, and when human "thought" will possess once more the rights which formerly belonged to it, it will appear that the changes and continuous flux of existence do not lead us necessarily to death and, in general, do not threaten us with any catastrophe. *Amor erga rem aeternam* [love for what is eternal] is not then to be considered what Spinoza and his predecessors imagined, as the only response that we could make to the questions which life puts before us. But in order that we may be capable of catching a glimpse, be it ever so vaguely, of the possibility of this new dimension of thought, we must have the courage to drive away our habitual terrors and cease to listen to the *a priori* of every kind that reason whispers to us. And then "there will no longer be anything impossible for us."

XXX: On the Usefulness of Philosophy

Men believe so little in the possibility of participating, no matter how partially, in the final truth that the deepest thirst to know, the most sincere searches— when they pass beyond certain limits—only excite their irritation and danger. Before you no one has found anything and, after you, no one will find anything either; why, then, disturb yourself and trouble the equilibrium of others? For every search begins with disquietude and ends with the loss of equilibrium.

One can, of course, interest himself in metaphysical problems and occupy himself with them, but on the condition of not connecting them with our own fate or that of humanity. Metaphysical systems must be constructed in such a way that they do not irrupt into life and do not shake the established order of existence, or, better yet, in a way such that they bless and sanctify the established order. And when a man arises to declare that metaphysics can discover a new truth and completely transform life, the whole world together throws itself upon him. Metaphysics must be useful to society, just like science and art and religion. A useless metaphysics, a useless religion—has anyone ever thus characterized the object of his final aspirations? And yet all those who seek have always known, and without the least doubt, that metaphysics *cannot* be useful and that there is nothing more terrible than to fall into the hands of God. But people do not speak of this, or only very rarely. Even the religion of the crucified God tries to imitate metaphysical systems, and Christians almost always forget, even though they wear a cross on their breasts, that the savior of the world cried out from the height of the cross, "My God, my God, why hast Thou forsaken me?" They believe that the savior must know this terrible despair, but that men may escape it. Men need a metaphysics which consoles and orders existence, and a religion which also consoles and orders existence. But no one cares for a truth of which he does not know beforehand what it will bring, nor for a religion which leads us into unknown territory. Even more than very rare, I repeat, are those who admit that religion and metaphysics may lead us ultimately toward anything worthwhile. Everyone demands that religion and metaphysics be visibly and indubitably useful right here, on the shores of time.

XXXI: The Limits of the Power of the Principles of Identity and of Contradiction

If we take it into our heads to say that "sound is heavy," the principles of identity and of contradiction immediately become involved in the matter and oppose their veto. It is impossible, they declare. But when we say that Socrates was poisoned, these two principles do not intervene. May it be that there is a reality in which the principles of identity and of contradiction would remain indifferent and inactive when sounds become heavy but rise up in rebellion when one kills the just? If such a reality is possible, these principles are not principles but simply "executive organs" and their role is completely different from that which people ordinarily ascribe to them.

It will be asked, "How is one *to know* if such a reality is possible or impossible, and if it is given us to penetrate into this reality?" Yes, this is just it: how is one to know. Obviously, if you ask, "Is such a reality possible?" people will answer you that it is impossible, that the principles of identity and of contradiction have always reigned autocratically and will always reign over the world, that there will never be heavy sounds, and that people will continue to kill the just. But try not to ask anything of anyone! Will you thus be able to realize the free will which the metaphysicians promise you? Or, to put it better, do you *want* this free will? It seems, indeed, that you would hardly have any desire at all for it, that "sacred Necessity" would be nearer and dearer to you, and that, after the manner of Schelling, you would see in *Herrschaft* the source of all *Herrlichkeiten*.

XXXII: The Human Truth and the Lie to God

Descartes affirmed that God could not be a deceiver, that the commandment "Thou shalt not lie" is observed by God also. However, God *does* deceive man. That is a fact. He shows man a sky—a blue, solid crystalline dome—which does not exist. Thousands of years have been required for man to free himself from this lie and to recognize the real truth. God often deceives us, and how difficult it is to escape from these deceptions! Yet, if God never deceived us, if no man ever saw the blue sky but knew only an infinite space, empty or filled with ether, if, instead of hearing sounds, men only counted waves—it is probable that they could not have gained much. It may even be that they would have ended by feeling disheartened by their truths and would have agreed to recognize that God may violate His own commandment.

Or would they not have agreed to this? Is the truth above all? Perhaps another idea would then have come to their minds: Is the truth really that which men themselves find, while that which God shows them is only a lie? To put it another way, may it not be that the sky *is* nevertheless a crystalline dome, the earth is flat, and sounds themselves exist and are essentially different from movement? May it not be that colors obey, not the laws of physics, but the will of God? Is it not possible that man may one day be called to this "knowledge," that he may renounce his demonstrated truths and return to the indemonstrable truths? And—who knows—will he not then find that the commandment "Thou shalt not lie" has only a relative and temporary value? No, it is not better to die than to speak falsehood, even if it be only once, as Kant taught; but it is better not to be born at all than to live in the world of our truths. In other words, a time perhaps will come (Plato many times spoke of it, but no one listened to him) when the "better" will triumph over our truths and our self-evidences.

XXXIII: THE POSSIBLE

Everything that has a beginning has an end, everything that is born must die: such is the unshakeable law of existence. But what about truths? For there are truths which have not always existed, which were born in time. Such are all truths that state matters of fact. Four hundreds years before Christ the truth, "the Athenians poisoned Socrates," still did not exist; it was born in the year 399. And it still lives, although it took place almost 2,500 years ago. Does this mean that it will live eternally? If it must disappear like everything that is born, if the general law that we apply with such assurance to everything that exists does not—as a truth *a priori*—admit of any exception, then there will come a moment when the truth about the poisoning of Socrates will die and cease to exist. And our descendants will then have the possibility of affirming that the Athenians did *not* poison Socrates, but that, quite simply (or, on the contrary, not "simply" at all) men lived a certain time, a very long time even, in an illusion which they took for an eternal truth because they forgot, through chance or intentionally, the law of birth and death and its ineluctable character.

XXXIV: DOCTA IGNORANTIA

We complain that we do not know whence we come, where we are going, what has been, what will be, what must be done, what must be avoided, etc., for we are convinced that it would be preferable for us to know these things. But it may be that it would be worse for us; knowledge would bind and limit us. Since we do not know, nothing binds us. The possibility is not even excluded that a day may come when we will be completely freed from knowing, that it will not be *we* who must adapt ourselves—as at present—to the "given" reality, but rather reality which will have to adapt itself to us: and then the *adaequatio rei et intellectus* (approximation of thing and intellect), to which knowledge is always reducible, will lose its element of constraint and make place for the free decision of men.

Certain people have already had a presentiment of this. The *docta ignorantia* [learned ignorance] had perhaps nothing other in view than the submission of *res* [things] to *intellectus* [intellect] and the deliverance of the *intellectus* from all its chains, and even from "first principles." We will no longer be obliged to adapt ourselves to things, but they, rather, will be ready to modify not only their form but also their substance at the word or demand of man. At present we can give a piece of wax the form of a chessman or of a seal; but then we shall be able to transform the wax into a piece of marble or into an ingot of gold by the power of our thought alone. It will then appear that the philosopher's stone was something quite other than the absurd dream of ignorant and superstitious men, and the legend of Pygmalion itself will then take its place in "history." This is what the *docta ignorantia* promises us and whereof Nicholas of Cusa probably had a presentiment.

XXXV: A Question

Did the great philosophers notice their own contradictions? Or did they not see them, and did only their successors take account of them? I speak of Plato, Aristotle, Plotinus. Of course, they were aware of their own contradictions but these hardly troubled them; they knew that this was not the most important thing.

XXXVI: "Simpletons" and "Possesseds"

The Russian people have always had their "simpletons" and "possesseds," and it is to be assumed that their stock is not about to die out. In the better organized, more cultivated countries, where life is relatively easier and where "thought" (the principle of order without which existence on earth would be so painful) acquired its rights well before it had obtained them among us, one hardly ever has occasion to be present at the crises of possessed persons or to observe the wandering and miserable existence of simpletons. The Cynics, about whom the history of philosophy gives us a rather large number of details, belong to a distant past and no longer interest anyone. Now in Russia, the people venerate and even love (one does not know why) their mental cripples. One might say that they somehow feel that the howlings of the possessed are not completely devoid of meaning and that the miserable existence of the simpletons also is not as absurd and repugnant as appears at first sight. And indeed, an hour will come when each of us will cry, as did the most perfect of men: "My God, my God, why hast Thou forsaken me?" And then we shall leave the riches we have accumulated and set out on the road like miserable vagabonds, or like Abraham, who, according to the word of the Apostle, departed without knowing where he was going.

XXXVII: Illegitimate Thoughts

It sometimes happens that a thought, rising one knows not whence but coming obviously from outside, suddenly presents itself to you and obstinately refuses to leave you—even though it has no connection with the psychological elements that constitute the ordinary material of your reflections. But do not hasten to drive this thought away, no matter how bizarre or strange it may appear to you. And do not demand that it furnish you proof of its legitimate birth. If the habit of verifying the origin of your thoughts is too deeply rooted in you, admit at least that illegitimate children may at times be closer to their parents than legitimate children. However, take care not to generalize: it is not a question of *all* illegitimate children but only of *some* of them. It is the same as in the case of the prodigal son. The prodigal son who has returned home is dearer to us than he who never left—at times, but not always.

XXXVIII: Theory and Fact

Was Socrates' demon a "fact"? To answer this question we must first have a theory of fact. Now people believe that "facts" precede "theory." Theory recognizes neither the demon of Socrates as "fact" nor the vision of St. Paul on the road to Damascus as "fact," because a fact is a fact that has been established; but it is theory that determines how one establishes facts. Despite the interdiction of theory, however, Socrates always considered that his demon was a real fact, just as St. Paul was always persuaded that he had really seen the Christ. Both even succeeded in convincing a very large number of people, so that history, which agrees to admit only what is important for a large number of people, has recorded the vision of Socrates and that of St. Paul and even reserved for them a place of honor. There is room to remark in this connection that Socrates and even more, infinitely more St. Paul, were personally interested that the memory of their visions, which theory refused to recognize as facts, should be preserved.

But everyone is not in the same situation; and the great majority of men are incapable, even if they wished it, of forcing history to admit their visions. Perhaps others besides Socrates have received the visit of some genie, of some demigod, perhaps even of the true God; but they said nothing of it, or else they tried to relate what they saw but the words were so flat and weak that they persuaded no one. And posterity knows nothing of them. Have these men failed?

In other words, what is more important: that Socrates should really have had relationships with a "demon," or that a great number of people should have believed in the reality of these relationships? History would certainly reply, and without the least hesitation, that the latter belief is the more important—that, indeed, it alone has any importance at all.

But Socrates himself and even St. Paul would, without any doubt, have said the contrary, even though history has given such an eminent place and accorded so high a value to everything that concerns their life and work. And both of them would have added—no longer for the historians but for the philosophers—that the *theory* of fact hides from men the most important realm of being, and that those facts which theory does not admit are precisely the most precious and the most significant. This statement would appear completely inadmissible because it disagrees with the fundamental principles of our conception of the world. Also, as long as we use this conception, we accept only the facts recognized by theory. But when we no longer have need of this conception, when it becomes an obstacle (which sometimes happens and more frequently than we imagine), we begin to admit facts without demanding authorization by theory.

Most of the time, it is true, we do not succeed in bringing those around us to recognize these facts: Socrates and St. Paul, as I have already said, are completely exceptional cases. Then we become accustomed little by little to do without the recognition of our neighbors. "Suddenly" we discover a blinding truth, as new as it is unexpected: just as the ancients recognized the gods by the sign that they did not touch the earth while walking, one can distinguish the truth by the sign that it cannot be recognized by "all," that unanimous recognition deprives it of that light and divine bearing which belongs only to the immortals but which mortals have always esteemed above everything else.

XXXIX: Debates over Truth

Why are men always debating? Debates are quite understandable when there are material interests involved. If it is a question of dividing up a legacy, for example, each of the opposing parties tries to prove his right in the hope of obtaining more. But the philosophers and the theologians also debate, though it seems that they have nothing to divide up. It appears, then, that they are fighting among each other rather than debating. But why, for what object, are they fighting? Must we believe that in order to fight it is not necessary to be fighting for something? War is the father and king of all, said Heraclitus: the chief thing is to fight; as for the object of the fight, that is a secondary matter. One man proclaims, "Man is the measure of everything that exists"; another immediately counters, "No, not man, but God is the measure of everything";

and, lo, war is declared. One person affirms "identical in essence," the other, "similar in essence"—and again there is a battle. The entire history of human thought, philosophical and theological, is the history of a relentless, mortal struggle. There is room to believe that the idea of truth as a thing which does not bear contradiction flows basically from men's passion for fighting. Old people (philosophers and theologians are usually old men) cannot fight with blows of the fist, and so they have invented the fiction that there is only "one" truth in order to be able to fight at least with words. Now the truth is not at all "one" and in no way demands that men fight on its account.

XL: To the Memory of the Most Soft-Spoken of Writers

The leitmotif of all of the last works of Chekhov is this: "You feel that men do not hear you well, that it is necessary to raise your voice and shout. But shouting is repugnant to you. So you begin to speak more and more softly, and soon you may be able to be completely silent."

XLI: Again the Principle of Contradiction

Yes, "again"; for no matter how much one says on this subject it is never enough. To *doubt* the principle of contradiction is not at all "the same thing" as to *deny* the principle of contradiction. It would be "the same thing" if, having conceived doubts on the matter, we should continue all the same to recognize its sovereign rights. But those who have felt in all their being, even if it be only at certain moments, that the power of the principle of contradiction is limited, know that this in no way obliges them to deny its utility and importance. But they refuse to see in it "the most unshakeable of all principles," as Aristotle expressed it. They refuse to admit that it must always and everywhere be appropriate, that it must be the supreme judge and master of man. For it is not the master, it is only the executor of someone's orders. Thus in certain cases it is all-powerful—not, however, by itself or by its "own nature"; its power is given to it by someone who is above it. Orpheus declared that Eurydice was Eurydice and that no other woman was Eurydice. And by the will of Orpheus, in this instance, the principle of contradiction becomes "the most unshakeable of all principles." Among the millions of women who have existed and who will exist no other can be Eurydice. Hell and the gates of hell themselves could not conquer the will of Orpheus and the power which it conferred on the principle of contradiction. But the statement "Giordano Bruno was burned alive," which up to now has enjoyed the protection of the principle of contradiction and has barred the road to the contrary statement—"Giordano Bruno was *not* burned alive"—can this statement be assured the eternal protection of the principle of contradiction?

Can it also assume that the gates of hell will never prevail against it? Or, let us take a more general statement: "It is impossible to make that which has been not to have been." Are we not free to admit that certain things among all those which have been will never be effaced, but that others *will* disappear and become non-existent, and that, consequently, the principle of contradiction, submitting to the commands of a superior principle, will to the end of time protect certain pages of the past and utterly destroy others, so that the past itself will be modified? We are free, of course, to admit this possibility. But we shall not admit it precisely because we "are afraid" (our thought is continually afraid of something) that it will result in a situation too difficult, too complicated, and that it would be necessary for us to transform our entire logic, or even (and this is what appears most terrible) to renounce the services of ready-made criteria and "lose our footing." Instead of asking, we would have to answer; and instead of obeying, we would have to command. We ourselves would have to choose our Eurydice and descend to hell in order to wrest from it the recognition of our rights. Is this not too much to ask of man, feeble and mortal man?

XLII: Commentaries

There come to me again the words of Occam: *Est articulus fidei quad Deus assumpsit naturam humanam. Non includit contradictionem, Deum assumere naturam asininam. Pari ratione potest assumere lapidem aut lignum.* ("It is an article of faith that God assumed human nature. It involves no contradiction for God to assume the nature of an ass. With equal reason he could take on the nature of stone or wood.")

What, at bottom, is the significance of Occam's thought? Why does it appear so daring, so unacceptable? What irritates us is not only the form which Occam gave to his thought, even though this form may be crude and offensive to all pious men: *Deum assumere naturam asininam* (for God to assume the nature of an ass) . . . Occam brings together terms which ought to be as far away as possible from each other and which would be found next to each other only in a dictionary where the words follow each other without any regard to their meaning. And yet it is not the form that is essential here—far from it. Occam is not among those who seek to strike the reader by some audacious, unexpected turn. It is not against others that he fights but against himself or, to use the language of Hegel, against the "spirit of his time."

It is generally believed that it was with Occam that the dissolution of scholasticism began. He is regarded as a "decadent." And, indeed, one does find in him certain traits which commonly characterize decadence. Albertus Magnus, St. Thomas Aquinas, Duns Scotus and the other *principes theologiae* [main theologians] had built splendid cathedrals to the glory of thought, when suddenly Occam arose with his questions which undermined the very foundations of the grandiose edifices of what was, from the spiritual point of view, the most creative of the centuries of the Middle Ages. This was the work of a "decadent." Are the decadent not recognized above all else by their passion for destruction, by their love of novelty, whatever it may be, by their need to contradict their time? . . . *Non includit contradictionem Deum assumere naturam asininam* [it does not include a contradiction that God should assume the nature of an ass]. If this is so, if the thesis of Occam is true, and if God may, by His will, become incarnate not only in a despised animal but in a piece of wood or in a stone, then why did all the *doctores angelici, subtillissimi* [angelic, most sublime doctors] etc. . . . . expend such tremendous efforts? Why did they call forth from the depths of the centuries the shades of Aristotle, Plato, Plotinus? Why all the *Summae,* the immense cathedrals, the monasteries, the universities? For all these were created by men only to explain and make acceptable to reason the fundamental dogma of the Christian religion. The Bible relates that the son of God became man, was treated like the worst of criminals, subjected to frightful humiliations, and died at last on the cross between two robbers. No one in the Middle Ages doubted the biblical account, and Occam himself also believed it, as his works prove and as does the very fragment which I have quoted and which begins with the words: *Est articulus fidei . . .* [it is an article of faith].

But it was not sufficient for men to "believe." They wished also to "reconcile" their faith with reason. They posed the question: *Cur Deus homo?* Why did God make Himself man? And they could not rest until they had found an answer to this question. But what did the term "an answer" mean to them? What it means to us is this: he "answers" who can show that what happened could not have not happened and could not have happened otherwise than it did happen. God had *necessarily* to become incarnate in man, for it was *impossible* to save man in any other way. In order that man might be deified, God had to become man. Despite their apparent diversity, all the answers to the question *Cur Deus homo?* were variations on one and the same theme: to show that what had happened was due to a *natural necessity.*

Man could not satisfy his need to know except with the nectar which goes by the name "explanation." To obtain it, men went to the farthest countries. It replaced that philosopher's stone of which the alchemists dreamed day and night. And then, suddenly, Occam's *non includit contradictionem* [it does not include a contradiction] and *pari ratione* [for the same reason], which ruin the foundations not only of medieval thought but of all rational "thought"! For if it is not given us to discover the necessary in the real, does not "thought" become impossible? How, then, can reason justify not its existence (existence has no need of justification), but its pretensions to a primary role? It was assumed, indeed, that it was precisely reason that prepared the divine draught which could quench the most ardent thirst for knowledge and does definitely and forever quench it: "Contentment with oneself can arise from reason, and that contentment which arises from reason is the highest possible." (Spinoza, *Ethics* IV, LII). Reason leads us to the boundary beyond which stretches the kingdom of Necessity, where all questions vanish of themselves and where man obtains the supreme peace which is the final goal of his aspirations. The *Summae*, the cathedrals, the solemn services—all these were created by the great minds of the Middle Ages only for the purpose of attaining this peace. And the role of reason also consisted in tranquilizing man, in extinguishing his doubts and anxieties. But reason can accomplish its work only if it succeeds in blending and becoming one with Necessity, for it is to Necessity, to Necessity alone, that there is given an absolute power over everything that exists, over the living and over the dead, over man and over God. *Cur Deus homo?* One can answer this question only when one recognizes *in advance* that God could not choose, that He was *obliged* to become incarnate, that it was impossible for Him not to become incarnate even if He had wished it.

All the effort of the Middle Ages, all its concentrated and immense spiritual labor, had for its end to render rationally explicable the mystery which Scripture contains. And man is so constructed that when he undertakes a task and gives himself up to it entirely, he begins to think that the object of his efforts is the most important and the most precious thing in the world for him and for others. The essential thing, it would seem, is that God became incarnate, that He came among men and revealed Himself to them—and it is precisely this that Scripture tells us. But the important thing for "thought" is what *it itself invents* and not what Scripture says; and it accepted Scripture only because it could understand and explain it. To put it otherwise, it could demonstrate that the biblical story in no way offended or contradicted the principles to which man has always been subject and which he proclaims to be eternal and unshakeable. If it had appeared, in the light of its principles, that it was *not* suitable for God to become incarnate, or that this was *impossible* for Him, one would have been obliged to renounce Scripture. Now this is exactly what happened at the end. It was discovered that the "proofs" and the "explanations" thought out by the medieval philosophers explained nothing and could explain nothing. It was discovered that it is impossible to defend, by means of reason, the truths of "revelation," that, in general, one cannot defend revealed truths, that they are indefensible. This means that one then has the choice: either to admit that the truths of revelation are not truths and that the Bible must be banished to the realm of poetic fiction, just like the stories of Homer—or else . . .

There was, there still is, an "or else"; there is still an escape. But this escape seems to such a degree contrary to human nature (not only to the "first" nature, perhaps, but also to the "second," following the dictum that habit is a second nature) that people do not even speak of it, or it is invoked only by those who are resolved in advance to speak without any hope of being understood. "It is not necessary to explain God, and one cannot justify Him." This is what Occam wished to say. And this is what no one heard. And if I now recall these words that people did not hear, it is not at all in the hope of drawing attention to them and of opening for them a way into the heart.

Here is a strange and troubling enigma. There are, indeed, words which are destined not to be heard, and yet, by some mysterious will, these words, it seems, must from time to time be pronounced in a loud voice. Let us recall the ancient *vox clamantis in deserto* [a voice crying out in the desert]. Perhaps it is not as useless and ridiculous as one imagines to recall to men at times those "heralds of the truth" whose voice possesses the magical power of transforming into deserts the most populous of regions. And then another still more mysterious "perhaps." Repeating the words of Tertullian, Pascal said that there is no place on earth for the truth, that the truth is condemned to wander among men who do not recognize it and refuse to accept it. What he meant was that truth is truth precisely because, by its very existence, it transforms populous cities into deserts. When the truth illuminates a man, he feels immediately that "all," that "human beings"—that is to say, those who transform deserts into populous cities—possess the gift or incomprehensible power of killing the truth. This is why Dostoevsky, in his better moments, had such a horror of, such a disgust for, "omnitude." That is why Plotinus speaks of the "flight of the one to the One." That is why all the theories of knowledge that have triumphed in the course of the centuries have always concealed the truth. We must leave them and turn toward the blessed men who, as Plato says, were better than we and closer to God, and whose thought soared freely in that second dimension which we discover only and, moreover, very rarely at the cost of the most painful *exercitia spiritualia*.

XLIII: OF DOGMATISM

What makes dogmatism unacceptable is not, as people ordinarily think, the indemonstrable propositions which it arbitrarily sets forth. Arbitrariness and contempt for demonstrations might, on the contrary, dispose men in favor of dogmatism. Whatever people may say, man in fact, by his nature, loves the arbitrary more than anything in the world and submits to demonstrations only when he cannot overcome them. One might then consider dogmatism the Magna Carta of human freedom. But it is precisely freedom which dogmatism fears above everything else, and it tries by all means to appear as obedient and reasonable as all other doctrines. It is just this that takes away all its charm, that even provokes our disgust—for if it dissimulates, it must be that it is ashamed and wishes that we should be ashamed also. To be ashamed of freedom and independence—can one pardon that?

XLIV: The Light of Knowledge

Salieri, says Pushkin, tested harmony by algebra, but it was not given to him to "create." And he was astonished, he was indignant even, that Mozart, who did not at all concern himself with testing, heard the heavenly songs that he, Salieri, did not succeed in hearing. Was not his indignation justified? Even in this life "the idle loafer" is admitted to the porch of paradise, while the honest and conscientious worker is left outside and waits vainly to be called. But it is said in an ancient book, "the ways of God are inscrutable." There was a time when men understood this, when they understood that the road which leads to the Promised Land does not reveal itself to him who tests harmony by algebra, to him who tests in general. Abraham departed without knowing general where he was going. If he had set about "testing" he would never have arrived at the Promised Land. Thus it is that testing, looking backward, the "light" of knowledge—these are not, contrary to what we have been taught, always what is best.

XLV: The Truths That Constrain

The great majority of men do not believe in the truths of the religion they profess. Plato already said, "Unbelief is proper to the mob." Thus they demand that those around them profess the very truths which they themselves officially believe and say the same things as they: that alone supports them in their "faith"; it is only from their environment that they draw the force of their convictions. And the less convincing the revealed truths appear to them, the more important it is to them that no one doubt these truths. It is for this reason that people who believe the least are ordinarily the most intolerant. While the criterion of ordinary, scientific truths consists in the possibility of making them binding upon all, there is room to believe that the truths of faith are true insofar as they are able to do without the consent of men, insofar as they are indifferent to recognition and demonstrations. However, the positive religions do not hold truths of this kind in very high esteem. They maintain them, for they cannot get along without them, but they rely on other truths, on those which constrain men; and they seek to place under the protection of the principle of contradiction even the revealed truths in order that these shall in no wise yield to ordinary truths.

As is known, the protection of the principle of contradiction appeared insufficient to Catholicism and it invented the Inquisition, without which it would not have been able to accomplish its immense historical work. It defended itself by means of "intolerance" and even made a virtue of its intolerance. It never occurred to the mind of Catholicism that that which requires the protection of the principle of contradiction or of executioners and jailers is outside the divine truth, and that what truly saves men is precisely that which, according to our human reckoning, is feeble, weak, and devoid of all protection. The truths of faith are to be recognized by this sign: that, contrary to the truths of knowledge, they are neither universal nor necessary and, consequently, do not have the power of constraining human beings. These truths are given freely, they are accepted freely. No one officially certifies them, they do not justify themselves to anyone, they do not make anyone afraid, and they themselves fear no one.

XLVI: Autonomous Morality

It is known that autonomous morality found its most complete and final expression in the doctrine of Socrates. Socrates affirmed that virtue has no need of reward, that it is of little importance whether the soul is immortal or not, that the virtuous man obtains everything that he needs from "the good." But I think that Socrates (quite like Kant, who, in his *Critique of Practical Reason*, walked in the footsteps of Socrates) stopped midway, and that "the good" will not be content with such signs of humility. He should have taken still another step; he should have admitted that the virtuous man has no need of "the immortality of the soul" and renounced immortality completely. In other words, he should have admitted that Socrates is mortal, since already here on earth he has obtained from "the good" everything that he could wish, but that Alcibiades and those who resemble him are immortal. The "good" gives them nothing or very little, and they exist by virtue of another principle which, in the course of this earthly life, does not succeed in accomplishing its promises and postpones the accomplishment of them to another life.

On this condition, *only on this condition,* will "the good" receive a complete satisfaction and will discussions on the subject of autonomous and heteronomous morality be finished. Let men of Socrates' type who willingly recognize the "good" as the supreme principle equally willingly renounce the future life, which they do not at all need, for the benefit of people of Alcibiades' type who, having submitted to a principle other than Socrates' "good," have a right to expect and demand that their existence should continue after death. Certainly from the point of view of Socrates, the Alcibidians lose by the exchange. A hundred lives deprived of "the good," no matter how happy they may be, are not worth one single life in "the good," no matter how painful and horrible it may be. Philosophy would then at last be able to celebrate its triumph. The Socratics and the Alcibidians would finally obtain complete satisfaction and all debates would cease.

XLVII: Thought and Being

The more positive knowledge we obtain, the more estranged we become from the mysteries of life. The more the mechanism of our thought perfects itself, the more difficult it becomes for us to recover the sources of being. Knowledge weighs heavily upon us and paralyses us, and perfected thought makes of us submissive, will-less beings who seek, see and appreciate in life only "order" and the laws and norms established by this "order." Our teachers and guides are no longer the prophets who spoke "as those who have power" but the scientists, for whom the supreme virtue consists in obeying the Necessity which they have not created and which never allows itself to be persuaded by anything or anyone.

XLVIII: "Our Own" and That Which Is Strange to Us

When we look at anything that is ours, that belongs to us, we "understand" it and even approve of it. When, however, we discover the same things in others, they often provoke our disgust. We willingly examine our own wounds while we turn away from those of others. But as we become more objective, our own wounds become as repugnant to us as those of others. Consequently? One has a choice between two "consequences": either to renounce objectivity, or else to learn to see others as we see ourselves—not to fear the wounds of others or the ugliness of others. Objectivity is not indisputably the way to truth, and fear is always a bad counselor.

XLIX: The Vice of Our Thought

In the theory of knowledge, it is the idea of Necessity that rules. In ethics it is the idea of Duty—which is, in fact, only Necessity diluted and weakened. Contemporary thought can make headway only on this condition.

L: Defeats and Successes

Plato was sure that the blessed wise men of antiquity were better than we and lived closer to God. Plato, it seems, was right. In any case, no one who has studied the history of philosophy will say that the millennial efforts of the human mind have brought us closer to the final truth, to the eternal sources of being. But this millennial struggle of the human soul with eternal mystery, a struggle which ends in nothing and which thus appears to many people completely useless, is for us a guarantee that the failures experienced by philosophy till now will not discourage men, that the struggle will continue. Whether we come closer to God or become estranged from Him, whether we become better or worse than our ancestors, we cannot give up our efforts and our searches. The failures will continue as in the past but, as in the past, they will not prevent new attempts. It is not given man to stop, it is not given him to cease searching. There is here, in this work of Sisyphus, a great enigma which we shall probably never succeed in resolving. It suggests to us, however, the idea that successes do not always have a final and decisive meaning in the general economy of human activity. The positive sciences have achieved immense and incontrovertible results. Metaphysics, on the other hand, has given us nothing solid or certain. And yet it is possible that metaphysics may, in some sense, be more useful and more important than the positive sciences. It may be that our abortive attempts to penetrate into the world which is forever hidden from us may have more value than the progress we make in the study of the world which extends visibly before us and reveals itself to all men on the condition that they manifest a certain persistence. If this be so, Kant's objections to metaphysics fall of themselves. Metaphysics has not given us a single truth obligatory upon all. That is true, but that is not an objection to metaphysics. "By its very nature" metaphysics does not wish to give us, and must not give us, truths obligatory upon all. Even more: its task consists, among other things, in devaluating the truths of the positive sciences, along with the very idea of constraint as the sign of truth. If, then, one decides to confront—as Kant wished to do—metaphysics and the positive sciences, it is necessary to reverse the problem and to put the question closer to the following way: In seeking the sources of being metaphysics has not been able to find universal and necessary truth, while in studying that which flows from these sources the positive sciences have discovered numerous "truths";—does this not signify that the "truths" of the positive sciences are false, or at least ephemeral—enduring only for a moment? . . .

I think that one cannot approach philosophical problems without ridding himself at the very outset of the idea of the bond, established by Kant, between metaphysics and the positive sciences. If we do not succeed in doing this, all the judgments that we shall try to make about the final problems of existence will remain fruitless. We shall always be afraid of failure, and, instead of coming closer to God, we shall become further estranged from Him. It is more than probable that Plato considered the ancient sages blessed because they were free of all fear of positive truths and still did not know the chains of the knowledge whose weight Plato himself so painfully experienced.

LI: The Empirical Personality

How are the rare moments when the "self-evidences" lose their power over man to be used for philosophy? These moments presuppose the existence of a very special kind of inward state wherein that which ordinarily appears to us as the most important, the most essential, and even as the only reality becomes suddenly insignificant, useless, fantastic. But philosophy wishes to be objective and despises "states of the soul." If, then, one runs after objectivity, one inevitably falls into the clutches of self-evidences; and if one wishes to rid himself of self-evidences he must, before everything else and contrary to tradition, disdain objectivity. Certainly no one will decide to do that. Everyone flatters himself that he has obtained a truth which, no matter how little, no matter how very little, will be a truth for all. It is only when we are alone with ourselves, under the impenetrable veil of the mystery of the individual being (the empirical personality), that we decide occasionally to renounce the real or illusory rights and privileges which we possess from the fact of our participation in the world common to all. It is then that there suddenly shine before our eyes the ultimate and the penultimate truths—but they appear more like dreams than truths. We forget them easily, as we forget dreams. And if it happens that we do retain a vague memory of them, we do not know what to do with it. And, to tell the truth, one cannot do anything with these truths. At the very most, one can try to translate them by means of a certain verbal music and listen to what those who, acquainted with these visions only by having heard others speak of them and not by their own immediate experience, transform them into judgments and, having thus killed them, make them necessary always and for everyone, that is, comprehensible and "evident." But they will then be truths quite different from those that were revealed to us in our solitude. It is no longer to us that they will belong, but to everyone, to that "omnitude" which Dostoevsky so hated and which his friend and disciple, Soloviev, for the sake of traditional philosophy and theology, made the basis of his system under the less odious name of "ecumenicity." It is here that there clearly appears the fundamental opposition between the thought of Dostoevsky and that of the school out of which Soloviev arose. Dostoevsky fled from "omnitude" to himself; Soloviev fled from himself to "omnitude." The living man, whom the school calls the "empirical personality," was for Soloviev the major obstacle on the road to the truth. He thought, or, to put it better, he affirmed (who can know what a man thinks?) that one cannot see truth as long as one has not completely rid himself of his "ego" (in other words, as long as one has not overcome and destroyed his empirical individuality). Dostoevsky, however, knew that truth is revealed only to the empirical personality. . . .

LII: DIALECTIC

Thought, said Plato, is a silent dialogue of the soul with itself. Obviously this is so, if thought is dialectical. Then, even while alone, a man can not remain silent and continues to speak: he imagines himself before an adversary to whom he must demonstrate something, whom he must convince or constrain, from whom he must wrest agreement. Plotinus, the last of the great Platonists, however, could no longer bear this kind of thought. He aspired to that true freedom wherein one no longer constrains and is himself no longer constrained by others. Is the idea of such freedom really only a fantasy, and, conversely, is the idea of Necessity which constrains—the idea on which dialectic lives—really as invincible as it appears to us? Certainly he alone can demonstrate and constrain who has taken in hand the sword of Necessity. But he who takes up the sword will perish by the sword. Kant succeeded in killing metaphysics only because metaphysics wished to constrain. And so long as metaphysics does not decide to lay down its weapons, it will remain the slave of the positive sciences. Thought is not a dialogue of the soul with itself. Thought is, or to put it another way, *may be,* much more than a dialogue and can do without dialectic. As Pushkin said, "And the seraph tore out of my mouth the tongue that added slander to lust for falsehood."

LIII: THE IDEA OF TOTAL UNITY

We live in narrowness and injustice. We are obliged to press close to each other and, in order to suffer the least possible, we try to maintain a certain order. But why attribute to God, the God whom neither time nor space limits, the same respect and love for order? Why forever speak of "total unity"? If God loves men, what need has He to subordinate men to His divine will and to deprive them of their own will, the most precious of the things He has bestowed upon them? There is no need at all. Consequently the idea of total unity is an absolutely false idea. And as philosophy cannot ordinarily do without this idea, it follows therefrom, as a second consequence, that our thought is stricken with a terrible malady of which we must rid ourselves, no matter how difficult it may be. We are all endlessly concerned with the hygiene of our soul; as far as our reason is concerned, we are persuaded that it is perfectly healthy. But we must begin with reason. Reason must impose upon itself a whole series of vows, and the first of these is to renounce overly great pretensions. It is not forbidden for reason to speak of unity and even of unities, but it must renounce *total* unity—and other things besides. And what a sigh of relief men will breathe when they suddenly discover that the living God, the true God, in no way resembles Him whom reason has shown them until now!

LIV: What Is Truth?

Shall one speak to stones in the hope that they will end by answering "Amen," as they did to the Venerable Bede? Or before animals, thinking that one will make himself understood by them through the power of his magic, the power which Orpheus possessed in olden times? For men apparently will not even listen; they are too busy. They are making history, and they have many other things on their minds besides truth. Everyone knows that history is infinitely more important than truth. Hence, this new definition of truth: truth is that which passes history by and which history does not notice.

LV: Logic and Thunder

Phenomenology, the faithful disciples of Husserl declare, ignores the difference between *homo dormiens* (sleeping man) and *homo vigilans* (waking man). This is true. It does ignore this difference, and herein lies the source of its power and persuasive force. It exercises all its efforts towards preserving its *docta ignorantia*. As soon, indeed, as phenomenology feels that not only *homo vigilans*, the man who has been awakened (it seems there has never yet been any such person on earth), differs from the man who is asleep, but that the man who is only beginning to awaken also differs from him *toto coelo*—it will be at the end of its success. Consciously and unconsciously, the man who is asleep tends to consider the conditions from which his dreams flow as the only possible conditions of existence. That is why he calls them "self-evidences" and guards and protects them in all kinds of ways (logic and the theory of knowledge: the gifts of reason). But when the moment of awakening comes (the rumbling of the thunder is heard: revelation), one will begin to doubt the self-evidences and to put up a struggle against them that is completely unreasonable—that is to say, one will do precisely what, for the man who is asleep, is the height of absurdity. Can there, indeed, be anything more absurd than to answer logic with claps of thunder?

LVI: Protagoras and Plato

Protagoras affirmed that man is the measure of all things; Plato said that it is God. At first blush it seems that Protagoras' truth is lowly while Plato's is exalted. However, Plato himself elsewhere says that the gods do not philosophize and do not seek wisdom, being already wise. But what does it mean to philosophize and to seek truth? Is it not to "measure" things? Is not, furthermore, such an occupation more suitable to weak and ignorant mortals than to the powerful and omniscient gods?

LVII: The Goals of Philosophy

The philosophers seek to "explain" the world in such a way that everything becomes clear and transparent and that life no longer has in itself anything, or the least possible amount, of the problematic and mysterious. Should they not, rather, concern themselves with showing that precisely what appears to men clear and comprehensible is strangely enigmatic and mysterious? Should they not try to deliver themselves and others from the power of concepts whose definiteness destroys mystery? The sources, the roots, of being lie, in fact, in that which is hidden and not in that which is revealed: *Deus est Deus absconditus* (God is a hidden God).

LVIII: The Possible and the Impossible

A round square or a wooden piece of iron is an absurdity and, consequently, an impossibility, for the connection of these concepts runs contrary to the principle of contradiction. But "the poisoned Socrates" is not an absurdity and, therefore, a possibility, for the principle of contradiction authorizes the bringing together of these concepts. Could one not beg the principle of contradiction to modify its decisions or even force it to do so? Or could not one discover a tribunal which would have the authority to set aside these decisions and which would establish that the poisoning of Socrates, being contradictory, is an absurdity and that, consequently, Socrates was not poisoned, while a round square is not at all absurd and, consequently, it is quite possible that it may someday be found? Or one might leave the wooden piece of iron and the round square to the principle of contradiction—let it do with them what it wishes—but on the condition that it recognize that the judgment "Socrates was poisoned" also contains within itself a contradiction and that, consequently, no matter what people say, Socrates was never poisoned. It is such questions that should occupy philosophy, and in olden times philosophy actually did concern itself with them. But today they have been completely forgotten.

LIX: The One Thing Necessary

"Prepare the way for God!" How prepare it? By observing fasts and festivals? By paying tithes or even distributing all of one's good to the poor? By mortifying one's flesh? By loving one's neighbor? By spending one's nights reading ancient books? All this is necessary and certainly good, but it is not the chief thing. The chief thing is to think that, even if all men without exception were convinced that God does not exist, this would not mean anything, and that if one could prove as clearly as two times two makes four that God does not exist, this also would not mean anything.

People will tell me that one cannot demand such things of men. Obviously! But God always demands of us the impossible, and it is in this that the chief difference between God and men consists. Or perhaps, on the contrary, the resemblance: is it not said that God created man in His image? It is only when man wishes the impossible that he remembers God. To obtain that which is possible he turns to his fellow men.

LX: Idle Questions

"I know what time is," says St. Augustine, "but when someone asks me what time is, I cannot answer and it then seems that I do not know." What St. Augustine says about time may be said about many other things. Man knows them as long as no one questions him or as long as he does not question himself about them. Man knows what freedom is, but ask him what it is and he will become confused and not be able to answer. He knows also what the soul is, but the psychologists, that is to say, scientists—people who are profoundly convinced that it is always useful and proper to raise questions—have succeeded in creating a "psychology without the soul." It should be concluded from this that our methods of searching for truth are in no way as infallible as we are sometimes accustomed to think, and that in certain cases our inability to answer a question that has been raised testifies precisely to our knowledge and the aversion to raising questions shows that we are near the truth. But no one will permit himself this conclusion. It would be a mortal offence to Socrates, Aristotle and all those who today write on the "science of logic." People have no desire to set themselves against the mighty of this world, be they living or dead.

LXI: Again on Idle Questions

Among the innumerable *a priori,* or evident, truths on which, as everyone believes, human thought is founded but which in reality have muddled human thought, one of the most firmly established is that one only asks questions in order to obtain answers. When I ask, what time is it? what is the sum of the angles of a triangle? what is the density of mercury? is God just? is the soul immortal? is the will free?, it is clear to everyone that I wish to obtain precise answers to these questions. But there are questions upon questions. He who asks, what time is it? or what is the density of mercury? needs, indeed, to be given a determinate answer, and this suffices for him. But he who asks if God is just or the soul immortal wants something quite other; and clear and distinct answers make him furious or plunge him into despair. How is one to make people understand this? How is one to explain to them that somewhere, beyond a certain limit, the human soul is so completely transformed that the very "mechanism" of thought becomes something quite other, or, to put it better, there is no longer any place for mechanism in this thought?

LXII: The Morality of Slaves and Masters

Socrates obeyed his demon, and he had at his side a demon who guided him. Alcibiades, however, although he had a profound respect for Socrates, did not have any demon, or, if he had, did not obey him. What should the philosophy which wishes to define and describe the moral "phenomenon" do? Should it be guided by Socrates or by Alcibiades? If it follows Socrates, the presence of the demon at man's side and man's complete submission to the orders of his demon will be considered a sign of moral perfection, and Alcibiades will be relegated to the category of immoral people. If it follows Alcibiades, Socrates must be condemned.

Here, I trust, is a perfectly legitimate question. I further trust that traditional philosophy will never succeed in resolving it. It does not even raise it. In other words, before setting out to describe a moral phenomenon, it already knows what morality is and how it is to be described. However, it may be that Socrates and Alcibiades cannot be put in the same category: "Not all persons are created equal; to some eternal life is preordained; to others eternal damnation" (Calvin). It is proper (it is ordained) for Socrates to let himself be guided by his demon, and it is proper (it is ordained) for Alcibiades to guide his demon. When Nietzsche spoke of the morality of slaves, he was much closer to Christianity than his critics imagined.

LXIII: The Stones Endowed with Consciousness

Spinoza said that if a stone were endowed with consciousness, it would imagine that it falls to earth freely. But Spinoza was mistaken. If the stone had consciousness it would be convinced that it falls to earth by virtue of the necessity of the stony nature of all being. "It follows from this" that the idea of Necessity could only have been born and developed in stones endowed with consciousness. And, as the idea of Necessity is so deeply rooted in the human soul that it appears to everyone primordial and the foundation, even, of being (neither being nor thought are possible without it), it also follows from this that the vast, overwhelming majority of men are not men, however they may seem to be such, but stones endowed with consciousness. And it is they—these stones endowed with consciousness, to whom everything is indifferent but who think, speak and act according to the laws of their petrified consciousness—it is precisely they who have created the environment in which all humanity finds itself obliged to live, that is, not only the stones endowed or unendowed with consciousness, but also living men. It is very difficult, impossible almost, to fight against the majority, especially considering that the stones are better adapted to the conditions of terrestrial existence and always survive much more easily. The result is that men must adapt themselves, in their turn, to the stones, flatter them and recognize as the truth and even as the good what appears true and good to the petrified consciousness. There is room to believe that the reflections of Kant on the subject of the *Deus ex machina*, as also the *sub specie aeternitatis seu necessitatis* of Spinoza, just like our ideas about the truth which constrains and the good which constrains, were suggested to living men by the stones endowed with consciousness that are mixed among them.

LXIV: DE SERVO ARBITRIO

After reading the first writings of Plato, Socrates, according to tradition, said, "How this young man has lied about me!" Plato, however, also tells us many true things about Socrates. To my mind the *Apology* reflects exactly the tone and content of the speech pronounced by Socrates before his judges. Socrates certainly told them that he accepted their verdict. As his demon demanded it of him, he had to submit to a judgment which he considered unjust and revolting, and to submit not only outwardly but inwardly. But even though Socrates himself submitted, this in no way imposes upon us the obligation to submit also. There still remains to us the right—and, who knows, perhaps even the possibility—of snatching Socrates from his fate, contrary to what he said, contrary even to what he desired—of snatching Socrates, against his will, from the hands of the Athenians. And if we (or someone stronger than we) snatch him away by force, does this mean that we have taken away from him his "free will"? At first blush it seems that we have, indeed, taken it away from him. Have we not wrested him from the hands of the Athenians against his will? And yet we have not really deprived him of his "will." On the contrary, we have given it back to him. . . . *Sapienti sat*, or is it still necessary to give some explanation? In that case, I should add this: the doctrine of Luther about the *servo arbitrio*, that of Calvin about predestination, and even that of Spinoza about "Necessity," aimed finally only to drive away from Socrates his demon who suggested to him that he must submit to Necessity not only externally through fear but inwardly through a sense of responsibility. Certainly Aristotle is right: Necessity does not allow itself to be persuaded. But does it follow from this that it is necessary to love Necessity with all one's heart, with all one's soul, and to submit to it out of a sense of responsibility? To submit to it through fear—that is another thing; but as far as a sense of responsibility, as far as conscience is concerned, it will always protest against all constraint. And "our conscience," the conscience that teaches us "to submit" and "to accept," is only a kind of fear made up and costumed. If, then, we succeed in driving away the demon of Socrates, if we (or someone else: we are not equal to this task) succeeded in wresting him from the hands of "history," we shall return to him his freedom, that freedom which every living being in the depth of his soul (at that depth to which the light of "our conscience" and all our "light" never attains and where the demons no longer have any power) esteems and loves above all else—even when he covers it with insults before others and brands it, in a loud voice, as arbitrariness and caprice.

LXV: Looking Backwards

Our thought consists essentially in turning around, in looking backward (in German "*Besinnung*"). It is born out of fear. We are afraid that behind us, under us, above us, there is something that threatens us. And indeed, as soon as man turns around and looks behind himself, he "sees" dangerous and terrible things. But what if these exist (will anyone admit this supposition?) only for him who turns around and only so long as he turns around? The head of Medusa presents no danger for the man who goes straight ahead on his way without looking backward, but it turns him who looks towards it to stone. To think without looking backward, to create the "logic" of the thought which does not turn around: will philosophy and the philosophers ever understand that it is in this that man's essential task consists, that here is the way which leads to "the one thing necessary?" Will they ever understand that inertia, the law of the inertia which is at the foundation of the thought which looks backward and is always afraid of possible surprises, will never permit us to escape from the somnolent, quasi-vegetative existence to which we are condemned by the history of our intellectual development?

LXVI: Commentary on That Which Precedes

Ten years before the publication of his *Critique of Pure Reason*, Kant wrote to his friend Herz that "in the determination of the origin and validity of our knowledge the *deus ex machina* is the most absurd supposition and, over and above the vicious circle in the conclusions of our knowledge, it presents the disadvantage that it gives aid to every caprice and every devout or brooding fantasy." And again, "to say that a Supreme Being (*höheres Wesen*) has wisely introduced into us concepts and principles of this kind (that is, what Kant called synthetic *a priori* judgments.—L.S.) amounts to destroying at its root the possibility of all philosophy."

All of Kant's "critique of pure reason," all of his *Weltanschauung* [world view], rests on this foundation. From where did Kant derive this assurance that the *deus ex machina* or *höheres Wesen* [higher being] is the most absurd of suppositions and that, in accepting them, one destroys the very foundations of philosophy? It is known that Kant himself declared on many occasions that metaphysical problems are reducible to three—God, the immortality of the soul, and free will. But the ground being so prepared, what can philosophy say about God? If one knows in advance that the *deus ex machina* or, what is the same thing, the *höheres Wesen*, is the most absurd of suppositions, if one knows in advance that he puts an end to all philosophy by admitting the intrusion into life of a supreme being, then there remains nothing further for metaphysics to do. It has been suggested to us in advance that God, like the immortality of the soul and free will, is only invention and fantasy (*Hirngespinst und Grille*) and that, consequently, metaphysics itself is only pure arbitrariness and fantasy.

But I ask once more: Who was it who gave Kant (and Kant stands for "all of us," Kant spoke in the name of all of us) this assurance? Whom did he question on the matter of the *deus ex machina* (*höheres Wesen*)? The answer can only be this: Kant (quite like "all of us") understood philosophy as a looking backward, as *Besinnung*. Now, to turn around and look behind one-self presupposes that what one seeks to see possesses a certain structure that is forever determined, and that it is given neither to man nor to any "supreme being" to escape the power of the "order of being" which was not created either by them or for them. Whatever this "order," which has been introduced by itself, may be, it is something given once for all that one cannot change, that one must accept and against which one cannot fight. The very idea of such a fight appears to Kant (and to all of us) inadmissible and absurd—inadmissible not only because we are condemned in advance to defeat and because the struggle is hopeless but also because the struggle is immoral and testifies to our spirit of rebellion and egotism. Caprice, arbitrariness, fantasy—says Kant, who, like all of us, is certain (because it has been suggested to us) that these things are much worse than necessity, submission, order.

And, indeed, it suffices merely to turn around to see immediately (intuition) that one cannot and must not fight, that one must submit. The "eternal order," like the head of Medusa crowned with serpents, paralyses not only the will but also the reason of man. And as philosophy has always been and is still now "a look thrown backward" (*Besinnung*) our final truths are found to be truths that do not liberate but rather enchain. The philosophers have always *spoken* much of freedom; almost none of them, however, has dared to wish for freedom. They have sought Necessity which puts an end to all searching, for it does not show respect for any thing or any person or according to Aristotle's formula: "Necessity does not allow itself to be persuaded" (*hê anankê ametapeiston ti einai*). He alone is capable of fighting against the Medusa and her serpents (the *anankê* of Aristotle, which inspired him as well as Kant with such a fear of the capricious and the fantastic) who has enough daring to march forward without turning around. Philosophy must not, then, be a looking around, a turning backward (*Besinnen*), as we have become accustomed to think—to look backward is the end of all philosophy—but it must go forward fearlessly, without taking account of anything whatever, without turning around to look at anything whatever. That is why the divine Plato said: "It is necessary to dare everything," without fearing, he adds, to pass as impudent. And Plotinus also tells us: "A great and final struggle awaits the soul." This is also what Nietzsche's "will to power" wished to be. Philosophy is not *Besinnen* but struggle. And this struggle has no end and will have no end. The kingdom of God, as it is written, is attained through force.

Lev Shestov—Biographical Timeline

1866

Lev Isaakovich Schwarzmann (alias Lev Shestov) was born in Kiev on 31 January (or 13 February according to the old Russian calendar), the first son of a respected Jewish family. The father, Isaak Moiseevich Schwarzmann, came from a modest background, but he established and ran an important textile business. His house was a meeting place for the most prominent cultural figures of Kiev and St. Petersburg at that time. He had a strong personality and the reputation of a free thinker in the Jewish community. Isaak Moiseevich's outstanding knowledge of Hebrew literature and, more generally, of the Jewish tradition made a lasting impression on Lev Isaakovich, whose later work significantly evolved around the alliance between Judaism and Christian Orthodoxism (as opposed to Greek wisdom).

1880–83

Secondary education in Kiev and Moscow (following his early involvement in a political affair he leaves Kiev and finishes his studies in Moscow).

1884

He enrolls in the Faculty of Mathematics but soon transfers to the Faculty of Law at the University of Moscow. Another conflict with the authorities, this time in the guise of a well-known Inspector of Students, forces Lev Isaakovich to return to Kiev.

1889

He finishes his studies at the Faculty of Law at Kiev University and graduates with the title Candidate in Law Sciences [*kandidat prav*]. He prepares a doctoral thesis on the working-class legislation in Russia, but is not awarded the title Doctor of Law, because the content of his dissertation is judged "revolutionary" and leads to its suppression by the Committee of Censors in Moscow.

Nevertheless, Kiev University accepts his thesis, and his name is inscribed on the official advocates list at St. Petersburg, but Lev Isaakovich has little interest in pursuing a career in law.

1890–91

He does his military service, and for a short time works as a trainee with an advocate in Moscow.

1891–92

He returns to Kiev, in order to save his father's textile firm from bankruptcy. This is also a time of inner turmoil and moral dilemmas for Lev Isaakovich. He starts a clandestine relationship with Aniuta Listopadova, a young woman of the Russian Orthodox religion, who is employed by the Schwarzmann family. In 1892, Aniuta gives birth to a son, Sergei Listopadov, and this further exacerbates Lev Isaakovich's struggle to uphold his own ideals against the inflexible authority of his father.

1892–94

He continues working in the family business and publishes a few articles on financial and economical issues. This is an important formative period, marked by intense reading of literature and philosophy works and by the discovery of his vocation as a writer. He frequents the literary circles of Kiev and Moscow and meets a young talented writer, Varvara Grigoryevna Malakyeva-Mirovitch, who was later to spend the summer of 1895 with the Schwarzmann family, as tutor to the children of Lev Isaakovich's sister, Sophia Balashovskaya.

1895

He starts publishing his first (anonymous) writings on literary and philosophical topics: "Вопрос совести (О Владимире Соловьеве)" [The problem of consciousness (On Vladimir Soloviev)] and "Георг Брандес о Гамлете" [George Brandes on Hamlet]. Toward the end of the year, he suffers a nervous breakdown (partly due to the increasing rift between his personal aspirations and the pressure of managing the family firm). However, the enigmatic manner in which he later described this event in his diary points to a much deeper personal crisis, probably related to a series of intellectual and emotional disappointments. Above all, the acknowledgment of his infatuation with Varvara Grigoryevna and her adamant refusal to believe him seems to have caused him considerable heartache (as the exchange of letters between them indicates).

1896

He travels abroad for treatment. He devotes his time to literary writing. His journey across Europe takes him to Vienna, Karlsbad, Berlin, Tréport, Paris, Munich, and again to Berlin. He starts working on his first book, *Шекспир и его критик Брандес* [Shakespeare and his critic Brandes]. In Rome, he meets Anna Eleazarovna Berezovskaya, a medical student, who will become his wife.

1897

He settles in Rome, and finishes writing *Шекспир и его критик Брандес* [Shakespeare and his critic Brandes]. He marries Anna Eleazarovna without his father's knowledge (as he would have never accepted that his son marry a Christian Orthodox woman). The same year, their first daughter, Tatiana, is born. During the next ten years, the couple will live in different cities to avoid disclosing their marriage to Lev Isaakovich's father.

1898

He publishes *Шекспир и его критик Брандес* [Shakespeare and his critic Brandes] at his own expense at A. Mendeleevich Publishing House in St. Petersburg. This is the first book he signs with the pseudonym Lev Shestov, which signals the symbolic break with the authority of the father—as mentioned in the author's conversations with his friend Aaron Steinberg and recorded by the latter in *Друзия моих ранник лет* [Friends from my youth]. He leaves Italy and goes to Switzerland. He works on his second book, *Добро в учении гр. Толстого и Фр. Нитше* [The good in the teaching of Count Tolstoy and Fr. Nietzsche], which he finishes toward the end of the year.

He returns to Russia. His earlier volume on Shakespeare and Brandes is more or less ignored by the critics.

1899

He spends time in Kiev and St. Petersburg, and establishes links with the literary circles. Despite great difficulties, he is able to publish his second book on credit, *Добро в учении гр. Толстого и Фр. Нитше* [The good in the teaching of Count Tolstoy and Fr. Nietzsche], at the Stasyulevich print house in St. Petersburg, thanks to Vladimir Soloviev's recommendation (this first edition of the book is dated 1900).

1900

In January, he leaves Russia and goes to Switzerland and Italy, where he concentrates on his literary activities, and in particular on the writing of his next book, Достоевский и Нитше [Dostoevsky and Nietzsche]. His daughter Natalia is born.

N. K. Mihailovki publishes two important essays on *Добро в учении гр. Толстого и Фр. Нитше* [The good in the teaching of Count Tolstoy and Fr. Nietzsche] in the February–March issue of the magazine *Русское богатство* [Russian wealth], which attract the attention of the critics and of the general public. In May the same year, Serge Diaghilev, the editor-in-chief of *Мир искусстба* [The art world], invites Shestov to contribute to this journal. Shestov sends him the manuscript of his book *Достоевский и Нитше* [Dostoevsky and Nietzsche], as well as two polemical articles on D. Merejkovsky's book, *Лев Толстой и Достоевский* [Lev Tolstoy and Dostoevsky].

1901

In September, he returns to Kiev, where he stays until 1908. He works in the family business and travels to Moscow and St. Petersburg. He gives talks and participates in debates. In Kiev, he forms a strong friendship with N. Berdyaev, S. Bulgakov, A. Lazarev, and G. Chelpanov. He is also close to a number of literary personalities of St. Petersburg, such as D. Merejkovsky, V. Rozanov, Z. Vengherova, and later, A. Remizov (one of his lifelong friends and correspondents).

1902

Достоевский и Нитше [Dostoevsky and Nietzsche] is published in six consecutive issues of *Мир искусства* [The art world].

1903

Достоевский и Нитше [Dostoevsky and Nietzsche] is published in book form (also including the study of Shakespeare's play *Julius Caesar*) at Stasyulevich, in St. Petersburg. He devotes his time to studying, reading, and preparing a new book, which will form the basis of his *Апофеоз беспочвенности* [The apotheosis of groundlessness], but his work in the family business prevents him from finishing this volume.

In February, he publishes in the magazine *Мир искусства* a virulently critical article on the second volume of D. Merejkovsky's work, *Лев Толстой и Достоевский* [Lev Tolstoy and Dostoevsky].

In spring, he leaves for Switzerland in order to continue working on *Апофеоз беспочвенности* [The apotheosis of groundlessness].

In November he returns to Kiev because of his father's illness.

1904

He continues writing *Апофеоз беспочвенности* [The apotheosis of groundlessness]. He works in his father's company.

1905

In February, *Апофеоз беспочвенности* [The apotheosis of groundlessness] is published, and becomes the subject of a fierce controversy in Russia. Book reviews by I. Eihenvald, N. Berdyaev, A. Remizov, and V. Rozanov are published in some of the most prestigious magazines of the time.

In March, Shestov publishes an article on Chekhov, "Творчество из Ничего" [Creation out of nothing], which was the best ever exegesis of the well-known writer's work, according to I. Bunin. Very positive comments from R. Ivanov-Razumnik and A. Bel'yi. N. Berdyaev publishes a substantial study of Shestov in the magazine *Вопросы жизни* [Life matters]. Several articles devoted to Shestov will come out in the same magazine (such as V. Bazarov's and V. Rozanov's articles that were of particular interest).

1906

In January he publishes an article on Dostoevsky.

1907

In April, he publishes a number of aphorisms and the article "Похвала глупости" [In praise of foolhardiness], devoted to N. Berdyaev.

1908

The family business is turned into a joint stock company, and Shestov becomes its managing director, in the hope that this will give him more freedom.

In September, he publishes *Начала и концы* [Beginnings and endings], a collection of articles that had come out in various magazines between 1905 and 1907. The same month, a substantial study on Shestov, by R. Ivanov-Razumnik, is published (*О смысле жизни* [On the meaning of life] [St. Petersburg: M. Stasyulevich, 1908], pp. 162–256).

In October, he begins writing *Великие кануны* [The great vigils] in Freiburg-in-Brisgau, where he has settled with his family.

During the last two months of the year, two articles containing violent attacks against Shestov's works are published: the first, by D. Filosofov, in *Московский еженедельник* [Moscow weekly] (15 November), and the second, by S. Frank, in the daily *Слово* [Word] (10 December).

1909

In January, he publishes a study on the occasion of Tolstoy's eightieth anniversary: "Разрушающиий и созидающий миры" [The destroyer and the builder of worlds].

1910

On 2 March he visits Tolstoy at Yasnaya Polyana.

In April, he leaves Kiev and settles in Switzerland, on the shores of Lake Leman (in Coppet, at the Villa des Saules), where he will live with his family until 1914. He thus comes to enjoy a period of peace, while managing the family business from afar. He continues the studies that he had begun in Freiburg: Greek philosophy, medieval mystic thinkers, Luther and theologians such as A. von Harnack, H. Grisard, and H. Denifle.

At the end of the year, his volume *Великие кануны* [The great vigils] (mainly gathering the articles he published in 1909 and 1910), is published at Shipovnik. The editors also propose to publish an edition of his complete works.

1911–12

Period of study in Coppet.

1913–14

He writes *Sola Fide* [Only by faith], which marks a significant shift in his thinking, and a predominant concern with religious philosophy as reflected in his recurring analysis of the conflict between the speculative drive behind the theological doctrine of salvation through works and the Biblical notion of salvation through faith alone.

1914

In July, he returns to Russia together with his family. Because of the outbreak of war, his library and the unfinished manuscript of *Sola Fide* are seized at customs and sent back to Switzerland. He will regain possession of them only when he emigrates from Russia in 1920.

He settles in Moscow and establishes contacts with the literary and philosophical milieux, where he meets again many of his old friends (Vyatcheslav Ivanov, S. Bulgakov, N. Berdyaev, G. Shpet, G. Chelpanov, M. Guershenson, S. Lourié, N. Butova, the sisters Evgenya and Adelayda Herzig , and others).

1915

He writes *Potestas Clavium* [The power of keys], in which he takes up a number of topics already discussed in *Sola Fide*.

In February, he becomes a member of the Moscow Society of Psychology, one of the centers for the study of religious philosophy in Russia.

In November, he gives a talk entitled "Potestas Clavium" to this society.

His son, Sergei Listopadov, who was serving in the army, is reported dead in action. Shestov goes to the front line but, despite sustained efforts, is unable to find him.

1916

On 4 November he gives a talk about Vyatcheslav Ivanov that arouses fiery debates.

A collection of his articles and essays, entitled *Anton Tchekhov and Other Essays,* and including his article on Chekhov and "the creation from the void" as well as "The Gift of Prophecy" (written on the occasion of the twenty-fifth anniversary of Dostoevsky's death), is published in English translation with Maunsel and Co. (Dublin and London), with an introduction by John Middleton Murry.

The same year, a collection of his articles from *Начала и концы* [Beginnings and endings], entitled *Penultimate Words and Other Essays,* is published by W. Luce in Boston.

1917

Toward the end of the year, he publishes an article on Edmund Husserl, entitled "Memento Mori." The February Revolution finds him in Moscow. He does not share in the general enthusiasm. He publishes thirty-eight aphorisms in various magazines, and writes little. The political climate is stifling. He is still in Moscow during the October Revolution.

1918

He leaves Moscow, where life has become too difficult, and settles in Kiev, at the home of his sister, Sophia Balashovskaya.

In winter, he works as a professor with the Popular University of Kiev, and teaches a course in Greek philosophy, which he will continue the following year.

1919

In January he writes the final draft of *Potestas Clavium,* which will not be published until 1923, in Berlin.

In autumn, he leaves with his family for Yalta (Crimea), where he will wait for an opportunity to go to Switzerland. He is Visiting Lecturer at the University of Simferopol.

1920

In January, he moves with his family to Sevastopol. There, he is able to secure places on a French cargo boat that takes them to Constantinople. From there, they travel to Genoa and Paris, and then to Geneva. In Geneva, they live at the home of Shestov's sister, Fanya Lovtzky. Shestov regains possession of his library and of the manuscript of *Sola Fide*. He copies the end of the first part, as a separate chapter devoted to Tolstoy, makes a few changes, and gives it the provisional title "Откровения смерти" [The revelations of death], which he will later change to "На страшном суде" [The final judgment]. The former title was already assigned to a volume that included the article on Tolstoy, as well as an essay on Dostoevsky (see bibliography). Shestov will not publish *Sola Fide* during his lifetime, perhaps because some of its themes had been taken up and developed in *Potestas Clavium*. The second half of *Sola Fide* was nevertheless published in French translation in 1957, and the Russian edition of the book came out in 1966 (based on an unfinished manuscript found in the Shestov archives after his death).

His book *Апофеоз беспочвенности* [The apotheosis of groundlessness] is published in English translation as *All Things Are Possible* (London: Martin Secker), with an introduction by D. H. Lawrence.

1921

In April, he leaves Geneva and settles in France, at Clamart. This marks the beginning of his longest time in exile, which will last until his death.

From May to September he writes an article devoted to Dostoevsky's centenary, "Преодоление самоочевидностей" [Overcoming self-evidences].

In November, he settles with his family in a modest flat in Paris (7, rue Sarasate, 15ème).

1922

In February, a substantial part of his article on Dostoevsky, "Преодоление самоочевидностей" [Overcoming self-evidences] is published in the *Nouvelle revue française*. This writing will play a significant part in Shestov's reception in France. Boris de Schloezer, his lifelong friend and most assiduous translator of his work into French, is the author of the translation, and of the introduction to Shestov's article for the *NRF*. The February issue of the French magazine also included articles by Gide and Jacques Rivière, and several texts by Dostoevsky.

He gives a series of talks on Dostoevsky, as well as on ancient philosophy, at the Society for Religion and Philosophy and at the Popular University.

He frequents the Russian émigré writers and is a member of the Academic Group, set up by the émigré professors. The artist Sorin paints his portray (presently at the Metropolitan Museum of New York). He establishes contacts with French literary circles and takes several trips to Berlin, where an important group of Russian émigré writers had settled. The publishing house Skify, based in Berlin, plans to publish several of his works in translation.

In April he is appointed professor in the Faculty of Russian Studies at the University of Paris (the Russian section of the Institute of Slavonic Studies). He will lecture there on philosophy from April 1922 to March 1936.

In October, Boris de Schloezer publishes an important study on Shestov ("Un penseur russe: Léon Chestov") in *Mercure de France*.

1923

In May, *Les révélations de la mort* [Revelations of death] is published with Plon, in the foreign authors collection, directed by Charles du Bos.

In June, Shestov's study "Descartes et Spinoza" is published in the *Mercure de France,* two years before its publication in the original Russian, in the magazine *Современные записки* [Contemporary papers], some of whose editors were opposed to his ideas.

In June, *La nuit de Gethsémani* [The night in the Garden of Gethsemane] is published by Grasset. Daniel Halévy, the director of the *Cahiers verts,* had asked Shestov to write this essay for Pascal's 300th anniversary.

Shestov's first two books in French translation enjoyed a warm reception, and were reviewed in *Mercure de France* and *La nouvelle revue française.*

Between 24 August and 3 September, he takes part in the Pontigny summer colloquium on the topic "Le trésor poétique réservé ou l'intraduisible" [The reserved poetic treasure or the untranslatable], at the invitation of the director of the Décades de Pontigny, Paul Desjardin, and of the editor of Plon, Charles du Bos, both of whom become his friends.

He gives a series of lectures at the Sorbonne, "Dostoevsky's and Pascal's Ideas," which he will repeat during the following academic year, 1924–25.

1924

In spring, he participates for the first time in the regular meetings organized by the philosopher and writer Jules de Gaultier. There he meets the Romanian-born French writer Benjamin Fondane, who had published a series of articles on Shestov before coming to Paris. Fondane was going to become Shestov's close friend and only disciple, who greatly contributed to the popularization of his ideas in France and wrote numerous articles as well as a book devoted to Shestov's memory, *Rencontres avec Léon Chestov* (Meetings with Lev Shestov).

In November, he moves to a new address in Paris, at 41, rue de l'Abbé Grégoire.

1926

In January, he moves to live with his sister Mme Sophia Balashovskaya, who lived in a spacious flat at 1, rue de l'Alboni, in Paris.

He begins a long-term collaboration with the *Révue philosophique de la France et de l'étranger,* run by Lucien Lévy-Bruhl. His first article, "Memento mori," which he had published in Russia in 1917, comes out in French translation in the January–February issue of the *Revue philosophique de la France et de l'étranger,* and is one of the first interpretations of Husserl's thought in France. Jean Hering responds to Shestov's existential critique of Husserl, by writing the article "Sub specie aeterni." He sends the manuscript of his article to Shestov, who writes "Что такое истина" [What is truth?]. Their polemic marks one of the most significant moments of Husserl's early reception in France.

He strengthens his links with the philosophical and literary circles in France and Germany. He organizes receptions for writers and philosophers in Paris. He often travels to Germany, where he is a member of the Kant-Gesellschaft and of the Nietzsche-Gesellschaft.

The Pléiade publishing house undertakes the project of publishing Shestov's complete works. Despite his growing reputation, Shestov finds it very difficult to get published, and only three volumes of the Pléiade edition will come out during his lifetime.

He starts writing *На весах Иова* [In Job's balances], which he will finish the following year. He also writes "Скованный Парменид" [Parmenides in chains], which will later be included in his book *Афины и Иерусалим* [Athens and Jerusalem].

1927

Shestov's second article on Husserl, "Qu'est-ce que la vérité" [What is truth?], is published in the January–February issue of the *Revue philosophique.* Several months later, the same article comes out in German translation, in the *Philosophischer Anzeiger* (no. 1, 1927), in which Jean Hering's article is also published (before its publication in France, in *Revue d'Histoire et de Philosophie Religieuse,* no. 4, July–August 1927).

1928

Between 15 and 23 April, Shestov participates in a philosophy conference in Amsterdam, where he gives a talk about Plotinus, and meets Husserl, who is interested in Shestov's articles on phenomenology, despite their virulent criticism. The two philosophers will become close friends and will continue to see each other regularly until 1933, either in Freiburg, where Husserl lives, or in Paris, where Husserl is several times invited to give talks, following arrangements made by Shestov.

Toward the end of the year, Shestov gives a conference on Tolstoy in Freiburg, which is attended by both Husserl and Heidegger. After the conference, Shestov meets Heidegger and talks to him about existential philosophy at Husserl's house.

Shestov discovers his deep intellectual affinities with Kierkegaard's work, thanks to Husserl.

1929

In May, he publishes the German and the Russian editions of *На весах Иова* [In Job's balances], which gathers a number of studies that he had written in Geneva and Paris between 1920 and 1927, some of which had been published.

1930

In September he moves to Boulogne-sur-Seine (at 19, rue Alfred Laurent), following his daughters' marriages. He will stay at this address until his death. He lives relatively withdrawn from the world, and although he is often ill, he remains active.

1931

J. Suys's doctoral thesis on Shestov is published in Amsterdam.

1932

In May, he finishes writing "В Фаларийском быке" [In the Bull of Phalaris], which he had probably begun in 1930, and whose last five chapters are devoted to Kierkegaard.

1935

He finishes writing his study of Kierkegaard, *Киргегард и экзистенциальная философия* [Kierkegaard and existential philosophy], which he had begun in 1930 or 1931.

In February, he finishes his study "О средневековой философии" [On the philosophy of the Middle Ages], devoted to Etienne Gilson's book, *L'esprit de la philosophie médiévale* [The spirit of medieval philosophy].

On 5 May he gives a conference on Kierkegaard and Dostoevsky, which will become the preface of his book on Kierkegaard.

1936

N. Berdyaev, A. Lazarev, B. Fondane, A. Remizov, and many others publish articles on the occasion of Shestov's seventieth birthday. The Committee of Lev Shestov's Friends is set up (the president is Lévy-Bruhl, the secretary is B. de Schloezer, and among the members are N. Berdyaev, P. Desjardin, A. Dobry, N. Eitingon, J. de Gaultier, A. Lazarev, and J. Paulhan). The aim of the committee is to launch a subscription in order to gather the funds necessary for the publication of the French edition of Shestov's book on Kierkegaard, which he had finished the previous year.

Between 23 March and 19 May, he travels to Palestine, where he is invited to give a series of talks.

In July the volume *Kierkegaard et la philosophie existentielle* is published at J. Vrin (the Russian original will not be published until 1939).

1937

Between 3 April and 1 May, he gives five conferences at Radio Paris, entitled "L'oeuvre de Dostoevsky" [Dostoevsky's work].

Between 21 October and 25 November, he gives another series of five conferences "Kierkegaard—philosophe religieux" [Kierkegaard—religious philosopher], at Radio Paris.

At the end of December, he suffers of an intestinal hemorrhage, and has a difficult recovery. He discontinues his courses at the Sorbonne.

1938

Publication of *Athènes et Jérusalem* [Athens and Jerusalem], a collection of studies written between 1928 and 1937, that have, in general, been previously published. The German edition comes out in Vienna (in April or May the same year). Shestov considers this volume to be his most important work, in which the opposition between knowledge and faith is most powerfully highlighted. The Russian edition of the book will not come out until 1951.

In the last years of his life, Shestov became interested in Indian philosophy, which he considered to be in many ways close to his own thought.

In autumn, his article in memory of Edmund Husserl (who died on 26 April) comes out in *Revue philosophique de la France et de l'étranger*.

On 20 November, Shestov dies at the Clinique Boileau, in Paris, and is buried in the new cemetery of Boulogne.

On 18 December, a meeting devoted to the memory of Shestov is held at the Academy of Religion and Philosophy. A number of articles (by N. Berdyaev, A. Remizov, I. Mandelstam, B. de Schloezer, G. Adamovich, and others) are published. In Jerusalem, Martin Buber speaks at a memorial service devoted to Shestov.

In December, the Committee for the publication of Shestov's work is set up. Since then thirteen of his works have been published, and numerous new editions and translations have come out in different countries (see bibliography for a partial list). The Shestov Archive, which has remained largely unpublished, is held in the Library of the Sorbonne University.

Notes

Introduction to the Second Edition by Ramona Fotiade

1. Benjamin Fondane, *Rencontres avec Léon Chestov*, comp. and ed. Nathalie Baranoff and Michel Carassou (Paris: Editions Plasma, 1982), p. 129 (all translations from the French are mine unless otherwise stated). Editions Non Lieu of Paris published a new edition in 2016. Fondane had entrusted the manuscript of the book to his friend Victoria Ocampo before his arrest and deportation in 1944, and the published work was compiled and edited by Shestov's daughter in collaboration with Fondane's copyright holder.

2. Gilles Deleuze and Félix Guattari, "1227: Treatise on Nomadology—The War Machine," chap. 12 in Deleuze and Guattari, *A Thousand Plateaus: Capitalism and Schizophrenia,* trans. Brian Massumi (London: Continuum, 2004), pp. 387–467.

3. Michel Foucault, "La pensée du dehors," *Critique*, no. 229 (June 1966): 523–46; translated as "Maurice Blanchot: The Thought from Outside" by Brian Massumi, in *Foucault/Blanchot* (New York: Zone Books, 1987).

4. Lev Shestov, *All Things Are Possible,* trans. S. S. Koteliansky, with an introduction by D. H. Lawrence (London: Martin Secker, 1920), part I, §22.

5. The family copy of the Septuagint or Greek Old Testament, included in the list of books in Shestov's personal library compiled by Nathalie Baranoff-Chestov, includes a number of handwritten annotations on 2 Maccabees 13, which recounts the victory of Judas Maccabeus against the Greek troops in 163 BCE (cf. *Vetus Testamentum, ex versione Septuaginta interpretum olim ad fidem,* vol. II, ex officina J. Heideggeri & Soc., 1731, in the Bibliothèque de la Sorbonne, Paris).

6. Lev Shestov, "Foreword," in *Athens and Jerusalem*, below, p. 59.

7. Lev Shestov, "In the Bull of Phalaris," chap. XIV, below, p. 197.

8. Ibid., p. 198.

9. Ibid., pp. 198–199.

10. 1 Corinthians 13, quoted in "A Thousand and One Nights (By Way of a Preface)," in *Potestas Clavium*, trans., with an introduction, by Bernard Martin (Athens: Ohio University Press, 1968), pp. 24–25.

11. Lev Shestov, "Parmenides in Chains," chap. I, below, p. 71.

12. Lev Shestov, "Разрушающий и созидающий миры. (По поводу 80-летнего юбилея Толстого)" [Destroyer and creator of worlds. (On Tolstoy's eightieth birthday anniversary)] in *Russkaia mysl,* no. 1 (January 1909): 25–40.

13. Ibid., §6.

14. See, for instance, "In the Bull of Phalaris," chap. VIII, below, p. 159; 205; 268: "Because man is presumptuous and imagines himself to be wise, righteous and holy, it is necessary that he be humbled by the law, that thus that beast—his supposed righteousness—without whose killing man cannot live, be put to death" (Luther, *Commentary on Paul's Epistle to the Galatians,* 3:23); "Therefore God must have a strong hammer to break the rocks, and a fire blazing to the middle of the heavens to overthrow the mountains, that is, to subdue that stubborn and impenitent beast—presumption—in order that man, reduced to nothing through his contrition, should despair of his power, his righteousness and his works" (Luther, *Commentary on Paul's Epistle to the Galatians,* 3:23).

15. Shakespeare, *Hamlet,* act 1, scene 5. Shestov quotes this verse in his obituary of Husserl, "In Memory of a Great Philosopher," published posthumously in Russian in *Russkie zapiski,* no. 12 (1938), and in French in *Revue philosophique de la France et de l'étranger,* no. 1–2 (January–February 1940), and recalls the conversations he had on this topic with Husserl in Paris in 1928: "Almost all of my conversations with Husserl revolved about these themes. When he visited me at my home in Paris, immediately after dinner (which he seemed not even to have noticed), he took me into another room and immediately plunged into philosophical discussion. At that time I was working on the first part of my book *Athens and Jerusalem,*—the section called 'Parmenides in Chains.'" See "In Memory of a Great Philosopher," in *Speculation and Revelation,* trans. Bernard Martin (Athens: Ohio University Press, 1982), p. 271.

16. This essay, which was originally part of Shestov's unfinished book on Luther, *Sola fide,* was first published in Russian in *Sovremennye zapiski* in 1920, then in French in 1923, with Editions Plon, and finally reprinted in the volume *In Job's Balances* (1929 for the Russian edition and 1932 for the first English edition, published by Dent & Sons; reprinted by Ohio University Press with a new introduction by Bernard Martin in 1975).

17. See Shestov, "Parmenides in Chains," chap. V, below, p. 69ff.

18. Maxim Gorki, "Souvenirs sur Tolstoï" [Memories of Tolstoy], in *La nouvelle revue française* 87 (1 December 1920), p. 894; the same passage is cited in Fondane, *Rencontres avec Léon Chestov,* p. 177.

19. Shestov, "Parmenides in Chains," chap. VI, below, p. 97–98.

20. The first chapter of *The Revelations of Death* was initially published in French translation in *La nouvelle revue française,* no. 101 (February 1922): 134–58, as an article entitled "Dostoievsky et la lutte contre les évidences" [Dostoevsky and the fight against the self-evident], which established Shestov's reputation in Parisian intellectual circles and earned him a number of accolades from prestigious writers and philosophers such as André Gide, Charles Du Bos, Lucien Lévy-Bruhl, and Daniel Halévy.

21. Lev Shestov, "A Letter from Lev Shestov to His Daughters," 13 April 1921, in *In Job's Balances,* trans. Camilla Coventry and C. A. Macartney, with an introduction by Bernard Martin (Athens: Ohio University Press, 1975), p. viii. Reprinted from the French edition of the volume published in 1971 with Flammarion.

22. Lev Shestov, "Children and Stepchildren of Time: Spinoza in History," in *In Job's Balances,* trans. Camilla Coventry and C. A. Macartney, with an introduction by Bernard Martin (Athens: Ohio University Press, 1975), part III, "On the Philosophy of History," p. 257.

23. Lev Shestov, "On the Philosophy of the Middle Ages," chap. III, below, p. 220–21.

24. Shestov, "In the Bull of Phalaris," chap. IX, below, p. 165.

25. Ibid., chap. X, p. 171.

26. Idem.

27. Shestov, "Foreword," below, p. 66–67.

28. Ibid., p. 51.

29. Ibid., part II, p. 66.

30. Unpublished notes on Tertullian, in MS2107, Fasc. 60 of the Shestov Archives, Bibliothèque de la Sorbonne.

31. See note 15 (Shestov, "In Memory of a Great Philosopher: Edmund Husserl," in *Speculation and Revelation,* trans. Bernard Martin).

32. The article, "Der gefesselte Parmenides: Über die Quellen der metaphysischen Wahrheiten" [Parmenides in chains: On the sources of metaphysical truth], was published in *Logos,* no. 1 (1931): 17–87.

33. Fondane, *Rencontres avec Léon Chestov,* 114. ["In another conversation, Shestov adds: 'I don't know if Heidegger's lecture *What is metaphysics?* is a follow-up to our encounter but in any case it does seem that something has shattered. I am still waiting for it . . .'"].

34. Shestov, "Parmenides in Chains," chap. III, below, p. 81.

35. Ibid., chap. IX, p. 110.

36. See the eponymous aphorism, "The Irrational Residue of Being," in the second part of *In Job's Balances,* "Revolt and Submission," § XLIII, pp. 221–25.

37. Shestov, "Foreword," part II, below, p. 64.

38. Lev Shestov, "The Autonomy of the Ethical," chap. XIV, in *Kierkegaard and the Existential Philosophy,* trans. Elinor Hewitt (Athens: Ohio University Press, 1969). The first drafts of chapters 14, 15, and 16 in the book on Kierkegaard date from 1930 to 1933. See also Nathalie Baranoff-Chestov, *Vie de Léon Chestov,* trans. from the Russian by Blanche Bronstein-Vinaver, vol. 2: *Les dernières années* (Paris: Editions de la Différence, 1993), pp. 101–2.

39. Shestov, "In the Bull of Phalaris," chap. X, below, p. 177.

40. Ibid., p. 175.

41. Ibid., chap. XIV, p. 196.

42. Shestov, "Foreword," part II, below, p. 64.

43. Lev Shestov, "On the Philosophy of the Middle Ages," chap. X, below, p. 280.

44. Ibid., chapter IX, p. 267.

45. Lev Shestov, "On the Sources of 'Conceptions of the World,'" aphorism XXVIII in *Athens and Jerusalem,* part IV, "On the Second Dimension of Thought," below, p. 303.

46. Cf. The aphorisms XXVIII "Ob istochnikah 'mirovozzrenia'" [On the sources of "Conceptions of the World"] and LXIV "Vybor" [The choice], in Lev Shestov, *Afini i Ierusalim* [Athens and Jerusalem], *Sochinenia,* vol. II (Moscow: Nauka, 1993), pp. 631–32; 659–60. See also "On the Sources of 'Conceptions of the World,'" in *Athens and Jerusalem,* below, pp. 303–4; and the first version of the same aphorism: "Le choix," in Lev Shestov, "Look Back and Struggle," in *Forum philosophicum,* no. 1 (1930): 107–11.

47. Cf. Shestov, part III, "Children and Stepchildren of Time," chap. 2, in *In Job's Balances,* pp. 253–59.

48. A reference to the "gentleman of retrograde and jeering physiognomy" in *Notes from the Underground* who mounts a virulent attack against reason in the name of individual freedom: "Well, gentlemen, why don't we reduce all this reasonableness to dust with

one good kick, for the sole purpose of sending all the logarithms to the devil and living once more according to our own stupid will!"

49. Shestov, "On the Sources of 'Conceptions of the World,'" below, p. 304.

50. Shestov, "A Thousand and One Nights," in *Potestas Clavium,* pp. 3–26. See also aphorism 15, "Rules and Exceptions," in the first part: "Philo was the first to insist on the rationality of Biblical doctrine. The *logos* of Greek philosophy, its eternal reason, is already completely contained in the revelation given to the Jewish people on Mount Sinai. God is rational, the essence of God is reason" (pp. 99–100).

51. Lev Shestov, "What Is Truth?" in *Potestas Clavium,* p. 361.

52. Lev Shestov, "Tchetvertoe Evangelie" [The fourth Gospel], in *Sochinenia,* vol. II (Moscow: Nauka, 1993), pp. 649–50.

53. See Shestov's letter to Fondane (31 July 1938), reproduced in Nathalie Baranoff-Chestov, *Vie de Léon Chestov* II, p. 212; and manuscript MS2107, Fasc. 57 page 24bis, in the Shestov Archives at the Bibliothèque de la Sorbonne.

54. Deleuze and Guattari, *A Thousand Plateaus,* pp. 376–77.

Introduction by Bernard Martin

1. With the exception of Benjamin Fondane who, because of his own early and tragic death, did not—as he might otherwise have done—succeed in publicizing his master's work.

2. Albert Camus, *The Myth of Sisyphus* (New York: Vintage Books, 1955; originally published in France in 1942 by Librairie Gallimard), p. 19.

3. Ibid., pp. 24–28. Camus here discusses what he calls Shestov's "leap" towards God, a leap which he himself rejects as an "escape" from an authentic awareness of the reality of the absurd.

4. *History of Russian Literature* (New York: Alfred A. Knopf, Fifth Printing, 1964), p. 426.

5. Although three of his books—*All Things Are Possible, Penultimate Words and Other Essays* (or, in the London edition, *Anton Tchekhov and Other Essays*), and *In Job's Balances*—were translated into English and published in the United States or Great Britain, they seem to have made hardly any impact when they first appeared many years ago and have long been out of print.

6. *Irrational Man: A Study in Existential Philosophy* (Garden City, NY: Doubleday and Company, 1958), p. 14.

7. For the facts of Shestov's life I have relied on Lowtzky's article "Lev Shestov as I Remember Him," published in Russian in the review *Grani,* no. 45 (1960) and no. 46 (1961) in Frankfurt-am-Main, and on personal conversation and correspondence with Shestov's daughters, Madame Natalie Baranov and Madame Tatiana Rageot of Paris.

8. Sergei Bulgakov's "Elements of the Religious Outlook of Lev Shestov" in *Sovremennye zapiski,* no. 68, Paris, 1939. Written on the occasion of Shestov's death.

9. Published in the journal *Kievskoe slovo* on February 22, 1895.

10. *All Things Are Possible* (New York: Robert M. McBride and Co., 1920), pp. 10–11.

11. Ibid., p. 9.

12. *Penultimate Words* (Boston: John W. Luce and Co., 1916), p. xi.

13. Ibid., p. xiii.

14. Quoted in Donald A. Lowrie, *Rebellious Prophet* (New York: Harper, 1960), p. 34.

15. All three essays are included in the collection entitled *In Job's Balances,* translated by Camilla Coventry and C. A. Macartney and published in London in 1932. *In Job's Balances* also contains important essays on Plotinus and Spinoza as well as fifty-two trenchant aphorisms on philosophy, science and religion collected under the heading "Revolt and Submission."

16. Fondane's manuscript *Sur les rives de l'Illisus,* containing accounts of his visits with Shestov, has not yet been published in full. Some excerpts appeared in the June 1964 issue of *Mercure de France* under the title *Rencontres avec Léon Chestov.* (The book was later published under that title by Editions Plasma in 1982; a new edition came out in 2016 with Editions Non Lieu, Paris. Fondane had entrusted the manuscript of the book to his friend Victoria Ocampo before his arrest and deportation in 1944, and the published work was compiled by Shestov's daughter Natalie Baranov and Fondane's copyright holder, Michel Carassou. [R.F.])

17. Especially the essays and aphorisms in the collection entitled *In Job's Balances.*

18. See the essay "Science and Free Inquiry" which serves as the Foreword to *In Job's Balances,* especially pp. xxv ff. Cf. also the first part of *Athens and Jerusalem,* entitled "Parmenides in Chains," below, pp. 69 ff.

19. Below, p. 62.

20. Below, p. 350, Foreword note 12. Cf. *In Job's Balances,* pp. 34 ff.

21. *Notes from the Underground,* translated by Andrew R. MacAndrew (New York: The New American Library, 1961), p. 99.

22. Below, pp. 60 ff.

23. Below, pp. 65 ff.

24. Below, pp. 66 ff.

25. Below, pp. 64–66.

26. *In Job's Balances,* p. 218.

27. Below, p. 65.

28. *In Job's Balances,* p. 82.

29. Below, p. 324–25.

30. Loc. cit.

31. *In Job's Balances,* p. 141.

32. Ibid., p. 230.

33. Loc. cit.

34. So he calls them in *Athens and Jerusalem.* See below, p. 43. In *In Job's Balances* Shestov insists that, though it has given us many gifts, science cannot give us ultimate truth for—in refusing to recognize the unique, the unrepeatable, the fortuitous—it has turned away from the realm in which real truth lies. "There is no need to renounce the gifts of the earth but we must not forget heaven for their sakes. However much we may have attained in science, yet we must remember that science can give us no truth because, by its very nature, it will not and cannot seek for the truth. The truth lies there where science sees the 'nothing,' in that single, uncontrollable, incomprehensible thing which is always at war with explanation, the 'fortuitous'" (p. 193).

35. Below, pp. 286–87, 325–26.

36. *Cosmos and History* (New York: Harper Torchbooks, 1959), pp. 161–62.

37. Cf. below, p. 300.

38. Below, p. 109.

39. Loc. cit.

40. *In Job's Balances,* p. 239.

41. Italics mine. [B.M.]

42. Pp. 40–44, above.

43. Below, p. 66.

Foreword by Lev Shestov

1. Spinoza, *Ethics,* V, Proposition XXXIII: "third kind of knowledge is eternal." [R.F.]

2. "Truths of reason" are similar to Descartes' eternal truths, because they are perfectly necessary and cannot be denied without contradiction, whereas "truths of fact" are merely contingent and can be subject to dispute. The central insight of Leibniz's system is that all existential propositions, based on experience, are truths of fact, not truths of reason. [R.F.]

3. Kant underlines *on faith.*

4. The expression, literally meaning "God from the machine," was coined from the Greek phrase ἀπὸ μηχανῆς θεός (*apò mēkhanês theós*), which designated the machine used to bring the actors playing the gods onto the stage. By extension, the term has evolved to mean a plot device, whereby an unsolvable problem (such as the existence of the world) is suddenly resolved by the contrived intervention of a character (which in the case of Leibniz's "pre-established harmony" corresponds to God's intervention). [R.F.]

5. Spinoza, *Ethics,* part IV, proposition 52. [R.F.]

6. Ibid., part III, preface. [R.F.]

7. Spinoza, *Political Treatise* I, 4. [R.F.]

8. Spinoza, *Ethics,* part IV, proposition 68. [R.F.]

9. Spinoza, *Treatise on the Emendation of the Intellect,* §1. [R.F.]

10. Spinoza, *Ethics,* part V, proposition 23, note. [R.F.]

11. Ibid., proposition 42. [R.F.]

12. Dostoevsky dared to do this. I have already indicated many times that the critique of reason was given us for the first time by Dostoevsky in *Notes from the Underground* and *The Dream of a Ridiculous Man,* whereas everyone believes that it is to be sought in Kant.

13. Mark 11:24.

14. 1 Corinthians 2:9.

I: Parmenides in Chains

1. *Republic,* 533C.

2. *Metaphysics,* 984b, 10.

3. *Metaphysics,* 1015a, 28 ff.

4. Psalms 137:5–6.

5. *Theaetetus,* 196D.

6. *Enneads,* II, 5, 3.

7. Plato, *Republic,* 476C.

8. Plato, *Protagoras,* 345D.

9. *Timaeus,* 41B.

10. *Enneads,* VI, 7, 41.

11. *Ethics,* IV, LXVII.

12. *Ethics,* IV, LII.

13. *Republic*, 519A.

14. *Phaedo*, 83D.

15. *Phaedo*, 80A.

16. *Republic*, 509B.

17. *Republic*, 582C.

18. *Republic*, 585E, 586A.

19. *Metaphysics*, 1072b, 23.

20. *Gorgias*, 484B.

21. *Timaeus*, 47B.

22. *Eth. Nic.*, 1139b, 10.

23. Italics mine. [L.S.]

24. Matthew 17:20.

25. Epictetus was far more candid in this matter. "The beginning of philosophy," he said, "is the recognition of its own powerlessness and of the impossibility of fighting against Necessity."

26. See Richard Kroner's outstanding book, *From Kant to Hegel*, the best of all that have been written on the history of German idealism.

II: In the Bull of Phalaris

1. *Ethics*, II, 49.

2. "If the heavens should collapse over him, the ruins would strike him unafraid" (Horace).

3. 1 Corinthians 15:32.

4. *Apology*, 38A.

5. *Ethica Nicomachea*, 1153b, 20.

6. *Enneads*, I, IV, 7, 8, 9.

7. *Ethica Nicomachea*, 1153b, 32.

8. *Metaphysics*, 980a, 21.

9. *Tract. Theo.-Polit.*, XV, 19f.

10. *Ethics*, I, App.

11. *Ethics*, IV, Praef.

12. *Ethics*, I, 33.

13. *Ethics*, I, 17.

14. *Ethics*, V, 36.

15. *Tract. Theol.-Polit.*, XIV.

16. *Tract. Theol.-Polit.*, XIV.

17. *Gr. Gal. Komm.*, WA I.S., 483.

18. *Beyond Good and Evil*, sec. 225.

19. *Beyond Good and Evil*, sec. 68.

20. *Principia Philosophiae*, Ed. 1678, I. 49.

21. *The Will to Power*, Book IV.

22. *Why I Am So Clever*.

23. No matter what certain commentators may think, the term "the Absurd" which is so characteristic of him was borrowed by Kierkegaard not from the German philosophers but from Tertullian, whom he greatly admired and to whom he attributed, as did almost everyone in the nineteenth century, the famous *credo quia absurdum* [I believe because it is absurd].

24. Italics mine. [L.S.]

25. Italics mine. [L.S.]

26. See the last chapter of my book *In Job's Balances.*

27. Speaking of the world of the "good" created by Socrates, I said in my book *Potestas Clavium:* "This world does not know frontiers and limits. It offers shelter to millions of men and fills them with a spiritual nourishment that satisfies all. All who wish to enter it are received like dear and longed for guests . . . There miraculous metamorphoses take place. The weak become powerful, the artisan a Philosopher, the poor rich, the ugly wondrously beautiful." When I wrote these lines about Socrates, I still knew nothing of Kierkegaard.

III: ON THE PHILOSOPHY OF THE MIDDLE AGES

1. Italics mine. [L.S.]

2. *L'esprit de la philosophie médiévale,* I, 49.

3. Ibid., p. 54.

4. Ibid., p. 71.

5. Ibid., p. 50.

6. Ibid., p. 71.

7. One could also refer to the passage of the *Stromata* where Clement says that if the knowledge of God could be separated from eternal salvation and if he had to choose between them, he would decide for the knowledge of God.

8. *L'esprit de la philosophie médiévale,* II, 205–6.

9. Ibid., I, p. 213.

10. Ibid., I, p. 224.

11. Ibid., II, p. 224.

12. *Metaphysics,* 981a, 26.

13. Cf. *Eth. Nic.,* 1140b, 31: "Scientific knowledge is intellectual perception of the universal and necessary." That is why "all true knowledge can be taught and its content transmitted to others." (Ibid., 1139b, 25.)

14. *Summa Th.* II, 1, 5, *ad quartum.*

15. *L'esprit de la philosophie medievale,* I, 63. The remarkable works of Meyerson are particularly significant in this respect. He also represents the human reason as being "obsessed" by the desire to subordinate everything to the principle of contradiction. Reason knows that this task is unrealisable, it knows that to wish the impossible is madness, but it is incapable of overcoming itself. This is no longer the *raison déraisonable* [unreasonable reason] of Montaigne—it is reason somehow become mad.

16. Ibid., I, p. 43.

17. Ibid., I, pp. 35–36.

18. *De Civ. Dei,* XIV, 12.

19. Italics mine. [L.S.]

20. *L'esprit de la philosophie médiévale,* I, 122.

21. Cf. *Parmenides in Chains.*

22. See *Enneads,* V, III.12.

23. See, for example, R. Seeberg's *Die Theologie des Joh. D. Scotus,* from whom I have borrowed the expression "*schlechthinnige und regellose Willkür.*" According to him, although Scotus flinches from such reproaches when he denies that anything can be good in

itself for the creature or throws out other scholastic quips of the same kind, the arbitrariness of God is in him limited by His *bonitas.*

24. *L'esprit de la philosophie médiévale,* II, 64.

25. And, referring to St. Augustine, Duns Scotus wrote: "The books of the holy canon are not to be believed except insofar as one must first believe the church which approves and authorizes those books and their content."

26. Italics mine. [L.S.]

27. *L'esprit de la philosophie médiévale,* I, 37.

28. *Summa Th.* II, Q. 4, 8, 3

29. *L'esprit de la philosophie médiévale,* II, 220.

30. Ibid., I, p. 24. Italics mine. [L.S.]

31. This is perhaps the moment to recall Kierkegaard's words: "to believe against reason is martyrdom."

32. *Dogmengeschichte,* II, 226.

33. *Summa Th.* I, Q. 25, 2.

34. Cf. *Eth. Nic.,* 1139b, 9.

35. Matthew 3:9.

36. Gilson, *L'esprit de la philosophie médiévale,* I, 140.

37. Ibid., II, p. 133.

38. *Metaphysics,* 1004a, 34.

39. *Eth. Nic.,* 1141a, 17.

40. *Metaphysics,* 1005b, 25.

41. Romans 8:20–21.

42. I call attention in this connection to Kierkegaard's remarkable book, *Repetition.* When Kierkegaard found himself confronting the question of the limits of God's omnipotence, he left the famous philosopher Hegel who was also "maestro di coloro che sanno" (master of all those who knew), and went to the "private thinker," Job. That Kierkegaard dared to include Job among the "thinkers" already appears to us as a gross presumption. But through Job Kierkegaard arrived at his Absurd and at the fundamental principle of his existential philosophy: God—this means that all things are possible. [R.F.]

43. *L'esprit de la philosophie médiévale,* I, 14.

44. Cf. his letters to Mersenne of 15 April and 27 May 1630. We read in the latter: "He (God) was also free to bring it about that it not be true that all the lines drawn from the center to the circumference of a circle are equal, just as He was free not to create the world."

45. Cf. the fragment of Tertullian quoted above.

46. Damian in another place says: "As we can therefore rightly say that God could bring it about that Rome, before it was built, not have been built, so we can say no less without contradiction that God may also bring it about that Rome, after it was built, not be built." It is also interesting that he allows himself to argue with Saint Jerome, from whom he borrows the example of the *virgo corrupta*: the hand of God means more to him than Saint Jerome.

47. *S. c. gent.* I, VII.

48. *L'esprit de la philosophie médiévale,* I, 238. At the end of his second volume (pages 214–218), Gilson returns once again to the idea of the biblical serpent and to those who wished to create a philosophy that should not be bound by the Greek principle and declares "the object of their wishes does not belong to the order of the possible." This, of

course, is certain if one admits in advance that it is given to the Greek speculation to determine once for all the limits of the possible and that the biblical "revelation" does not pass beyond the limits of what appeared possible to the Greeks.

49. *Summ. Th.* I, Q. 47, 3 *ad pr.*

50. *Phaedus,* 82D.

51. *Apology,* 22C.

52. *Phaedo,* 82C.

53. St. Augustine at times allowed himself to become infected with the "foolishness" of St. Paul's faith. He did not write, it is true, the phrase that is so often attributed to him, *virtutes gentium splendida vitia sunt,* but *potius vitia sunt.* The idea is there, nevertheless.

54. Cf. *Eth. Nic.* (1111b, 20): "Man does not aspire to the impossible, and if he does, everyone will consider him weak in mind." From this follows: "to aspire only to what is in our power."

55. It is known that the text of Exodus (X, 20), "The Lord hardened Pharaoh's heart," gave a great deal of trouble not only to the theologians but also to the philosophers, and particularly to Leibniz.

56. *Notes from the Underground,* 1st Part, Chapter III.

57. *L'esprit de la philosophie médiévale,* II, 99.

58. *Eth. Nic.* 1178b, 21. When Karl Werner said of Saint Thomas Aquinas, in his tremendous work written with so much respect and love, that his conception of beatitude is only the transcription into Christian language of the Aristotelian conception of the beatitude of contemplative activity, he had certainly in mind this passage of the Ethics that I have just quoted as well as certain corresponding passages of Aristotle's *Metaphysics.*

59. *L'esprit de la philosophie médiévale,* II, 85.

60. *Theaet.*, 176A.

61. It would not be exaggerated to regard Kierkegaard as the spiritual double of Dostoevsky. If in my former writings I have not mentioned Kierkegaard in speaking of Dostoevsky, it is only because I still did not know him; I have known Kierkegaard's works only in the last few years.

62. Cf. de Wulf, *Histoire de la philosophie médiévale,* p. 474: "The tone of his (St. Thomas') refutations in the *De unitate intellectus* is of a vehemence that is not elsewhere met in his works."

63. *De Anima* III, 430a, 17.

64. When St. Thomas Aquinas writes (*S. Th.* I, 16, 7): "no created truth is eternal, but only the truth of the divine intellect which alone is eternal and from which its truth is inseparable" or "it must be said that the laws of the circle and that two and three make five have eternity in the divine mind" etc., it is difficult not to see in this the *intellectus separatus* (or *emancipatus*) *a Deo.*

65. From this comes Spinoza's "we feel and experience ourselves to be eternal."

66. *L'esprit de la philosophic médiévale,* I, 123.

67. Ibid., I, p. 124.

68. Ibid., I, p. 117. Italics mine. [L.S.]

69. Ibid., I, p. 124. Italics mine. [L.S.]

70. As in Spinoza: "Contentment with oneself can arise from reason and that contentment which arises from reason is the highest possible."

71. *Eth. Nic.,* 1098b, 2.

72. *Summa Th.* I, 84, 5, *concl.*

73. Two historians as different as J. Tixeron and Harnack, who both, however, had the greatest admiration for St. Augustine, cannot prevent themselves from emphasizing "his habit of reflecting on his faith" (*Histoire des dogmes*, II, P. 362) and to remark that in him, "the moral point of view dominates the religious point of view" (Harnack, III, 216).

74. *Summa Th.* I, 1 and 2.

75. *Summa Th.* I, 96 ad sec.

76. *L'esprit de la philosophie médiévale,* II, 70.

77. Ibid., p. 71.

78. *Ethics,* V, XXXVI.

79. Gilson cites (II, 222 and 278) some examples of the crude fashion in which Luther treated Aristotle. But we must not forget that Luther was the son of the declining Middle Ages and that the writers of the Middle Ages expressed themselves very crudely. We read, for example, in Duns Scotus: "What the Saracens, the most common swine, the pupils of Mohammed—as their scriptures make clear—expected when they awaited beatitude is that which is appropriate to swine, namely, gluttony and whoring."

80. *L'esprit de la philosophie médiévale,* II, 221.

81. *ad. Galatas,* II, 14.

82. Ibid., p. 18.

83. *Theodicy,* sec. 37.

84. *Nouveaux essais* IV, Ch. XVII, sec. 25.

85. *Nouveaux essais* IV, Ch. XVIII, sec. 5.

86. *Confessions,* VI, 5, 7.

87. *Theodicy,* II, sec. 121.

Bibliography

Lev Shestov's Main Works and Translations into English, French, and German

1.a. *Шекспир и его критик Брандес* [Shakespeare and his critic Brandes]. St. Petersburg: A. M. Mendelevicha, 1898. Second edition, St. Petersburg: Shipovnik, 1912.

1.b. *Shakespeare and His Critic Brandes*. Translated by Stephen Van Trees and Margaret Tejerizo, with an introduction by Ramona Fotiade. Athens: Ohio University Press, forthcoming in 2017.

2.a. *Добро в учении гр. Толстого и Фр. Нитше: Философия и проповедь* [The good in the teaching of Count Tolstoy and Fr. Nietzsche: Philosophy and preaching]. St. Petersburg: M. M. Stasyulevich, 1900.

2.b. *L'idée de bien chez Tolstoï et Nietzsche: Philosophie et prédication* [The idea of the good in Tolstoy and Nietzsche: Philosophy and preaching]. Translated by T. Beresovski-Chestov and G. Bataille, with an introduction by Jules de Gaultier. Paris: Ed. du Siècle, 1925.

2.c. *Tolstoi und Nietzsche*. Translated by Nadja Strasser. Cologne: Marcan-Block Verlag, 1923. 2nd ed. Berlin: L. Schneider, 1931.

3.a. *Достоевский и Нитше: Философия трагедии* [Dostoevky and Nietzsche: The philosophy of tragedy]. St. Petersburg: M. M. Stasyulevich, 1903.

3.b. *La philosophie de la tragédie: Dostoïevski et Nietzsche* [The philosophy of tragedy: Dostoevsky and Nietzsche]. Translated by Boris de Schloezer. Paris: Editions de la Pléiade, 1926.

3.c. *Dostoevsky, Tolstoy and Nietzsche: The Good in the Teaching of Tolstoy and Nietzsche: Philosophy and Teaching & Dostoevsky and Nietzsche: The Philosophy of Tragedy*. Translated by Bernard Martin and Spencer E. Roberts, with an introduction by Bernard Martin. Athens: Ohio University Press, 1969.

3.d. *La philosophie de la tragédie: Dostoïevski et Nietzsche* [The philosophy of tragedy: Dostoevsky and Nietzsche]. Translated by Boris de Schloezer. New edition, with a preface and annotations by Ramona Fotiade, and a postface by George Steiner. Paris: Le Bruit du Temps, 2012.

4. *Начала и Концы* [Beginnings and endings]. St. Petersburg: M. M. Stasyulevich, 1908.

5.a. *Великие кануны* [The great vigils]. St. Petersburg: Shipovnik, 1910.

5.b. *Les grandes veilles*. Translated by Sylvie Luneau and Nathalie Sretovitch. Lausanne: L'Âge d'Homme, 1985.

6.a. *Апофеоз беспочвенности: Опыт адогматического мышления* [The apotheosis of groundlessness: Essay in adogmatic thinking]. St. Petersburg: Obchestvennaja pol'za, 1905; Shipovnik, 1911.

6.b. *All Things Are Possible.* Translated by S. S. Koteliansky, with an introduction by D. H. Lawrence. London: Martin Secker, 1920.

6.c. *Sur les confins de la vie: L'Apothéose du dépaysement* [On the outposts of life: The apotheosis of estrangement]. Translated by Boris de Schloezer. Paris: Librairie philosophique J. Vrin, 1936.

6.d. *All Things Are Possible & Penultimate Words and Other Essays.* Translated by S. S. Koteliansky, with an introduction by Bernard Martin. Athens: Ohio University Press, 1977.

6.e. *All Things Are Possible.* Translated by S. S. Koteliansky, with an introduction by D. H. Lawrence. Leopold Classic Library, 2015.

7.a. *Anton Tchekhov and Other Essays.* Translated by S. S. Koteliansky. Introduction by John Middleton Murry. Dublin and London: Mansel & Co., 1916.

7.b. *Penultimate Words and Other Essays.* (US title for 7.a; see also 6.d.) Boston: John W. Luce and Co., 1916.

7.c. *Chekhov and Other Essays.* Introduction by Sidney Monas. Ann Arbor: University of Michigan Press, 1966.

8.a. *Щто такое большевизм* [What is Bolshevism?]. Berlin/Geneva: Otto Elsner, 1920.

8.b. *Qu'est-ce que le bolchevisme?*[What is Bolshevism?]. In *Mercure de France,* no. 533 (1 September 1920): 257–90.

8.c. *Qu'est-ce que le bolchevisme?* [What is Bolshevism?], followed by "Les oiseaux de feu" [The firebirds] and "Les menaces des barbares d'aujourd'hui" [Menacing barbarians of today]. Translated by Sophie Benech, with a preface by Ramona Fotiade and a postface by Jean-Louis Panné. Paris: Le Bruit du Temps, 2015.

9.a. *Власт ключей.* [Potestas Clavium]. Berlin: Skify, 1923.

9.b. *Potestas Clavium; oder Die Schlüsselgewalt.* Translated by Hans Ruoff. Munich: Verlag der Nietzsche-Gesellschaft, 1926; Lambert-Schneider, 1930.

9.c. *Le pouvoir des clés* [Potestas clavium]. Translated by Boris de Schloezer. Paris: Schiffrin, 1928.

9.d. *Potestas Clavium.* Translated by Bernard Martin. Athens: Ohio University Press, 1968.

9.e. *Le pouvoir des clés* [Potestas clavium]. Translated by Boris de Schloezer. New critical edition with a preface, annotations, and a concluding study by Ramona Fotiade. Paris: Le Bruit du Temps, 2010.

10.a. *На весах Иова: Странствования по душам* [In Job's balances: Pilgrimages through souls]. Paris: Sovremennye zapiski, 1929.

10.b. *In Job's Balances: On the Sources of the Eternal Truths..* Translated by Camilla Coventry and C. A. Macartney, with a note on the author by Richard Rees. London: Dent & Sons, 1932.

10.c. *In Job's Balances: On the Sources of the Eternal Truths.* Translated by Camilla Coventry and C. A. Macartney. Edited, with an introduction, by Bernard Martin. Athens: Ohio University Press, 1975.

11.a. *Kierkegaard et la philosophie existentielle: Vox clamantis in deserto* [Kierkegaard and existential philosophy: A voice crying in the desert]. Translated by T. Rageot et B. de Schloezer. Paris: Ed. Les Amis de Léon Chestov & Librairie philosophique J. Vrin, 1936.

11.b. *Киргегард и экзистенциальная философия: Глас вопиющего в пустыне* [Kierkegaard and existential philosophy: A voice crying in the desert]. Paris: Dom knigi i Sovremennye zapiski, 1939.

11.c. *Kierkegaard and the Existential Philosophy.* Translated by Elinor Hewitt. Athens: Ohio University Press, 1969.

12.a. *Athènes et Jérusalem: Un essai de philosophie religieuse* [Athens and Jerusalem: An essay in religious philosophy]. Translated by Boris de Schloezer. Paris: J. Vrin, 1938; Flammarion, with a preface by Yves Bonnefoy, 1967.

12.b. *Athens und Jerusalem: Versuch einer religiösen Philosophie* [Athens and Jerusalem: An essay in religious philosophy]. Translated by Hans Ruoff. Graz: Verlag Schmidt-Dengler, 1938.

12.c. *Афини и Иерусалим* [Athens and Jerusalem]. Paris: YMCA-Press, 1951.

12.d. *Athens and Jerusalem.* Translated, with an introduction, by Bernard Martin. Athens: Ohio University Press, 1966.

12.e. *Athènes et Jérusalem: Un essai de philosophie religieuse,* followed by "L'obstination de Chestov" [The stubborness of Shestov] by Yves Bonnefoy. New edition, with a preface and annotations by Ramona Fotiade. Paris: Le Bruit du Temps, 2011.

13.a. *Умозрение и откровение: Религиозная философия Владимира Соловьева и другие статьи* [Speculation and revelation: The religious philosophy of Vladimir Soloviev and other essays]. Paris: YMCA-Press, 1964.

13.b. *Spekulation und Offenbarung* [Speculation and revelation]. Translated by Hans Ruoff, with an introduction, "Der Grundgedanke der Philosophie Schestows" [The fundamental idea of the philosophy of Lev Shestov], by Nikolaj Berdjajew. Munich: Verlag Heinrich Ellermann, 1963.

13.c. *Spéculation et révélation* [Speculation and revelation]. Translated by Sylvie Luneau. Paris: L'Age d'Homme, 1981.

13.d. *Speculation and Revelation.* Translated by Bernard Martin. Athens: Ohio University Press, 1982.

14.a. *Сола Фиде—Только верою* [Sola fide—By faith alone]. Paris: YMCA-Press, 1966.

14.b. *Sola fide: Luther et l'église* [Sola fide: Luther and the Church]. Translated by Sophie Seve. Paris: Presses Universitaire de France, 1957.

15. *A Shestov Anthology.* Edited, with an introduction, by Bernard Martin. Athens: Ohio University Press, 1970.

16. *Тургенев* [Turgenev]. Ann Arbor, MI: Ardis, 1982.

Index

CPSIA information can be obtained
at www.ICGtesting.com
Printed in the USA
BVHW072021210120
569693BV00001B/4